Private International Law in Montenegaro

Private International Law in Montenegaro

Maja Kostić-Mandić

This book was originally published as a monograph in the International Encyclopaedia of Laws/Private International Law.

Founding Editor: Roger Blanpain
General Editor: Frank Hendrickx
Volume Editor: Bea Verschraegen

Wolters Kluwer

Published by:
Kluwer Law International B.V.
PO Box 316
2400 AH Alphen aan den Rijn
The Netherlands
E-mail: lrs-sales@wolterskluwer.com
Website: www.wolterskluwer.com/en/solutions/kluwerlawinternational

Sold and distributed by:
Wolters Kluwer Legal & Regulatory U.S.
7201 McKinney Circle
Frederick, MD 21704
United States of America
E-mail: customer.service@wolterskluwer.com

ISBN 978-94-035-1586-1

e-Book: ISBN 978-94-035-1316-4
web-PDF: ISBN 978-94-035-1326-3

The Author

Maja Kostić-Mandić graduated from the University of Montenegro, Faculty of Law in 1991 as a student of a generation. She obtained a Master's (1995) and a Doctoral (2001) in the field of Private International Law (PIL) at the Faculty of Law of the Belgrade University, Serbia. Currently, she is Professor of Private International Law and Environmental Law at the University of Montenegro, Faculty of Law. Among other things, she is a Van Calker scholar of the Swiss Institute of Comparative Law, a Chevening scholar of the University College London and a scholar of the Max Planck Institute for Comparative and International Private Law. She used to be a member of the Parliament of Montenegro in one mandate (2006–2009) and a member of its three committees. She coordinated and worked on a large number of international projects. She is on the list of arbitrators of foreign trade arbitrations with the chambers of commerce of Montenegro, Serbia and Slovenia. She was involved in drafting Montenegrin PIL Act, and she is the author of the first comprehensive treaties on PIL in Montenegro (2017). She is a member of the Board for Legal and Political Sciences of the Montenegrin Academy of Sciences and Arts and a Vice President of the Montenegrin Association of Lawyers. Her mother tongue is Montenegrin (Serbian/Croatian/Bosnian), and she is fluent in English, Italian, French and German. More information is available at: https://www.ucg.ac.me/objava/blog/17174/objava/1.

The Author

Table of Contents

List of Abbreviations

CEAC	Central European Aluminum Company
ECJ	European Court of Justice
ECHR	European Convention of Human Rights
ECtHR	European Court of Human Rights
EU	European Union
FRY	The Federal Republic of Yugoslavia (1992–2003)
GPC	The General Pecuniary Code of Montenegro (1888)
LA	Law on Arbitration
LB	The Law on Bankruptcy
LBE	The Law on Bills of Exchange
LC	The Law on Cheques
LCC	The Law on Commercial Companies
LCP	The Law on Civil Procedure
LCRR	Law on Copyright and Related Rights
LESC	The Law on Enforcement and Securing of Claims
LF	The Law on Family
LFLA	The Law on Free Legal Aid
LFI	The Law on Foreign Investment
LFLF	The Law on Financial Leasing, Factoring, Purchase of Claims, Microcredit and Credit Guarantee Business
LMIN	The Law on Maritime and Inland Navigation
LO	The Law on Obligations
LOPRAT	The Law on Obligations and Basic Ownership Relations in Aerial Transport
LPD	The Law on the Prohibition of Discrimination
LRCL	The former Yugoslav Law on Resolution of Conflict of Laws with Regulations of Other Countries (1982–2014)
LS	The Law on Succession

List of Abbreviations

LSSLP	Law on Same-Sex Life Partnership
PIL	Private International Law
PIL Act	The Private International Law Act (2014)
SFRY	The Socialist Federative Republic of Yugoslavia, former Yugoslavia (1963–1992)

General Introduction

§1. Historical Development

1. The development of Private International Law (PIL) in Montenegro, with regard to the sources of law, can be divided into four time periods: the period of validity of the General Pecuniary Code for the Principality of Montenegro; the period of application of the norms of PIL from different sources (1946–1983); the period of validity of Yugoslav Law on Resolution of Conflict of Laws with Regulations of Other States (1983–2014); and application of the PIL Act of Montenegro (from 9 July 2014).

2. The beginnings of PIL in Montenegro relate to provisions that regulate private legal relations with a foreign element contained in the General Pecuniary Code for the Principality of Montenegro (GPC) from 1888.[1] At the time of the adoption of GPC, the basis of the rule of law in Montenegro was laid. Contacts with foreigners in general and in particular civil law relations with a foreign element are still sporadic. The idea of drafting the rules of PIL was not a reflection of the needs and the overall social and economic reality of Montenegro at that time, and in particular the state of the legal system, yet the work of a distinguished law professor, Valtazar Bogišić,[2] who has created a codification for the future. The predominant part of the provisions, relating to PIL is contained in Part I ('Introductory Rules and Orders') and Part VI, entitled 'Explanations, Decisions and Amendments'. Bogišić explains that, regardless of the name given above, these rules are of the same nature as those contained in the 'main' five parts of the Code and that they are rules 'about the details of any regulations', 'abstract or rarely applicable rules (and a little known to the general public)',[3] which best described the situation in the field of PIL at the time.

---

1. Maja Kostić-Mandić, *Mjerodavno pravo u Opštem imovinskom zakoniku za Knjaževinu Crnu Goru* u *120 godina OIZ-a u Crnoj Gori* (The Applicable Law in the General Pecuniary Code for the Principality of Montenegro). In *120 years of GPC in Montenegro*, Podgorica: Univerzitet Crne Gore, Pravni fakultet, Udruženje pravnika CG, 2009, 95–106.
2. Valtazar Bogišić was prominent South Slav professor with Russian University in Odessa. The Code included the great legal achievements of that time and in the field of PIL provides for twenty articles inspired by work of Savigny and Mancini. Maja Kostić-Mandić, *The New Private International Law Act of Montenegro, Yearbook of Private International Law*, Vol. XVI, 2014/2015, 429.
3. Valtazar Bogišić, *Izabrana djela, tom: Studije i članci* (Selected Works, Volume: Studies and Articles), Podgorica: CID, 2004, 14.

3. The General Pecuniary Code contains a series of general rules of PIL (on the application of foreign law, determining and proving the content of foreign law, the public policy exception, retorsion).[4] This Code, in accordance with its subject matter, contains basic rules for all major areas of PIL: conflict of laws, conflict of jurisdictions and the rights of foreigners to enter into civil law relations. Among others, the Code determines the applicable law to ownership and other real rights, legal entities, the business capacity of natural persons, contracts,[5] non-contractual obligations and the form of legal acts.[6] In the area of conflict of jurisdiction, the Code deals only with the issue of recognition and enforcement of foreign court decisions. The effect of foreign court decisions equals the effect of domestic decisions, and conditions are established for the recognition of foreign court decisions, most of which still apply.[7]

4. Before 1983 and the beginning of the implementation of the Law on Resolution of Conflict of Laws with Regulations of Other States in Certain Relations (LRCL),[8] which for the first time completely codified PIL, there was a legal particularism in this area. The provisions of the GPC were applied in the form of legal rules[9] for all relations that were not regulated by conflict rules or other norms mainly contained in substantive legislation.

5. The Law on Resolution of Conflict of Laws represents the first codification of PIL in the region. In addition to the abbreviation LRCL, this law is often referred to in the literature as the PIL Act, as it was the title of the law proposal, changed in the legislative procedure subsequently. At the time of its adoption, the LRCL is considered internationally as high-quality text. And one of the reasons is that the provisions of the GPC dedicated to PIL were a starting point. The LRCL contained the most significant innovations present in the comparative law and in the theory of PIL. The development of the text of the law has lasted for several decades, and the most prominent experts from this field from Croatia and Serbia[10] were involved in the work. The LRCL had minor changes in 1996, when, among other things, it was abbreviated to the title ('certain relations' were dropped). The law has codified in detail the field of applicable law and civil procedure with a foreign element, while it did not contain provisions on the rights of foreigners to enter into civil law relations. The LRCL was applied in Montenegro from 1 January 1983 to 9 July 2014, when the implementation of the PIL Act (*Zakon o međunarodnom privatnom*

4. Articles 5–9 GPC.
5. *See infra* Contractual Obligations, Party Autonomy.
6. Articles 786–794, 798–799 GPC.
7. Articles 795, 796, 797 GPC.
8. Law of Resolution of Conflict of Laws with Regulations of Other States, Belgrade, Službeni list SFRJ No. 43/82, 72/82 and Službeni list SRJ No. 49/96.
9. Based on the Law on Non-validity of Laws Enacted Prior to 6 Apr. 1941, of 1946.
10. *See* also: Maja Stanivuković & Mirko Živković, *Međunarodno privatno pravo: opšti deo* (Private International Law: General Part), Belgrade: Službeni list SCG, 2004, 53.

pravu)[11] had started. The LRCL, though, as a national piece of legislation still applies in Serbia and Bosnia and Herzegovina.

6. Changes in State sovereignty did not significantly affect the implementation of the LRCL in Montenegro. The LRLC was applied as the federal law on the territory of the former Socialist Federative Republic of Yugoslavia (SFRY, former Yugoslavia), and later on the Federal Republic of Yugoslavia (FRY, consisting of Serbia and Montenegro) with only minor amendments in 1996). Without any changes, this law was applied in Montenegro as a national piece of legislation, first based on the Constitutional Charter of the State Union of Serbia and Montenegro, and later after the declaration of independence of Montenegro, until the implementation of the PIL Act in 2014.

7. On 21 May 2006, Montenegro held a referendum to seek full independence and following the results of the referendum Montenegro Parliament formally declared independence on 3 June 2006. In October 2007 the new Constitution of Montenegro was adopted and by the end of the year, the Stabilization and Association Agreement with the European Union (EU)[12] was signed. All these new developments reflected the PIL of Montenegro and resulted in adopting the new piece of legislation in the field strongly influenced by the European PIL.

§2. International and Supranational Legal Framework

8. In order to avoid problems and issues which entail the existence of an international element and the putting into operation of mechanisms of national PIL, in those areas that are of particular importance, which are most commonly encountered in legal practice, a unique solution for the laws of several States is sought, the instrument being the conclusion of international treaties (conventions). For Montenegro, in addition to international treaties, of particular importance is the EU law.

9. Montenegro is bound by a number of international treaties, among others in the field of international sales, international commercial arbitration, air, road and rail transport and partly maritime traffic, bill of exchange, check, copyright and industrial property rights,[13] and others. The unification of PIL at the global level is mostly

11. Podgorica, Službeni list Crne Gore No. 1/2014, 6/2014, 11/2014, 14/2014 and 47/2015 – others laws, *see infra* Annex I.
12. Stabilization and association agreement between the European communities and their Member States and the Republic of Montenegro of 15 October 2007, [2010] OJ L 108/3.
13. The relevant treaties will be addressed under respective titles *infra.* For general overview *see* Maja Kostić-Mandić, Maja Stanivuković & Mirko Živković, *International Encyclopedia of Laws: Private International Law*, Kluwer Law International, Supplement 38: Montenegro, B. Verschraegen ed., Alphen aan den Rijn: Kluwer Law International, 2013, (Kluwer Monograph on PIL of Montenegro of 2013), paras 54–55.

carried out under the frame of the Hague Conference on Private International Law. And Montenegro, as a contracting party, is bound by a significant number of conventions.[14]

10. The EU law is significant for Montenegro on several grounds. Sources of law that undoubtedly bind Montenegro as a candidate country are international treaties concluded with the EU (primarily the Stabilization and Association Agreement). The application of the EU law also occurs through the positive legislation of Montenegro, harmonized with the EU law, the best example being the PIL Act. On the other hand, in some cases, the application of national law provisions originating from EU law is postponed until Montenegro becomes an EU member. Thus, in 2019 amendments to the Law on Civil Procedure (LCP) and the Law on Enforcement and Securing of Claims (LESC)[15] have been made in order to mirror the EU regulations in the field of judicial cooperation. The new provisions of the LCP are now aligned with the European Service Regulation (No. 1393/2007), the European Evidence Regulation (No. 1206/2001), the European Payment Order Regulation (No. 1896/2006), the European Small Claims Procedure Regulation (No. 861/2007) and the European Regulation amending European Payment Order Regulation and European Small Claims Procedure Regulation (No. 2015/2421) and the relevant provisions of the LESC with the European Enforcement Order Regulation (No. 805/2004), the European Payment Order Regulation (No. 1896/2006), the European Small Claims Procedure Regulation (No. 861/2007) and the European Regulation amending European Payment Order Regulation and European Small Claims Procedure Regulation (No. 2015/2421). Also, the new Law on Commercial Companies[16] regulates cross-border mergers, in accordance with the relevant EU Directives.[17] However, the chapters of these laws containing specific provisions on the implementation of judicial cooperation / cross-border mergers in the EU shall apply only from the date of accession of Montenegro to the EU.[18]

11. One of the ways in which the acquis is implemented is also by taking into account the case law of the Court of Justice of the European Union, that is of the European Court of Justice (ECJ) and of the national courts of the EU Member States.

12. Montenegro formally became a candidate for the EU membership after the entry into force of the SAA between the EU and Montenegro (1 May 2010). Based on this agreement, which is essentially atypical, *sui generis* international treaty,[19] Montenegro has undertaken the obligation of harmonization, transposition and adequate implementation of its existing and future legislation with the acquis of the

14. https://www.hcch.net/.
15. *See infra* Table of Statutory Instruments.
16. Podgorica, Službeni list Crne Gore No. 65/20.
17. *See infra* Cross-Border Transformation.
18. Part IV of the LCP pursuant to Art. 511 and Chapter IIIa of the LESC pursuant to Art. 295a).
19. Maja Stanivuković, *Pojedinac pred sudom Evropskih zajednica* (Individual before the ECJ), Belgrade: Službeni glasnik, 2009.

EU.[20] In principle, the SAA, as well as other international treaties that fulfil the condition that they are ratified and published, can be directly applied before Montenegrin courts if its provisions are apt for direct application, especially when it comes to the teleological interpretation of the norms of internal law. Furthermore, there are also international agreements between the EU and Montenegro, which are ratified by the Parliament of Montenegro and are also legally binding. In the field of PIL, the EU also appears as a member of multilateral treaties (e.g., as a member of the Hague Conference, under whose auspices a number of conventions have been adopted), which are also binding on Montenegro.

§3. Nature and Scope

13. It is indisputable that the PIL is a branch of national law that deals with private law relations with an international element. The term 'private law' is used as common for civil, labour and commercial[21] relations. The term 'civil law relations' is also used equally encompassing traditional relations of real, obligations, succession and family law, as well as: commercial, labour, intellectual, consumer, transport and other laws.[22] In the legal tradition of the former Yugoslav legal space, and in the law of Montenegro, the subject of PIL consists of the conflict of laws, the conflict of jurisdictions (international civil procedure, international legal assistance and recognition and enforcement of foreign decisions included) and the rights of foreigners in private legal relations with a foreign element. Also, it is customary to study international commercial arbitration in the framework of PIL.

14. The legal norms which regulate the relations of PIL are imperative in nature, and this also applies to conflict rules. Pursuant to the positive law of Montenegro, the foreign law applicable on the basis of a conflict rule is treated as a law and not as a mere fact. Therefore, the PIL Act establishes the obligation for a competent authority to ascertain the content of foreign law and to apply foreign law ex officio and provides the legal remedies[23] if there would be a breach of those obligations. Having in mind that it is not always easy to determine the content of foreign law, various forms of assistance are provided for to help the body that applies the conflict rules. The judicial or other authority shall determine the content of applicable law in accordance with international treaties and may seek information on foreign law from the ministry responsible for justice affairs as well as opinions from experts and specialized institutions. Parties to a proceeding may also file documents on the content of foreign law or otherwise assist the judicial or other authority (the PIL Act, Article 6).

20. Article 72 of the Stabilization and Association Agreement.
21. The term commercial law better reflects the type of relationships that fall under private law relations than the term economy law, but it is not accepted in the positive law of Montenegro.
22. Vladimir V. Vodinelić, *Građansko pravo* (Civil Law), Belgrade: University Union, Faculty of Law, 2014, 37.
23. *See infra* Legal Consequences.

15. The PIL Act does not contain an alternative in the case where it is not possible to determine the content of foreign law. The legislature did not provide a subsidiary rule such as the application of *lex fori*, bearing in mind the prospective risk of abuse of such a rule. It is understandable that the judiciary and other bodies are not indifferent whether they should apply domestic or some foreign law and the 'homeward' trend is always an issue. However, the prevailing view of the working group drafting the provision was that the trend of applying domestic law even when the conflict rule points to the application of a foreign law could not be revised if the competent authorities had an opportunity to apply *lex fori* as a subsidiary rule.

§4. Characteristics of National PIL

16. The PIL of Montenegro represents a blend of tradition and new achievements in the comparative law and especially in European PIL.[24]

17. Montenegro heritage the tradition of PIL of the former Yugoslavia. This is reflected in succeeding to almost all of the international treaties concluded before regaining independence.[25] Also, the provisions on the applicable law of certain special laws from the former Yugoslavia are still in force. The connection between the legal space of the former Yugoslavia is also explained by the fact that in the period before the adoption of the PIL Act there was no significant number of doctrinal works in the field published in Montenegro,[26] so there was a significant influence of the doctrine from Serbia and Croatia.

18. Building on tradition, the new PIL Act retains the structure of the LRCL. The first part in nine chapters regulates applicable law in great details (Articles 1–98); the second part contains rules on jurisdiction and procedure (Articles 99–140); the third part regulates recognition and enforcement of foreign decisions (Articles 141–158); the fourth part addresses competences of the diplomatic-consular organs (Articles 159–163) and the fifth part contains transitory and final provisions (Articles 164–169). A number of LRCL articles are literally imported from that law to the PIL Act. Also, for certain institutes, basic solutions have been upgraded and improved in accordance with the best comparative practice (such as the public policy institute, Article 9 of the PIL Act), while some solutions have been completely altered (e.g., significantly reduced possibility of applying the renvoi by specifying for which type of relations it is not permitted, Article 4 of the PIL Act).

19. However, some of the main features of the PIL Act in the field of conflict of laws include: a significantly increased number of articles and a substantial change

24. *See infra* Supranational Law.
25. *Ibid.*
26. Montenegro with its 620,029 inhabitants (according to the Census of Population, Households and Dwellings in 2011, https://www.monstat.org/userfiles/file/popis2011/saopstenje/saopstenje(1).pdf (accessed 14 Apr. 2022) has very scarce human resources in the field of PIL.

in the content of many provisions in order to take into account the new developments in the comparative law, international conventions and the EU law. One of the main features of the PIL Act is a significant extension of the applicability area of choice of law to contractual obligations and introducing a limited choice of law in following matters: non-contractual, divorce, matrimonial property regimes, name and succession. The most important new institutes introduced by the PIL Act include: the escape clause (Article 8), the overriding mandatory rules (Article 9) and habitual residence (definitions are contained in Articles 12, 40 and 51).

20. The PIL Act, in accordance with Article 80 of the SAA, is aimed at harmonizing national law with the EU law. The PIL Act provides the application of the EU law in two different ways: by incorporating provisions of the EU regulations into national law in certain areas and for certain types of relations with certain changes,[27] but also by direct reference to the EU law. When Montenegro becomes a Member State of the EU, all EU regulations in the field of PIL[28] will be directly applicable in the country. During the drafting of the new PIL Act and deciding on the degree of harmonization of its provisions with the EU law, there was a different approach to the type of matter that is the subject of European regulations, depending on the prevailing national interests. Thus, in the field of determining the applicable law for contractual and non-contractual obligations, a reception of the EU law was made, with only the necessary adjustments. The judiciary and other bodies in Montenegro will have time to become familiar with the practice of the EU law in this field. In determining the applicable law to maintenance obligations, the provisions of the 2007 Hague Protocol on the applicable law for maintenance obligations (Hague Maintenance Protocol)[29] have been fully transposed. Furthermore, the areas which have undergone the most changes include succession, both in the domain of applicable law and international jurisdiction, and exclusive jurisdiction which is now regulated in a completely new way.

21. In contrast to the above, with regard to the rules for determining the applicable law for other private law relations, as well as the rules on international jurisdiction, national interests, legal tradition and legal security needs prevailed.

§5. Domestic Authorities Involved, Interpretation and Application of PIL

22. In Montenegro there are no special courts in the field of PIL. The cases are adjudicated by the courts of general jurisdiction (basic courts)[30] – civil division and

27. In the domain of the applicable law for contracts, non-contractual obligations, maintenance and succession.
28. For the texts of all acts, *see* http://ec.europa.eu/justice/civil/law/index_en.htm (accessed 14 Apr. 2022).
29. Hague Protocol of 23 Nov. 2007 on the Law Applicable to Maintenance Obligations.
30. In Montenegro there are fifteen basic courts, some of them being competent for several municipalities. Also, there are three misdemeanour courts having local units in most of the Montenegrin municipalities.

the Commercial Court in Podgorica. The second instance courts are: the Higher Court in Podgorica and Higher Court in Bijelo Polje for civil matter cases and the Court of Appeal of Montenegro for criminal and business-related cases. Furthermore, there is the Administrative Court of Montenegro, a specialized court based in Podgorica (there are no basic/primary administrative courts in Montenegro). Its decisions are final and may be subject only to extraordinary legal remedies.

23. The Supreme Court of Montenegro as the highest instance court in Montenegro decides on extraordinary legal remedies against decisions of the courts in Montenegro (except for the retrial of the procedure where the court that issued a decision in the first instance shall decide).

24. The Constitutional Court of Montenegro is empowered to review domestic legislation as to its conformity with the Constitution and international treaties (abstract constitutional review), while a constitutional appeal is a legal remedy for instituting proceedings before the Constitutional Court for the protection of human and minority rights and freedoms guaranteed by the Constitution, after all other efficient legal remedies have been exhausted.

25. In their practice some judges used to disregard the existence of foreign elements in civil and commercial matters resulting in regular application of *lex fori* to many cases, instead of the rules of the LRCL. Until the adoption of the PIL Act in 2014, there was no specialization of judges in this field. However, the new codification triggered the attention of the specialized national body in charge of training and education of judges (and prosecutors),[31] and Ministry of Justice, in the course of fulfilling obligations from the European integration process, so that regular trainings for judges are organized several times per year. The judges specialize by attending courses on PIL.[32] The trainees are mostly judges of the first instance (basic courts, Commercial court) and higher courts, and presently they are best suited to adjudicate PIL cases. Also, the trainings are organized for newly elected judges and even for prosecutors. However, in spite of the above said and the fact that since 2017 practitioners can benefit from the treaties on Private International Law of Montenegro[33] in their native language the examples of unfamiliarity with basic institutes can still be found. Thus, in a recent case,[34] the Higher Court in Podgorica pointed out that the Court of First Instance is obliged to distinguish between two legal institutes of international law – jurisdiction and applicable law. It further instructs that the sole fact that the court of Montenegro has international

31. www.cosdt.me (accessed 14 Apr. 2022).
32. Most of the trainings from 2015 to 2017 dealt with issues of recognition and enforcement of foreign judicial decisions. See in more details Maja Kostić-Mandić, Cross-border Recognition and Enforcement of Foreign Judicial Decisions in South East Europe and Perspectives of HCCH 2019 Judgments Convention, Skopje: GIZ, 2021, 121–122.
33. Maja Kostić-Mandić, *Međunarodno privatno pravo* (Private International Law), Podgorica: Univerzitet Crne Gore Pravni fakultet, 2017.
34. Higher Court in Podgorica, Gž.br. 5360/18 of 29 Oct. 2018.

jurisdiction does not mean that a priori the Montenegrin substantive law is applicable, and therefore it is necessary to determine governing law for each of the claims.

26. In addition to the courts, PIL matters are usually addressed by certain authorities performing non-judicial functions, such as the Ministry of Justice, notaries, public execution officers, public authorities in charge of family law matters (centres for social welfare), international commercial arbitration tribunals[35] and so forth.

27. The Ministry of Justice, which is also the Central Authority for all HCCH conventions ratified by Montenegro, can be addressed by the court in order to obtain information on a foreign law (in accordance with the European Convention on Information on Foreign Law of 1968); if service is needed (in accordance with the HCCH 1965 Service Convention), or if assistance in some other way is needed. Furthermore, the Ministry of Justice prepares an annual general report on the application of the PIL Act as an obligation in the course of European integration, and collects data on case law of the Montenegrin courts. However, the data are only of a general nature.

28. Notarial service in Montenegro is established as public service pursuant to the Law on Notaries.[36] In addition to drafting and issuing notarial acts and keeping deposits of certificates, securities, money and other movables they are in charge of performing services conferred to them with the court decisions.[37] In the field of PIL, the most important role of notaries is in the field of contracts and succession. The Law on Notaries provides for a notarial form as a prerequisite of validity of a number of the most significant contracts in the area of succession, family and obligations law.[38] Notarial deed on any legal transaction shall acquire the status of public document and under certain conditions, it may also obtain the status of executive title. However, if a foreign notary deed is to be performed in Montenegro, it is not necessary to conduct an exequatur procedure. A foreign notarial deed has, subject to reciprocity, the same legal effect as a notarial deed drawn up in Montenegro. Furthermore, notaries acting as court commissioners have been entrusted by court decisions with the procedure of ruling on succession.

35. *See infra* International Arbitration.
36. Article 52 para. 1 of the Law on Notaries, Podgorica, Službeni list Crne Gore No. 68/05, 49/08 and 55/2016, https://www.paragraf.me/propisi-crnegore/zakon-o-notarima.html (accessed 14 Apr. 2022). For more information on practical aspects of their work related to PIL *see* Maja Kostić-Mandić, *Primjena međunarodnog privatnog prava u notarskoj praksi* (Application of Private International Law in Notaries' Practice), Podgorica: GIZ, 2021.
37. Article 4 of the Law on Notaries.
38. *See infra* Contractual Obligations, Form. *See* Velibor Korać, Notarial Form *Ad Solemnitatem* in Montenegrin Law, Annals FLB – Belgrade Law Review, Year LXIV, 2016, No. 3. https://www.researchgate.net/publication/312353465_Notarial_form_ad_solemnitatem_in_Montenegrin_law (accessed 14 Apr. 2022).

29. The Law on Enforcement and Security, which began to be implemented in 2014, introduced into the legal system of Montenegro a new legal profession – a public enforcement officer as an independent holder of a function with public authority. The provisions of the LESC clearly distinguish between the jurisdiction of the court and the public enforcement officer and specify their respective powers (Article 4). This basically abandoned the so-called system of 'court executions' as public enforcement officer shall be competent to decide in enforcement procedure, to levy enforcement, as well as to enforce securing of claims, except in the cases that competency of the court is prescribed for by law (Article 3). However, the competence for recognition of foreign judgments remains exclusively with the competent court (PIL Act, Article 152 (1), (2), (3)) and therefore public enforcement officer may not decide on the recognition of the foreign judgments as a preliminary question in enforcement procedure.[39]

30. Centres for social welfare as custodial bodies are in charge of 'providing expert assistance and protecting the rights and interests of the child and of other members of the family, for resolving disputes between family members, as well as in all other cases where family relationships are disturbed'.[40] Furthermore, for the above-mentioned matters the court and the person authorized for mediation shall also be competent.

31. The Law on Courts[41] of 2015 in Article 25 enumerates the powers of the Supreme Court of Montenegro, one of them being a power to provide a legal position in principle in relation to a contentious legal issue, which has arisen from the case law for the purpose of providing uniform application of the law by the courts.

32. The PIL Act remains silent on the prospective law which should apply to the interpretation of the conflict rules if the applicable law has not been ascertained yet. One of the reasons is that by automatism, it starts from the view that the court or other authorities applying a conflict rule, as well as any other legal norm, interpret it according to the *lex fori*. In addition to this reason, which implies an interpretation of the conflict provisions under domestic law, avoiding the formulation of a specific rule is motivated by leaving the possibility for the court to act differently in certain situations. In the doctrine, there are other opinions, among others that the interpretation of the connecting factor should be done according to the law of the State with which the connecting factor is in the closest connection.[42] So, in principle, the interpretation of the conflict rules, until the applicable law is determined, is done according to the domestic law.

33. When the applicable law has already been ascertained, the rule of interpretation is contained in the PIL Act, which provides that the interpretation of terms

39. *See infra* Recognition and Enforcement of Foreign Decisions.
40. Article 14 of the Law on Family, https://www.paragraf.me/propisi-crnegore/porodicni-zakon.html (accessed 14 Apr. 2022).
41. Podgorica, Službeni list Crne Gore No. 11/15, 76/20.
42. Krešimir Sajko, *Međunarodno privatno pravo* (Private International Law), Zagreb: Narodne novine, 2009, 180.

and institutes of foreign applicable law will be conducted under that law.[43] The specificity of the PIL Act is also the possibility of choosing the applicable law to interpret a Joint Will or Succession Agreement (Article 74, paragraph 4), and in particular, an explicit statement that the provisions of the chapter on the applicable law for contractual and non-contractual obligations are interpreted and applied in accordance with the Rome I Regulation and Rome II Regulation[44] (Articles 49 and 67 of the PIL Act, respectively).

34. The PIL Act contains a number of definitions of legal institutes for the purposes of that law: habitual residence of a person; habitual residence of companies and other entities which are performing commercial activities for contractual relations and for non-contractual relations; definition of damages for non-contractual obligations[45] and other. Also, in most of the chapters on conflict of laws, the PIL Act contains the provisions on the scope of applicable law. This approach, which clarifies the scope of conflict rules in a particular area, is present for the status relations of legal entities and organizational forms without the character of a legal entity, real rights, contractual relations, non-contractual relations, succession and maintenance.[46]

35. The question of interpretation of international treaties is regulated by the Vienna Convention on the Law of Treaties of 1969,[47] which starts from textual and teleological interpretation.

43. Article 7 para. 1 of the PIL Act states: 'Foreign law shall be interpreted and applied in the way it is interpreted and applied in its State of origin.'
44. Regulation (EC) No. 593/2008 of the European Parliament and of the Council of 17 June 2008 on the law applicable to contractual obligations (Rome I), [2008] OJ L 177/6; Regulation (EC) No. 864/2007 of the European Parliament and of the Council of 11 July 2007 on the law applicable to non-contractual obligations (Rome II), [2007] OJ L 199/40.
45. *See* Arts 12, 40, 51 and 50 of the PIL Act.
46. *See* Arts 21, 34, 48, 64, 76 and 97 of the PIL Act.
47. *See* the general interpretation rule and the supplementary means of interpretation in Arts 31 and 32 of the Vienna Convention on the Law of International Treaties.

Part I. General Principles (Choice of Law Technique)

Chapter 1. Sources of PIL

§1. Public International Law

36. Legal sources of Public International Law are of great importance to PIL. This stands especially for international treaties (such as the Vienna Convention on the Law of International Treaties) providing for legal framework for treaties concluded between States or under the auspices of international organizations, but with the subject matter in the field of private law relations with an international character.

37. The relationship between Public International Law and PIL can also be seen as a relationship between two legal disciplines that in modern times have much in common. There are a number of sources and institutes of Public International Law that are relevant to PIL, such as: international treaties, general legal principles, human rights, immunity, reciprocity and more. Also, diplomatic or consular agents apply the rules of PIL to marriage, custody, drafting a will and more.

38. Article 9 of the Constitution of Montenegro states that in addition to ratified international treaties '... generally accepted rules of international law are directly applicable and shall have precedence over the law of Montenegro'. The phrase presumably refers primarily to customary international rules and general principles of law accepted by civilized nations (i.e., to Public International Law sources other than treaty law). There are no cases interpreting or applying this rule yet.

39. There are specific references to Public International Law as a source of law in some domestic laws. For example, the LCP (Article 28) provides that the rules of Public International Law shall govern the question of the jurisdiction of Montenegrin courts to adjudicate cases against foreign citizens protected by immunity and against foreign states and international organizations.

§2. Supranational Law

40. The European integration process in Montenegro has had a significant impact on the national PIL, helping to set priorities and adopting the Montenegro PIL Act that is in most fields harmonized with the EU law. The new PIL codification either incorporates several provisions of the EU regulations into national law with only minimum adjustments or transposes the basic concepts of the regulations depending on two facts – the prevailing national interest to be protected by the provisions of the new codification, and the different approach to be applied to certain fields and types of relations.

41. In the field of conflict of laws, the EU law has had the most significant impact on those provisions of the Montenegrin PIL Act, which effectively adopted the rules of the Rome I and Rome II Regulations with the necessary adjustments. The same can be said for the conflict of law provisions of the Hague Maintenance Protocol while the conflict rules for succession were inspired by the provisions of the Succession Regulation.[48]

42. In the area of international jurisdiction, the new solutions are harmonized with solutions of the Brussels I Regulation[49] and the Lugano Convention[50] while in other matters, regard has been had to the relevant regulations.

§3. National Law

43. International treaties ratified (in the form of a statute) and promulgated in accordance with the Constitution constitute part of the internal legal order and shall have the supremacy over the statutory law and will be directly applicable when regulating certain relations differently than the internal law. This rule is expressly provided by the 2007 Constitution of Montenegro (Article 9). International treaties are published in an official periodical publication (*Službeni list Crne Gore, Me unarodni ugovori*), together with the promulgating act. The power to ratify international treaties belongs to the Parliament of Montenegro (Article 89(17) of the Constitution).

44. The Decision on Proclamation of Independence on 3 June 2006 explicitly states that Montenegro will be bound by international conventions and agreements concluded and succeeded by the State Union of Serbia and Montenegro, when they relate to Montenegro and do not contravene with its legal order. At that time, letter

48. Regulation (EU) No. 650/2012 of the European Parliament and of the Council of 4 July 2012 on jurisdiction, applicable law, recognition and enforcement of decisions and acceptance and enforcement of authentic instruments in matters of succession and on the creation of a European certificate of Succession, [2012] OJ L 201/107.
49. Council Regulation (EC) No. 44/2001 of 22 December 2000 on jurisdiction and the recognition and enforcement of judgments in civil and commercial matters, [2001] OJ L 12/1.
50. Lugano Convention of 30 October 2007 on jurisdiction and the recognition and enforcement of judgments in civil and commercial matters, [2007] OJ L 339/3.

on notification on succession with enclosed list of conventions[51] ratified by the previous State (State Union of Serbia and Montenegro) with the priority list of conventions has been sent to the United Nations and other relevant institutions. However, presently, neither Ministry of Foreign Affairs nor Ministry of Justice of the Government of Montenegro keeps a steady record on international treaties binding on Montenegro, available to the general public.[52]

45. Montenegro became a Member State of the Hague Conference on Private International Law retroactively since 1 March 2007 and succeeded to the conventions previously ratified by SFRY[53] as of 3 June 2006. Presently[54] the following conventions are binding on Montenegro:

- Convention of 1 March 1954 on civil procedure;
- Convention of 5 October 1961 on the Conflicts of Laws Relating to the Form of Testamentary Dispositions;
- Convention of 5 October 1961 Abolishing the Requirement of Legalisation for Foreign Public Documents;
- Convention of 15 November 1965 on the Service Abroad of Judicial and Extrajudicial Documents in Civil or Commercial Matters;
- Convention of 4 May 1971 on the Law Applicable to Traffic Accidents;
- Convention of 18 March 1970 on the Taking of Evidence Abroad in Civil or Commercial Matters;
- Convention of 2 October 1973 on the Law Applicable to Products Liability;
- Convention of 25 October 1980 on the Civil Aspects of International Child Abduction;
- Convention of 25 October 1980 on International Access to Justice;
- Convention of 29 May 1993 on Protection of Children and Co-operation in Respect of Intercountry Adoption;
- Convention of 19 October 1996 on Jurisdiction, Applicable Law, Recognition, Enforcement and Co-operation in Respect of Parental Responsibility and Measures for the Protection of Children;
- Convention of 30 June 2005 on Choice of Court Agreements; and
- Convention of 23 November 2007 on the International Recovery of Child Support and Other Forms of Family Maintenance.

46. Montenegro is also a Contracting Party to a number of conventions concluded in the framework of the United Nations, such as:

51. The list of conventions is not available to the general public.
52. Information provided by the Ministry of Foreign Affairs.
53. Civil Procedure Convention; Legalization Convention; Testamentary Dispositions Convention; Traffic Accident Convention; Product Liability Convention; Child Abduction Convention and Access to Justice Convention.
54. The new accessions to the Hague Conventions by Montenegro include: Service Convention; Evidence Convention; Adoption Convention, Child Protection Convention, Maintenance Convention and Choice of Court Agreements Convention.

- Convention on the Recovery Abroad of Maintenance of 1956;
- Convention on Consent to Marriage, Minimum Age for Marriage and Registration of Marriages of 1962;
- European Convention on International Commercial Arbitration of 1961;
- Convention on the Recognition and Enforcement of Foreign Arbitral Awards of 1958; and
- Convention on Contracts for the International Sale of Goods of 1980.

47. Montenegro is a contracting party to a certain number of conventions of the Council of Europe including:

- Convention on Information on Foreign Law of 1968;
- Convention on the Liability of Hotel-Keepers Concerning the Property of Their Guests of 1962;
- European Convention on Recognition and Enforcement of Decisions Concerning Custody of Children and on Restoration of Custody of Children of 1980;
- Convention for the Protection of Human Rights and Fundamental Freedoms of 1950;
- European Convention on Nationality of 1997;
- European Convention on the Avoidance of Statelessness in Relation to State Succession of 2006, and so forth.

48. Montenegro is a contracting party to the Convention on the Settlement of Investment Disputes between States and Nationals of Other States (the ICSID Convention) of 1965.

49. Bilateral agreements relating to PIL are encountered in the area of international legal assistance, recognition and enforcement of foreign decisions and arbitral awards, consular affairs and legal protection of foreign investments. Most of the legal assistance conventions regulate service of process and taking of evidence, contain provisions on abolishing the requirement of legalization for foreign public documents and security for costs (cautio iudicatum solvi), and provide for access to justice, legal aid and exchange of information on the content of laws of the contracting parties or all of it.

50. Montenegro is a party to the following bilateral treaties on legal assistance in civil procedures concluded with: Austria, Belgium, Bosnia and Herzegovina, Cyprus, Czech Republic, France, Greece, Hungary, Italy, Macedonia, Poland, Romania, Serbia and Slovakia.[55] In all of these cases, with the exception of Serbia,

55. They apply to Montenegro in relation to Austria 1954 (Sl. list FNRJ, Dodatak 8/55), Belgium 1971 (Sl. list SFRJ, 55/72), Bosnia and Herzegovina 2010 (Sl. list CG, MU 15/2010), Croatia 1997 (Sl. List SFRJ, MU 1/98), the Czech Republic 1964 (Sl. list SFRJ, Dodatak 13/64), France 1969 (Sl. List SFRJ, Dodatak 7/72), Hungary 1968, 1986 (Sl. list SFRJ, Dodatak 3/68, Sl. list SFRJ, MU 1/87), Italy 1960 (Sl. list FNRJ, Dodatak 5/63), Macedonia 2016 (Sl. list CG, MU 22/2016), Poland 1960 (Sl. list FNRJ, Dodatak 5/63), Romania 1960 (Sl. list FNRJ, Dodatak 8/61), the Russian Federation 1962 (Sl. list FNRJ, Dodatak 5/63), Serbia 2009 (Sl. list CG, MU 4/2009) and Slovakia 1964 (Sl. list SFRJ, Dodatak 13/64). *See infra* section on Bilateral Treaties.

Bosnia and Herzegovina and Macedonia, Montenegro became a party by way of a declaration on succession in respect of conventions binding the Former Yugoslavia (i.e., the State Union of Serbia and Montenegro). The Ministry of Justice of Montenegro factually applies the treaties of the former Yugoslavia with Croatia[56] and with the Russian Federation.[57]

51. Furthermore, there are four bilateral treaties dealing exclusively with recognition and enforcement of foreign decisions and arbitral awards, concluded with: Austria, Belgium, France and Greece: the Agreement with Austria on the Mutual Recognition and Enforcement of Arbitral Awards and Settlements Reached Before Arbitral Tribunals in Commercial Matters (1960, in force since 1961); the Convention with Austria on the Recognition and Enforcement of Maintenance Judgments (1961, in force since 1962); the Convention with Belgium on the Recognition and Enforcement of Maintenance Judgments (1971, in force since 1976), the Convention with France on the Recognition and Enforcement of Judgments in Civil and Commercial Matters (1971, in force since 1972); the Agreement with Greece on the Mutual Recognition and Enforcement of Judgments (1959, in force since 1960).

52. Special bilateral treaties deal with certain issues in narrower areas, such as status and family law relations with a foreign element, such as the Convention with France on Jurisdiction and Applicable Law in the Field of Status and Family Matters (in force since 1972) and the Convention with Belgium on the Issuance of Extracts from Marriage Registers and Abolishing the Requirement of Legalization (in force since 1972).

53. Some issues relevant to PIL are addressed in consular conventions[58] (such as drafting of testament, determining the custody, the use of documents, and so forth). Furthermore, in Montenegro, there are a number of bilateral agreements in the field of social security,[59] and numerous agreements on free trade, economic cooperation, and legal protection of foreign investments.[60]

56. The Agreement between Federal Republic of Yugoslavia and Croatia on Legal Assistance in Civil and Criminal Matters (in force since 1998).
57. The Agreement with the USSR on Legal Assistance in Family, Civil and Criminal Matters (in force since 26 May 1963). The issue of the succession of international treaties with the Russian Federation has not been concluded, so we have no official confirmation from the Russian side that the agreement is in force.
58. Consular treaties concluded with: Austria, Bosnia and Herzegovina, Belgium, Bulgaria, Greece, Croatia, Italy, China, Poland, Romania, Russian Federation, Slovakia, Serbia, Switzerland, Turkey. *See* Maja Kostić-Mandić, *Međunarodno privatno pravo* (Private International Law), Podgorica: Univerzitet Crne Gore, Pravni fakultet, 2017.
59. Social security treaties concluded with: Austria, Bosnia and Herzegovina, Belgium, Bulgaria, Denmark, France, the Netherlands, Croatia, Italy, Kosovo, Luxembourg, Hungary, Macedonia, Germany, Norway, Poland, Slovakia, Slovenia, Turkey, United Kingdom.
60. Bilateral treaties by the way of succession with: Austria, France, Greece, the Netherlands, Israel, Cyprus, Lithuania, Germany, Poland, Romania, the USA, Slovakia, Spain and Switzerland. Following the declaration of independence, treaties were also concluded with: Azerbaijan, the Czech Republic, Danemark, the Economic Union of Belgium – Luxembourg, Finland, China, Macedonia, Malta, Moldova, Serbia and the United Arab Emirates. *Ibid.*

54. The statutory sources of positive PIL of Montenegro are numerous and come from different epochs. The basic law regulating PIL in the area of applicable law and civil proceedings with a foreign element is the PIL Act, which replaced the Law on Resolution of Conflict of Laws. The new PIL Act applies since 9 July 2014. In the area of determining applicable law, the PIL Act is applied primarily. In the field of civil procedure, on those relations that are not regulated by the PIL Act, as well as in the field of rights of foreigners, special laws apply. However, the Constitution of Montenegro and the ratified bilateral or multilateral international treaties will have primacy in application in relation to the PIL Act, but also in relation to the other statutory instruments.

55. The 2007 Constitution of Montenegro has established a hierarchy of sources of law. The Constitution provides that ratified and published international treaties shall have the supremacy over the domestic law and will be directly applicable when regulating certain relations differently than the internal law. The Constitution of Montenegro explicitly provides the application of generally accepted rules of international law.[61] The Constitution contains important principles and provisions that apply in the field of PIL such as the prohibition of discrimination, gender equality, the right to legal remedy, and so forth. The Constitution guarantees human rights and especially the right of a foreigner to be a subject of property right in accordance with the law.[62] Human rights are protected by the constitutional complaint before the Constitutional Court,[63] and the Constitutional Court in its decisions refers to international conventions, primarily to the European Convention for the Protection of Human Rights and Fundamental Freedoms (European Convention on Human Rights (ECHR)) and to the practice of the European Court of Human Rights (ECtHR). This Convention guarantees fundamental rights and freedoms, some of them playing an important role in PIL: the right to a fair trial (Article 6), the right to respect for private and family life (Article 8), the right to marry (Article 12), the right to an effective remedy (Article 13), prohibition of discrimination (Article 14), protection of property (Article 1 of Protocol Number 1), prohibition of imprisonment for debt (Article 1 of Protocol Number 4), prohibition of the collective expulsion of foreigners (Article 4 of Protocol Number 4), procedural safeguards relating to expulsion of aliens (Article 1 of Protocol Number 7), equality of spouses (Article 5 of Protocol Number 7), general prohibition of discrimination (Article 1 of Protocol Number 12) and other. The ECtHR is in charge of supervising the enforcement of the Convention and it examines the petitions of individuals in international legal proceedings.[64]

---

61. The Constitution was published in Službeni list Crne Gore No. 1/2007. The Constitutional Court of Montenegro is competent to decide on the conformity of laws with the Constitution and confirmed and published international agreements – Art. 145 of the Constitution of Montenegro.
62. Article 61 of the Constitution of Montenegro.
63. Ivana Jelić, Siniša Bjeković & Maja Kostić-Mandić, *Grundrechte in Montenegro,* Handbuch der Grundrechte – in Deutschland und Europa, Band IX, Heidelberg: Hg. Merten/Papier, 2016, 481–535.
64. Article 34 of the European Convention on Human Rights.

56. In current practice, the Constitutional Court has applied the ECHR and the legal positions of the ECtHR in two ways: directly applying the relevant provision of the Convention and by accepting the interpretation of the content and scope of certain legal principles and institutes by the ECtHR in applying the Convention. Regarding the practice of the biggest court of general jurisdiction in Montenegro, the Basic Court in Podgorica, out of the twenty-two analysed final decisions in which international law was applied, in eighteen cases the ECHR was applied, two decisions related to the application of the United Nations Convention on the Rights of the Child, and the remaining two to the application of other instruments of international law. In most cases, the subject was a claim for compensation of non-pecuniary damage due to violation of the honour and reputation of the plaintiff through printed media and violation of the freedom of expression.[65]

57. Furthermore, so far, the Constitutional Court of Montenegro has decided in only a few cases[66] on issues in which the subject of challenge was the decisions of regular courts which decided on the request for recognition of foreign decisions in civil / commercial matters. In all cases, decisions on the merits were made (rejection of the constitutional complaint); however, in none of them was a violation of constitutional or convention rights found in the proceedings that preceded the constitutional court.

58. Apart from the PIL Act, the most important laws comprising the provisions on applicable law are as follows: the Law on Bill of Exchange of 2005 (LBE) (*Zakon o mjenici*), whose Articles 95 to 101 apply analogously to conflict of laws for checks; the Law on Maritime and Inland Navigation of 1998 (LMIN) (*Zakon o pomorskoj i unutrašnjoj plavidbi*); the Law on Obligations and Basic Ownership Relations in Aerial Transport of 2011 (LOPRAT) (*Zakon o obligacionim odnosima i osnovama svojinsko-pravnih odnosa u vazdušnom saobraćaju*), the Law on Bankruptcy of 2011 (LB) (*Zakon o stečaju*), the Law on Financial Collateral of 2012 (*Zakon o finansijskom kolateralu*) and the Law on Capital Market of 2018 (*Zakon o tržištu kapitala*).[67]

59. Also, for civil procedures with foreign element, the provisions of the following laws are relevant: LCP of 2004 (*Zakon o parničnom postupku*), the Law on Extra-Judicial Procedure of 2006 (*Zakon o vanparničnom postupku*), the LESC of 2011 (*Zakon o izvršenju i obezbjeđenju*), LB (*Zakon o stečaju*) and the Law on Arbitration of 2015 (LA) (*Zakon o arbitraži*).[68]

60. The most important laws that are the source of norms for the rights of foreigners in private law relations are: the Law on Family (LF) (2007); the Law on

65. Maja Kostić-Mandić, *Implementation of International and European Law in Montenegro*, In *EU Law Application by the National Courts of the EU-Membership Aspirant Countries from South-East Europe*, Skopje: South East European Law School Network, GIZ, 2014, 136–137.
66. The Constitutional Court of Montenegro, Už-III br. 447-12, Už-III br. 69-13, U-III br. 479-16 and U-III br. 917-17.
67. *See infra* Table of Statutory Instruments.
68. *Ibid.*

Succession (LS) (2008); the Law on Obligations (LO) (2008); the Law on Ownership Relations (2009); the Law on Foreigners (2018); the Law on Labour (2019); the Law on Commercial Companies (LCC) (2020); the Law on Foreign Investment (LFI) (2011); the Law on Concessions (2009); the Law on Patents (2015); the Law on Trademarks (2010); the Law on Copyright and Related Rights (2011) and others.[69]

61. A large number of laws adopted since 2007 have been translated into English and are available either on the official website of the Montenegrin courts or other domestic or international organizations or institutions. However, those translations, as well as the text of statutes in Montenegrin on the official sites of Montenegrin institutions are often not regularly updated to encompass the latest amendments (which in some cases may be of a substantial nature) and therefore it is always important to access the site of companies providing for databases on legislation.[70]

62. In terms of the hierarchy of the sources of law, although the Constitution of Montenegro prescribes supremacy of international treaties over the legislation, due to a comprehensive codification of PIL as well as the adoption of concrete solutions from certain multilateral conventions, the cases in which multilateral international treaties are directly applicable are relatively rare in practice.

63. The PIL Act explicitly states that it will not apply to relations regulated by an international treaty (or other law),[71] while Article 3 of the Code provides that, in the event of a legal gap for determining the applicable law, 'the provisions and principles of this law, the principles of the legal order of Montenegro and the principles of Private International Law[72] shall apply accordingly'. The international treaties binding on Montenegro are limited to certain areas and a limited number of countries, so in practice, the provisions of the PIL Act will most often be applied.

64. Article 30 of the Vienna Convention on the Law of Treaties addresses application of successive treaties relating to the same subject matter.

§4. Case Law

65. In Montenegro previous court judgments are not formally recognized as a source of law and there is no system of binding precedent. However, the Law on Courts in Article 25 enumerates the powers of the Supreme Court of Montenegro,

69. *Ibid.*
70. According to the author's experience, the best partly open database was available at: www.paragraf.me. However, the company is not operational in Montenegro anymore, so the latest updates of the legislation available online are from 31 March 2021, but the already existing texts are still available online. In our view, one of the most reliable paying database is 'Katalog propisa' (https://www.katalogpropisa.me/).
71. Article 2 of the PIL Act.
72. *See infra* Principle of the Closest Connection.

one of them being a power to provide legal position in principle in relation to a contentious legal issue, which has arisen from the case law for the purpose of providing uniform application of the laws by the courts (ex officio or upon the request of the court). The creative role of the courts is predominantly reserved for the domain of filling gaps in statutory law and the interpretation of general and ambiguous statutory provisions.[73]

§5. DOCTRINE

66. Jurisprudence is not officially a source of law in Montenegro, since courts are not entitled to cite opinions of legal authors as the basis for their decisions. However, courts may refer to opinions of established legal scholars when explaining the reasons for a certain general position with respect to a particular issue of law.

67. In Montenegro, as well as in the region, the far-reaching role of the doctrine is in active contribution of experts in drafting legislation. The Montenegrin PIL Act as well as its predecessors (the GPC and the LRCL) are pieces of legislation written by experts in the field. And the 2014 codification was the joint work of experts and professors of PIL, judges of the Supreme Court of Montenegro, with the assistance of the Max Planck Institute for Comparative and International Private Law in Hamburg. Also, colleagues from Serbia, Bosnia and Herzegovina, and Croatia, as well as Serbian draft of PIL codification[74] were consulted for some specific issues.

§6. CUSTOMARY LAW

68. 'Usages' are an indirect source of law, because they can have binding force upon the parties and the court in international civil and commercial matters only if provided so by law. The PIL Act does not make any reference to usages as a potential source of law. Usages are most frequently referred to in domestic contract, tort, and commercial law, and rarely in family, property, or succession law. Some of these references may be relevant to cases with a foreign element.[75] A good example of such a reference can be found in the rules of the 1980 UN Convention on the International Sale of Goods, which has been a law in force in Yugoslavia (Montenegro) since 1 January 1988. Article 9 of the Convention incorporates widely known and regularly observed usages in international trade, unless the parties agreed otherwise, that is, unless they excluded the application of usages to their sale contract. A further example is provided by the 2015 Arbitration Rules of the Arbitration Court at the Chamber of Commerce of Montenegro. Article 24 stipulates in paragraph 4:

73. *See* Kluwer Monograph on PIL of Montenegro of 2013, para. 44.

74. *Encyclopedia of Private International Law*, vol. 4, Jürgen Basedow, Giesela Rühl, Franco Ferrari & Pedro de Miguel Asensio eds Chetenham, UK, Northampton, MA, USA: Edward Elgar Publishing, 2017, (Encyclopedia of PIL of 2017), 3717–3764.

75. Kluwer Monograph on PIL of Montenegro of 2013, para. 63.

'The arbitral tribunal shall decide in accordance with the provisions of the arbitration agreement and shall take into account the usages of the trade applicable to the transaction in relation to which the dispute arose.'

Chapter 2. Determination of the Applicable Law

§1. Conflict of Law Rules

69. PIL is the only national legal discipline where domestic courts or other public authorities may directly apply foreign substantive law when applying conflict rules. That may be the case with marriages concluded before the registrar. If both persons are citizens of Montenegro, the Montenegrin LF will apply to the substantive conditions for concluding their marriage. However, if one of the future spouses does not hold a Montenegrin citizenship, that fact will trigger application of Montenegrin conflict rules in order to select the appropriate legal system whose substantial rules will govern the case. In this matter, legal category, as a part of conflict rule is 'substantive conditions for conclusion of marriage'. A conflict rule of the PIL Act (or a bilateral treaty, if applicable) provides for connecting factor, linking this legal category to the applicable law. Substantive conditions for conclusion of marriage shall be governed by the national law of each party at the time of marriage (the PIL Act, Article 77).

I. Types of Conflict of Law Rules

70. In Montenegro, conflict rules are generally regarded and accepted as binding, irrespective of the will of the persons. Depending on whether the connecting factor leads to the exclusive application of domestic law, or leads to the application of one or more laws of any country, we distinguish unilateral and multilateral conflict rules.

71. The unilateral conflict rule regulates a certain type of legal relation only from the aspect of domestic law, as they determine that domestic law will always apply to these relations. The fact that one conflict rule is formulated as unilateral indicates the special interest of the State to regulate a certain kind of relation on the basis of domestic law. There are only a few unilateral conflict rules in the PIL of Montenegro. Thus, the LMIN provides in Article 1035 that real rights on the vessel which is being constructed in Montenegro are governed by Montenegrin law. The same law further provides in Article 1036 that the labour relations between ship crew members are governed by Montenegrin law, and in Article 1049 that Montenegrin rules on salvage are applicable to salvage of goods sunken beyond territorial and internal waters of Montenegro, if the goods are owned by the State of Montenegro, natural or legal person and if they are saved by a Montenegrin enterprise, or another legal or natural person. There are other unilateral conflict rules in this Code, as well as in the LOPRAT. This latter law enumerates certain situations in Article 179 paragraph 2 in which the law of Montenegro must be applied to insurance contracts.[76]

76. *See infra* Insurance Contracts.

72. Multilateral conflict rules, which may point to the application of any law, either domestic or foreign (or cumulative application of both laws, or the application of several foreign laws, depending on the type of connection), regulate private legal relations with an international element by using abstract connecting factors. The great majority of conflict rules in Montenegrin law are of a multilateral character. In some cases the conflict rule contains a single connecting factor. However, in case of several connections in a conflict rule, their relationship can vary so they can be cumulative, alternative and subsidiary connections.[77]

II. Connecting Factors

73. In PIL of Montenegro, characteristic connections for certain categories of legal relations are:

- for status, family and succession matters: citizenship, habitual residence, party autonomy;
- for property matters: place where the property is located;
- for contracts: party autonomy, habitual residence of the party effecting the characteristic performance, principle of the closest connection, place of conclusion of the contract;
- for torts: place where the damage occurs, principle of the closest connection, habitual residence, party autonomy.[78]

74. As Montenegro adheres to the European Continental Legal Tradition, conflict of laws rules used to be drafted in a way to be 'blind' in relation to the substantive result of their application, by using classical multilateral conflict rules, which makes the application of domestic or foreign law only dependent on the circumstances of an individual case. Therefore, the conflict rules of Montenegro used to point to the judiciary of a country, with which the concerned case has the closest connection. However, the modern PIL of Montenegro adheres also to alternative connections in order to achieve a certain substantive result. This alternative binding may be aimed at protecting the weaker party and ensuring the use of law that is more favourable to a party.[79]

III. Time Factors

75. The importance of the time factor in PIL can be discussed in various aspects.[80] Here we shall address variable connecting factors and institute of the mobile conflict of laws (*conflit mobile*).

77. *See infra* Combination of Connecting Factors.
78. *See infra* Choice of Law, and Objective Connecting Factor.
79. *See infra* Combination of Connecting Factors.
80. *See also* Michael Pryles, *The Time Factor in Private International Law*, 3 Monash U. L. Rev. 225–243 (1980).

76. The mobile conflict of laws is a phenomenon in PIL that occurs at connecting factors that are not fixed in time. Over time, there may be a change in the facts on which the connecting factor is based, so it should be determined which fact is relevant for the application of the governing law. When a movable item is being displaced from one country to another, it can be disputed whether to apply the law of the country where the movable was originally located or the law of the country where the item is located when the question arises. Also, if a change occurs, for example, in citizenship or habitual residence, the question arises whether to apply the law of earlier or present nationality or habitual residence of a person. In these cases, the connecting factors do not change, but only the facts that make up their background are altered (e.g., citizenship, habitual residence, place where the property is located).

77. The simplest way to avoid this problem is to turn the variable connecting factors into permanent ones in the conflict rule itself, by specifying which moment is relevant for determining the applicable law for a particular relation. The PIL Act resorts to this method by specifying as a relevant moment for:

- torts: the habitual residence of the tortfeasor and a victim in the same State at the time when the damage occurs (Article 52, paragraph 2);
- succession: the habitual residence of the deceased at the time of his death (Article 70);
- marital property relations: citizenship or habitual residence of the spouses at the time the question arises (Article 81, paragraph 2), and so forth.

78. In addition to the mentioned cases, the mobile conflict of laws is especially pertinent to real rights on movables where a special solution is envisaged.[81]

79. Another way of resolving this problem, which implies a general solution that would be applied in all cases, regardless of the type of relation, is not accepted in either doctrine or the legislation of Montenegro.

IV. Dépeçage

80. The concept of dépeçage is traditionally linked to contractual relations. LMIN provides for numerous possibilities of dépeçage in its Articles 1033–1050. On the contrary, the LRCL in Article 19, contained only a general rule on choice of law for contractual relations (unless otherwise is provided by that law or by international contract). At that time, the opinions of the doctrine[82] on the possible dépeçage for contractual obligations under the LRCL were divided.

---

81. *See infra* Moveable Property.
82. Mihajlo Dika, Gaša Knežević & Srđan Stojanović, *Komentar Zakona o međunarodnom privatnom i procesnom pravu* (Commentary of the PIL Act), Belgrade: Nomos, 1991, 75.

81. Pursuant to the PIL Act, parties may choose the applicable law for a whole range of relations. However, only the provision about the choice of applicable law for contractual relations, borrowed from the Rome I Regulation, contains an explicit possibility that 'By their choice the parties can select the law applicable to the whole or to part only of the contract.'[83] Furthermore, the application of this institute is not called into question for succession. Here, in addition to the rules that, for the succession as whole, a testator may choose the law of the country of which he is a citizen or the law of the country in which he habitually resides at the time of choice of law or at the time of death, the PIL Act also provides the possibility for testator, for the succession of the immovable estate, to choose the law of the country where the immovable property is situated (Article 72, paragraph 2). In this case, dépeçage is an exception to the regime of unitary succession. Other areas where parties may be entitled to a scission of applicable law may include Article 63 of the PIL Act, on choice of law for non-contractual obligations, modelled after Article 14 of the Rome II Regulation. However, the line of interpretation of this PIL Act provision will depend on the prevailing attitude in the application of its model provision.

V. Legal Consequences

82. Article 7, paragraph 1 of the PIL Act provides that when the competent authority ascertains the content of foreign law, it shall be applied 'according to its own sense and the terms that it contains'. Paragraph 2 of the same article provides that legal remedies may be used in case of non-application, misinterpretation, or misapplication of foreign law.

We can picture a number of situations:[84]

- The court (or other body) did not apply the conflict rule at all, but instead it applied the domestic substantive law, and on the basis of the conflict rule, the foreign law should have been applied. The foreign law was not applied at all because the judge neglected or overlooked the existence of a foreign element due to which the rules of PIL should have been applied in the case, and the conflict rule that should have been applied, refers to the application of a foreign law.
- The court (or other body) erroneously applied the conflict rule (e.g., it did not apply the conflict rule from an international treaty or it erroneously submitted facts under a certain legal category of conflict rule), which led to the application of another foreign law.
- It is also possible that the correct conflict rule was applied, but there was a misinterpretation and misapplication of foreign law.

In all three above-listed cases, the legal consequences are identical as to the misapplication of the domestic substantive law. Therefore, the legal remedies include

83. *See* Article 38(1)3of the PIL Act and Art. 3(1)3 of the Rome I Regulation.
84. Maja Stanivuković & Mirko Živković, *Međunarodno privatno pravo: opšti deo* (Private International Law: General Part), Belgrade, Službeni list SCG, 2004, 310–311.

appeal and revision.[85] However, the revision shall be rejected when the conflict rule was not applied, but its application would lead to the application of domestic law, which was applied in the first place. On the contrary, erroneously or incompletely determined state of facts can only be a ground for the appeal.[86]

§2. Relevant Contact and Evasion of the Law

83. A foreign element may appear as a fact that triggers the application of the rules of PIL in any of the factors of a legal relationship: persons, res, and events or actions (rights and obligations). Each of the above-listed foreign elements should be considered as relevant in order to apply the rules of PIL. However, this general theoretical principle, widely accepted in the literature[87] has not always been applied by the competent courts and other public authorities. This principle is tested every year, especially in the second half of December and during the summer holidays, when Montenegrin courts in some municipalities are busy with divorce disputes between domestic nationals 'temporarily employed abroad', who never renounce their domicile in Montenegro. During these holidays a number of Montenegrin nationals come to this country from abroad, wishing to solve part of their problems in front of domestic courts in a potentially less costly and time-consuming manner. Since these cases involve Montenegrin citizens having habitual residence abroad it may be asked whether the existence of the foreign element based on the fact of foreign habitual residence has any influence upon resolution of these disputes. Pursuant to the LRCL[88] the answer would be negative, while pursuant to the PIL Act[89] even when the issue of the divorce of two Montenegrin citizens who have habitual residence abroad is raised before a Montenegrin court, the rules of PIL should be applied. However, the same result would be reached by ignoring the foreign element, that is, by the application of domestic law of divorce.

84. The institute of evasion of the law will be addressed under the separate title,[90] and here we will briefly look at another phenomenon. In practice, the implementation of the LRCL often resulted in a homeward trend. Namely, in numerous cases, a foreign element in a concrete dispute has been disregarded and did not trigger the application of the rules of PIL, but domestic substantive or procedural[91] law. After the adoption of the PIL Act and numerous training of judges, it is expected that the number of such cases will be significantly reduced.

85. Article 366 para. 1(3) and Art. 400 para. 1(3) of the Law on Civil Procedure.
86. Article 400, para. 3 of the Law of Civil Procedure.
87. Mihajlo Dika, Gaša Knežević & Srđan Stojanović, *Komentar Zakona o međunarodnom privatnom i procesnom pravu* (Commentary of the PIL Act), Belgrade: Nomos, 1991, 10–11.
88. Article 61, para. 1(1), (3); para. 2.
89. Articles 85 and 130.
90. *See infra* Evasion of the Law.
91. For example, decision of the Basic Court in Kotor, Posl. br. P. 93/08.

§3. Choice of Law

85. The choice of law in the law of Montenegro represents a connecting factor which determines the applicable law and includes the application of both dispositive and imperative rules of that contracted law. Parties may agree on the application of substantive domestic, foreign law or non-national law. This subjective connection, the application of which depends on the expressed or implied will of the parties, has the same effect as all other connections established by the legislator, the restrictions being public policy exception, mandatory rules that cannot be derogated from or overriding mandatory rules, in certain types of relationships in which there is a special interest of the country to apply its own law.[92]

86. The choice of law is increasingly gaining importance in the PIL of Montenegro, as well as in conventional and comparative law. Pursuant to the PIL Act, the party autonomy, in addition to the domain of contractual obligations with a foreign element (Article 38), occurs in areas where it was previously excluded or where other connections were prevalent. Thus, choice of law is now possible in some family relationships (marital property relations (Article 82), divorce (Article 86)); maintenance (Article 95); succession (Article 72); non-contractual obligations (Article 63) and for personal name (Article 17, paragraph 4).

87. The LMIN provides in Article 1038 that 'contracts on navigation relationships' are governed by the law chosen by the parties, and the LOPRAT provides in Article 177, paragraph 1, that its rules on contracts of carriage of passengers and goods by air do not apply to contractual relationships in international air traffic, if the parties have agreed upon application of another law.

88. The choice of law, where it is permitted, achieves its primary goal: it allows the parties to choose the law to their own relationship and to avoid conflict of laws, which ultimately leads to predictability in ascertaining the applicable law and legal certainty. In addition, unlike contractual relationships, where party autonomy is the most important connection and where its scope is the broadest, the other types of relationships are characterized by the limited party autonomy, so that the parties can make choice of law in accordance with the possibilities prescribed by the legislator.

§4. Objective Connecting Factor

I. Principle of the Closest Connection

89. The principle of the closest connection may have different functions in the PIL of Montenegro.[93] This principle is one of the basic principles of a domestic

92. *See infra* Public Policy, and Overriding Mandatory Rules.
93. Maja Kostić-Mandić, *The Closest Connection Principle in 1983 PIL Act in Theory and Practice,* In *Twenty Years of the Private International Code,* Niš: Univerzitet u Nišu, Pravni fakultet, 2004, 104–117.

legal system that can be used for filling legal gaps. Also, the principle of the closest connection appears as a connecting factor and a tool that allows the correction of the system of PIL, by triggering an escape clause mechanism.

90. The principle of the closest connection is a flexible connecting factor. The way in which this connection is to be applied is left to the judiciary or other competent authority. However, the Montenegrin doctrine dealt with this issue in detail.[94] The first step in applying this connection is to establish all contacts that one relationship has with different legal systems. The following step is the process of evaluation of these contacts in order to determine one or more of them, indicating the closest link with a legal system of a single country. The final step is to answer the question on the basis of which criteria this evaluation will be carried out and here two possibilities are identified. According to the first one, the bare counting of the contacts to different countries is taking place so that the governing law shall be the one to which the greatest number of contacts is pointing to. By applying the latter approach, the special regard in ascertaining the applicable law using the closest connection test should be paid to the quality of connections that the disputed relationship has with different legal systems. Thus, each case is treated independently from others, so that circumstances once qualified as decisive, based whether on territorial or personal ties, in another case based on different facts may be found irrelevant.[95] In conclusion, the procedure of applying the closest connection test consists of ascertaining all the contacts pointing out at different legal systems and then their valorization depending on the quality and relevance of the contacts to a specific case.

91. In the PIL Act, the principle of the closest connection appears in the formulation of 'close or closer connection'. The most common is in the form of an escape clause: general escape clause (Article 8) and special escape clauses in: contractual (Article 39, paragraph 3), non-contractual (Article 52, paragraph 3), and maintenance obligations (Article 92). The principle of the closest connection also appears as a subsidiary solution in provisions on: States with multiple legal orders[96] (Article 5, paragraph 2), citizenship (Article 11, paragraphs 3 and 6), and in case of a legal gap in the contract (Article 39, paragraph 4) and it is also a part of the provision on overriding mandatory rule (Article 10, paragraph 2).

II. Nationality

92. Citizenship as a legal relationship between a person and a country is addressed in detail in the Law on Montenegrin Citizenship. Citizenship does not imply nationality, and there are four grounds for acquiring citizenship, which have

94. Maja Kostić-Mandić, *Opšta klauzula odstupanja od redovno mjerodavnog prava: u savremenom me unarodnom privatnom pravu* (General Escape Clause: in Contemporary Private International Law), Podgorica: University of Montenegro, Faculty of Law, 2012.

95. *See infra* Sales Contract.

96. *See infra* Reference to the Law of States with Multiple Legal Orders.

different practical significance and reflect the dominant political interests of the legislator. The basic way of acquiring citizenship is by origin. In contrast, the acquiring of Montenegrin citizenship by birth in the territory of Montenegro is of exceptional character and is primarily aimed at preventing statelessness (apatridia).[97] The acquiring of Montenegrin citizenship on the basis of international treaties is limited in its scope to only a small number of countries. However, the naturalization (admission) is the sole ground that causes controversy due to uneven practice and strict policy in some cases.[98]

93. In practice only certain issues in relation to citizenship actually affect the ability of citizens to exercise their rights. The issue of facilitated naturalization and the possibility of acquiring dual citizenship have evolved over time in the national laws and practices of the countries of the region.[99] The contemporary legal moment of Montenegro is characterized by the continuous liberalization of the legal regime for acquiring citizenship (which is restrictive) in order to harmonize national legislation with the European Convention on Nationality and the European Convention on the Avoidance of Statelessness in Relation to State Succession.

94. In the domain of regulation of private law relations with a foreign element for certain types of relationships, nationality principle gives way to a habitual residence as a principle which guarantees non-discriminatory application of the law to persons, regardless of citizenship. The legislator also wants to ensure the application of domestic law to citizens residing abroad, as well as access to domestic courts.[100] Citizenship as a connecting factor in status, family, and succession relationships also relates to the compliance with human rights, as a basis of the cultural identity of a natural person. And the right to cultural identity falls under the privacy rights.[101]

97. *See* Art. 7 of the Law on Montenegrin Citizenship, Podgorica, Službeni list Crne Gore, No. 13/2008, 40/2010, 28/2011, 46/2011, 20/2014– decision of the Constitutional Court and 54/2016 and 73/2019. https://www.paragraf.me/propisi-crnegore/zakon-o-crnogorskom-drzavljanstvu.html.

98. Even ten articles of the law have been devoted to this issue (Arts 8–17), and all amendments to this law were primarily or exclusively related to a certain category of persons acquiring citizenship by naturalization.

99. Maja Kostić-Mandić, *Državljanstvo, sredstvo ili prepreka za ostvarivanje prava građana na prostoru bivše Jugoslavije*, u: *Regulisanje otvorenih pitanja između država sukcesora bivše SFRJ* (Citizenship, means or obstacles for exercising the rights of citizens in the territory of the former Yugoslavia, In *Regulating open issues between successor countries of the former SFRY)*, Belgrade: Institute for International Politics and Economy, 2013, 518–545.

100. Maja Stanivuković, *Srpsko međunarodno privatno pravo u vremenu tranzicije: promenjen značaj državljanstva i prebivališta*, u: *Državljanstvo i međunarodno privatno pravo; Haške konvencije*, urednici: G. Knežević, V. Pavić (Serbian Private International Law at the time of transition: the changed significance of citizenship and residence, In *Citizenship and International Private Law; The Hague Conventions*), G. Knežević, V. Pavić, eds., Belgrade: Univerzitet u Beogradu, Pravni fakultet, Službeni glasnik, 2007, 46–47.

101. Aleksandar Jakšić, *Državljanstvo i prethodno pitanje*, u: *Državljanstvo i međunarodno privatno pravo; Haške konvencije* (Citizenship and Previous Question, In *Citizenship and International Private Law; The Hague Conventions*), *Ibid,* 99.

95. In Montenegrin PIL, the terms 'nationality' and 'citizenship' are used interchangeably, with the same meaning.[102] The nationality principle has a traditionally primary role as connection for certain types of relationships. The LRCL provided for this connecting factor in both, narrower area of personal status of natural persons: for legal and business capacity, declaring missing persons dead and in wider area, on: marital relations, validity of marriage, divorce, adoption, legalization, maintenance and succession in general.

96. The rules of Montenegrin PIL have been modernized under the influence of the European and comparative law. Significant changes occurred in the area of determining the applicable law to succession and maintenance obligations, where shift was made from nationality to the habitual residence principle. However, such fundamental changes did not significantly affect the formulation of connections for status and family relations, where nationality principle remains the basic connecting factor.

97. In the PIL Act, nationality principle retains its primacy in status and family relations and is used to determine the applicable law for:

- legal capacity (Article 13);
- business capacity (Article 14, paragraph 1);
- guardianship (Article 16);
- name (Article 17, paragraph 1);
- declaration of missing person dead (Article 18);
- terms of conclusion of marriage (Article 77);
- annulment of marriage (Article 79);
- relations between spouses (Article 80, paragraph 1);
- law applied to property relations between spouses (Article 81, paragraph 1);
- divorce (Article 85, paragraph 1);
- family status of a child (Article 87, paragraph 1);
- relations between parents and children; (Article 88) and
- adoption (Article 89).[103]

In these types of relationships nationality principle is the basic connecting factor and indicates a significant intensity of connections between a person and the country of their citizenship.

98. In addition, for certain types of relationships, the PIL Act envisages the possibility of applying nationality principle as a result of choice of law, but also as a more favourable substantive law. For the contractual property relations of spouses, for divorce, maintenance obligations, and succession, one of the listed laws to be elected encompass the national law of a person.[104] Substantive effects of a more

102. *See also* Encyclopedia of PIL of 2017, vol.2, 1289–1290.

103. *See infra* Nationality/Habitual Residence/Domicile.

104. Article 82, para. 1(1), Art. 86, Art. 95, Art. 72, para. 1 of the PIL Act.

favourable national law of a person are taken into account for: paternity disputes, relationships between parents and children, and the maintenance obligation.[105]

99. Issues that may pose a problem when applying nationality principle are when there is a so-called positive or negative conflict of laws regarding citizenship (multiple citizenships and statelessness).[106] In modern times, it is not unusual for a person to have multiple citizenships. The PIL Act distinguishes between two situations: whether it is a person with multiple citizenships, one of which is Montenegrin, or a person has only foreign citizenships.[107] If one of the citizenships is Montenegrin, it will be considered that the person has only Montenegrin citizenship, and no effective citizenship will be established. In cases of multiple citizenships, in the case of a person who is not a Montenegrin citizen and who has more foreign citizenships, it is envisaged that he will be considered to be a citizen of the country with which he has the closest connection based on all circumstances, and in particular his habitual residence. When citizenship as a starting criterion cannot be applied because the person is stateless or citizenship cannot be determined, as well as in the case of refugees and asylum seekers, the PIL Act provides for the habitual residence as the main connection. If the habitual residence of these persons cannot be determined, the law of the country with which this person is in the closest connection shall apply.

III. Residence

A. Domicile (of Origin, of Choice, of Dependence)

100. Domicile used to be a widely used connecting factor in Montenegrin PIL as a criterion for designating the applicable law. The adoption of the PIL Act marked the switch from domicile principle to habitual residence principle so that presently, except in the area of international jurisdiction, the importance of domicile principle is insignificant. Namely, in contrast to the LRCL, where the domicile was a subsidiary connection for a whole range of relationships, in the new codification of PIL, it gives way to a more flexible connection – the habitual residence and is prescribed as connection only in one case, for the validity of the form of the will.[108] In contrast, in the field of international jurisdiction, domicile as a basis for international jurisdiction retains its prominent place, as a general forum.[109] The PIL Act does not contain a definition on domicile either for the purposes of applicable law or for jurisdiction. However, the PIL Act allows for a possibility that a person has no domicile at all. Thus, pursuant to Article 99, paragraph 2 if the defendant is not domiciled in Montenegro or in any other country, the court will have jurisdiction if

105. Articles 87 para. 2, 88 and 95 para. 5 of the PIL Act. For maintenance obligations, if according to the general rule and special rules for the benefit of individual creditors it is not possible to obtain maintenance from the debtor, the law of the country of their common citizenships shall apply.
106. Article 11 of the PIL Act.
107. *Ibid.*
108. Article 73 para. 3 of the PIL Act.
109. *See infra* Statutory Forums.

the defendant resides on the territory of Montenegro. Furthermore, there are neither any express provisions on possibility of having more than one domicile at a time, nor can any conclusions be drawn from the interpretation of its provisions.

101. The Law on Registers of Domicile and Residence (LRDR)[110] provides a definition of domicile for the purposes of that law. The place of domicile is a place in the territory of Montenegro in which a Montenegrin citizen settled with the intent to live there permanently, which is the centre of his life activities and with which he has a lasting connection (Article 2, paragraph 2). This definition comprises two standard elements of the notion of domicile: the objective and the subjective element (corpus and animus). However, this definition of domicile incorporates the third element, the factual vital and continuous connection with the place of settlement. It may be concluded by interpretation of Article 2, paragraph 2 of this law, that nobody can have more than one domicile at a time. However, pursuant to Article 12, paragraph 1, a Montenegrin citizen 'may' make a notification of abandoning the old domicile when he moves to live in another country, but it is not mandatory. And in practice, Montenegrin nationals living and working abroad for a longer time retain a domicile in Montenegro as if they were only temporarily employed abroad. Similarly, in the jurisprudence of the countries of the region, the place of domicile approached the notion of citizenship because of this category of persons who were considered to be domiciled in their countries of origin.[111]

B. Habitual Residence

102. Since the adoption of the PIL Act, the habitual residence has become one of the most important connections in PIL of Montenegro. This concept was not used by the Law on Resolution of Conflict of Laws, which only provides for a domicile and a (temporary) residence. However, habitual residence has been used as a connecting factor in certain Hague Conventions ratified by this country, such as the Hague Testamentary Dispositions Convention, the Hague Traffic Accidents Convention, and the Hague Products Liability Convention.[112]

103. The PIL Act attaches great importance to the habitual residence as a connecting factor. The Code contains as many as three definitions of habitual residence

110. The Law on Registers of Domicile and Residence, Podgorica, Službeni list Crne Gore No. 46/2015.

111. Maja Stanivuković, *Srpsko međunarodno privatno pravo u vremenu tranzicije: promenjen značaj državljanstva i prebivališta*, u: *Državljanstvo i međunarodno privatno pravo; Haške konvencije*, urednici: G. Knežević, V. Pavić (Serbian Private International Law at the time of transition: the changed significance of citizenship and residence, In *Citizenship and International Private Law; The Hague Conventions*), G. Knežević, V. Pavić, eds., Belgrade: Univerzitet u Beogradu, Pravni fakultet, Službeni glasnik, 2007, 46–47.

112. A habitual residence is present also in procedural conventions such as, Convention on International Access to Justice (1980) and the Convention on the Civil Aspects of International Child Abduction (1980).

pertaining to this codification: (general – for natural persons, as well as special definitions for contractual and non-contractual obligations for natural and legal persons performing commercial activity) and a large number of provisions where habitual residence is a connecting factor (about thirty articles). For contractual and non-contractual relations, succession, as well as the maintenance obligation the habitual residence as a connecting factor, was imported from the European regulations. Furthermore, for personal and property marital relations, as well as divorce, this connection has replaced domicile principle, while for other family law relations it is combined with citizenship principle.

104. Pursuant to the general definition, the habitual residence is a place where a natural person habitually resides, regardless of the entry in the records of the competent authority or the approval of residence or settlement, and regardless of whether the stay is time-limited. The PIL Act specifies that, when determining a habitual residence, account should be taken of circumstances of a personal or professional nature that indicate more permanent connections to that place or the intention to create such relationships (Article 12). The decisive factor for determining the habitual residence of a person is whether that person made a particular place the centre of his professional activities and his social contacts. A habitual residence should always coincide with the closest connection, and the emphasis should be on the durability and stability of the stay in a particular place. The time factor is also important, but the length of stay required to establish a habitual residence should be determined in accordance with the circumstances of a case in question.[113] The minimum length of stay is not prescribed, and shorter temporary leave will not affect the habitual residence. When determining a habitual residence, account must be taken of the circumstances of a personal or professional nature, which indicate more permanent connections to that place or the existence of such intentions. On the one hand, it is required that a stay in the territory of a country is of a lasting character, even if this does not necessarily mean permanent residence. If a relationship with a country is serious and the actions to achieve it are intense, a more significant time span is not required for the establishment of a habitual residence. For example, in the case of Russian citizens who purchase a real estate on the Montenegrin coast, register a company, relocate their family to Montenegro, enrol the children in school, open a bank account, enrol a language course, it can be considered that in a very short time Montenegro became the centre of their private and professional life where they acquired a habitual residence (regardless of their domicile in Russia, and their formal legal status as foreign nationals in Montenegro).

105. For contractual relations, the habitual residence of a natural person performing commercial activity is his principal place of business, and for companies – the place of their central administration. If a contract is concluded or executed

113. A natural person has a habitual residence in a country in which he lives for a certain period of time, even if this period of time has been limited – Art. 20 para. 1(b) of the Swiss PIL Act.

within the business of a branch, agency, or other business units, the habitual residence shall be the place where that unit is located.[114] In order to avoid a mobile conflict, the Code specifies that the relevant point in time for determining habitual residence is the time of the conclusion of the contract. In the case of non-contractual obligations, similar rules, now imported from the Rome II Regulation apply.[115]

106. The habitual residence appears as a connecting factor for almost all types of relationships, both as the main and as the subsidiary connection. For succession[116] and maintenance,[117] it fully takes on the primacy in relation to citizenship. Furthermore, it is also the sole connection for the personal belongings of the passengers.[118] In contractual relationships,[119] habitual residence appears as the most important subsidiary connection in the absence of choice of law. Its role as subsidiary connection is also significant for family,[120] non-contractual obligations,[121] as well as for certain status relationships (for the personal name[122] and declaring a missing person dead[123]). Furthermore, the habitual residence is introduced as a basis for special jurisdiction for status of persons, consumer contracts, succession, and family matters.[124]

107. There is a record that not all the judges master the concept of habitual residence. In one case[125] the second instance court had to point out that the habitual residence is not the same as the domicile and cannot be proved in the same manner.

C. *Temporary Residence*

108. The concept of temporary residence is not of particular importance to the modern PIL of Montenegro. The PIL Act does not provide a single conflict rule with temporary residence as a connecting factor. However, temporary residence appears as a subsidiary ground for general jurisdiction (Article 99, paragraph 2 of the PIL Act) and in the recognition and enforcement of foreign decisions (Article 153, paragraph 6): 'The court shall not serve a decision recognizing a foreign judgment on divorce to the other party if the party seeking recognition is a Montenegrin national, and the other party has no domicile or residence in Montenegro.'

114. Article 40 of the PIL Act mirrors Art. 19 of the Rome I Regulation.
115. Article 51 of the PIL Act mirrors Art. 23 of the Rome II Regulation.
116. Article 71, Art. 72 para. 2, Art. 73 para. 1(4) of the PIL Act.
117. Articles 90–93, 95 of the PIL Act.
118. Article 30 para. 2 of the PIL Act.
119. Articles 40–41, 44–45 of the PIL Act.
120. Articles 80–82, 84–88 of the PIL Act.
121. Article 52 para. 2, Art. 55, Art. 62 of the PIL Act.
122. Article 17 para. 2, Art. 17 paras 4 and 5 of the PIL Act.
123. Article 18 of the PIL Act.
124. *See infra* Statutory Forums.
125. Higher Court in Podgorica, Gž.br. 5360/18 of 29.10.2018 rendered a decision revoking the judgment of the Basic Court in Podgorica P. br.1536/17 of 26.07.2018.

109. Pursuant to the Law on Registers of Domicile and Residence, residence is a place and the address on which a Montenegrin citizen temporarily resides (Article 2(3)). On the contrary, the Law on Foreigners[126] provides for temporary residence of a foreigner, as opposed to ninety days residence and permanent residence (Article 33).

IV. Registered Office

110. By choosing the connecting factor that should apply to legal persons, national legislators, and case law usually adhere to two systems: the application of the law of the country in which the legal person is established or the law of the country in which the legal person is actually located. Applying the law of incorporation implies that one legal entity is created, operates, and ceases to exist according to the law of the country where it is established. The place of establishment most often coincides with registered, statutory seat. Founders can choose for the location of the head office of a company some other country, regardless of whether there is any connection between the founders, property, business, and that country, so that this type of seat can be completely fictitious (e.g., a registered seat in a country that is known as an offshore destination). The real seat criterion implies that legal persons belong to the country in which they have a real seat and that the precondition for their constitution is to meet all the conditions that the law of that State provides for the establishment and operation of that type of enterprise. Thus, the real seat most often coincides with the place of establishment, as well as with the seat mentioned in the founding act or the statute. Here, the party autonomy[127] is excluded and there is always an objectively determined connecting factor: a real seat. Moving a real seat to another country leads to the application of the law of a new real seat. In comparative law, a real or effective seat is determined on the basis of performing activities in the territory of a particular country, which can be expressed in terms of the location of the head office, as well as the presence of the employees, the management body and so forth. Otherwise, the actual centre of administration takes into account the interests of third parties and the country in which the business is being performed, either as an adjacent circumstance or as an independent connecting factor, unlike the establishment theory.

111. The aforementioned finds its elaboration in the law of Montenegro, where the rules on the applicable law for the status relations of legal persons are contained in the PIL Act. It addresses ascertaining of the applicable law for the status relations of legal persons by its distinctive conflict rules which remain the same as in the LRCL. A legal person is primarily governed by the law of the State under which it was established. However, if a legal person has its real seat in a State other than the

126. Law on foreigners, Podgorica, Službeni list Crne Gore No. 12/2018, https://www.paragraf.me/propisi-crnegore/zakon_o_strancima.html.

127. Stephan Rammeloo, *Corporations in Private International Law*, Oxford: Oxford University Press, 2001, 11, 39, 72.

State of its establishment, and according to the law of that other State its law is applicable, then it will be deemed a legal person of the State of its real seat.[128]

V. *Lex Loci Delicti*

112. The law of the place where the harmful act was performed used to be a widespread connecting factor in national laws but also in conventional law. In a situation where more and more cases have been reported where tortfeasor take several actions in different countries, as well as in case of objective liability, it is not easy to determine in a definite way which country will be considered as the country where the tortious act was committed. Furthermore, in comparative law, there is no single solution that would apply when elements of the case gravitate to different legal systems (such as when a tortious act is committed in one country, while a harmful consequence occurs in another or in other countries). Pursuant to the LRCL the governing law for non-contractual obligations was the law of the place where the harmful act was performed or the law of the place where the consequence occurred, depending on which of these two laws is more favourable to the injured person (Article 28, paragraph 1). According to views expressed in judicial practice, the more favourable law is determined at the initiative of the injured person, rather than at the court's own initiative, and the injured person may choose the applicable law until the closing of the main hearing; however, the injured person may not request a combined application of these two laws in order to attain a more favourable solution.[129]

113. The PIL Act's conflict rules on non-contractual obligations mirror the Rome II Regulation with only minimal adjustments. Moreover, pursuant to Article 67 of the PIL Act, it has been envisaged that the provisions of the Code dedicated to the applicable law for non-contractual obligations shall be interpreted and applied in accordance with the Rome II Regulation. However, this does not apply to the subject matters regulated by the relevant Hague Conventions.[130] The PIL Act introduces as a general rule the application of the law of the State where the direct damage occurs and to a certain extent and under certain conditions also allows for the use of a habitual residence (for which there is a special definition for commercial law relations[131]), and an escape clause. The party autonomy is elaborated in great detail. Also, a number of rules are provided for different types of non-contractual obligations.[132]

128. *See infra* Incorporated Organizations.
129. Opinions of the Commercial Courts of Serbia, *Pravo i privreda*, Nos 7–8 (June), 1993, 145. *See* Maja Stanivuković, *Yugoslavian PIL at the End of the 20th Century: Progress or Regress*? In *Private International at the End of the 20th Century: Progress or Regress?* S. Symeonides ed., The Hague/London/Boston: Kluwer Law International, 2000, 470.
130. Articles 58 and 59 of the PIL Act.
131. Article 51 of the PIL Act.
132. *See infra* Non-contractual Obligations.

VI. *Lex Rei (Cartae) Sitae*

114. The place where the property is located (*lex rei sitae*, *lex situs*) is traditionally the most important connecting factor for determining the applicable law for property relations, movables and immovables, alike. This is a rule in PIL of Montenegro since the time of Bogišić's General Pecuniary Code (Article 791); the tradition continued with the Law on Resolution of Conflict of Laws (Article 18, paragraph 1), and then with the PIL Act. The movable or immovable nature of the property is determined according to the law of the country where the property is located (Article 28 of the PIL Act).

115. The *lex situs* is the only connecting factor for immovable property, whether it is the acquisition, the termination, the content, or the exercise of real rights. However, in the case of special legal bases for the acquisition of property, on the basis of an agreement on the acquisition of ownership, succession, or division of the joint property of a spouse in case of divorce or death of one of the spouses, the conflict rules for these types of legal relations shall apply.

116. Pursuant to the PIL Act, *lex situs* also applies:

- to an estate without a claimant (Article 75);
- when spouses agree in writing to subject their contractual property relations in relation to immovable property to the law of the country where it is located (Article 82, paragraph 1(4)); and
- when the deceased for the succession of immovable property chose the law of the country where it is situated (Article 72, paragraph 2).

117. When a moveable property is being displaced from one country to another, it can be disputed whether to apply the law of the country where the item was originally located or the law of the country where the item is located when the question arises. The PIL Act resolves these mobile conflict of laws.[133]

118. The *lex situs* does not apply to some specific categories of movables: goods in transit, the means of transport (ships and aircraft, as well as railways),[134] and cultural property.

119. The law of Montenegro does not contain a special conflict rule for acquiring and terminating ownership rights on securities. In the doctrine, the unanimous attitude is that the *lex cartae sitae* shall apply.

---

133. *See infra* Movable Property.
134. *Ibid.*

§5. CHANGES IN THE CONNECTING FACTORS; CHANGES IN THE *LEX CAUSAE*

120. The impact of the changes in the connecting factors of the forum is addressed in the Transitional and Final Provisions of the PIL Act. Article 166 stipulates that: 'first-instance proceedings on a cause of action involving an international element which is still pending on the date the implementation of the present Act begins shall be governed by the law provided for by the present Act'.

121. Another situation involves changes in the internal law of the governing legal system when a decision as to whether the *lex cause* will be applied as it presently exists or as it formerly existed should be made. The foreign transitional rule will be applied not only when there are successive changes in the foreign substantive rules, but also when there are such changes in the foreign conflict rules.

122. The issue of application of the old or the new conflict rules of foreign law may arise in the course of implementation of the doctrine of renvoi. For example, if a Montenegrin conflict rule orders application of German law, and German conflict rule has been recently changed, so that it now refers back to Montenegrin law, while it did not refer to that law before, the judge will have to consult German transitional rules in order to determine whether to take into account the former or the present conflict rule in the particular case.[135]

§6. COMBINATION OF CONNECTING FACTORS

123. In some cases the conflict rule contains a single connecting factor. However, in case of several connections in a conflict rule, the way in which these connections are applied is determined by the conflict rule itself contained in a piece of legislation or in an international treaty. Their relationship can vary so they can be cumulative, alternative or subsidiary connections.

124. The cumulative application of connections leads to the case where several laws may be simultaneously applied as the applicable law, depending on the circumstances of a particular case (in the following example, provided that persons have different citizenships): 'As regards the conditions for entering into marriage the governing law for each person is the law of the State whose citizen that person is at the time of marriage.' (Article 77 of the PIL Act). When persons have different citizenships, two laws are cumulatively applied, but in a way that the fulfilment of these conditions is valued for each of the persons according to the law of their citizenship, and it is a so-called distributive cumulation. Ordinary cumulation would exist if all conditions from both national laws would apply to both persons. In this case, it would in fact lead to application of the law providing for stricter conditions and therefore this type of cumulation is avoided in modern Montenegrin PIL.[136] The only example of ordinary cumulation is Article 89 of the PIL Act on adoption which

135. Kluwer Monograph on PIL of Montenegro of 2013, para. 161.

136. *See infra* Heterosexual Marriage, Substance.

in its paragraph 1 states: 'The terms of establishment, effect, and termination of adoption of a child shall be governed by the law of the State of nationality of the adoptive parent' and in its paragraph 3 stipulates: 'The child's consent, in addition to the applicable law as designated under paragraph 1 of Article 89, shall be governed by the law of the State of the child's nationality.' Here cumulative connecting is aimed at preventing the creation of legal relations that would be valid according to the law of one country and null and void according to the law of another country.

125. In the case of an alternative application of the connections, a conflict rule contains two or more connections that are usually separated using the word 'or'. As a result, only one connection is applied. The application of alternative connections is aimed at achieving a certain substantive result. Alternative binding may be aimed at protecting the weaker party and ensuring the use of law that is more favourable to a party, as in the following example: 'The parent child relations shall be governed by the law of the State in which the child has habitual residence or the law of the State of the child's nationality, where so more favourable to the child (Article 88 of the PIL Act).' The use of alternative connections is frequent when it comes to the matters of form of legal relationship. The typical example is a large number of alternative connections in order to maintain the will in force, and it is sufficient that conditions are met pursuant to any law to which application directs any of the connections. Pursuant to the PIL Act, Article 73, which essentially takes over the solution from the Hague Testamentary Dispositions Convention, the will may be declared valid as to form if it is considered valid under at least one of the numerous alternatively applicable laws. Similarly, pursuant to Article 23 of the PIL Act, legal transaction and legal action shall be considered valid as to form if they satisfy formal requirements of either the law of the place where they were concluded/initiated, or of the law which is applicable to the content of such legal transaction or action.

126. Connections from the same conflict rule can be formulated in a subsidiary manner. By the very nature of the matter, subsidiary connections have been created to 'cover' those situations where the conditions for the application of the main connection are not fulfilled. A characteristic example is related to contractual relations, where the choice of law is the main connection, and the use of subsidiary connections occurs only if the parties have failed to make such a choice for their contractual relation (Article 39 of the PIL Act).

Chapter 3. Basic Terms

§1. Characterization (Classification)

127. There are significant misalignments in the literature of the former Yugoslavia on the relationship between the classical procedure of interpreting the conflict rule, on the one hand, and the qualifications of legal concepts and relations, on the other hand.[137] However, it is undisputed that legal qualification is in fact subsuming of a fact under legal concepts, while the interpretation defines the exact meaning of legal as well as conflict rule. In most cases, there will be no problem to subsume a certain factual relationship under the legal category of a certain conflict rule. However, the problem of qualification in PIL can occur if the legal concept or institute in domestic and foreign substantive law are treated differently or fall under different branches of law. Thus, for example, questions may arise as to whether an agreement on life support will be subject to a conflict rule on succession or contractual obligations (presently this contract is regulated by LO, while previously was traditionally regulated by LS); will the donation contract concluded between the spouses qualify as a family law question, to which the conflict rules for personal and property relation of spouses apply, or as a matter falling within the scope of the contract law? Also, the question may arise: do you qualify a particular question as substantive or procedural (proxy marriage)?

128. The problem of qualification also occurs when foreign substantive law contains a legal institute unknown in domestic law (e.g., whether the dowry from Sharia law will be treated as a condition for the conclusion of a marriage, or the conflict rules for the matrimonial property regime or, in case of a divorce, the conflict rule for the maintenance of the former spouse will be applied).[138]

129. The positive PIL of Montenegro does not contain a general rule on how to solve the problem of qualification. This allows flexible approach depending on the circumstances of a particular case. In practice, often, the problem of qualification is solved on the basis of legal understandings of domestic law (by *lex fori*), if there is not a special rule for a particular type of relationship. And the PIL Act in Article 28 contains a special rule which provides that the qualification of a property as movable or immovable shall be governed by the law of the State where the property is located – by *lex causae* (Article 11). When performing qualification of an institute that is unknown in domestic law, the *lex causae* should be combined with the *lex fori* qualification (functional qualification).

---

137. Natko Katičić, *Ogledi o međunarodnom privatnom pravu* (Essays on Private International Law), Zagreb: Narodne novine, 1971, 130–131. Tibor Varadi, *Međunarodno privatno pravo* (Private International Law), Novi Sad: Forum, 1990, 62; 272. Maja Stanivuković & Mirko Živković, *Me unarodno privatno pravo: opšti deo* (Private International Law: General Part), Belgrade, Službeni list SCG, 2004, 245–260.
138. Aleksandar Jakšić, *Međunarodno privatno pravo* (Private International Law), Belgrade: Dosije, 2008, 265–266.

130. Also, in a series of international treaties that bind Montenegro, there are definitions of legal institutes or concepts that have different legal meanings for the contracting parties. In that manner, autonomous concepts that have a predetermined meaning only for a specific international treaty are being established independently of the concepts of national law. Thus, for example, the Hague Traffic Accidents Convention provides a definition of what is considered a road traffic accident, which is an autonomous concept only for that convention.[139] Certain Hague Conventions autonomously determine the applicable law for certain concepts. Furthermore, the Hague Testamentary Dispositions Convention specifies that, for the purposes of the Convention, it will be considered that the rules restricting the recognized forms of the testamentary disposition, relating to age, citizenship or other personal attributes of the testator, fall into the question of form, and the same applies to the 'qualifications that must be possessed by witnesses required for the validity of a testamentary disposition'.[140] The PIL Act literally copied this provision (Article 73, paragraph 3).

§2. Preliminary Question

131. The preliminary question often arises in the domain of domestic law, but only if the dispute has an international character the existence of this incidental question may provoke a problem: whether that incidental question should be governed by the conflict rule of the law applicable to the main question (*lex causae*) or by the domestic conflict rule (*lex fori*)? The preliminary question is most commonly reported in the sphere of marital relations, which are related to other rights that arise in the dispute as the main issues (maintenance, succession). Supposing that a Montenegrin court is deciding on a succession with a foreign element and a foreign law is the applicable law for succession, successors being the wife and children of the deceased. In this matter the question may arise whether the marriage is valid or whether the children are born in or out of wedlock. In this example, the main issue relates to the succession statute, but its solution depends on the existence of other, previous legal relationships, of family legal character.[141]

132. The application of the *lex fori* conflict rule to this incidental question implies it is independent, while the application of the *lex causa* conflict rules that it is in a dependent relation to the main question. The law of Montenegro lacks the normative solution of this problem, while in the comparative case law on the European continent, and even doctrine, the *lex fori* prevails. Nevertheless, in these legal systems, it is generally accepted in the doctrine and practice that if the acquisition or loss of citizenship depends on certain status relationships, for example, the validity of marriage, then those preliminary questions should be decided by the conflict rule of the State of their citizenship.

139. *See* Art. 1, para. 2 of the Convention.
140. *See* Art. 1 para. 3; Art. 5 of the Convention.
141. Krešimir Sajko, *Međunarodno privatno pravo* (Private International Law), Zagreb: Narodne novine, 2009, 219.

133. A particular possibility of solving a problem is by applying the escape clause to the conflict rule applicable to the main legal relationship, which can have a twofold effect. On the one hand, it can eliminate the problem raised by the phenomenon of the preliminary question, in so far as it may lead to the application of domestic law to the main legal relationship. On the other hand, the application of the escape clause may lead to a departure from the application of the domestic law, in favour of foreign law, which may raise the issue of the preliminary question.

§3. Substance and Procedure

134. In Montenegrin PIL in most cases the line between matters pertaining to substance or procedure is unambiguous. Thus, for example, the statute of limitation of the claim in most legal systems, and in the law of Montenegro, is considered to be a question pertinent to substance and not a procedure and therefore is governed by *lex causae*. However, it may happen that a substantive or procedural nature of a particular issue has to be addressed as a problem of legal qualification, such as proxy marriages. The positive law of Montenegro does not give an answer to the question of whether a proxy marriage falls within the substantive or formal conditions of the validity of marriage. In the doctrine, the prevailing attitude is the proxy is entitled only to represent an absent spouse in concluding a marriage with a given spouse without any initiative and discretion right, and therefore this issue should be regarded as pertaining to the form of conclusion of a marriage.[142]

135. As previously addressed, certain Hague Conventions autonomously determine what falls into the question of procedure, such as the Hague Testamentary Dispositions Convention.

§4. Renvoi

136. Renvoi is an institute of positive PIL of Montenegro since 1983, when the LRCL, stipulating full renvoi, began to apply, but its content, scope and manner of application with regard to the formulation contained in the LRCL caused different interpretations.[143] There was no agreement among scholars on the scope of this institute, and this was also expressed in various versions of the draft that preceded the adoption of the final text of the provision (including the prohibition of the application of this institute). However, it is also a legal institute that, on the basis of available information, has never been applied in Montenegro.

137. The PIL Act adopts a modern concept of renvoi that leaves no room for doubt when this institute should be applied (Article 4). The PIL Act has opted for

142. Bernadet Bordaš, *Porodičnopravni odnosi u međunarodnom privatnom pravu* (Family Law Relations in Private International Law), Novi Sad: Forum, 2000, 57.

143. Mihajlo Dika, Gaša Knežević, Srđan Stojanović, *Komentar Zakona o međunarodnom privatnom i procesnom pravu* (Commentary of the PIL Act), Belgrade: Nomos, 1991, 25–30.

selective renvoi in one step. Where under the PIL Act reference is made to foreign law, the legislation, including conflict rules, of that State, shall apply unless otherwise provided for by the PIL Act or some other statute. If it reverts to our law, domestic substantive law shall apply, and if a foreign conflict rule redirects to the law of a third country, the substantive law of a third country shall apply.

138. However, the PIL Act lists the areas or issues for which the renvoi is excluded. Thus, even if on the basis of our conflict rule, foreign law is applicable, foreign conflict rule shall not apply if it comes under one of the exceptions referred to in Article 4, paragraph 2, that is: legal status of legal persons and forms of organization without legal personality; form of legal transactions; choice of applicable law; maintenance; contractual relations, and non-contractual relations.

139. The PIL Act prescribes mandatory application of the renvoi, except in the cases which are listed explicitly. Those are types of relations where the interests of legal certainty and the protection of the parties prevail. It would not be justifiable to apply the renvoi for cases where the parties have made choice of law, or where the aim of the conflict rule is to achieve a particular substantive solution in order to protect the weaker party (in the case of maintenance or non-contractual obligations) or to ensure the validity of the form of a particular legal transaction. Greater importance is given to the protection of these interests than to the interest of international harmony in decision-making. The choice of law, with certain limitations, is envisaged in the PIL Act for a large number of relations in almost all areas of private law relations regulated by this statute. When parties in a private law relation with a foreign element choose a national law as applicable, they choose the substantive law of a particular country, and not its conflict rules and therefore there is no room for the renvoi. Furthermore, contractual and non-contractual relations are also singled out due to the fact that it is envisaged that the provisions of the PIL Act in this area will be interpreted and applied in accordance with the Rome I and Rome II Regulations, and for these relations, as well as for the maintenance obligations, the EU law excludes the application of the renvoi.

140. One of the few recent Hague Conventions that recognizes renvoi and is binding on Montenegro is the Hague Child Protection Convention.[144]

141. It seems that Montenegrin judges are becoming more aware of this institute. The recent case addressed the renvoi although it was not applied in this particular case.[145]

144. Article 21 para. 2 of the Convention.
145. Higher Court in Podgorica, Gž.br. 5360/18 of 29.10.2018 rendered a decision revoking the judgment of the Basic Court in Podgorica P. br.1536/17 of 26.07.2018.

§5. General Conflict Rule/Special Conflict Rule

142. One of the features of the PIL Act is a very detailed regulation of conflict of laws. The general conflict rules, characteristic of the LRCL have been substituted by a large number of special conflict rules. The scope of the changes is explained best by the fact that the PIL Act in the applicable law field contains a total of 134 provisions (including the Basic Provisions), of which fewer provisions are not conflict rules, compared to the LRCL, which was almost completely based on general conflict rules (the applicable law section had thirty-two provisions). Furthermore, the LRCL regulates the applicable law within one head, while the PIL Act contains nine heads, some of which are divided into several sections (non-contractual relations, family relations). Not only the PIL Act significantly increased the number of conflict rules, but they also regulate relations in a detailed manner (the conflict rules for contractual, non-contractual obligations, and family relations, in particular).

143. For the first time some issues are regulated by special conflict rules for: name (Article 17), business capacity of entrepreneurs (Article 15), unincorporated organizations (Article 20), contractual representation (Article 24), cultural property (Article 33), contracts of carriage (Article 41), consumer contracts (Article 42), individual employment contracts (Article 43), unfair competition and acts restricting competition (Article 53), environmental damage (Article 54), violation of right of person (Article 55), industrial action (Article 56), special rules for maintenance (Articles 91–92) and others.

144. In some areas, the general conflict rules are retained, and this relates, in the first place to the rules on real rights, as well as to the new rules on intellectual property rights (Articles 35–37).

145. If the PIL Act does not contain a conflict rule for some kind of relations, the provisions of this law should be applied accordingly (as well as the principles of: the PIL Act, legal order of Montenegro and PIL (Article 3)).

146. In addition to the PIL Act, special conflict rules are also contained in a number of international treaties[146] and other laws: LBE (Chapter XVI also applies to conflict of laws relating to checks), LMIN (Articles 1033–1050), LOPRAT (Articles 177–182); the Law on Financial Collateral (Article 19), the Law on Capital Market (Article 406). According to the *lex specialis derogat lege generali* principle these specific conflict rules have primacy in application for relations they regulate over the provisions of the PIL Act.

§6. Assimilation

147. Problem of coordination of legal systems occurs when the legal relationships created under one law have to produce their effects in another legal system.

146. *See supra* Supranational Law.

For instance, if a national of the country whose law allows polygamy acquires citizenship of Montenegro by naturalization, and establishes habitual residence together with his three wives in Montenegro, Montenegrin law shall govern personal and pecuniary effects of his marriage, maintenance and succession matters. The question is how to deal with this situation where three wives are involved. Similar problems may occur when domestic law provisions have to be applied to a legal category unknown to the domestic legal system, like trust.[147]

148. In the cases described *supra*, we are dealing with different concepts existing in each of the involved laws: the task is to determine whether the particular foreign category represents a generic counterpart of a domestic category sufficiently similar to enable substitution or transposition. In the first example, Montenegrin courts will recognize the right of the second and third wives to inherit the property of the deceased and the maintenance right, but they will neither recognize their right to social security benefits nor will they order these wives to live together in the same household. In the second example, the courts may not be willing to make a transposition of categories coming from the English law, because of *numerus clausus* of real rights in the Montenegrin law.[148]

149. Judicial practice of the region treats the problem of assimilation (as well as the problem of substitution or transposition) empirically, without bothering to name it as such. In those rare cases, when courts attempt to identify the problem, they usually associate it with the doctrine of public policy.[149]

§7. *Ordre Public* (Public Policy)

150. Public policy is a general doctrine of the Montenegrin PIL which may be used as a ground for non-application of the foreign law, non-recognition of foreign judgments, or arbitral awards, setting aside the domestic arbitral award,[150] and denying the legal assistance to a foreign court.

151. The national legal history gives us more insight into how the public policy concept in PIL reflected the current legal attitudes of the time when the legal texts were adopted. A striking example of attempts to define this institute is provided by the GPC of 1888 in Article 8, which reads:

Foreign laws will not be recognized in Montenegrin courts when they contravene the Montenegrin laws on public policy and security. Foreign laws that would be contrary to ordinary humanity and justice, or would privilege an inhuman institution (such as slavery) that is not tolerated in Montenegro, shall not be recognized.

147. Kluwer Monograph on PIL of Montenegro of 2013, para.170–181.
148. *Ibid.*
149. *Ibid.*
150. *See infra* International Arbitration.

152. Almost 100 years later, the LRCL contained an abstract definition and stipulated: 'The law of the foreign State shall not be applied if its effect would be contrary to the basic principles of social organization laid down by the Constitution of the Federal Republic of Yugoslavia.' Furthermore, it provided for a similar provision on the recognition and execution of foreign court and arbitration decisions (though without stipulating 'effects' as a prerequisite for their application).[151]

153. The PIL Act addresses the institute of public policy in its basic provisions, as a general institute in the field of applicable law: 'Where a provision of foreign law regarding its effect is manifestly contrary to the public policy of Montenegro, that provision shall not apply' (Article 9). In addition to this general provision, there are also special provisions dealing with public policy as a condition, that is, the obstacle to the recognition and enforcement of foreign judgments,[152] and foreign arbitral awards.[153] In both cases, those decisions shall not be recognized if the effect of their recognition would be manifestly contrary to the public policy of Montenegro.

154. Public policy exception to application of foreign law is also contained in the Hague Testamentary Dispositions Convention, Article 7; the Hague Traffic Accident Convention, Article 10; the Hague Product Liability Convention, Article 10, and the Hague Child Protection Convention, Article 22.

155. The integral part of the national public policy is the basic values guaranteed by international sources of law such as, for example, some international treaties (ECHR), general principles (principle bona fides) or soft law (Universal Declaration of Human Rights of the United Nations).

156. Characteristic examples that may trigger application of public policy exception in the domain of marital law relate to rules of foreign substantive law, which permit polygamy, same-sex marriage,[154] as well as if divorce is not permitted or religious form for divorce has been applied. In the field of succession, examples that trigger public policy exceptions are if, under the applicable law, out of wedlock children cannot be heirs, or when the institute of the compulsory portion is unknown in foreign law. For contractual relations, the example may be, if a foreign law does not protect the rights of consumers (who enjoy special protection under the Constitution and the legislation of Montenegro). Pursuant to the PIL Act the mere fact that a rule of foreign law contravenes the public policy of Montenegro is not enough to trigger the application of the public policy clause. It is necessary that the effects of the rules of a foreign applicable law are manifestly contrary to the domestic public policy.

151. *See* Art. 91 and 99, para. 1(3) of the LRCL.
152. Article 147 of the PIL Act.
153. The Law on Arbitration, Art. 52, para. 2(1).
154. It would not encompass registered partnership of persons of the same sex as in 2020 Montenegro adopted the law on registered partnerships. Though, more than 20 different pieces of legislation still have to harmonize with that law.

157. It is undisputable that the domestic law should be applied instead of foreign law which contravenes domestic public policy. However, the question may be to what extent: whether only partially in order to replace the rule of foreign law which is contrary to the public policy or to the relation as a whole. The doctrine is unanimous the application of domestic law should be limited to replacing a specific rule of foreign law. This will be the case when a foreign applicable law regulates some legal institute but denies rights to certain categories of persons, and then the application of domestic law is justified by referring to a public policy exception in order to recognize that person's right, and all other issues should be governed by foreign law.

158. In the recognition and enforcement of a foreign court or arbitral decision, the institute of public policy appears as an obstacle to a foreign decision to obtain an exequatur if the effect of the foreign decision would be manifestly contrary to the domestic public policy. These are situations when a domestic authority deciding on the recognition and enforcement of a foreign decision establishes whether in the process of adopting a foreign decision there has been a violation of the principles that constitute the procedural public policy of the home country. It is also possible that the foreign decision is contrary to the domestic substantive public policy, since the very merits of the decision are such that the effects of such a decision would be contrary to the domestic public policy. Foreign decisions that are contrary to the substantive public policy most often concern status and family relations. The violation of substantive public policy is very rare, due to ongoing harmonization of national legal systems under the influence of international treaties and the EU law.

159. Now we are listing one example from the former Yugoslav practice when the recognition and enforcement of a court decision from the United States of America (USA) were refused due to the public policy.[155] In the USA case, the defendant was 'Zastava' Factory from Kragujevac, who designed and manufactured the passenger car of the 'Yugo' brand, 1987 model, which was exported and distributed in that country. The plaintiff who commenced an action for damages was a passenger in that type of vehicle, who suffered serious body injuries (quadriplegia) during a crash with the 'Bjuik' vehicle, although the car was moving at a low speed. The court in New Jersey found that the plaintiff's disability was a direct consequence of a defect in the design of the vehicle, which refers to safety (the defect was latent and could not be recognized by the buyer but was or should have been known to the manufacturer), and issued a decision, whose recognition was sought in Yugoslavia, for the plaintiff to pay approximately USD 13 million for punitive damages. The recognition and enforcement of this decision by the Yugoslav court were rejected with reference to a public policy, since the institute of compensation for damages, which has a punitive character, is contrary to the public policy of the domestic country.

155. Biljana Vukoslavčević, *Priznanje i izvršenje sudskih i arbitražnih odluka, komparacija sistema SAD-a i Srbije i Crne Gore* (Recognition and enforcement of court and arbitration decisions, comparisons of the US and Serbia-Montenegro system), Podgorica: *Univerzitet Mediteran*, 2012, 139–140.

§8. Overriding Mandatory Rules

160. Overriding mandatory rules doctrine is introduced in Montenegrin positive law by the PIL Act in 2014. Article 10 of the PIL Act states:

The provisions of Montenegrin law whose application is deemed particularly significant to the protection of public interest, such as political, social, or economic system of the State, shall apply to all the cases that the provisions refer to, irrespective of the applicable law designated.

By way of exception, a court may take into account the direct application provisions of another State that the legal relationship is closely connected to.

In deciding to take into consideration the provisions from paragraph 1 of this Article, the court shall take into account their nature and purpose, as well as the consequences of their application or non-application.

161. In a situation where the PIL Act provides the possibility of choice of the applicable law even for those types of relations where previously it was not allowed (non-contractual obligations, succession, maintenance, divorce, name), there is a need for certain restrictions in the choice of applicable law, as well as for formulating instruments aimed at protecting the interests of the home country. This is achieved in two ways: by stipulating limited choice of law for the said relations and by introducing a general institute of PIL, which serves to protect the interests of the home country, apart from the choice of the applicable law. The PIL Act tends to be a modern national codification and, to the extent that it is adequate, is in line with the EU PIL regulations. It introduces the positive law of Montenegro provision on the overriding mandatory rules. This rule is modelled after provisions of comparative legal codifications of PIL[156] in which this type of rule constitutes a positive concept for many years, the relevant rule[157] of Rome I Regulation, and the case law of the ECJ.

162. The legislator has chosen a wider approach in regulating a provision on overriding mandatory rules, which also includes defining this concept as rules whose application is imposed independently of the applicable law, since it is essential for the protection of the political, social, or economic system of which they are a part. The application of these rules is imposed independently of the conflict of law method, if the test of the necessity of applying these rules for private legal relations with a foreign element is fulfilled, but also for the protection of the public interest of Montenegro. In addition, the concept of overriding mandatory rules is narrower than the concept of imperative norms and includes only those norms for which there is a fundamental interest of the country to apply them for the protection of the public interest, irrespective of the applicable law.[158]

156. *See* Arts 18 and 19 of the Swiss PIL Act, Art. 46 of the Bulgarian PIL Act and Art. 20 of the Belgian PIL Act.

157. Article 9 para. 3 of the Rome I Regulation.

158. Recital 37 of the Rome I Regulation states that the concept of overriding mandatory provisions should be distinguished from provisions which cannot be derogated from by agreement and should be interpreted narrowly.

163. Therefore, Article 10 paragraph 1 of the PIL Act starts from the traditional concept of overriding mandatory rules, which has been confirmed in the *Arblade* case before the ECJ.[159] However, paragraph 2 goes one step further providing for the possibility of applying the overriding mandatory rules of the other State with which the relation is closely connected. In the same paragraph, it is also specified that when deciding on taking account of these rules, the court shall take into account their nature and purpose, as well as the consequences of their application or non-application.

164. Article 10 of the PIL Act establishes two regimes in the application of overriding mandatory rules. Overriding mandatory rules of domestic law apply in all cases while the application of overriding mandatory rules of the law of the State with which there is a close connection (and which is neither a domestic law nor an applicable law whose imperative rules apply as an integral part of the applicable law) depends on the case and judge's assessment. Therefore, judiciary has a significant, but also demanding role in deciding whether to apply a foreign law rule that is closely related to a particular legal relation, bearing in mind its content and the result of its application.

§9. Evasion of the Law

165. Montenegrin PIL acknowledges the general doctrine of evasion of the law, both in the field of conflict of laws and substantive law. However, the PIL Act does not provide for a specific provision addressing evasion of the law, while LMIN states: 'Foreign law that would be applicable according to the provisions of this law shall not apply if its application was exclusively for the purpose of avoiding the application of the law of the Federal Republic of Yugoslavia (Article 1050).'

166. Previously, the LRCL contained a general clause on evasion of the law, stipulating in its Article 5 that the law of a foreign State that would be applicable pursuant to the provisions of that or any other federal law shall not be applied if the purpose of their application would be to evade the application of the Yugoslav law.

167. While working on the text of the PIL Act, it was concluded that it was not necessary to provide a special provision on evasion of the law since the codification is based on the principle of the closest connection, and the escape clauses allow for intervention, if necessary. Furthermore, by definition, the evasion of the law should protect the application of imperative conflict rules of domestic law from legally permitted actions of a party aimed at exercising the law of another country that is more favourable to the party. Now when the parties can make choice of law for a large number of relations, there is no more place for this institute. Finally, in those rare cases where the clause on evasion of the law may have been applied, the same function can perform a public policy clause. This attitude is similar to the position of

159. ECJ 23 Nov. 1999, C-369/96, *Jean-Claude Arblade and Arblade & Fils SARL* and C-376/96 *Bernard Leloup, Serge Leloup and Sofrage SARL*, [1999] ECR I-08453.

doctrine in those countries providing for the escape clause. Thus, the Swiss,[160] Quebec and Slovenian PIL codifications do not contain a provision on evasion of the law, although this institute is widely accepted in their doctrine.

168. The evasion of the law, in the form of prohibition of abuse of law, as a general legal institute, is formulated by statutes in the field of substantive property and obligatory relations. Pursuant to these legal texts, it shall be prohibited to exercise the ownership rights and other property rights/a right arising from obligation relations, contrary to the purpose they are created or recognized for by law (Article 5 of the LPR and Article 6 LO,[161] respectively).

§10. Reference to the Law of States with Multiple Legal Orders

169. The PIL Act copied the provision of the LRCL (Article 10) on the reference to the law of States with multiple legal orders. Article 5 of the PIL Act provides a rule that when the conflict rule points to the law of the country with multiple legal orders the judge must apply the law system within that country to which the conflict rule directly leads. If the conflict rule does not directly lead to any specific law system within that country, the applicable law shall be determined according to the internal conflict rules of that country. If this proves to be impossible (e.g., because there are no such internal rules at the federal level or because the internal conflict rules would lead outside of that country), the law system within that country that has the closest connection with the case should be applied.

170. Some Hague conventions in force in Montenegro also include provisions regulating this issue: the Convention on the Conflict of Laws Relating to the Form of Testamentary Dispositions (Article 1), the Convention on the Law Applicable to Traffic Accidents (Article 12), the Convention on the Law Applicable to Products Liability (Article 12), the Convention on Civil Aspects of International Child Abduction (Articles 31 and 32), the Convention on Protection of Children and Cooperation in Respect of Intercountry Adoption (Articles 36–38), the Convention on Jurisdiction, Applicable Law, Recognition, Enforcement and Cooperation in Respect of Parental Responsibility and Measures for the Protection of Children (Articles 46–49), the Convention on the International Recovery of Child Support and Other Forms of Family Maintenance (Articles 46–47).

---

160. The evasion of the law is sanctioned by Art. 2 of the Swiss Civil Code, which applies also to private legal relations with an international character. Alfred Eugène Von Overbeck, *Les questions générales du droit international privé a la lumière des codifcations et projets récents*, Recueil des Cours, Académie de droit international, the Hague/Boston/London: Martinus Nijhoff Publishers, 1982, 207.

161. Text in English available at: https://www.ano.me/en/index.php?option=com_phocadownload&view=category&id=7:&Itemid=110 (accessed 14 Apr. 2022).

§11. General Escape Clause

171. The escape clause is one of the most important new institutes introduced by the Montenegrin PIL Act (Article 8). The escape clause is designed in a way similar to the Swiss general escape clause, stating that the law designated by the present statute by way of exception does not apply if it is clear from all the circumstances that the matter has only a slight connection with the designated law but is closely connected to another law. Naturally, this does not apply where the parties have made a choice of law.

172. In addition to these law-stipulated cases, the escape clause will not apply in case of conflict rules aimed at securing a particular substantive result for the special protection of a particular category of person, in the case of a unilateral conflict rule, and in case when a close connection principle is a connecting factor.[162]

173. In Montenegro, as it is in a large number of other countries, the commitment to introduce this institute is not based on national judicial practice,[163] but rather aims at modernizing national law, in accordance with the tendencies in comparative national laws, as well as harmonizing our law with the EU law. The underlying ratio of this institute is to provide for flexible system of conflict of law rules in order to achieve equity in an individual case. However, as pointed out by the comparative practice, the value of introducing this institute into positive law, as well as the influence of the judiciary on the development of the national PIL, can be ascertained only after a certain period of time.

174. In addition to the general escape clause from Article 8, the PIL Act also provides special escape clauses: a general rule for contracts in the absence of a choice of law (Article 39, paragraph 3), for non-contractual obligations (Article 52, paragraph 3), and for a special rule for maintenance obligation between spouses and former spouses (Article 92). These escape clauses are identical to those of the corresponding articles of the Rome I and Rome II Regulations, as well as to the escape clauses from the Hague Maintenance Protocol.

175. The closest connection is primarily valued[164] on the basis of objective criteria (citizenship, domicile, residence, habitual residence, *lex solutionis*), and in addition to these personal and territorial connections, other circumstances (such as time factor) are also taken account of. Furthermore, regard shall be had of other facts which are not decisive for localizing a certain legal relation in a particular legal

162. Maja Kostić-Mandić, *Opšta klauzula odstupanja od redovno mjerodavnog prava: u savremenom međunarodnom privatnom pravu* (General Escape Clause: in Contemporary Private International Law), Podgorica: University of Montenegro, Faculty of Law, 2012, 54–55.

163. *Ibid.*

164. *See supra* Principle of the Closest Connection.

system but serves to reinforce the effects of another objective factor, such as the language in which the contract is drafted; referral to certain legal institutes characteristic of a particular legal system; for family law relations, facts such as the language spoken by the persons in question, religious affiliation, respecting of certain customs.

176. The prospective role of subjective circumstances, such as the legitimate expectations of the parties and acquired rights, when assessing the quality and quantity of the case's connection with the laws of several countries, was not addressed in the domestic doctrine. The general escape clause is formulated based on the 'Swiss model' and not the 'Belgian model', and according to the recent practice of the Swiss Federal Court, the legitimate expectations of the parties as criteria in determining the closest related law should not be taken into account.[165]

177. Characteristic cases where the need for applying the escape clause can be indicated are when there is spatial and temporal isolation of the connecting factor, as well as in the case of dependent and independent legal relations. The application of the escape clause to situations where the connecting factor, envisaged by the appropriate conflict rule, is found spatially and temporally isolated in relation to other circumstances of the given case can be pertinent to the succession, family and obligation relations.

178. The application of an escape clause can also be justified in cases where one, independent legal relation, is closely related to some other, or more legal relations, as well as when those relations constitute a relation as a whole.[166] For economically related independent contracts, which form a chain of contracts created to fulfil the same objective, the possibility of applying an escape clause is reduced to exceptional cases where the relationship of these contractual relations and their mutual dependence is obvious to all contracting parties. Contrary, in the case of those legal relations where several contracts occur, of which one can easily differentiate those who are in the function of a single contract, and in this case, we distinguish the 'main' contract and the contracts that serve to ensure the execution of that contract, it is understandable that there is a higher probability of applying the escape clause, with the aim of submitting dependent contracts to the law of the 'main' contract. Also, in the case of family and succession relations, by applying the escape clause the matrimonial property regime and the succession of the deceased spouse are subjected to the same law.

165. http://www.bger.ch (accessed 14 Apr. 2022).
166. Cristina Campiglio, *L'esperienza svizzera in tema di clausola d'eccezione*: L'Art. 14 del progetto di riforma del diritto internazionale privato, Rivista di diritto internazionale privato e processuale, 1985, 55–56.

Part II. Conflict of Law Rules

Chapter 1. Persons

§1. Natural Persons

I. Legal Capacity

179. The principle of nationality is traditionally the most important connecting factor for the status of natural persons in Montenegrin law. The PIL Act contains several conflict rules for this area, so, special conflict provisions are established for: legal capacity, business capacity, business capacity of the entrepreneur, guardianship, name and declaring a missing person dead (Chapter II of the PIL Act).

180. Legal capacity of a natural person is governed by the law of his citizenship (Article 13). The Code does not address *commorientes* and *nasciturus* and for these matters one should adhere to the prevailing doctrine. In the case of *commorientes* the law of citizenship shall apply. In Montenegrin law, there is a rebuttable presumption that persons have died at the same time and that they cannot inherit one another. For the *nasciturus*, prevailing attitude of doctrine is that *lex causae* should apply.[167]

181. The PIL Act in Article 14 provides that citizenship is also a basic connecting factor for business capacity of a natural person. The said rule relates to general business capacity, but if the applicable law provides for specific conditions on business capacity for a particular legal relation, these conditions will apply. This refers to contractual capacity, non-contractual liability capacity, capacity to conclude marriage, capacity to compose the will and so forth.

182. The PIL Act provides that, if a contract was concluded by persons present in the same State, the person who according to the law of that State has business capacity, may not claim his business incapacity according to the law of a third country, unless the other contractual party was aware of business incapacity at the time the contract was concluded and when the person was not aware of it for a reason of gross negligence.[168] This prohibits a person to refer to incapacity, either by virtue of

167. Mihajlo Dika, Gaša Knežević, Srđan Stojanović, *Komentar Zakona o međunarodnom privatnom i procesnom pravu* (Commentary of the PIL Act), Belgrade: Nomos, 1991, 53.
168. Article 14(2) of the PIL Act.

the law of his citizenship, domicile or habitual residence, and the burden of proof is on that person who needs to prove that the other contractual party had known about it. Here, due to the principle *in favorem negotii*, the PIL Act deviates from the personal principle and applies the territorial principle – the law of the country where the contract was concluded. The fact that a party is according to the law of citizenship or some other personal law considered to be business incapable shall not have legal effect if he has a business capacity under the law of the country where the contract was concluded.

183. The PIL Act specifies that the above-mentioned rule of applying the territorial principle shall not apply to legal transactions related to family and succession relations, or to legal transactions relating to the rights in rem in an immovable property located in a third State, rather than a State where the contract was concluded.[169]

184. The PIL Act introduces a special rule for individuals pursuing business activity. Their business capacity shall be governed by the law of the State where the person is registered as an entrepreneur. Where no registration is required, business capacity shall be governed by the law of the State where the natural person has the principal place of business (Article 15).

185. In comparative law, the protection of interests of business incompetent persons is most often regulated by the personal law of the warder (the law of citizenship, domicile, or habitual residence). The PIL Act provides that the law of the State of which the person under guardianship is a citizen shall apply to the placement under guardianship and the termination of guardianship. The same law applies to relations between a guardian and persons under guardianship. On the contrary, the law of Montenegro shall be applied in respect of provisional protection measures against a foreigner, as well as for the protection of the property of an absent foreigner (this also applies to persons without citizenship who are present in Montenegro).[170]

186. In a case[171] involving representation of a person in a process for deprivation of legal capacity of a Montenegrin national domiciled in Montenegro, initiated by a son residing in Belgrade, Republic of Serbia, the Higher Court in Podgorica stated that the Court of First Instance was obliged to eliminate all omissions made regarding representation in order to best protect rights and interests of a party. The Higher Court points to the reasoning of the ECtHR judgment in *Ivanović v. Croatia*[172] that 'in cases of mentally disabled persons the States have an obligation to ensure that they are afforded independent representation, enabling them to have their Convention complaints examined before a court or other independent body'.

169. Article 14(3) of the PIL Act.
170. Article 16 of the PIL Act.
171. Higher Court in Podgorica Gž.br. 2811/16 of 07.06.2016. revoked the decision of the Basic Court in Cetinje Rs. br.12/2016 of 22.04.2016 and referred the case back to the trial court for retrial.
172. Application No. 13006/13 of 18.09.2014.

The court also refers to the Convention on the Rights of Persons with Disabilities of 2006, whose Article 12(3) stipulates that States Parties 'shall take appropriate measures to provide access by persons with disabilities to the support they may require in exercising their legal capacity'.

187. The principle of nationality also applies to declaring a missing person dead, while for stateless persons their last habitual residence applies. A person who has habitual residence in Montenegro may be declared dead, according to Montenegrin law, if it is requested by a person who has a legal interest in it.[173]

II. Name

188. The applicable law for the individual name was not previously regulated by a special conflict rule, and therefore the general rule for other status relations – *lex nationalis* used to apply. The new conflict rule of the PIL Act is complex and regulates in detail the applicable law for an individual name.[174] Determining or changing of an individual name is governed by the law of citizenship of the person concerned, while the law of newly acquired citizenship will be applied in determining the effect of changing of citizenship on an individual name. For two types of relations, it is also possible to choose the applicable law (for the individual name of the spouse and the last name of the child). In both cases, spouses or holders of parental rights have a limited possibility of choice of law in Montenegro (pursuant to the law of the country of citizenship of either of them or pursuant to the Montenegrin law if either of them has habitual residence in Montenegro), and the choice of law must be performed in a special form. Instead of the general rule (the law of citizenship of the person concerned), they may designate as applicable the law of citizenship of one of the spouses or Montenegrin law as the place of the habitual residence of one of the spouses. In both cases, the statement on changing an individual name when concluding marriage and changing the last name of the child must be given in a certain form – before the registry officer or later, in the form of a public document. For the effect of choosing an individual name, that is, the last name of a child, if it is changing the last name of a juvenile person who has reached the age of 10, his consent is required if he is able to express his opinion.

189. The protection of an individual name shall be governed by provisions on non-contractual liability from Chapter VI of the PIL Act.

173. Article 18(3) of the PIL Act.
174. Article 17 of the PIL Act was inspired by German, but also by Bulgarian and Belgian codification of PIL.

III. Nationality/Habitual Residence/Domicile

190. The new PIL of Montenegro has a foundation built of traditional concepts, and it preserves nationality principle[175] as a primary connecting factor for personal status relations of natural person while habitual residence replaced domicile as a connecting factor.

191. The PIL Act stipulates nationality principle as the only relevant criterion of ascertaining applicable law for natural person regarding legal capacity (Article 13), guardianship (Article 16(1)), and declaring a missing person dead (Article 18(1)). Thus, legal capacity of a natural person shall be governed by the law of the State of which the natural person is a national; Placement under guardianship and cessation of guardianship, as well as relationships between a guardian and persons under guardianship shall be governed by the law of the State of which the person under guardianship is a national; declaring a missing person dead shall be governed by the law of the state of which the person was a national at the time he disappeared.

192. On the contrary, nationality principle has its specifics regarding business capacity (Article 14(1)) and name (Article 17(1)). In principle, civil capacity of a natural person shall be governed by the law of the State of which the natural person is a national. But, if applicable law for a particular matter envisages specific provisions on civil capacity, that law shall apply. Furthermore, if contract was signed by persons present in the same State, the person who according to the law of that State has civil capacity may not claim his civil incapacity according to the law of a third country, except where the other contractual party was aware of civil incapacity at the time the contract was concluded, and where the person was not aware of it for reason of gross negligence.

193. Nationality principle applies to determination or change of name of a person while the effect that a change in nationality has on one's name shall be governed by the law of the State of which that person has obtained nationality. Moreover, spouses may make choice of law on determination or a change in name either at the time or after the conclusion of their marriage in Montenegro, and one of the legally prescribed possibilities is the national law of one of the spouses.

194. For legal status of a natural person habitual residence is a subsidiary connecting factor in Montenegrin PIL Act. Habitual residence of a natural person is ascertained according to the general definition of habitual residence (Article 12), while habitual residence of a natural person pursuing a business activity shall be subject to Articles 40 and 51 of the PIL Act which provide for special definitions of habitual residence for contractual and non-contractual relations.

175. *See* Maja Kostić-Mandić, *Državljanstvo, sredstvo ili prepreka za ostvarivanje prava građana na prostoru bivše Jugoslavije*, u: *Regulisanje otvorenih pitanja između država sukcesora bivše SFRJ* (Citizenship, means or obstacles for exercising the rights of citizens in the territory of the former Yugoslavia, In *Regulating open issues between successor countries of the former SFRY)*, Belgrade: Institute for International Politics and Economy, 2013, 518–545.

195. For legal status of a natural person habitual residence is a subsidiary connecting factor in the general provision on nationality (Article 11 of the PIL Act). These exceptions refer to particular situations where the use of nationality principle, which would normally apply to that category of legal relations is not possible or adequate. If a person is stateless or their nationality cannot be established, applicable law shall be designated according to their habitual residence, and for refugee or asylee, instead of nationality, applicable law shall be the law of the State where that person has habitual residence.

196. Furthermore, regarding applicable law to name (Article 17 of the PIL), habitual residence applies to different types of situation and with a different aim. For a stateless person in order to prevent mobile conflict and to adhere to the presumptive will of the person, the effect of a change in habitual residence on the name shall be governed by the law of the State where the person has his new habitual residence. Regarding choice of law spouses may subject the determination or a change in name on the occasion of or after the conclusion of their marriage in Montenegro to the law of Montenegro if one of the spouses has habitual residence in Montenegro; and holders of parental rights may make a statement before the registry officer that the child's surname shall be governed by the law of the State in which one of the spouses has habitual residence if that is Montenegro.

197. Habitual residence is also subsidiary connecting factor for declaring dead: a stateless missing person (Article 18(1)), as well as a person who has habitual residence in Montenegro, according to Montenegrin law where so required by the person who has a legal interest in it (Article 18(3)).

IV. Stateless Persons and Refugees

198. The problem of statelessness in Montenegro is mostly related to the status of persons who, due to the war and political instability in the former Yugoslavia, had found shelter in Montenegro, and previously did not have citizenship, or they renounced their previous citizenship and did not acquire citizenship of Montenegro. The increase in this problem has been caused by the fact that the countries which were formed in the territory of the republics of the former Yugoslavia have predicted[176] or are still predicting very restrictive conditions for acquiring their citizenship, as well as the obligation to renounce previous citizenship as a prerequisite for the possible acquisition of their citizenship.[177]

176. Serbia and Croatia, in particular have changed their restrictive policy following the Yugoslav conflicts in the 1990s (of the twentieth century) to that respect and they are presently generous in granting citizenship to those who meet the minimum requirements. Therefore, a significant number of Montenegrin citizens have more than one citizenship.

177. *Ibid.*

199. A large number of legal sources in Montenegro apply to the stateless persons. Montenegro succeeded to the 1954 Convention Relating to the Status of Stateless Persons. Montenegro also ratified the 2006 Council of Europe Convention on the Avoidance of Statelessness in relation to State Succession and the 1997 European Convention on Nationality. Montenegrin legislation guarantees basic rights to stateless persons. Thus, the Montenegrin Law on Citizenship provides for the facilitated naturalization of stateless persons. A number of provisions of the Law on International and Temporary Protection of Foreigners from 2017[178] are applied to stateless persons, who are also guaranteed legal protection, while the Law on the Prohibition of Discrimination (LPD) from 2010[179] prohibits discrimination based on nationality (Article 2). Furthermore, the Law on Free Legal Aid (LFLA)[180] (Article 12(2)), provides for free legal aid to the stateless persons based on this law, and it is limited to court procedures.

200. Regarding applicable law, the PIL Act attaches great importance to regulate relations of stateless persons, which is a novelty in comparison to the former LRCL. As a general rule it stipulates that for stateless person (as well as if their nationality cannot be established), applicable law shall be designated according to their habitual residence (Article 11(4)). Other conflict rules for this category of persons relates to guardianship, personal name and declaring a missing person dead. In all three cases, the PIL Act operates with timely fixed connecting factors: current presence *lex fori*, the last/the new habitual residence.

201. In line with practical reasons, the law of Montenegro shall apply to provisional protection measures with respect to a stateless person, but under the condition that a person is present in Montenegro. Those measures last until the State whose judicial or other authority is competent issues a decision and takes the necessary measures. This rule also applies to the protection of property of a stateless person who is present in Montenegro (Article 16(2)).

202. Another rule addresses the effects of a change in habitual residence on the name of a stateless person. By the way of analogy with the nationals, where the law of new nationality applies, for stateless person the governing law is the law of the person's new habitual residence (Article 17(2)). On the contrary, the law of the last habitual residence of a stateless person shall apply to the terms and effects of declaring the missing person dead (Article 18). Stateless persons are also addressed in the PIL Act provisions on special jurisdiction, on actions relating to the existence of marriage, divorce or annulment of marriage (Article 130(3)), and regarding cautio iudicatum solvi, where a stateless person without a domicile in Montenegro institute civil proceedings before a Montenegrin court (Article 137(1)).

178. Podgorica, Službeni list Crne Gore No. 2/2017 and 3/2019.
179. Podgorica, Službeni list Crne Gore No. 46/2010, 40/2011– other laws, 18/2014 and 42/2017, https://www.paragraf.me/propisi-crnegore/zakon-o-zabrani-diskriminacije.html (accessed 14 Apr. 2022).
180. Podgorica, Službeni list Crne Gore No. 20/2011 and 20/2015.

203. The issue of refugees is the current question for Montenegro, which, especially during the conflict in the territory of the former Yugoslavia, had received a large number of persons who were categorized as 'displaced persons' and 'internally displaced persons' which did not meet the international standards of the 1951 Refugee Convention in terms of access to rights. As a result, for some time, they had limited access to important economic and social rights.[181] Today, the situation is different. In the course of the past several years, the problem of refugees is connected with the refugee crisis where Montenegro is a transit country for numerous persons wishing to reach Western European countries.

204. Montenegro is bound by the 1951 Refugee Convention and its 1967 Protocol, while the 2007 Montenegrin Law on Asylum is superseded by the Law on International and Temporary Protection of Foreigners which is in line with international standards in this field. In the domain of conflict of laws, the PIL Act stipulates where a person has the status of a refugee or asylee, the applicable law shall be the law of the State where that person has habitual residence (Article 11(5)).

V. Transsexuals

205. Montenegro is a traditional society and its legislation does not address legal status of transsexuals. Nevertheless, the adoption of the 2010 LPD and the Law on Gender Equality[182] influenced the interpretation and application of other laws. The LPD provides an extensive definition of discrimination, including gender-based discrimination and discrimination based on sexual orientation or any other personal characteristics (Article 19) and lays down procedural guarantees for those facing discrimination. Adoption of this law was one of the requirements the country had to meet for the prospective EU membership.

206. On the basis of the Law on Personal Name[183] and its general norm stipulating that every person has the right to change his personal name, the Ministry of Internal Affairs of Montenegro allows for transgender persons to change their name before hormonal therapy and surgical operation (the first case recorded in 2013). Also, the identification card and personal documents are issued unhindered after the change of sex. However, certain problems still occur in practice. In the 2017 case, the Ministry did not allow a transsexual person who did not have medical documentation of gender change, to change the name in what she wanted, but only to gender neutral name. In that case[184] the Ombudsman gave his opinion with the recommendation. The explanation states that the public authorities and administrative bodies in the process of deciding on the rights and obligations of citizens must 'with

181. Submission by the United Nations High Commissioner for Refugees for the Office of the High Commissioner for Human Rights Compilation Report – Universal Periodic Review: Montenegro, available at: http://www.refworld.org/pdfid/4ffd355f2.pdf 3 (accessed 14 Apr. 2022).
182. Podgorica, Službeni list Crne Gore No. 46/2007, No. 73/2010 – other law, 40/2011 – other law and 35/2015.
183. Podgorica, Službeni list Crne Gore No. 47/2008, 40/2011 – other law and 55/2016.
184. Ombudsman of Montenegro, Opinion No. 01-293/17-2, Podgorica, 30.06.2017.

due care, respect their gender self-determination, or their gender identity, which necessarily does not have to follow the biological gender at the time when the person was born'. The Ombudsman has made recommendations to the Ministry in all future cases, 'to act in accordance with the Law on Personal Name, LPD and the Law on Gender Equality, in accordance with which transgender persons shall not be restricted or denied the right to change the name to the desired, as long as they fulfil the conditions for it'.[185]

207. In view of the above, the provisions of the PIL Act, which are applicable to the status (in the narrower sense) of natural persons, apply to transgender persons accordingly. The same should apply to the general rule for determining or changing a personal name (Article 17(1)), but not for provisions on the change of personal name in relation to marriage and parental relations where a transsexual person is involved, which are not allowed on the basis of substantive norms of the family law of Montenegro.

§2. Legal Persons

208. Legal persons include companies and other forms of organizations of civil law nature such as professional associations, chambers, funds and so forth and therefore there is a number of laws in Montenegro that contain substantive law provisions on the status of legal entities. Before we deal with determining the applicable law for legal entities under the PIL Act, we will briefly look at some of the most important laws in this field, among others: LCC,[186] LFI[187] and the Law on Non-governmental Organisations[188] (LNGO).

209. The LCC defines a commercial company as a legal form for conducting commercial activity (Article 2). Forms of commercial companies recognized by that law are the following: partnerships, limited partnerships, public limited companies ('joint-stock company'), private limited companies ('limited liability company'), and parts of foreign companies. The part of a foreign company in Montenegro does not have the status of a legal entity.

210. The Montenegrin LFI provides that foreign investors may: establish their own company (alone or jointly with other investors), establish part of foreign companies, acquire interests and shares in a company and purchase a company (Article 4). With respect to conditions for establishing a company, foreign investors enjoy national treatment (Article 6). A company established on the basis of foreign investment must be entered in the register kept by the Commercial Court of Montenegro.

185. *Ibid.*
186. Podgorica, Službeni list Crne Gore No. 65/2020, https://www.paragraf.me/propisi-crnegore/zakon-o-privrednim-drustvima.html (accessed 14 Apr. 2022).
187. Podgorica, Službeni list Crne Gore No. 18/2011, 45/2014 and 73/2019.
188. Podgorica, Službeni list Crne Gore No. 39/2011 and 037/2017, https://www.paragraf.me/propisi-crnegore/zakon-o-nevladinim-organizacijama.html (accessed 14 Apr. 2022).

211. Special conditions are provided for establishing banks and insurance companies.[189] Pursuant to the Law on Credit Institutions,[190] a bank with its registered office in Montenegro or a branch of a credit institution with its registered office in EU Member State or a third country conducting business on the territory of Montenegro may be established (Article 2(2). A permit for operation of a bank is issued by the Central Bank of Montenegro. As to the establishment of broker-dealer companies and stock exchanges, the provisions of the Law on Capital Market must be observed, in addition to the provisions of LCC and LFI.

212. For legal persons of a non-commercial nature, the most important source is the Law on NGOs which provides that non-governmental associations and non-governmental foundations may be established by foreign natural or legal persons, while a foreign NGO is considered to be a legal person with a seat in another country, and which is established under the laws of that State. This law does not apply to political parties, trade unions, sport organizations, religious communities, business associations, organizations and foundations established by the State, as well as to other forms of association that are established by a special law. However, it applies to the issues which are not regulated by these special laws (Article 5).

I. Incorporated Organizations

213. When it comes to the applicable law, the dichotomy between the place of incorporation (establishment, registration) and the place of the real seat and the underlying interests from comparative law reflects in Montenegrin law. For the legal position of legal entities, the renvoi is excluded (Article 4(1) of the PIL Act).The PIL Act adheres almost literally to the wording of the former LRCL.[191] Pursuant to Article 19 of the PIL Act applicable law for a legal person shall be the law of the State of its incorporation. However, if legal person has its real seat in another State and if that State considers it as its own, the real seat criterion will prevail. The PIL Act starts from the place of establishment of a legal person. Therefore, for the status relations of legal persons the law of the country in which it is incorporated shall apply. But, unlike those systems in comparative law that envisage a pure system of incorporation, in Montenegrin PIL, the place of the real seat of the company may prevail if certain conditions are met. Thus, if a legal person is established by the law of one country and has a real seat in another country, the applicable law for that legal person will depend on the substantive law of the country of the real seat. If a country of the seat considers it its own, the law of the seat shall apply. However,

189. *See* Art. 4 of the Law on Insurance, Podgorica, Službeni list Crne Gore No. 78/2006, 19/2007, 53/2009, 40/2011, 45/2012, 6/2013, 55/2016 and 146/2021.

190. Podgorica, Službeni list Crne Gore No. 72/2019, 82/2020 and 8/2021.

191. However, Art. 17 of the LRCL refers to 'nationality' of a legal person. For different meanings of terms, affiliation, citizenship and nationality of the legal entity *see* Maja Stanivuković & Mirko Živković, *Međunarodno privatno pravo: opšti deo* (Private International Law: General Part), Belgrade, Službeni list SCG, 2004, 126.

most often this will not be the case, since the company is not established in a country where it now has a real seat, and the applicable law will nevertheless be the law of the country of incorporation.[192]

214. However, the new LCC has opted for the concept of registered, statutory seat instead of the real seat theory. Thus, pursuant to the Article 13 of the LCC, the seat is the place in Montenegro from which the business of the company is managed or the place where the company permanently performs its activity, which is determined by the founding act or the statute of the company and which is registered in the Central Register of the Commercial Court (CRPS) in Montenegro. Now,[193] it is envisaged that a company may have only one seat and if the management of the company or the place where the company permanently performs its activity is located in a place other than the place registered as the seat of the company, the seat shall be considered the place registered in CRPS, provided that third parties against the company may also establish the jurisdiction of the court according to the place where the management of the company is located or the place where the company permanently performs its activity. For the legal position of legal entities, the renvoi is excluded (Article 4(1) of the PIL Act).

II. Unincorporated Organizations

215. According to the LCC, mercantile partnerships do not have the status of a legal person in Montenegro (Article 3). The PIL Act provides a special conflict rule for unincorporated organizations: the law of the country in which they are entered into the register or established (Article 20 of the PIL Act). This rule applies to all matters covered by the rule from Article 21 on the scope of the applicable law, as well as to issues that are not explicitly stated. For the legal position of the unincorporated organization the renvoi is excluded (Article 4(1) of the PIL Act).

III. Scope of the *Lex Societas*

216. The PIL Act also provides useful guidance to some of the issues to which the applicable law applies. This list is not final and serves only to point out to the most important issues that arise in this field. Article 21 specifies that the applicable law for legal persons and unincorporated organizations relates in particular to: establishment, legal nature and legal organizational form; name or title; legal subjectivity and system of management; establishment, competence and functioning of the bodies of the legal person or unincorporated organizations; proxy; acquisition and loss of membership, and related rights and obligations with them; liability for

192. Mihajlo Dika, Gaša Knežević, Srđan Stojanović, *Komentar Zakona o međunarodnom privatnom i procesnom pravu* (Commentary of the PIL Act), Belgrade: Nomos, 1991, 64.

193. Previously, according to the Article 4a of the 2002 LCC, the seat was defined as the place where the commercial company performs the activity, and if the activity is performed in several places, the seat is considered to be the place where the head office of the company's management is located.

obligations; consequences of any violations of law or of founding acts; reorganization and cessation of a legal person or unincorporated organizations.

217. Bilateral treaties binding on Montenegro contain different solutions, so, for example, the establishment criterion is adopted in the treaties on legal aid with Romania, the Czech Republic and Slovakia, while the seat criterion was adopted in the treaties with Poland and Hungary.

IV. Liability

218. In accordance with the provision on the scope of the *lex societas* the law of the country to which the company belongs, determined in accordance with Article 19 of the PIL Act shall govern liability of a company. The application of the *lex societas* to non-contractual liability of the company is implicitly provided for by the Rome II Regulation Article 1.2(d), which stipulates the following, among others, shall be excluded from its scope:
Non-contractual obligations arising out of the law of companies and other bodies corporate or unincorporated regarding matters such as the creation, by registration or otherwise, legal capacity, internal organization or winding-up of companies and other bodies corporate or unincorporated, the personal liability of officers and members as such for the obligations of the company or body and the personal liability of auditors to a company or to its members in the registered audits of accounting documents.
Even if Montenegro is still not an EU country, this provision is relevant pursuant to the PIL Act Article 67 providing for interpretation and application of its provisions on applicable law for non-contractual obligations in accordance with the Rome II Regulation.

219. The *lex societas* governs the liability of the shareholders and managers when they act in that function. On the contrary, the tort statute governs the responsibility for rules applicable to everyone as well as the attribution of delict behaviour to the company. The liability for the violation of specific corporate obligations is governed by the *lex societas.*[194]

220. Legal persons may appear in the role of the plaintiff or the defendant in different types of disputes. In Montenegro in addition to civil and administrative liability, legal persons can also be criminally liable on the basis of the Law on Liability of Legal Persons for Criminal Offenses.[195] A potential criminal liability may stand with: a commercial company, a foreign company and a part of a foreign company, a public enterprise, a public institution, a domestic and a foreign non-governmental organization, an investment fund, another fund (excluding a fund that exclusively

194. *Vorschläge und Berichte zur Reform des europäischen und deutschen internationalen Gesellschaftsrechts*, Sonnenberger, Hrsg., Tübingen: Mohr Siebeck, 2007, 475.
195. Podgorica, Službeni list Crne Gore No. 2/2007, 13/2007, 30/2012, 13/2007, 30/2012 and 39/2016.

performs public competencies), a sports organization, a political party, another association or organization that permanently or occasionally realizes or acquires funds and disposes of them in the course of its business (Article 4(1)). The law stipulates that the following entities are exempted from criminal liability: State, State bodies and local self-government bodies, as well as a legal person entrusted with the exercise of public authority, for the criminal offence committed in the exercise of such powers.

V. Relocation

221. A commercial company may, for various reasons, make a decision on relocation. These reasons include, among others, a reduction in production costs, and application of more favourable tax legislation. The LCC does not contain a single conflict rule for commercial companies. Nevertheless, the formation of a commercial company is governed by its personal law which is determined on the basis of connecting factors contained in Article 19 of the PIL Act. A company duly formed in its home country will be recognized as such by the Montenegrin legal system and it will enjoy legal and procedural capacity it was endowed with under the personal law.

222. Currently, there is no legal option for transferring a seat of company from abroad to Montenegro without such company being forced to undergo foundation and registration procedure as prescribed by the Montenegrin legislation (LCC).

223. In its Article 318, the LCC provides for a definition of a part of a foreign company. It is a part of a company established and registered outside of Montenegro, through which that company carries on commercial activity in the territory of the country. Such foreign company has a duty to conduct its business in compliance with the relevant legislation of Montenegro. Parts of foreign companies have to be registered with the Commercial Court in Podgorica and they have to appoint the representatives to represent the company in legal proceedings.

224. The LB provides for conflict rules modelled on the respective provisions of the Insolvency Regulation.[196] Thus, the law applicable to a bankruptcy procedure and its effects is the law of the country where the bankruptcy procedure has been commenced (Article 179(1) of LB), while the law applicable to effects of the bankruptcy procedure on employment contracts is the law applicable to the employment contract (Article 179(3)).

---

196. Council Regulation (EC) No. 1346/2000 of 29 May 2000 on Insolvency Proceedings, [2000] OJ L 160/1.

VI. Cross-Border Transformation

225. Regarding cross-border transformation, Montenegrin company law is yet to be aligned with the newest regulatory development in the EU law (EU Directive No. 2019/2121 amending the former Directive No. 2017/1132 on cross-border conversions, mergers and divisions). Presently, the LCC features only regulatory framework for cross-border mergers and divisions fully aligned with EU company law (Directive 2005/56/EC consolidated by the Directive 2017/1132). However, this legislative framework will become applicable in Montenegro only when Montenegro reaches full EU membership.

226. The LCC regulates mergers of public limited companies by its Chapter VII, section B, as one of the forms of restructuring but it does not include any conflict rule. Generally, Article 19 of the PIL Act regulating legal status of companies should be applied here, but due to the complex situation of ascertaining the personal law in case of cross-border transformation, the solution that could be applied in case of mergers of foreign and domestic companies, as a general principle of PIL, is the cumulative application of both laws that govern the status of the legal persons that intend to be merged. The merger would be validly effectuated only if it complied with provisions of both of these laws.

Chapter 2. Obligations

§1. Contractual Obligations

227. Contractual relations have traditionally been one of the most regulated areas in PIL of Montenegro. As an illustration of the previous statement, the Law on Resolution of Conflict of Laws contained provisions on: the party autonomy; the application of the domicile of the debtor of the characteristic performance and the principle of the closest connection to the nineteen designated contracts; the rule for contracts relating to immovable property; subsidiary rule on the use of the *lex contractus* to determine the moment of acquiring the rights to products and fruits, as well as the risk transfer; subsidiary rule for the method of handing over of goods; for effects of assignation and subrogation, accessory legal transaction and unilateral legal transaction (Articles 19–26 of the LRCL).

228. The PIL Act copied a great number of provisions from the Rome I Regulation. Therefore, the positive law of Montenegro in this area contains provisions parallel to the provisions on the law applicable to contractual obligations under the Rome I Regulation, with the minimum adjustments. Furthermore, Article 49 of the PIL Act explicitly provides that the interpretation and application of the provisions relating to contractual obligations shall be carried out in accordance with the Rome I Regulation. This means that Montenegrin judges and other competent authorities are already obliged to directly apply the acquis in this field, although Montenegro has only a candidate status for the EU membership.

229. The conflict rules pertinent to contractual obligations are also contained in other pieces of legislation: LMIN, LOPRAT and LBE, whose Articles 95 to 101 apply analogously to conflict of laws for checks.

I. Party Autonomy

230. In Montenegro's law, party autonomy is traditionally the most important connecting factor to contractual relations. The influence of the development of social relations and the advancement of technology to conflict rules can be tracked in the span of three centuries. Party autonomy for contractual relations was first stipulated by Article 792 of the GPC of 1888, which distinguishes the explicit, implicit and hypothetical autonomy of will.[197] Paragraph 2 of the same article lists 'places', that is laws that can be applied and thus introduces restrictions in this sphere, as connection is required between the law chosen and the parties or their transaction. According to the GPC, parties may choose to apply the law of the country where the contract is concluded, the law of the country where the contract is

197. *See also* Maja Kostić-Mandić, *Mjerodavno pravo u Opštem imovinskom zakoniku za Knjaževinu Crnu Goru* u *120 godina OIZ-a u Crnoj Gori* (The Applicable Law in the General Pecuniary Code for the Principality of Montenegro) In *120 years of GPC in Montenegro*, Podgorica: Univerzitet Crne Gore, Pravni fakultet, Udruženje pravnika CG, 95–105.

executed, the law of the country of the court or the law of the country where the centre of gravity of the contract is. With this formulation, the legislator opted for the concept that party autonomy is the basic and practically the only connecting factor to contractual relations, since all other connections are merely its expression.

231. Almost a century later, the provision on party autonomy for contractual relations was provided by the LRCL in 1982. It is important to note that, unlike other conflict rules of the GPC, which were almost literally taken over by the LRCL, there were significant changes in the scope of the contract, but the basic idea of Article 792 of the GPC has been retained. The LRCL provides the party autonomy as the main connecting factor to the contracts, unless provided otherwise by LRCL or an international treaty predicts so. The LRCL excludes the party autonomy if the subject of the contract are immovables (Article 21), so *lex situs* was applied equally to the property and obligation effects of contracts relating to immovables. Although the LRCL did not contain a definition of the types of party autonomy, in the doctrine it is indisputable that the choice can be exercised explicitly or tacitly and parties are free to choose the law of any country. The doctrine unanimously allows the application of different laws to different parts of the contract – scission of the contract, as well as the option of changing the choice of the applicable law in the course of the contract duration.[198] As to the time of choice, there is general agreement, confirmed by the arbitral practice of the former Yugoslav Foreign Trade Arbitration (FTA) in Belgrade, that the choice of applicable law can be made or altered after the contract is concluded, and even at the time when the lawsuit has already begun.[199]

232. The PIL Act of 2014 goes a step further. As already mentioned, for the contractual obligations it mirrors the main provisions of the Rome I Regulation, with minimal corrections, and explicitly establishes the obligation to interpret these provisions and apply them in accordance with the Rome I Regulation (Article 49). Article dedicated to the party autonomy of the PIL Act is slightly adjusted Article 4 of the Rome I Regulation. Pursuant to Article 38 of the PIL Act, party autonomy as the main connecting factor retains its primacy and is regulated in detail. It is envisaged that the choice of law must be exercised explicitly or unambiguously stemming from the provisions of the contract or the circumstances of the case (tacit choice of law); also, the possibility of scission of the applicable law is envisaged, which implies the choice of different laws for certain parts of the contract, as well as the possibility of contracting and changing the applicable law at any time during the validity of the contract. In addition, it is specified that the change of the applicable law after the conclusion of the contract does not affect the validity of the form and the rights of third parties. The same article of the PIL Act contains the provision on the application of the provisions of the law of another country, which cannot be derogated from by agreement, with which all other elements of the factual situation at the time of the choice of the law are connected (Article 38(3)). Also, it

198. Mihajlo Dika, Gaša Knežević & Srđan Stojanović, *Komentar Zakona o međunarodnom privatnom i procesnom pravu* (Commentary of the PIL Act), Belgrade: Nomos, 1991, 72–77.
199. *Ibid.*

is envisaged that the existence and validity of the parties' agreement on the applicable law shall be valued by the following general provisions: on the existence and material validity of the contract (Article 44), the validity of the form of the contract (Article 45) and the contractual capacity of the contractors located in the same country (Article 14(2)).

233. In addition to these general rules on the choice of the applicable law for contracts, the PIL Act contains special rules for certain types of contracts. The Code provides for the choice of the applicable law for contracts where the object is the real right to immovable property or lease of immovable property, which was not possible before.[200] In a situation when the fundamental provisions of the Rome I Regulation are almost fully copied, the introduction of party autonomy in this area has its own justification, and the protection of the interests of Montenegro, as well as the weaker parties, can be effectively implemented on the basis of the application of Article 38(3) of the PIL Act. With certain specificities and limitations, the party autonomy is also addressed in provisions on contract on the carriage of goods and transport of passengers, consumer contracts and individual employment contracts.[201]

234. The right of the parties to freely choose the law that will govern their contract is also provided by Article 1038 of the LMIN, and Article 178(1), of the LOPRAT. There are several provisions of the LOPRAT and the LMIN providing for the parties' possibility to choose different laws with respect to different parts of the contract or to choose a law that will not cover all the issues arising from contract.[202]

235. If an arbitration of a contractual dispute is taking place in Montenegro, the European Convention on International Commercial Arbitration (1961) in Article VII, paragraph 1, guarantees freedom of the parties to agree upon the law to be applied by the arbitrators to the substance of the dispute. A similar provision is found in LCP (Article 493, paragraph 1) and in the Arbitration Rules of the Arbitration Court at the Chamber of Economy of Montenegro (2015), Article 24, paragraph 1.[203] If an ad hoc arbitration to which the European Convention does not apply decides, there is no specific rule, but such an arbitration could also refer to the conflict rules of the PIL Act, the Montenegrin LCP, the LMIN or the LOPRAT respectively, to recognize the parties' choice as valid.

236. Party autonomy is excluded or limited for the following specific types of contracts:

200. The LRCL in Art. 21 provides that contracts related to immovables are exclusively governed by the lex situs.

201. *See infra* under the respective titles.

202. See in particular the LMIN, Arts 1040, 1041 and 1045–1047, and the LOPRAT, Art. 178(1). However, after adoption of the PIL Act, a provision guaranteeing participants in foreign trade the right to choose the applicable law contained in The Law on Foreign Trade (2004, as amended 2007, Art. 10) ceased to exist.

203. http://www.privrednakomora.me/sites/pkcg.org/files/multimedia/main_pages/files/2012/09/final_eng_montenegro_arbitration_rules_draft_galic_docx_en_0.pdf (accessed 14 Apr. 2022).

- Contracts on exploitation of ships; the parties are free to agree upon the applicable law subject to limitations contained in the LMIN, Article 1039; further limitations of a similar nature exist with respect to contracts on salvage of ships (the LMIN, Article 1042), general average (the LMIN, Article 1045(2)) and contracts on marine insurance (the LMIN, Article 1047(2)).
- Contracts on transport of passengers and goods by air; the parties are also free to agree upon the applicable law, subject to limitations contained in the LOPRAT Article 179(2) for contracts on insurance in aerial transportation.
- Contracts on transportation of goods by road; autonomy of the parties is excluded for contracts which fall within the scope of application of the Convention on the Contracts for the International Carriage of Goods by Road (CMR).
- Contracts for transportation of passengers and luggage by road which fall within the scope of the Convention on the Contracts for the International Carriage of Passengers and Luggage by Road (CVR) (pursuant to Articles 41 and 23, respectively).

II. Form

237. The PIL Act mirrors the rules of the Rome I Regulation on the formal validity.[204] Article 45 of the PIL Act contains rule for the form of contracts concluded between the present (paragraph 1) and absent persons (paragraph 2) and for unilateral legal acts related to the contract (such as tender, paragraph 3), as well as special rules for two types of contracts: consumer contracts (paragraph 4) and contracts where the object is the real right to immovable property or lease of immovable property (paragraph 5).

238. The general rule for formal validity of contracts irrespective of whether they are concluded between present and absent persons is that the form is valid if it meets the formal requirements of the law applicable to the substance of that contract (based on the party autonomy or subsidiary connecting factors). If the form of a contract would not be valid according to this law, alternative connecting factors are envisaged which aim to strengthen as many contracts as possible. Then the validity of the contract will be assessed according to the law of the country where it is concluded, that is, for a contract between absent persons, under the law of the country in which at the time of the conclusion of the contract, any party or its representative (if the contract is concluded by a representative) is present or in which one the parties had a habitual residence. A special rule for contracts concluded between absent persons will help to avoid the problem of legal qualification.

239. The validity of the form of unilateral legal acts relating to a contract, already concluded or still to be concluded will be valued according to: the law applicable to the substance of a contract or the law of the country in which that act was done or the law of the country in which the person who did the act at that time had a habitual residence.

204. *See* Art. 11 of the Rome I Regulation.

240. The main feature of these solutions is that they strive to convalidate as many contracts as possible regarding the validity of their form.

241. A rule that is established for the form of consumer contracts – the country of the habitual residence of the consumer has another objective: the protection of a weaker party. Therefore, the form of the consumer contract will be valid only if it is valid under the law of the place of habitual residence of the consumer and it is not possible to convalidate the form under any other law.

242. A special rule was also drafted for a contract where the subject is the real right to immovable property or lease of immovable property. The form of these agreements is an important condition for the validity of a legal transaction. It is envisaged that the contract is formally valid if it meets the requirements of the form prescribed by the law of the country in which the immovable property is situated, if, under that law, these conditions: (1) apply regardless of the country in which the contract is concluded and which law is applicable for the contract; and (2) fall under imperative regulations that cannot be derogated from by agreement.

243. According to the Montenegrin Law on Notaries, the following contracts have to be concluded in mandatory form of a notarial deed: (1) marital contracts and contracts on property relations between persons living in the extramarital community; (2) contracts on disposition of property belonging to juvenile persons and persons without capacity to contract, the scope of which are immovable property or valuable movables and rights; (3) contracts on distribution and use of assets during lifetime, contracts on lifelong maintenance; (4) sales contracts by retaining ownership right; (5) promised gifts and agreements on gift in cases of death; (6) contracts regulating transfer or acquisition of ownership or other in rem rights over immovable property.[205]

III. Validity and Formation

244. Substantive contract law of Montenegro stipulates that the conclusion of the contract should meet the general conditions regarding: the capacity to contract, the agreement of the will of the contracting parties, the subject of the contract is possible, allowed and determined or determinable and that the legal causa of the contract is allowed.

245. Article 44 of the PIL Act on consent and material validity mirrors Article 10 of the Rome I Regulation. Thus, the basic rule stipulates that existence and validity of a contract, or of any term of a contract, shall be determined by the law which would govern if the contract or term were valid. The law of the contract (*lex contractus*) applies in case parties made choice of law or when the applicable law should be ascertained according to the subsidiary connecting factor for a specific type of contract. Nevertheless, a party, in order to establish that he did not consent,

205. Article 52 para.1 of the Law on Notaries.

may rely upon the law of the country in which he has his habitual residence if it appears from the circumstances that it would not be reasonable to determine the effect of his conduct in accordance with the law of the contract. Thus, habitual residence may prevail over *lex contractus* regarding silence and conduct of either of the parties as to the formation of the contract if other conditions are met.

246. The provision of the PIL Act on choice of applicable law (Article 38(4)) stipulates that the existence and validity of the agreement of the parties on applicable law shall be governed by its:

- Article 14(2) (on business capacity, which mirrors Article 13 of the Rome I Regulation providing for limited possibility of invoking incapacity resulting from the law of country other than the country where parties, both of them being present, concluded the contract);
- Article 44; and
- Article 45 (on the form of contract, which mirrors Article 13 of the Rome I Regulation).

The object and causa of the contract are governed by the law of the contract.

IV. Performance

247. Regarding not exhaustive list of the matters which fall within the scope of the law applicable to the contract (*lex contractus*) from Article 12 of the Rome I Regulation, which are literally taken over in Article 48 of the PIL Act dedicated to scope of the applicable law, the provision on the obligation to interpret and apply this article of the law in accordance with the law of the EU shall apply. Below we point out only the basic solutions, and for a more comprehensive elaboration of these questions, we refer to the commentaries of the Rome I Regulation.[206]

248. The PIL Act mirrors Rome I provision on scope of the applicable law (Article 12) and among others it provides that the law applicable to a contract by virtue of the Code shall govern in particular performance of the obligations arising from the contract (Article 48(1)2). Thus, the basic rule for performance is the *lex contractus*. However, the *lex solutionis* (the law of the State in which performance takes place) shall be taken into account in relation to the type and manner[207] of performance and the steps to be taken by the creditor in the event of defective performance.

206. Schulze, *Art. 12 Rome I*, In *Rome Regulations* 2nd Edn, Calliess ed., Alphen aan den Rijn: Kluwer Law International, 2015, Lüttringhaus, *Art. 12 Rome I*, In *Rome I Regulation: Pocket Commentary*, Ferrari ed., Sellier European Law Publishers, 2015.
207. Ferrari/Lüttringhaus, Rome I Regulation (2015), Art. 12, 422.

249. The term 'performance' refers to the totality of the conditions, resulting from the law or from the contract, the completion of which is essential for the fulfilment of the respective obligation.[208] Under Article 12(1) of the Rome I and Article 48(1)2 of the PIL Act, the performance of the obligations arising from the contract encompasses in particular:[209]

- the conditions relating to the place and time of performance;
- the diligence with which the obligation must be performed;
- the identification of the creditor and the debtor of a claim and the extent to which the obligation can be performed by a person other than the contracting party;
- how and under which conditions certain special types of obligations may be fulfilled, such as when it comes to joint or several obligations, alternative obligations, divisible and indivisible obligations or pecuniary obligations;
- the illegality of performance and its consequences;
- conditions and the time of the passing of the risk with regard to the obligations arising from the contract;
- whether a contracting party may refuse performance, such as on the basis of a right of retention or a plea of non-performance and so forth.

In cases where performance consists of the payment of a sum of money, the law of the contract governs the conditions under which the debtor making the payment is freed from his obligation, the appropriation of the payment and other issues, such as requirements relating to the receipt of payment (including the currency of the debt).[210]

V. Breach of Contractual Obligations (Including Damages)

250. The PIL Act reflecting the Rome I Regulation adheres to a unitary approach, subjecting the existence, assessment and qualification of damages to the substantive law applicable to the contract as a whole.

251. Article 48(3) of the PIL Act addressing the scope of the applicable law stipulates the law applicable to contractual relations shall govern in particular: within the limits of the powers conferred on the court by its procedural law, the consequences of a total or partial breach of obligations, including the assessment of damages in so far as it is governed by rules of law. The PIL Act in its Article 70, which provides provisions common to contractual and non-contractual obligations, copies Article 18 of the Rome I Regulation on burden on proof so that governing law shall apply to the extent that it contains rules which raise presumptions of law or determine the burden of proof. However, the legal effect of an act may be proven by any mode of proof recognized by the law of the forum or by any of the laws

208. Report Giuliano/Lagarde, O.J. 1980 No. C 282/1, Art. 10, 37.
209. Ferrari/Lüttringhaus, Rome I Regulation (2015), Art. 12, 408–411.
210. *Id.* 409.

referred to in Article 45 of the PIL Act under which that contract is formally valid, provided that such mode of proof can be administered by the forum.

252. Within the limits set by the procedural law of the competent court the law applicable to the contract governs questions relating to the amount of compensation, mitigation of loss, modalities of the compensation payments (i.e., periodic payments or a lump sum), remoteness of damage, admissible heads of damage, rules limiting the amount of compensation payable and so forth.[211]

253. In Montenegrin substantive law the rules on non-contractual liability are to be applied accordingly to rules on contractual liability (Article 276 of the LOO). Thus, the rules on non-contractual liability are structured as general rules on liability for damages inflicted, while the rules on contractual liability are structured as more specific ones.[212] Under Article 197 of the LO 'the court shall determine damages in the amount necessary to restore the material state of the person sustaining damage into the state it would have been without the damaging act or omission' (the principle of full indemnification).

VI. Rescission

254. In Montenegrin substantive law a contract may be extinguished:[213] by its (complete) performance; by mutual agreement; by lapse of time or reaching of the stipulated objective; by notice of termination; in case of death of one of the parties; in case of confusion; ex lege in case of breach or in case of other occurrences causing the contract to end ex lege; by unilateral rescission as a result of breach; in case of changed circumstances, impossibility of performance and gross disparity; in case of voidance.

255. The PIL Act mirroring Rome I provision on the scope of the applicable law stipulates that the law applicable to the contract applies to various ways of extinguishing obligations (Article 48(4)), while prescription and limitation of actions are dealt with under the same article, numbers 5 and 6, respectively. The *lex contractus* governs the various ways of extinguishing obligations, but it does not apply to set-off by operation of law, which is governed by the law applicable to the claim against which the right to set-off is asserted (Article 47 of the PIL Act). Another category

211. Dicey/Morris/Collins, *Conflict of Laws* 15th ed. London: Sweet and Maxwell, 2012, para. 32-154 and 7-45.
212. For key differences between contractual and tortuous liability in Montenegrin law *see* Oliver Antić, *Obligaciono pravo, 8. izdanje* (Obligations), 8th edn, Belgrade: Pravni fakultet Univerziteta u Beogradu, Dosije studio, 2014, 454–459; Jakov Radišić, *Obligaciono pravo, opšti deo, 6. izdanje* (Obligations, General part), 6th edn, Belgrade: Nomos, 2000, 183–187.
213. *See* Vladimir Savković, *International Encyclopedia of Laws – Contracts: Montenegro*, Alphen aan den Rijn: Kluwer Law International, 2017, Chapter 5, The Extinguishment of the Contract.

of relations where *lex contractus* may not apply is the one regarding effects of bankruptcy procedure to contracts. LB provides for conflict rules modelled on the respective provisions of the Insolvency Regulation.[214] Thus, the law applicable to a bankruptcy procedure and its effects is the law of the country where the bankruptcy procedure has been commenced (Article 179(1) of LB), unless otherwise provided by the same act. However, the LB does not contain provisions similar to those of the Insolvency Regulation that the law of the State of the opening of proceedings shall determine, in particular, '(e) the effects of insolvency proceedings on current contracts to which the debtor is party' and '(k) creditors' rights after the closure of insolvency proceedings'. The LB does not contain any special provisions regarding the effects of insolvency proceedings on contracts relating to immoveable property.[215]

256. In the period of 2018 to 2020, the Commercial Court adjudicated in two cases on limitation period in the international sale of goods. In one case where the plaintiff was a company from Serbia and defendant company from Montenegro, the Convention on the Limitation Period in the International Sale of Goods has been applied,[216] while in the second case[217] where the plaintiff was a company from Croatia, which is not a signatory to the Convention, by applying the PIL Act, applicable law was the substantive law of Croatia – the Law on Obligations.

VII. Representation

257. The PIL Act provides for provision on contractual representation, which is contained in its tale III 'Legal Affairs, Representation and Statute of Limitations'. This conflict rule is inspired by the 1978 Hague Convention on the Law Applicable to Agency (Montenegro is not a Member Party to this convention).

258. Pursuant to Article 24 of the PIL Act relationships between the grantor of attorney and a third party, the existence and scope of authority given to a representative, as well as effects arising out of the usage or alleged usage of such authority, shall be governed by the law chosen by the grantor and the third party, under condition that the choice made is known or could have been known to the representative. In the absence of a choice of law, those matters shall be governed by the law of the State where the representative acted and if the representative acted in conduct of his professional activity, applicable law shall be the law of the place where the representative had his seat, under condition that the place is known or could have been known to the third party.

214. Council Regulation (EC) No. 1346/2000 of 29 May 2000 on Insolvency Proceedings, [2000] OJ L 160/1.
215. Ferrari/Lüttringhaus, Rome I Regulation (2015), Art. 12, 416.
216. Commercial Court P.br.288/18, Pž.br.864 /18.
217. Commercial Court P.br.1113/18, Pž.br.675/19.

259. The same applicable law also governs the relationship between the representative and the third party that arise out of the fact that the representative acted within the scope of his authority, that he has exceeded such authority, or that he has acted without any authority.

260. However, those rules do not apply where the subject of representation is the right to immovable property. In that case relationships between the grantor of attorney and a third party, the existence and scope of authority given to a representative, as well as effects arising out of the usage or alleged usage of such authority, shall be governed by the law of the State where the immovable property is situated.

VIII. Interpretation

261. Interpretation of the contract (Article 48(1)) is also governed by the *lex contractus*. The law applicable to the contractual obligation governs the interpretation of the entire contract, including declarations of rescission and notices of termination. Interpretation includes the resolution of potential ambiguities in contract clauses as well as the supplementation of the agreement where the parties did not make any stipulations with respect to specific issues.[218]

IX. Third Parties and Multiparty Agreements

262. The PIL Act does not contain a conflict rule for third parties and multiparty agreements as stipulated by Rome I Regulation, Article 4(1)h. Moreover, it does not have a special conflict rule for contracts concluded in favour of third parties (beneficiaries), although the LO has general provisions on such contracts in Articles 143–147 and particular provisions on certain insurance contracts of this kind in Articles 994 and 1054–1062. Consequently, the applicable law for these contracts in the absence of choice of law will be determined pursuant to the rules and principles contained in Article 39 of the PIL Act. This law will presumably determine the effects of these contracts in relation to the beneficiary.

X. Assignment and Subrogation

263. There are in fact only two rules in the Montenegrin PIL Act that regulate the applicable law to relationships that may arise between parties to a contract and third parties (assignment and subrogation). Article 46 of the PIL Act mirrors Article 14 of the Rome I Regulation. Thus, the relationship between assignor and assignee under a voluntary assignment or contractual subrogation if parties did not make choice of law agreement shall be governed by the *lex contractus*. However, the main rule is subject to exception. Thus, the law governing the assigned claim shall determine its assignability, the relationship between the new creditor and the debtor, the

218. Ferrari/Lüttringhaus, Rome I Regulation (2015), Art. 12, 406–408.

conditions under which the assignment can be invoked against the debtor and the conditions under and the manner in which the debtor can discharge his obligations. The same provision applies to contractual subrogation, while legal subrogation is governed by Article 68 of the PIL Act mirroring Article 15 of the Rome I Regulation. The assignment of claims includes outright transfer of claims, transfers of claims by way of security and pledges or other security rights over claims.

§2. Particular Contracts

264. Article 39 of the PIL Act provides the same solutions as Rome I in Article 4 (on applicable law in the absence of choice). The only difference is that PIL Act does not contain point h) (on a contract concluded within a multilateral system in accordance with Directive 2004/39/EC of the European Parliament and of the Council of 21 April 2004 on markets in financial instruments). In addition to the rules applicable to the largest number of contracts, the PIL Act also contains special rules for certain types of contracts (transport contracts, consumer contracts, individual employment contracts), but does not contain the provisions on the applicable law for insurance contracts regulated by the Rome I Regulation.[219]

265. The LMN and the LOPRAT apply to contracts in their respective field, and their conflict rules as *lex specialis* have primacy over the PIL Act.

I. Sales Contract

266. The PIL Act's conflict rules for sales contract mirrors Regulation Rome I Article 4(1)(1), and pursuant to Article 49 of the PIL Act, the interpretation and application of these provisions shall be done in accordance with the Rome I Regulation. The basic connecting factor to the sales contract is the party autonomy, while the subsidiary rules include lex venditoris and the principle of the closest connection.

267. For this type of contract, all the foregoing regarding party autonomy as connecting factor in contractual relations generally, applies.

268. Article 39(1)1 of the PIL Act provides that, if the parties have not made the choice of law, the contract of sale of goods shall be governed by the law of the country where the seller has his habitual place of residence. The application of the law of the party required to effect the characteristic performance of the contract was also prescribed by the LRCL, but in the form of a domicile for natural persons, or the seat for the legal entities. The PIL Act, in accordance with the Rome I Regulation, also contains a definition of what is considered to be the habitual place of residence of a contracting party whose obligation is characteristic to that type of contract and

219. Article 7 of the Rome I Regulation.

which makes a particular type of contract different from other types of contract.[220] For contractual relations, the habitual place of residence of a natural person performing a business activity is his principal place of business, and for companies – the place of central administration. If a contract is concluded within the business of a branch, agency or other business units, or one of the units is under the contract responsible for its performance, the habitual place of residence is considered to be the place where that unit is located. In order to avoid a mobile conflict, it is specified that for contractual relationships the habitual residence is valued by the time the contract is concluded. In a situation where the principal contractual obligation of one party is expressed in money (payment of goods), the obligation of the other contracting party, which carries out the delivery of goods, is characteristic for that type of contract.

269. In addition to the habitual residence of the seller, the principle of the closest connection appears as a subsidiary connecting factor in two cases: if it is clear from all the circumstances of the case that the contract is obviously more closely connected to another country or when the applicable law cannot be determined on the basis of the lex loci venditoris rule. In the first case, this principle appears as a part of a special escape clause. Pursuant to Article 39(3) of the PIL Act a prerequisite for the application of the escape clause, is that it is unambiguous that the contract is more closely connected to another country (and not with some other law, as foreseen by the general escape clause under Article 8 of the PIL Act) in relation to a country whose law would otherwise govern the case. When establishing closer connections with another country, Recital 20 of the Rome I Regulation specifies that 'account should be taken, among other things, of whether the contract in question has a very close relationship with another contract or contracts'. In the second case, the principle of the closest connection occurs if the applicable law cannot be determined under the lex loci venditoris rule (Article 39(4) of the PIL Act).

270. The PIL Act, in accordance with the Rome I Regulation (Article 4(1)(f)), also provides for a subsidiary rule for contracts relating to a right in rem in immovable property or to a tenancy of immovable property. In the absence of the choice of law those contracts will be governed by the law of the country where the property is situated. However, in case of a tenancy of immovable property concluded for temporary private use for a period of no more than six consecutive months the contract shall be governed by the law of the country where the landlord has his habitual residence, provided that the tenant is a natural person and has his habitual residence in the same country (Article 39(1) points 3 and 4, respectively).

271. The PIL Act, in accordance with the Rome I Regulation, also contains special rules for the contract on the sale of goods at the auction – the law of the country where the auction is held, if that place can be determined (Article 39(1) point 7).

272. In the former Yugoslavia, as well as in the countries that applied the LRCL, the party autonomy, with all the characteristics discussed, was used as a basic rule

220. *See* Art. 19 of the Rome I Regulation.

and in practice did not cause problems. This could not be said of the method of application of subsidiary connecting factors. In practice, the courts used to directly apply the domicile of the debtor of a characteristic performance and did not determine the closest connection, while the arbitration practice applied the principle of the closest connection.[221] Based on the experience of the judges of the Commercial Court in Podgorica,[222] the impression is that the 'special circumstances', which was the terminology of the LRCL for the closest connection principle did not come to life in court practice and that the judges directly applied the law of domicile of the debtor of a characteristic performance. As for the arbitration practice of the former Foreign Trade Arbitration at the Chamber of Commerce of Yugoslavia when the parties did not make the choice of law, it was documented that the principle of the closest connection was applied in several cases.[223] The arbitration practice of Foreign Trade Arbitration at the Chamber of Commerce of Montenegro did not have opportunity to comment on these issues.

II. Service Contract

273. In the law of Montenegro a conflict rule for this type of contract mirrors Regulation Rome I Article 4(1)(b), and pursuant to Article 49 of the PIL Act, the interpretation and application of these provisions is carried out in accordance with the Rome I Regulation. The PIL Act provides that, if the parties have not made choice of law, a contract for the provision of services shall be governed by the law of the State where the service provider has his habitual residence (Article 39(1)(2)). In addition to the habitual residence, the principle of the closest connection appears as a subsidiary connecting factor in two cases. In the first case, this principle appears as part of a special escape clause. Article 39(3) of the PIL Act provides that, if it is clear from all the circumstances of the case that the contract is in an obviously closer connection with another country than the one above, the law of that other country shall apply. In the second case, the principle of the closest connection occurs if the applicable law cannot be determined under the rule that the contract shall be governed by the law of the State where the party required to effect the characteristic performance of the contract has his habitual residence (Article 39(4)).

274. According to the experience of the judges of the Commercial Court in Podgorica, the principle of the closest connection from the LRCL had never been tested in practice, and judges directly applied the law of domicile of the debtor of a characteristic performance. This is also supported by the 2010 decision of the same court,[224] where for the contract for work (*locatio operis*), or the construction

221. For a more detailed overview of court and arbitration practice, *see*: Maja Kostić-Mandić, Kostić-Mandić, M. *Opšta klauzula odstupanja od mjerodavnog prava: u savremenom međunarodnom privatnom pravu* (The General Escape Clause from the Applicable Law: in Contemporary Private International Law), Podgorica: Pravni fakultet, 2012, 205–208.
222. Until 2015 there were two commercial courts in Montenegro.
223. Yugoslav Foreign Trade Arbitration T-55/76, T-190/82, T-4/02. Its successor, the Serbian Foreign Trade Arbitration, continued the same practice in cases: T-2/04, T-14/04 and T-15/04.
224. Commercial Court P. br. 513/10.

contract, the law of the place where the seat of the employer was located at the time of acceptance of the offer was directly applied, pursuant to Article 20, paragraph 1, point 2 LRCL.

III. Consumer Contracts

275. Prior to the adoption of the PIL Act, the conflict rule for consumer contracts was contained in 2007 Law on Consumer Protection providing for party autonomy as the main connecting factor for consumer contracts stipulated on the territory of Montenegro when one of the parties is a foreign national (Article 3(1)). As a subsidiary rule in cases when parties failed to choose the applicable law paragraph 2 provided for the application of the law of Montenegro. Before 2007, the law applicable to consumer contracts used to be determined pursuant to general conflict rules of the LRCL depending on the type of contract involved (sale, insurance, transportation, etc.). With the adoption of the PIL Act, the listed article ceased to apply.

276. Consumer contracts should also be interpreted and applied in accordance with the Rome I Regulation (its Article 6). However, there are certain specificities here. The PIL Act Article 42, paragraphs 1–3, fully takes over the provisions of Article 6 of the Rome I Regulation, except for the definition of the consumer and trader, which the PIL Act does not contain. Also, the exceptions mentioned in paragraph 4 of these two sources are not identical.

277. The habitual residence of consumers prevails as a connecting factor for consumer contracts while the role of party autonomy differs compared to the general rules on the choice of law for contracts.[225] The habitual residence is determined in the same way as for other contracts, and relevant is the one that existed at the time of the conclusion of the contract, so that the subsequent change of the habitual place of residence does not affect the application of the governing law. In order for the consumer to enjoy the protection of the law of the State where he has his habitual residence, provided for by Article 42 of the PIL Act, certain conditions must be fulfilled. There is a need for a significant connection between a trader and that country, which will exist (1) when a trader carries out his trade or professional activity in the country of the habitual residence of the consumer, or (2) when in any way directs such activity to that country or to several countries, including that country, and the contract falls within the scope of such activities. If one of the stated conditions for the application of the law of the habitual residence of a consumer is not fulfilled, general rules on the law applicable to contracts (party autonomy or subsidiary connecting factors) will be applied.

278. Unlike the Rome I Regulation, which provides five exceptions to the aforementioned rules,[226] on the basis of the PIL Act,[227] exemptions from the application

225. *See infra* Consumer Contracts.
226. Article 6(4) of the Rome Regulation I.

of the law of the consumer's habitual residence or the law that the parties would choose on the basis of their autonomy, relate to three types of contracts:

1. Service contracts, where the above-described rules will not apply if these services are provided to the consumer solely in a country other than the country of the place of his habitual residence. When there is a strong connection with the country where the services are provided (such as, when a consumer directly makes a reservation and pays the price of accommodation in a foreign hotel), the consumer does not want to be placed in an unfavourable position by the service provider. Also, the consumer cannot expect the protection of the law of the country of his habitual place of residence because this connection is not relevant when the service is fully provided in another country, and not the country where the consumer has a habitual residence.
2. Contracts of carriage. This applies to all types of transport of passengers and goods, regardless of whether the transport is carried by road, rail, sea or air traffic, except for contracts for which a combined travel and accommodation service is provided for the unique price. Protection is provided also in the case of free transport.[228] In the field of international transport, there is a large number of international conventions that contain uniform substantive rules. However, the specific consumer protection provided for in Article 42, paragraphs 1 and 2 of the PIL Act, shall apply to travel package, organized excursions and package arrangements.[229] This would include arrangements that, in addition to the combined travel and accommodation services, also envisage language learning,[230] but not contracts that include only accommodation service or, as we already saw, only the transport service.
3. Contracts relating to the real right to immovable property or a tenancy of immovable property, except for the contract on the time-limited usage of immovable property (timesharing).An exception that provides non-application of the basic rules for contracts on real property rights in immovables or a tenancy of immovable property is established because of the importance, complexity and connection with the law of the country where the real estate is situated. A consumer who buys real estate abroad, even if the advertising of real estate sales is in the country of the place of his habitual residence, cannot expect the application of his law. Furthermore, he will certainly seek the help of an expert (lawyers, notaries) and the registration of property rights has to be done in the country where the real estate is situated. On the other hand, in case of timesharing, there is no such strong connection with the law of the country where the real estate is situated, so for these contracts the basic rules governing other consumer contracts apply.

---

227. Article 42(4) of the PIL Act.
228. Francesca Ragno, *Article 6*, In *Rome I Regulation*, *Pocket Commentary*, F. Ferrari, S. Leible, eds. Munich: Sellier, 2009, 140.
229. Article 6(3)(b) of the Rome I Regulation.
230. Francesca Ragno, *Article 3*, In *Rome I Regulation, Pocket Commentary*, F. Ferrari, ed., Munich: Sellier European law publishers, 2015, 141.

279. Unlike in other types of contracts, the importance of party autonomy is significantly reduced in consumer contracts. The contracting parties may choose another law as applicable (instead of the law of habitual residence of the consumer), but such a choice may not deprive the consumer of the protection afforded to him by provisions of the law of his habitual residence that cannot be derogated from by agreement. This means that the judge must ex officio determine whether the choice of the applicable law leaves the consumer without protection which, if there was not the choice of law, would have been given to him by the law of country of his habitual residence. The judge should compare the content of the law of the habitual residence of the consumer with the content of the law chosen by the parties and apply those legal rules that are more favourable to the consumer.

IV. Employment Contracts

280. The PIL Act contains a special conflict rule (Article 43) for individual employment contracts. The established rules mirror Article 8 of the Rome I Regulation. Previously, the employment contract was, according to the LRCL, regulated in a less detailed manner.[231]

281. The PIL Act envisages the party autonomy as a basic connecting factor and refers to the application of the general provision on the choice of law for contracts. It is also specified that the choice of law may not deprive the employee of the protection afforded to him by provisions that cannot be derogated from by agreement by virtue of the law which, in the absence of choice, would have been applicable. Therefore, parties are not limited in terms of the law that they can choose as applicable, but there is a limitation that the choice of law cannot avoid the application of protective substantive rules that would be applicable on the basis of objective connecting factors, if the party autonomy was not exercised. In this type of contract, the judge should compare the content of these laws and apply those legal rules that are more favourable to the employee.

282. When the law applicable to the individual employment contract has not been chosen by the parties, the contract shall be governed by the law of the country in which an employee, by fulfilling an employment contract, usually performs his job or, if that is not the case, from which the employee, normally fulfilling his job, performs job. In the case where an employee is temporarily hired in another country, he is considered to be at work in the country in which he is normally performing his job. If the applicable law cannot be determined by applying the aforementioned rule, the contract shall be governed by the law of the country in which the business unit is located through which the employee is engaged.

231. Article 20(19) of the LRCL states that applicable law for property claims arising from an employment contract is the law of the country in which the work is carried out or was carried out.

283. The PIL Act does not contain a special escape clause as the Rome I Regulation, but a general escape clause from Article 8 of the PIL Act may apply. However, the PIL Act stipulates more stringent conditions than Article 8(4) of the Rome I. Pursuant to Article 8 of the PIL Act escape clause should be applied by way of exception if there is significantly closer connection of the contract to other law and a manifestly weak connection to that law (and not the country).

V. Contracts of Carriage

284. The PIL Act includes a general choice of law rule for contracts of carriage in Article 41, which mirrors Article 5 of the Rome I Regulation. This rule applies if there are no specific conflict rules on the particular contract of carriage in international treaties or other laws. Pursuant to Article 49 of the PIL Act its conflict rule for contracts of carriage shall be interpreted and applied in accordance with the Rome I Regulation.

A. Carriage of Persons

285. The PIL Act introduces the conflict rule for carriage of persons (Article 41(2) and (3)). This rule provides for limited party autonomy. The parties may choose as the law applicable to a contract of carriage of persons only the law of the State where: the passenger has his habitual residence; or the carrier has his habitual residence; or the carrier has his place of central administration; or the place of departure is located, or where the place of destination is located.

286. Subsidiary rules include habitual residence of the passenger or the carrier. The law of the State where the passenger has his habitual residence shall apply under condition that either the place of departure or the place of destination is located in that State. Where these requirements are not met, the law of the State where the carrier has his habitual residence shall apply. The provision of the PIL Act does not contain the special exception clause, but the general exception clause from Article 8 of the Code may apply.

B. Carriage of Goods

287. In the field of international carriage of goods, Montenegro succeeded to numerous conventions ratified by the former Yugoslavia: the 1956 Convention on the Contract for the International Carriage of Goods by Road (CMR, in force since 1961), the 1973 Convention on the Contract for the International Carriage of Passengers and Luggage by Road (CVR, in force since 1977), the 1980 Convention Concerning International Carriage by Rail (COTIF, in force since 1985) and its annexes, the Uniform Rules on the Contract for International Carriage of Merchandise by Rail (CIM), and the Uniform Rules on the Contract for International Carriage of Passengers and Luggage by Rail (CIV)), the 1924 International Convention for the Unification of Certain Rules Relating to Bills of Lading, Convention on International Civil Aviation (Chicago, 1944), Convention on the International Recognition of Rights in Aircraft (Geneva, 1948), Convention on Damage Caused by Foreign Aircraft to the Third Parties on the Surface (Rome, 1952). Furthermore, Montenegro ratified in 2007 and 2009 respectively, Multilateral agreement between EC and its Member States, Albania, Bosnia and Herzegovina, Bulgaria, Croatia, Macedonia, Island, Montenegro, Norway, Romania, Serbia and UN Mission to Kosovo on the establishment of a European common aviation area, and the 1999 Montreal Convention for the Unification of Certain Rules for International Carriage by Air.[232]

288. There are several laws that regulate applicable law to contracts of carriage of goods in the law of Montenegro. Conflict rules on the subject matter are contained in the PIL Act, the LMIN and the LOPRAT.

289. The PIL Act Article 41(1) contains general rules for contracts of carriage of goods which mirrors Article 5(1) of the Rome I Regulation. Thus, the PIL Act stipulates primacy of party autonomy, and as a subsidiary connecting factor – the law of the State of habitual residence of the carrier, provided that the place of receipt or the place of delivery or the habitual residence of the consignor is also located in that State. Where those requirements are not met, governing law will be the law of the State where the place of delivery as agreed by the parties is located. The provision of the PIL Act does not contain the special exception clause, but the general exception clause from Article 8 of the Code may apply.

290. Depending on the type of traffic, choice of law rules for contracts of carriage by air are found in the LOPRAT, Articles 177–179, and for contracts of carriage by sea or inland waterways in the LMIN, Articles 1038–1040 apply.

291. Contracts of carriage by railway are still regulated by the Law on Contractual Relationships in Railway Traffic (2010).[233] Contracts of carriage by road are now regulated by the Law on Carriage by Road (2017)[234] which addresses both national and international carriage of goods and passengers. However, these two statutes include only substantive rules.

292. Parties are given freedom to choose the law applicable to their contracts in the field of maritime and inland navigation pursuant to the LMIN, Article 1038. This freedom is limited, because certain issues of the contract on exploitation of ships must be regulated by this law, such as the issue of the ship operator's liability for the damage, loss, or shortage of cargo, provided that the port of loading or the port of destination is in Montenegro and the issue of liability towards the passenger, if the passenger would be put into a less favourable position by application of some

232. Kluwer Monograph on PIL of Montenegro of 2013, §2 Multilateral and Bilateral Treaties, para. 54.
233. Podgorica, Službeni list Crne Gore No. 41/10.
234. Podgorica, Službeni list Crne Gore No. 71/17 and 67/2019 https://www.paragraf.me/propisi-crnegore/zakon-o-prevozu-u-drumskom-saobracaju.html (accessed 14 Apr. 2022).

other law. A contract concluded in contravention of these mandatory provisions is void (Article 1039). Subsidiary connecting factors for contracts on the exploitation of ships provided in the LMIN (Article 1040) are concentrated around several issues. If the law chosen by the parties cannot be applied to the whole contract or to certain relations arising from the contract, or if the parties failed to choose the applicable law, and their intention for the applicable law cannot be inferred from the circumstances of the case, the contract is governed:

(a) by the law of the place where the contract was concluded (the *lex loci contractus*), with respect to principal rights and obligations of the contractual parties;
(b) by the law of the ship operator's nationality, if the contract of carriage of goods or passengers was concluded on the basis of the ship operator's general conditions;
(c) by the law of the place where the acts were performed, or were supposed to be performed, with respect to the manner of performance of accessory rights and obligations (i.e., the manner of loading and delivery of cargo, counting lay days and days of demurrage, the manner of payment of freight, and so forth);
(d) the contract on towage is governed by the provisions of the LMIN.

293. If the particular contract of carriage or an issue arising from this contract falls beyond the scope of ratified treaties, the governing law will be determined pursuant to the choice of law provisions of the LOPRAT. According to this law, contracts on carriage of goods and passengers by air are primarily governed by the law chosen by the parties. However, provisions of the LOPRAT have to be applied, pursuant to Article 177 if parties have not stipulated some other law as applicable or if the international treaty provides so. If the chosen law cannot be applied to the whole contract, or if no express choice has been made, and the intention of the parties cannot be undoubtedly ascertained from the circumstances of the case, the contract is subsidiarily governed by the law of the closest connection. Unless pertinent circumstances point to a different conclusion, the law of the carrier's domicile or seat at the time of conclusion of the contract of carriage is considered to be the most closely connected law with respect to principal rights and obligations. Accessory rights and obligations are governed by the law of the place where the acts were performed, or where they were supposed to be performed (the LOPRAT, Article 178).

VI. Insurance Contracts

294. The Law on Insurance[235] and the Law on Obligatory Insurance in Traffic[236] are the main sources of Montenegrin insurance law. Their substantive rules include several provisions devoted to questions connected with the occurrence of foreign element. As to other substantive law rules, the provisions of LO, as well as LOPRAT

235. Podgorica, Službeni list Crne Gore No. 78/2006, 19/2007, 53/2009 – other law, 40/2011 – other law, 45/2012, 6/2013, 55/2016 and 146/2021.
236. Podgorica, Službeni list Crne Gore No. 44/2012 and 146/2021.

and LMIN may also apply to some issues. In addition, Montenegro concluded or succeeded to a number of bilateral treaties on 'social' insurance[237] (i.e., health, retirement and disability insurance).

295. The PIL Act does not provide for a specific rule on the applicable law to insurance contracts. Thus, the PIL Act's general conflict rule for contracts applies to insurance contracts. To the extent that the law applicable to the contract has not been chosen by the parties in accordance with Article 38 of the PIL Act, the governing law shall be the law of the habitual residence of the insurer, as a party required to effect the characteristic performance (Article 39(2)). Also, it is possible to apply the closest connection principle, pursuant to Article 39(3) and (4).

296. The PIL Act recognizes the injured person's right to a direct action if it exists either in the law of the tort or in the law of the insurance contract. Article 66 of the PIL Act states: 'The person having suffered damage may bring his claim directly against the insurer of the person liable to provide compensation if the law applicable to the non-contractual obligation or the law applicable to the insurance contract so provides.' This provision practically eliminates the problem of characterization.

297. The LMIN contains choice of law rule for contracts on marine insurance in Article 1047. According to this rule, parties are free to choose the applicable law, unless all interested parties in the contract are Montenegrin nationals resident in Montenegro, or legal persons having their seat in Montenegro, and insurance concerns the property, which is exposed to insured risks exclusively within the territory of Montenegro (Article 1047, paragraph 1, item 1, and paragraph 2). The law of the insurer's seat will govern the contract if the parties have not expressly made their choice of the applicable law, or if their intention in that respect cannot be inferred from the circumstances of case, or if the chosen law cannot be applied to the whole contract or to certain relationships under that contract (but in the latter case, the law of the insurer's seat governs solely that part of the contract or relationship which is not covered by the chosen law).

298. The LOPRAT provides very similar provision for contracts on insurance in aerial navigation (Article 179), the main difference being in wording and adding the place of incorporation in Montenegro for legal persons.

237. *See* Maja Kostić-Mandić, Maja Stanivuković & Mirko Živković, *International Encyclopedia of Laws: Private International Law*, Kluwer Law International, Supplement 38: Montenegro, B. Verschraegen ed., Alphen aan den Rijn: Kluwer Law International, 2013, (Kluwer Monograph on PIL of Montenegro of 2013), paras 54–55.

VII. IP Contracts

A. Licence Agreement

299. Intellectual property rights are regulated by international treaties, special laws, and the licence agreement is regulated by the general law – LO (Articles 778–803). The subject of the licence agreement is to transfer, in whole or in part, the right to exploit the invention, technical knowledge and experience, trademark, sample or model. Licence agreement is also governed by the special law, the Law on Patents (Article 121).

300. The previous codification, LRCL, contained a special conflict rule on applicable law to licence agreements (Article 20(18)). This rule explicitly stipulated the application of the law of the state in which the party who acquires the technology has its domicile or seat at the time of receipt of the offers (unless the parties have chosen the applicable law). The *ratio* of this rule was to protect the weaker party, that is the domestic importer. The conflict rule of the PIL Act which applies to the licence agreement differs from the LRCL regarding the party whose obligation is considered to be characteristic and the domicile, as a criterion, is replaced with the habitual residence.

301. The PIL Act stipulates the same rule to all contracts relating to intellectual or industrial property rights. Thus, pursuant to Article 37 of the PIL Act, contracts relating to intellectual or industrial property rights shall be governed by the *lex contractus* (i.e., the rules of Chapter V and VII of the PIL Act). Since the PIL Act does not provide a special rule for licence agreement, general rules for contracts are applied: party autonomy (under Article 38) and subsidiary, the law of the country where the party required to effect the characteristic performance of the contract has his habitual residence (Article 39(2)). Also, it is possible to apply the closest connection principle, pursuant to Article 39(3) and (4).

302. The PIL Act also contains a special rule which provides that the law applicable to an individual employment contract shall also apply to a holder of an intellectual or industrial property right (licence agreement included) if the subject of the right was created in the context of employment (Article 36).

B. Trade Mark Agreement

303. The applicable law to trade mark agreements, as for other contracts relating to intellectual or industrial property is the *lex contractus* (Article 37 of the PIL Act). Since the PIL Act does not provide a special rule for this type of contract, general rules for contracts are applied: party autonomy (under Article 38) and subsidiary, the law of the country where the party required to effect the characteristic performance of the contract has his habitual residence (Article 39(2)). Also, it is possible to apply the closest connection principle, pursuant to Article 39(3) and (4). The PIL Act also contains a special rule which provides that the law applicable to an individual employment contract shall also apply to a holder of an intellectual or industrial property right if the subject of the right was created in the context of employment (Article 36).

VIII. Hybrid Contracts

A. Leasing

304. In Montenegro, financial leasing is regulated by the Law on Financial Leasing, Factoring, Purchase of Claims, Microcredit and Credit Guarantee Business (LFLF).[238] This law does not contain a conflict rule for a leasing contract. Since the PIL Act does not provide a special conflict rule for this type of contract, the general rules for contracts of the PIL Act apply: the party autonomy (pursuant to Article 38) and subsidiary, the law of the country where the party required to effect the characteristic performance of the contract has his habitual residence (Article 39(2)). Also, it is possible to apply the closest connection principle, pursuant to Article 39(3) and (4).

305. The obligation of the leasing provider is considered as the characteristic performance for the financial leasing contract. Considering that Article 8 of the LFLF stipulates that the leasing provider may be a company with a head office in Montenegro, so that a company from another country (directly or through a branch established in Montenegro) cannot provide financial services of leasing in the territory of Montenegro, financial leasing matters can only be dealt by leasing companies of Montenegro that are under the supervision of the Central Bank.

306. Article 42 of the PIL Act applies to the leasing contract concluded with the consumer.

B. Factoring

307. The LFLF contains substantive norms on factoring but does not contain conflict of law rules. The provisions on rights and obligations of the contracting parties (Articles 63–73) have been borrowed from the UNIDROIT Convention on International Factoring and the UN Convention on the Transfer of Claims in International Trade.

308. The basic conflict rule is party autonomy (pursuant to Article 38 of the PIL Act). The PIL Act, as well as the Rome I Regulation, does not specifically designate this type of contract, so in the absence of the choice of law the governing law is the law of the country where the party required to effect the characteristic performance of the contract has his habitual residence, either by reference to Article 39(2) or by

238. Podgorica, Službeni list Crne Gore No. 73/2017 and 44/2020.

the qualification of this type of contract as a service contract (Article 39(1)(2)). Also, it is possible to apply the closest connection principle, pursuant to Article 39(3) and (4).

C. *Franchise*

309. For the franchising agreement, the basic conflict rule is the party autonomy (pursuant to Article 38 of the PIL Act). The PIL Act, in accordance with the Rome I Regulation (Article 4(1)(e)), if the parties failed to choose the applicable law, provides a special conflict rule – a franchise contract shall be governed by the law of the country where the franchisee has his habitual residence (Article 39(1)(5)).

D. *Publishing Contract*

310. The publishing contract is substantially regulated by the Law on Copyright and Related Rights[239] (Articles 86–94), and LO as a general source. Since these laws as well as the PIL Act do not contain a special conflict rule, the basic rule is the party autonomy (pursuant to Article 38 of the PIL Act). Subsidiary, the law of the country where the party required to effect the characteristic performance of the contract has his habitual residence, either by reference to Article 39(2) or by qualifying this type of contract as a service contract (Article 39(1)(2)) shall apply. In both cases, the result is the same because publisher's performance is the characteristic obligation for this type of contract. Also, it is possible to apply the closest connection principle, pursuant to Article 39(3) and (4).

E. *Distribution Contract*

311. The PIL Act, in accordance with the Rome I Regulation (Article 4(1)(f)), provides a rule for distribution agreement, on the basis of which, in the absence of choice of law, the law of the country of the habitual residence of the distributor shall apply (Article 39(1)(6)). Furthermore there is a possibility of applying the closest connection principle under Article 39(3) and (4).

IX. Negotiable Instruments

A. *Bills of Exchange*

312. In Montenegro, bills of exchange are regulated by the Law on the Bills of Exchange (2005) which incorporated the provisions of the Geneva Convention Providing a Uniform Law for Bills of Exchange and Promissory Notes (1930) and the

239. Podgorica, Službeni list Crne Gore No. 37/2011, 53/2016 and 145/2021.

Geneva Convention for the Settlement of Certain Conflicts of Laws in Connection with Bills of Exchange (1930).[240] Previously, the 1946 Law on the Bills of Exchange applied. The conflict rules in the 2005 Law are modelled after the 1946 Law provisions and regulate the following issues: capacity, form, effects of obligations under a bill, right of recourse, limitations of acceptance and partial payment, relation of the bill to the underlying contract and loss or theft of the bill.

313. The capacity of a person to bind himself by a bill of exchange is determined by the national law. If the conflict rules of that law point to a different State, the renvoi is allowed, and the law of the other State will govern (Article 95, paragraph 1). The second paragraph of Article 95 provides for the alternative applicability of the *locus regit actum* rule. If a person is incapable of binding himself by a bill of exchange under the national law, or under the law to which the national law points, he still may be considered bound, if the law obtaining in the country where he signed the bill of exchange declares him capable. The LBE did not incorporate the reservation from Article 2, paragraph 3 of the Geneva Convention, according to which the application of the *lex loci actus* may be excluded with regard to domestic nationals. The rule will, therefore, have application in cases when the citizens of Montenegro incapable under the Montenegrin law enter into engagements under bills of exchange abroad.

314. The form of obligations arising from a bill of exchange is governed by the law of the State in which the obligation has been accepted (Article 96, paragraph 1). In this case the *lex loci actus* prevails imperatively. Furthermore, the principle of independence of obligations under a bill of exchange requires that the validity of each obligation be ascertained separately and independently of other obligations. When the place of actual signature differs from the place named in the text of the instrument, the place of actual signature should be considered as the place in which the obligation has been accepted.

315. There are two exceptions to the rule that form is governed by the *lex loci actus*. First, if an obligation is formally invalid according to the *lex loci actus* but complies with the laws of a State in which a subsequent obligation was accepted, the formal invalidity of the previous obligation does not entail invalidity of the subsequent obligation (Article 96, paragraph 2, item 1). The prevailing view in the doctrine is that this exception does not apply to formal invalidity of the basic obligation under a bill of exchange, that is, the obligation of the drawer or of the maker of a promissory note. If the basic contract is invalid no subsequent obligation can be treated as valid. The second exception concerns obligations under a bill of exchange undertaken between citizens of Montenegro abroad. If these obligations are formally valid under the LBE, they will be treated as valid even if the law obtaining in the State where they were taken was not observed (Article 96, paragraph 2, item 2). This exception is more narrowly framed than the reservation existing under the Geneva Convention, Article 3, paragraph 2, because it requires that both the debtor

240. This section is taken from Kluwer Monograph on PIL of Montenegro of 2013, paras 284–291.

and the creditor be domestic nationals. In contrast, under the Geneva Convention, it suffices that the debtor is a national of the forum State, while the nationality of the creditor is irrelevant.

316. Form and time periods for protest as well as the form of other acts necessary for enforcement or preservation of rights under a bill of exchange are governed by the law of the State where the protest has to be made or the act has to be done (the LBE, Article 97).

317. The LBE, Article 98, regulates the legal effect of obligations under a bill of exchange. The legal effect of obligations of the acceptor of a bill of exchange or the maker of a promissory note is determined by the place of payment (Article 98, paragraph 1). The law of the State where the party has signed the bill governs obligations of all other debtors (drawer, endorser, avaliser and intervenient) (Article 98, paragraph 2).

318. Time periods as to recourse are determined, with respect to all debtors, by the place where the bill was issued (the LBE, Article 99, paragraph 1). The relationship of the bill of exchange to the underlying contract is regulated by Article 99, paragraph 2. According to this provision, the law where the bill was issued determines whether the holder of a bill of exchange acquires the claim which gave rise to issuing of the bill.

319. The LBE regulates the limitation of acceptance and partial payment in Article 100. The question whether acceptance of a bill may be limited to a part of the amount and whether the holder of a bill has a duty to receive partial payment is determined by the law of the place of payment (Article 100, paragraph 1). The law of the place of payment also governs partial payment of a promissory note (Article 100, paragraph 2), and measures to be taken in case of loss or theft of a bill of exchange (Article 101).

B. Cheques

320. The basic source in this area of law is the former federal Law on Cheques (LC) (1946, as amended 1965, 1971, 1973, and 1996). The LC contains only one provision dealing with applicable law. Pursuant to Article 23(1)(15) of the LC the conflict rules of the LBE should be applied to cheque in accordance with the legal nature of cheque (Articles 95–101).[241]

241. For some specific characteristics, *see* Kluwer Monograph on PIL of Montenegro of 2013, paras 292–298.

C. Letters of Credit

321. Montenegrin law does not have a special conflict rule for letters of credit and therefore the general rules for contracts apply: party autonomy (pursuant to Article 38) and subsidiary, the law of the country of the habitual residence of the contracting party which is required to effect the characteristic performance of the contract (Article 39(2)). Also, it is possible to apply the closest connection principle, pursuant to Article 39(3) and (4).

X. Agency Contracts

322. The PIL Act contains a conflict rule (Article 24) on agency contracts which was modelled after the 1978 Hague Convention on the Law Applicable to Agency. Party autonomy is the primary connecting factor (on condition that the choice made is known or could have been known to the representative). When parties did not choose the applicable law the law of the State where the representative acted shall apply. If the representative acted in the conduct of his professional activity – the law of the place where the representative had his business seat applies (on condition that the place is known or could have been known to the third party).

323. The applicable law will govern: relationships between the grantor of attorney and a third party, the existence and scope of authority given to a representative, as well as effects arising out of the usage or alleged usage of such authority, the relationship between the representative and the third party that arise out of the fact that the representative acted within the scope of his authority, that he has exceeded such authority, or that he has acted without any authority.

324. Where the subject of representation is the right to immovable property, relationships between the grantor of attorney and a third party, the existence and scope of authority given to a representative, as well as effects arising out of the usage or alleged usage of such authority, shall be governed by the law of the State where the immovable property is located.

§3. Non-contractual Obligations

325. The relevant provisions determining the law applicable to non-contractual obligations are contained in the PIL Act (Articles 50–70), the LMIN (Articles 1043 and 1044) and the LOPRAT (Article 182). In addition, this area is regulated by international sources: the Hague Convention on the Law Applicable to Traffic Accidents, the Hague Convention on the Law Applicable to Products Liability and certain other multilateral treaties (the non-exhaustive list including: the 1910 Brussels Convention on Unification of Certain Rules Concerning Collision between Vessels, the 1960 Geneva Convention Relating to the Unification of Certain Rules Concerning Collision in Inland Navigation, 1963 Convention on Civil Liability for

Nuclear Damage, 1992 Convention on Civil Liability for Oil Pollution, 1972 Convention on International Liability for Damage Caused by Space Objects). In terms of the hierarchy of the legal sources the PIL Act explicitly states in Article 2 that it will not apply to relations that are regulated by an international treaty (or other law), so the conflict rules of the LMIN and the LOPRAT are applied as lex specialis.

326. The PIL Act's conflict rules on non-contractual obligations mirror the Rome II Regulation with only minimal adjustments. Moreover, these provisions shall be interpreted and applied in accordance with the Rome II Regulation (Article 67 of the PIL Act). The PIL Act introduces as a general rule the application of the law of the State where the damage occurs and to a certain extent and under certain conditions also allows for the use of a habitual residence (for which there is a special definition for commercial law relations[242]), and an escape clause. The party autonomy is elaborated in great detail. Also, a number of rules are provided for different types of non-contractual obligations.

327. Previously, based on the LRCL the governing law for non-contractual obligations was the law of the place where the act was performed or the law of the place where – the consequence occurred, depending on which of these two laws is more favourable to the injured person (Article 28(1)).

I. Party Autonomy

328. The possibility of choosing the applicable law for non-contractual obligations is a significant novelty introduced by the PIL Act mirroring the Rome II Regulation. Unlike contractual relations where party autonomy is the basic connecting factor, the significance of this institute in non-contractual relations is different. Parties are entering the contractual relations consciously and intentionally, so it is logical that they are planning the law applicable to their contract in advance. As non-contractual obligations are occurring without the will of the parties, it is considerably less likely to decide in advance on the applicable law.

329. The PIL Act in Article 63, with certain exclusions and limitations, introduces possibility of party autonomy for non-contractual obligations, regardless of whether they are a result of a tort or unjust enrichment, *negotiorum gestio* or *culpa in contrahendo*. However, the parties cannot exercise the choice of law in the case of non-contractual obligations arising out of an act of unfair competition, nor because of infringement of intellectual property rights.

330. The PIL Act stipulates that the choice of the applicable law must be expressed or clearly derived from the circumstances of the case. One of the restrictions on party autonomy relates to the time of choice of law. The PIL Act stipulates as the basic rule that the parties may agree on the applicable law to the non-contractual obligation after the event that caused the damage occurred. This time

242. Article 51 of the PIL Act.

limit has been set in order to protect the weaker parties,[243] such as customers and employees and to exclude the imposition of such a choice in standard form contracts. However, if all parties perform commercial activity, an agreement on the choice of law is possible even before the event that caused the damage occurred, as it is considered that professionals can in advance assess the potential risk of consent to the application of the law of a particular country.

331. The choice of law may not prejudice the rights of third parties. This limitation to party autonomy is applicable to direct lawsuits against the insurer of the responsible person. Thus, the agreement of the injured party and the person that caused injury on the law applicable to their non-contractual relationship does not apply in case of a direct claim against the insurer of the responsible person.[244]

332. However, party autonomy is not limited in terms of adhering to a particular law. There is no requirement for a connection between the chosen law and other facts of the relation (harmful event, parties and so forth), so if the parties agree, the applicable law may be some neutral law which may best suit their interests. But, if all other elements of the relevant situation, at the time when the event that caused the damage occurs, are related to another country, and not to the country whose law was elected, the choice of the law cannot exclude the application of provisions of the law of that other country that parties cannot derogate from by their agreement.

II. Objective Connection

333. Objective connections depend on the type of non-contractual obligation. Below (under *lex loci delicti*) are elaborated the objective connections based on the general rule for torts (Article 52 of the PIL Act), which is modelled after Article 4 of the Rome II Regulation.

334. The specific conflict rules of the PIL Act address: violation and restriction of competition, environmental damage, violation of rights relating to the personality, industrial action, as well as: unjust enrichment, *negotiorum gestio* and *culpa in contrahendo* (Articles 53–62). These rules reflect the relevant articles of the Rome II Regulation. However, unlike the Rome II Regulation, the PIL Act regulates the applicable law for violations of rights relating to the personality, as well as for damage to a ship on the high seas or on an aircraft. On the contrary, the Code neither contains specific rules for relations regulated by the Hague Convention on the Law Applicable to Traffic Accidents, nor the Hague Convention on the Law Applicable to Products Liability, to which application it directs. Also, the provisions of the PIL Act do not apply to the matters regulated by other international conventions on civil liability.

---

243. *See* Recital 31 of the Rome II Regulation.
244. Andrew Dickinson, *The Rome II Regulation*, Oxford: Oxford University Press, 2008, 556.

III. Law of Torts

A. *Lex Loci Delicti*

335. The general rule in Article 52 paragraph 1 of the PIL Act stipulates that the applicable law for a non-contractual obligation arising out of a tort is the law of the country in which the damage occurs, regardless of the country in which the event that caused the damage occurred and regardless of the country or countries in which indirect consequences of the event occur. Therefore, out of the three elements of the non-contractual obligation: the place of a direct damage, the place of a harmful event and the place of the indirect consequences, only the *lex loci damni* is relevant.

336. The Recital 17 of the Rome II Regulation explains that in cases of physical injury or material damage, the State in which the damage was caused should be the State in which the physical injury was sustained or the country where the material damage occurred.[245] According to the Court of Justice of the EU[246] for damages for unlawful deprivation of liberty and confiscation of property – direct damage occurs in that country, regardless of the material financial damage occurring in the country where the person is domiciled,[247] and in the case of the goods damaged during the combined transport of goods, a direct damage occurs at the place where the shipping company was obliged to deliver the goods and where it was found at the end of the transport operation that they were damaged.[248] The relationship with the country in which the imminent damage was created establishes a fair balance between the interests of the person to whom responsibility is established and the victim, and also reflects the contemporary approach to civil liability, which includes equally objective as well as the subjective liability.[249]

337. Article 52 paragraph 2 of the PIL Act provides a derogation from the *lex loci damni* rule when a person claimed to be responsible and a person sustaining damage have their habitual residence in the same country at the time when the damage occurs. In that case the law of country of their habitual residence shall apply. It is deemed to correspond to the legitimate expectations of the parties to apply the law which is close to them. Based on the PIL Act, the habitual residence for a natural person is determined on the basis of Article 12, and Article 51 of the PIL Act applies to legal entities and unincorporated organizations performing business activity. As with contractual obligations, companies have a habitual residence in place of their central administration. But if a harmful event occurs or a damage arises within the business of a branch, agency or other business unit, the habitual residence is

245. Peter Stone, *The Rome II Proposal on the Law Applicable to Non-contractual Obligations*, The European Legal Forum (E) 4/2004, 220. http://www.simons-law.com/library/pdf/e/518.pdf (accessed 14 Apr. 2022).
246. ECJ deliberated on this matter when adjudicating jurisdiction on the basis of Brussels Convention or Brussels I Regulation.
247. ECJ 19 Sep. 1995 – C-364/93 – *Marinari v. Lloyd's Bank*, [1995] ECR I-2719.
248. ECJ 27 Oct. 1998 – C-51/97 – *Réunion Européenne v. Spliethoff's Bevrachtingskantoor*, [1998] ECR I-6511.
249. Recital 16 of the Rome II Regulation.

where that unit is located. By specifying as relevant a habitual residence at the time when damage occurs, a possibility of mobile conflict is avoided.

338. However, the mere fact that a person who caused the damage and injured person have a habitual residence in the same country does not mean that this law will always apply, as the escape clause from Article 52 paragraph 3 of the PIL Act may apply. In fact, paragraph 2 of Article 52 constitutes a specific escape clause. There are opinions that a common habitual residence is given too great significance, calling into question the possibility of applying the escape clause from paragraph 3, and that it would be better if this rule was foreseen in paragraph 3 as a fact which, depending on the circumstances, can lead to a derogation from the basic rule referred to in paragraph 1.[250]

339. The escape clause is contained in Article 52 paragraph 3 which provides that where it is clear from all the circumstances of the case that the tort is in an obviously closer relationship with another country than the law of the country in which the damage occurred and the common habitual residence, that closer connected law shall apply. It also specifies that an apparent closer relationship with another country may be based on a prior relationship between the parties, such as a contract that is closely related to the tort. Although the PIL Act emphasizes only contractual, the previously established relationships include the effects of marriages, relationships between parents and children,[251] and even those relating to another tort. When determining whether there is an apparent closer connection between the tort and the law of another country, account should be taken of the circumstances that link the tort with that country,[252] the durability or short-term character of the connection, the nature of the circumstances in question, as well as the damage suffered by a person or property in a country pursuant to the law applicable on the basis of paragraph 1 or paragraph 2 of Article 52 of the PIL Act. The legitimate expectations of the parties or the substantive result of the application of one or another law should not be taken into account.

340. The PIL Act, under the influence of the Rome II Regulation, did not adopt the principle of favouring the victim as a basic rule, thereby allowing the injured party to choose the law which is most favourable to him. The solution finally adopted is a compromise between the two 'extreme' solutions:[253] the application of the law of the place where the event giving rise to the damage occurs and giving the victim the option.

250. This position was represented by Austria, Spain, Ireland and the United Kingdom, as well as by Dickinson. *See* Andrew Dickinson, *The Rome II Regulation*, Oxford: Oxford University Press, 2008, 337, f. 221.

251. I. Bach, *Torts/Delicts*, u: Rome II Regulation, Pocket Commentary, ed. Peter Huber, Munich: Sellier, 2011, 104.

252. Andrew Dickinson, *The Rome II Regulation*, Oxford: Oxford University Press, 2008, 342.

253. *Explanatory Memorandum of the Commission Proposal for a Regulation of the European Parliament and the Council on the Law Applicable to Non-Contractual Obligations ('Rome II')*, Brussels, 22. 7. 2003, COM (2003) 427 final 2003/0168 (COD), 11–12. http://eurlex.europa.eu/LexUriServ/LexUriServ.do?uri=COM:2003:0427:FIN:EN:PDF.

B. Scope of Application

341. The PIL Act mirrors Regulation Rome II provision on scope of the applicable law (Article 15). Article 64 of the PIL Act stipulates non-exhaustive list of non-contractual obligations that shall be governed by the applicable law: the basis and extent of liability, including the determination of persons who may be held liable; the grounds for exemption from liability, limitation and division of liability; the existence, the nature and the assessment of damage or the remedy claimed; pursuant to *lex fori* the measures which a court may take to prevent or terminate injury or damage or to ensure the provision of compensation; transferability of a right to claim damages or a remedy, succession included; persons who are personally entitled to compensation for damage; liability for the acts of another person; the manner in which an obligation may be extinguished and rules of prescription and limitation, including rules relating to the commencement, interruption and suspension of a period of prescription or limitation.[254]

342. However, the PIL Act shall not apply to relations that are regulated by an international treaty or by the LMIN and the LOPRAT.

C. Damages (Compensation)

343. The PIL Act's provisions on damages are generally modelled after the Rome II Regulation, with some peculiarities. Thus, the PIL Act adheres to a unitary approach, subjecting the existence, assessment and qualification of damages to the substantive law applicable to the tort as a whole.[255] Furthermore, the same principle is stated in the Hague Convention on the law applicable to traffic accidents and the Hague Convention on the law applicable to products liability (Article 8, respectively). The PIL Act in its Article 70, paragraph 1 copies Article 22, paragraph 1 of the Rome II Regulation on the burden of proof so that applicable law shall govern this matter 'to the extent that it contains rules which raise presumptions of law or determine the burden of proof'. However, Article 70, a rule common to contractual and non-contractual obligations alike, in its paragraph 2 addresses only contractual relations. Furthermore, the PIL Act does not contain a provision similar to Article 21 of the Rome II on the formal validity of unilateral act. Therefore, the law of the country in which the act is performed is not explicitly listed as applicable law for 'acts intended to have legal effect to be proved by any mode of proof recognized by that law'. However, the law of the country in which the act is performed may be applied by operation of the general clause of exception from Article 8 of the PIL Act.

344. Also, the PIL Act addresses the insurance matters only in a single article on direct action against the insurer of the person liable (Article 66). And Commercial Court has already adjudicated on compensatory damages from the insured case.

254. *See* Arts 148–235 of the LO for rules of substantial law.
255. Encyclopedia of PIL of 2017, Vol. 1, 518.

The Commercial Court rejected the plaintiff's request that the defendant is obliged to jointly compensate the plaintiff non-pecuniary damage on the basis of mental pain suffered due to non-payment of compensation on the basis of the insured case and basic salary.[256] In addition to numerous international conventions, the court also referred to Article 66 of the PIL Act. In this particular case, applicable laws for the non-contractual obligation are the Panamanian (flag of the ship) and Spanish (territorial waters of Spain in which the ship was located at the time of the incident), neither of which gives the seafarer the right to the direct lawsuit against the P&I Club. The applicable law for the insurance contract is the English Law – The Third Parties (Rights Against Insurers) Act of 1930, together with the Rules (conditions) of insurance of the first defendant from 2009, which also do not provide the right to a direct lawsuit against the P&I Club.

345. If Montenegrin law is the governing law, the rules of LO shall apply to damages and compensation in general. In Montenegrin substantive law non-contractual liability is regulated by mandatory rules so that liability may not be excluded or limited by a prior agreement between the parties. Punitive damages are not admissible and they are subject to the public policy exception.

D. Insurance and Social Security Law

346. Rules in international social security law are unilateral in nature and courts and authorities are bound to apply the Montenegrin law. However, the principle of equivalence present in the form of substitution or adaptation, help to integrate foreigners and foreign facts and legal relations into the ambit of a State law.[257]

347. In Montenegro insurance and social security matters of an international character are mainly dealt with by bilateral Social Security Agreements. Those agreements mainly regulate the following areas of social security: health insurance rights, pension and disability insurance rights, rights in the event of work injury or occupational disease, maternity rights, rights in case of unemployment, child welfare rights.

The main principles of these agreements include:

- the principle of insurance under which benefits are provided at the expense of insurance carrier of the Contracting State in which a person is insured, or who has been paid the required contributions;
- the principle of adding periods of insurance or other relevant periods for entitlement to benefits;
- the principle of equal treatment of foreign nationals according to its own nationals;
- the principle of payment of pension benefits acquired in the territory of another Contracting State.

256. P.br.1041/12, Pž.br. 420/20.
257. Encyclopedia of PIL of 2017, Vol. 2, 1652.

348. These agreements have been concluded with the following countries: Austria, Belgium, Bosnia and Herzegovina, Bulgaria, Croatia, Czech Republic, Denmark, Egypt, France, Germany, Hungary, Italy, Kosovo, Libya, Luxembourg, Macedonia, the Netherlands, Norway, Poland, Romania, Slovakia, Slovenia, Sweden, Switzerland, Turkey and the United Kingdom. Some of the agreements are the so-called Complete Social Security Agreements which regulate all the above-mentioned social security fields (with Bosnia and Herzegovina, Macedonia, Luxembourg, Serbia, etc.). However, certain agreements govern just some social security branches (those concluded with Romania, Libya, Egypt regulating the health insurance field).

IV. Unfair Competition

349. The conflict rule on unfair competition and acts restricting the competition from Article 53 of the PIL Act borrows from Article 6 of the Rome II Regulation, with some adjustments. Party autonomy is excluded for this type of relations. The applicable law to a non-contractual obligation arising out of an act of unfair competition shall be the law of the State where competitive relations or the collective interests of consumers are, or are likely to be, affected. However, where an act of unfair competition affects exclusively the interests of a specific competitor, the general rule from Article 52 of the PIL Act shall apply. The provisions of Article 53, paragraph 4 of the PIL Act addressing law applicable to a non-contractual obligation arising out of a restriction of competition adjust multilateral conflict rule from Article 6 paragraph 3(b) of the Rome II Regulation to the needs of a conflict rule of a national codification. As a general rule a non-contractual obligation arising out of a restriction of competition shall be governed by the law of the State where the market is, or is likely to be, affected. The Montenegrin law may be applicable if the person seeking compensation for damage chooses to base his claim on the Montenegrin law, provided that the market of Montenegro is among those directly and substantially affected by the restriction of competition (out of which the non-contractual obligation on which the claim is based arises), but only if the defendant has his domicile in Montenegro. Furthermore, where the claimant sues more than one defendant, he can choose to base his claim on the Montenegrin law if the restriction of competition on which the claim against each of these defendants relies directly and substantially also affects the market in Montenegro. By this wording, the conflict rule addressing Member States of the EU from the Rome II Regulation has been transformed into a conflict rule addressing Montenegro.

V. *Negotiorum Gestio*

350. Unlike many national legislations, the Montenegrin PIL has a tradition of having a separate conflict rule for *negotiorum gestio*. Thus, the LCRC provided the application of the law of the place in which the action of the *negotiorum gestio* was performed (Article 27(2)) and the same rule governed the relationships between the dominus negotii and the gestor. However, non-contractual liability for damages arising out from *negotiorum gestio* pursuant to Article 28(2) of the LRCL was governed by the general rule for delicts: lex loci delicti commissi and the rule on more favourable law.

351. The PIL Act introduces the new special rule for the *negotiorum gestio* (actions taken without the necessary authority in relation to the affairs of another person) mirroring Article 11 of the Rome II Regulation, in case the general rule on the party autonomy referred to in Article 63 of the PIL Act is not applicable. This rule contains a basic connection and subsidiary connections if the basic one cannot be applied which should be interpreted and applied in accordance with the Rome II Regulation (Article 67 of the PIL Act). However, unlike the Rome II Regulation, the PIL Act does not provide special escape clauses for *negotiorum gestio*, but the general escape clause from Article 8 may apply.

352. The main rule for *negotiorum gestio* is based on a previous relationship between the parties, and it is required that the non-contractual obligation arises from that previous relationship, so that for these non-contractual obligations rules for prior contractual or non-contractual relations shall apply. When the applicable law cannot be established in this way, two subsidiary connections are envisaged:

(1) the habitual residence of parties in the same country at the time when the event giving rise *negotiorum gestio* occurs; or
(2) the law of the country in which the *negotiorum gestio* was carried out.

To the *negotiorum gestio*, general institutes of PIL (overriding mandatory rules and public policy) may apply.

VI. Unjust Enrichment

353. The LCRC provided the conflict rule for unjust enrichment (Article 27(1)) stipulating the application of the law that would be applicable to the legal relation which was created, expected or supposed, and that served as a reason for enrichment. This law governed the requirements for determining the unjust enrichment as well as the relationship between enriched party and the party on whose expenses the enrichment has occurred (e.g., the claim for restitution and the obligation for returning what has been unjustly enriched). However, the *lex loci delicti commissi* and the rule on more favourable law of Article 28(2) LRCL applied to non-contractual liability for damage arising out of unjust enrichment.

354. The PIL Act introduces the new special rule for the unjust enrichment (Article 60) mirroring Article 10 of the Rome II Regulation, in case the general rule on the party autonomy referred to in Article 63 of the PIL Act is not applicable. Those rules should be interpreted and applied in accordance with the Rome II Regulation (Article 67 of the PIL Act). The main rule for unjust enrichment including the payment of undue amounts is based on a previous relationship between the parties, and it is required that the non-contractual obligation arises from that previous relationship, so that for these non-contractual obligations, rules for prior contractual or non-contractual relations shall apply. The underlying rationale is expediency. When the applicable law cannot be established in this way, two subsidiary connections are envisaged:

(1) the habitual residence of parties in the same country at the time when the event giving rise to unjust enrichment occurs; or
(2) the law of the country in which the unjust enrichment took place.

Unlike the Rome II Regulation, the PIL Act does not provide special escape clauses for unjust enrichment, but the general escape clause from Article 8 may apply. Also, other general institutes of PIL (overriding mandatory rules and public policy) may apply.

VII. *Culpa in Contrahendo*

355. The PIL Act for the first time explicitly regulates applicable law for the *culpa in contrahendo* (Article 62) mirroring Article 12 of the Rome II Regulation. It does not provide for a definition of this legal institute which includes violation of the obligation to provide information and termination of contract negotiations. The conflict rule contains a basic connection and subsidiary connections if the basic one cannot be applied and will be applied if parties failed to choose the applicable law in conformity with the Article 63 of the PIL Act. Those rules should be interpreted and applied in accordance with the Rome II Regulation (Article 67 of the PIL Act). In comparison to the other quasi-delicts, the conflict rule for *culpa in contrahendo* is expected to be most often applied. For a non-contractual obligation arising from the conduct that preceded the conclusion of the contract, regardless of whether the contract is concluded or not, the governing law is the law applicable to the contract or which would be applicable to the contract if it was concluded. Subsidiary rules include the application of the law of the State in which the damage occurred, or the law of the State in which both parties have a habitual residence at the time when the event that caused the damage occurred (Article 62 of the PIL Act). Unlike the Rome II Regulation, the PIL Act does not provide special escape clauses for *culpa in contrahendo*, but the general escape clause from Article 8 may apply. Also, other general institutes of PIL (overriding mandatory rules and public policy) may apply.

VIII. Other

A. *Violation of Rights of Personality*

356. The PIL Act introduces a special conflict rule for the law applicable to obligations arising out of the violation of rights relating to the personality by way of the media while this issue is not regulated by the Rome II Regulation (due to the lack of consent of the Member States of the EU).[258] The conflict rule applies only to violations of rights of personality by press, radio, television or other media and infringement of rights related to personal data protection. In accordance with comparative practice,[259] the PIL Act (Article 55) provides that the injured party may choose as applicable law the law of the country:

(1) in which he has his habitual residence;
(2) where the damage occurred; or
(3) in which the person responsible has his habitual residence or place of residence (*mjesto stanovanja*).

The same rule applies to obligations arising out of the infringement of rights relating to the protection of personal data.

357. The option for the injured party to choose the applicable law between the three variants established by the PIL Act is aimed at protecting him to the fullest extent and enabling him to choose the most favourable law. The interests of the person claimed to be responsible are protected in a way that if the injured party chooses the law of the country of their own habitual residence or the *lex loci damni*, the precondition to apply one of the above laws is that the person claimed to be responsible could reasonably expect that the damage will occur in one of these two places.

358. The benefits of applying the law of the habitual residence of the injured party are that he is familiar with the legal system and wants to protect his reputation in his chosen social environment, and since the compensation for damages will be fulfilled in that country, it is logical that the law of the same country applies to determining and assessment of damage. The negative side of this solution is that a person may have a habitual residence in a country, for example for a reason of tax exemption, and that the person is not actually integrated into that social environment, which is often the case with well-known personalities from the entertainment or sporting world. Also, media reporting on persons from different countries must be aware of these laws in advance.[260] Regarding the location of the damage, it can be problematic when damage occurs in several countries because the laws of all these countries will have to be applied on a distributive basis; therefore, each law applies to injuries inflicted on its territory. This would apply, for example, in case of defamation published in newspapers distributed in several countries; or for defamation contained in a television show broadcast in several countries; or in case of defamation contained on a website downloaded from the server by a person in several

258. For a comparative view *see*: Geert van Calster, *European Private International Law*, Oxford and Portland: Hart Publishing, 2013, 160.

259. *See* Art. 108 of the Bulgarian PIL Act.

260. Thomas Thiede, *A Topless duchess and caricatures of the Prophet Mohammed, a Flexible conflict of laws rule for cross-border infringements of privacy and reputation*, Yearbook of Private International Law, vol. XVI/2012/2013, 258–259.

countries.[261] The third option, the habitual residence or place of residence of the tortfeasor, will often be the place where the tort occurred.

359. Although Article 55 of the PIL Act is not subject of interpretation of the acquis, since this issue is not regulated by the Rome II Regulation, the preliminary opinion of the ECJ in the *Fiona Shevill*[262] case of the Brussels Convention may be of importance to Montenegrin judiciary. The ECJ took a stance that the place where the harmful event occurred in the case of a violation of reputation by a newspaper article is the State in which the publication was distributed and where the alleged injury to reputation of that person occurred.

360. The PIL Act provides for a special rule on the right to publish a correction for violation of rights of personality by way of the media: governing law is the law of the country where the violation occurred.

B. Damage on Vessel in Open Sea or on Aircraft

361. The PIL Act, as well as its predecessor,[263] the LRCL, provides for a special rule for damage on vessel in open sea or on aircraft. Pursuant to Article 59 of the PIL Act:
If the event giving rise to an obligation to compensate for the damage caused occurred on a vessel in an open sea or on an aircraft, the law of the place where the facts giving rise to the obligation of compensation of damage occurred shall be considered the law of the State of the flag or the law of the State in which the aircraft is registered.

C. Liability for Damages in Case of Collision of Ships

362. The issue of liability for damages in case of collision of ships is regulated by the LMIN (Articles 1043 and 1044). The law of the State in whose territorial and internal waters the collision occurred is the governing law (Article 1043(1)(1)). If the collision happened on high seas, liability for damages is governed by the *lex fori* (Article 1043(2)(1)). Nevertheless, the indicated laws will not be applied if all the ships that participated in the collision flew the same flag – the lex bandarae will be applied instead. The same rule will apply if the ships that collided flew different flags, but the laws of the countries whose flags they flew are the same.

363. Article 1044 of the LMIN regulates certain special situations of collision by mandatory norms. This Article reads as follows:

---

261. Peter Stone, *The Rome II Proposal on the Law Applicable to Non-Contractual Obligations*, The European Legal Forum (E) 4/2004, 220.
262. ECJ 7 Mar. 1995, C-68/93, *Fiona Shevill and others v. Press Alliance SA* [1995] ECR I-415.
263. Article 29 of the LRCL.

Notwithstanding provisions of Article 1043, which may call for the application of a foreign law to the question of damages arising from collision,

1. the provisions of this Law will be applicable if all the interested persons are Yugoslav nationals or Yugoslav legal entities, or if one of the ships that collided is a Yugoslav warship or a Yugoslav State ship;
2. the provisions of Article 793, paragraph 2, Article 794, paragraph 1, and Articles 795–801 of this Law will always be applicable;
3. the provisions of the federal statute of limitations will be applicable, unless provided otherwise by this Law.

D. Liability for Damages Caused by Aircraft

364. Article 182 of the LOPRAT provides that the law of the State on whose territory the damage was inflicted governs the liability for damages referred to in Article 114(1) of the same Law. Article 114 regulates liability for damages caused to third parties by aircraft in the course of flight. According to Article 114(1) the air carrier is liable to compensate damages occurring on the surface because of the death, health impairment or bodily injury of a third person, and because of damage to property, caused by an aircraft in the course of flight or by persons or objects fallen or thrown out of the aircraft in the course of flight, if the injuries directly resulted from these facts.

Chapter 3. Property

365. In Montenegrin law property relations are governed by the PIL Act, the LMIN, the LOPRAT, a few bilateral treaties[264] and the Law on Ownership Relations. Conflict rules provide for application of *lex situs* for immovables and movables alike, while the PIL Act provides for special rules on mobile conflict of laws for movables. Furthermore, special rules are stipulated for goods in transit, means of transport and cultural property.

366. Montenegrin substantial property law – Law on Ownership Relations (LOR) is based on numerus clausus of property rights. They encompass: right of ownership, right of easement, security interest in movable (pledge) and immovable property (mortgage) and fiduciary ownership right on movable and immovable property.

367. Some of the case law reflects the Montenegrin political and economic conditions in the second half of the twentieth century. In a recent, typical case, the plaintiff, a US citizen, sought to establish that the contract on the transfer of capital assets and the right to use the parcel was absolutely null and void, that she was the owner of the parcel and the building and asked for damages for not being able to use the disputed plot.[265] Her ancestors emigrated to the US at the beginning of the twentieth century, and they leased the property with the house to a family, which bought certain plots from the money they sent (which was also confirmed by witnesses from the village). However, based on the situation in the case file, the court found that the plaintiff had not proved the existence of the right of ownership over the real estate in question in favour of her legal predecessors, her father and grandfather in any of the ways provided by law. There was no evidence of the existence of a legal business as a basis for acquiring property rights that were necessary for the acquisition of property rights on the real estate at the time of their transfer to state ownership (1948), and in accordance with the legal rules contained in the General Property Code of 1888 which was then applied in accordance with the provision of Article 4 of the Law on the Invalidity of Legal Regulations Adopted Before 6 April 1941, through 1946. In addition, no evidence was provided regarding the acquisition of property by maintenance in terms of the above legal rules. Namely, in the procedure it was established that the plaintiff's father left Montenegro in 1914 and went to America where he lived until his death in 1949, as well as that the plaintiff was born in America in 1933, where she still lives today. Thus, the immediate possession of the plaintiff and her legal predecessor have undoubtedly not existed since 1914, while the indirect possession required for extraordinary possession under the then rules (30 years), and in terms of the said lease with the family has not been proven until the disputed real estate passes into the state property regime.

264. Bilateral treaties on judicial assistance with the Czech Republic, Slovakia, Hungary and Poland.
265. Supreme Court Rev. br. 545/19. The revision does not explicitly address PIL Act.

§1. *Lex Rei Sitae*

368. In Montenegro, the place where the property is situated (*lex situs*) is traditionally the basic connecting factor for the property-legal relations. The 1888 GPC provided for elaborate conflict rules for property:

- Article 786 determines the law applicable to ownership;
- Article 790 determines the law applicable to ownership and other real rights related to immovable property (*lex situs*);
- Article 791 determines the law applicable to real rights on movable property (paragraph 1 – in principle: *lex situs*, paragraph 2 – in case of changes in the situs: *lex situs* when the action or facts that are invoked as basis of the acquisition occur, and paragraph 3 – the law governing prescription – *lex situs* at the moment when prescription has started).

369. The 1982 LRCL did not contain such sophisticated rules for property and the whole subject field was regulated by only one article with three paragraphs (Article 18). In addition to the basic solution for ownership relations and other real rights – *lex situs*, which was applicable to movables and immovables alike, special rules were provided only for ownership relations in matters of transit of goods and for means of transport.

370. The 2014 PIL Act regulates in detail the applicable law for ownership relations (Articles 26–34). The place where the property is situated is the basic connecting factor for immovables and movables alike. In addition to the general rules for movables, special rules are also foreseen in order to prevent a mobile conflict of laws, which will be discussed below. The *lex situs* also applies to: existence, type, content and scope of rights; holders of rights; transferability of the rights; ways of acquiring, transferring and termination of rights; the obligation of registration and the possibility of opposing third parties.[266] Also, the qualification of properties as movable or immovable shall be done according to the law of the country where the property is situated.[267] Furthermore, for the validity of registration by which the rights are acquired, transferred or terminated, the applicable is the law of the country in which the property was situated at the time the legal transaction was concluded (Article 32 of the PIL Act). The place where the property is situated is the only connecting factor for immovable property, whether it is the acquisition, the termination, the content or the exercise of real rights. However, in the case of special legal bases for the acquisition of property, on the basis of an agreement on the acquisition of ownership, succession or division of the joint property of a spouse in case of divorce or death of one of the spouses, the conflict rules for these types of legal relations shall apply.

371. Pursuant to the PIL Act exceptions to the application of the *lex situs* rule to the immovable property are:

266. Article 34 of the PIL Act.
267. Article 28 of the PIL Act.

- where parties have chosen the law to govern their contract on real rights in immovable property and tenancy of immovable property. Although the PIL Act in its Article 38 does not explicitly address this issue, the choice of law has been introduced with importing rules from the Rome I Regulation. Previously, the LRCL provided that contracts relating to immovables are exclusively governed by the law of the State in which the immovable property was situated (Article 21);
- in case of choice of law for succession of the immovables. Based on the principle of a unitary succession, Article 72, paragraph 1 of the PIL Act provides that a deceased for the succession as a whole may choose the law of the country of which he is a citizen or the law of the country in which he has habitual residence at the time of the choice of law or at the time of his death.

The *lex situs* rule does not also apply to some specific categories of movables: goods in transit, the means of transport and cultural property.

§2. Movable Property

372. Real rights on movables are governed by the *lex situs* (the PIL Act, Article 27(1)). This general rule is supplemented by special provisions on the mobile conflict of laws. Foreign citizens may acquire ownership of movables located in Montenegro under the same conditions as nationals of Montenegro (the LOR, Article 413). Special rules are stipulated for goods in transit, means of transport and cultural property.[268] Furthermore, there are special statutory rules which regulate acquisition of real rights on ships and aircraft by foreigners and applicable law to real rights on these specific types of movables.[269]

373. The mobile conflict of laws are particularly important in real rights on movables.[270] When a movable property relocates from one country to another, it can be disputed whether to apply the law of the country where the movable was originally located or the law of the country where it is located when the legal question arises. The basic conflict rule remains *lex situs*, but it needs to be determined whether to apply the former or actual place of movables. Since the laws governing this issue apply different rules to the mobile conflict of laws, depending on whether it is about acquiring/terminating or about the content (effects) of real rights, the doctrine makes the difference between the simple and complex (qualified) mobile conflict of laws.[271]

268. *See infra* ss II, III.
269. *See infra* s. IV.
270. *See* Maja Stanivuković & Petar Đundić, *Međunarodno privatno pravo, posebni deo* (Private International Law, Special Part), Novi Sad: Univerzitet u Novom Sadu, Pravni fakultet, 2008, 41–44.
271. This distinction is characteristic of German doctrine, which has many proponents in the region. *See* Slavko Đorđević, *Rešavanje mobilnih sukoba zakona u stvarnopravnim odnosima sa elementom inostranosti* (Solving Mobile Conflict of Laws in Real Right Relations with a Foreign Element), Kragujevac: Univerzitet u Kragujevcu, Pravni fakultet, 2015, 14.

374. In the case of a simple mobile conflict of laws, this is a so-called terminated factual state that for rights in rem means that the movable was first located in country A, in which the real right was acquired, and then it was moved to country B, where this real right should produce effects. The example may be a buyer who in good faith purchased a movable in Montenegro and bring it with him to Germany. In Montenegro, a buyer acting in good faith has acquired property on stolen property according to the rules of acquiring from non-owners, while German law does not provide for the institute of acquiring property from non-owners on stolen goods. Here the question arises: which of these two laws apply to the content and to the effects of that right in rem? The content and exercise of the real right to movable property previously acquired in another country shall be governed by the law of the place where the property is located at the moment when the question arises – the current place (in our example, the law of Germany).

375. In the case of complex mobile conflict of laws, unlike the previous case, the real right to movables transferred from State A to State B has not been yet acquired or ceased to exist under the law of State A, and the question arises: by which of these two laws should be completed acquisition, or termination of rights? This type of *conflit mobile* is particularly evident in case of acquisitive prescription when the laws of States A and B provide for different rules (when for example, the law of State A provides for a six-year period and the law of State B stipulates three-year period of prescription for acquiring adverse possession). In a comparative law, those legislations that address this problem require the application of the law of the country where the movable is located when a question arises (the law of State B).[272] However, if, under the law of State A, the real right could not have been acquired (e.g., in the case of acquiring from non-owners, if the buyer acting in good faith has bought in Germany the movable and brought it with him to Montenegro), the transfer to State B would not establish the real right on this movable – the law of the former place where the item was located will be applied.

376. A simple mobile conflict of laws refers to the impact of changing the place where the movable is situated on the applicable law to the content and the exercise (effects) of the real right to the item on which the ownership has already been legally acquired in another country (the final state of facts). The content and exercise of real right to an item previously acquired in another country will always be governed by the law of the place where the movable is situated at the time when the question arises – the current *lex situs*. This can be the law of the country where the right has been acquired while the movable is in that country, and if the item is moved to another country, for the content and exercise of the law, the law of that other country, where the item is situated when the question arises, is applicable (the law of the new, last place where the movable is situated).

377. A particular problem with this kind of mobile conflict of laws exists if the item on which the real right is validly acquired in another country, has been moved

---

272. *See* Art. 43 of the German PIL Act, Art. 100 of the Swiss PIL Act, Art. 87 of the Belgian PIL Act, Art. 64 of the Bulgarian PIL Act etc.

to Montenegro and our law does not acknowledge this kind of real right. The PIL Act provides that this acquired real right is recognized if our law knows the real right which by its content and effects is equivalent to the real right acquired in another country.[273] The transposition of foreign real right into the legal order of the home country is done by comparing the content of foreign real right with domestic law institutes in order to find a related domestic law institute that achieves the same goal and function.[274] If the appropriate domestic law institute is found, our law will apply to the content, exercise and registration of the real right to movable. In the absence of an equivalent institute, real right acquired abroad cannot produce effects while the movable is in Montenegro.

378. The Montenegrin legislator also provides for a rule in case of transposition of real right to secure the claim[275] which is not provided for by the law of Montenegro (e.g., the institute of Italian law, pledge without –possession on cars, which is entered into the public register of cars and in the traffic licence and licence extension[276]). In order that this kind of real right produce the effect if the vehicle has been transferred to our country, it is necessary to determine that it is by its purpose and function equivalent to the corresponding domestic security institution – registered pledge or fiduciary transfer of ownership, and then to be entered into the domestic register.[277] In order to preserve the rights of the foreign creditor over domestic creditors, it is established that if it is a real right that must be registered and if it is registered within thirty days from the date when the movable entered Montenegro, it shall be deemed that the date of registration is the day when the item arrived in Montenegro.

379. In both cases of mobile conflict of laws listed above the law of Montenegro applies to the content, exercise and registration of real right to movables.

380. A complex *conflit mobile* refers to the impact of a change in the location of a movable to the applicable law for the acquisition or termination of real right. The PIL Act contains special rules aimed at resolving this problem. It stipulates that governing law for the acquisition and termination of a real right to a movable is the law of the country in which the movable was situated at the time of the taking of an act or when the circumstances, on which the acquisition or the termination of the real right is based, occur. If certain acts or circumstances necessary for the acquisition or termination of a real right to a movable were initiated in one country, they shall

273. Article 29 para. 1 of the PIL Act.

274. *See*: Slavko Đorđević, *Pogled na opšta koliziona pravila za stvarna prava na pokretnim stvarima u novom Zakonu o međunarodnom privatnom pravu Crne Gore, u:,,Usklađivanje pravnog sistema Srbije sa standardima Evropske unije', urednik S. Đorđević* (View of general conflict rules for real rights on movables in the new Private International Law Code of Montenegro, In *Harmonization of the legal system of Serbia with the standards of the European Union*), S. Đorđević ed., Kragujevac: Univerzitet u Kragujevcu, Pravni fakultet, 2014, 590; Aleksandar Jakšić, *Međunarodno privatno pravo* (Private International Law), Belgrade: Dosije, 2008, 281.

275. Article 29 para. 3 of the PIL Act.

276. Đorđević (2015), *supra*, 115.

277. Đorđević (2014), *supra*, 591–594.

be considered to have been realized in another country in which the last act or circumstance on which the acquisition or the termination of real right is based occurred.[278]

381. A particular kind of complex mobile conflict exists when acquiring property from non-owners when all the relevant facts made in the country of the original situs have not led to the establishment of a real right under that law, and the movable is transferred to the country under whose jurisdiction these same facts are sufficient for the establishment of that right. Examples can be found in case law.[279] For example, a domestic citizen with domicile in Montenegro travels to Germany with the intention to buy a used car from an authorized car dealer. He concluded a contract in Germany, paid the price, took over the vehicle, a vehicle permit and accompanying documents and drove the car to Montenegro. But during the vehicle registration procedure it is established that the traffic licence is not genuine and the competent authority seized the vehicle. The buyer who acted in good faith files a lawsuit for the return of a vehicle. It is indisputable that the issue of ownership rights on a vehicle should be governed by the *lex situs*, but is it the original place – Germany or the current place – Montenegro? According to German substantive law,[280] the buyer could not acquire ownership from the owner from whom the item was stolen or lost in any other way, regardless of the fact that the buyer acted in good faith and that the car was purchased from an authorized dealer. Since all relevant facts occurred in Germany as the original situs, removing vehicle to the territory of Montenegro under which law[281] this buyer would acquire the ownership will not produce legal effects. Therefore, for this type of complex mobile conflict of laws, the law of the original situs is the most appropriate.

382. When the real right to movable transferred from State A to State B is still not acquired, but there is a valid ground for acquiring, the initiated acquisition should be terminated under the law of State B as the last place where the item is located. In addition, according to the legal fiction applicable to this case, all relevant facts for the acquisition of real right have been exercised under the law of State B, irrespective of when and where they were achieved and whether the law of State B is the law of Montenegro.[282] For this type of complex mobile conflict of laws, the applicable is the law of the new, last place where the item is located. Also,

278. Article 27 paras. 1–2 of the PIL Act.

279. *See*: Slavko Đorđević, *Rešavanje mobilnih sukoba zakona u stvarnopravnim odnosima sa elementom inostranosti* (Solving Mobile Conflict of Laws in Real Right Relations with a Foreign Element), Kragujevac: Univerzitet u Kragujevcu, Pravni fakultet, 2015, 30–34; Zoran Rašović, *Komentar Zakona o svojinsko-pravnim odnosima* (Commentary on the Law on Ownership Relations), Podgorica: Univerzitet Crne Gore, Pravni fakultet, 2009, 285–304.

280. Article 935, para. 1 of the German Civil Code.

281. Article 60 of the Law on Ownership Relations; Zoran Rašović, *Komentar Zakona o svojinsko-pravnim odnosima* (Commentary on the Law on Ownership Relations), Podgorica: Univerzitet Crne Gore, Pravni fakultet, 2009, 278–284.

282. *See* Slavko Đorđević, *Pogled na opšta koliziona pravila za stvarna prava na pokretnim stvarima u novom Zakonu o međunarodnom privatnom pravu Crne Gore, u:,,Usklađivanje pravnog sistema Srbije sa standardima Evropske unije', urednik S. Đorđević* (View of general conflict rules for real rights on movables in the new Private International Law Code of Montenegro, In *Harmonization*

when the real right to movable transferred from State A to State B has not been terminated under the law of State A, the termination of the right must be governed by the law of State B.

I. Collateral

383. Collateral as a real guarantee right is governed by the general rule of the PIL Act for property relations – *lex situs*. This law shall also apply to: existence, type, content and scope of rights; holders of rights; transferability of the rights; ways of acquiring, transferring and termination of rights; the obligation of registration and the possibility of opposing third parties.

384. As noted above, for the acquisition and termination of the collateral right on movables the applicable law is the law of the country in which the movable was situated at the time of the taking of an act or when the circumstances, on which the acquisition or the termination of the real right is based, occur. The content and exercise of the collateral right on a movable that has previously been legally acquired in another State are governed by the law of the place where the item was located at the time when the question arises – the current *lex situs*.

385. Since a lien over the movable property is most often created on the basis of a contract on pledge, this contract shall be governed by *lex contractus* (the party autonomy and subsidiary, the law of the habitual residence of the debtor of the characteristic obligation or the principle of the closest connection).

386. However, in case of a financial collateral the provisions of the Law on Financial Collateral apply. Its conflict of law rule mirrors EU Directive 2002/47/EC on financial collateral arrangements, Article 9. The Law on Financial Collateral in its Article 19 stipulates 'if securities in electronic form, including the rights to such securities, are given as financial collateral and when the rights over such securities are recorded in the register or in the corresponding account, the applicable law is the law of the State in which the register or account is kept'. The scope of applicable law includes determining the type of securities and rights based on those securities; the requirements for concluding financial collateral arrangement relating to securities in electronic form and issuing collaterals in securities in electronic form in accordance with that arrangement; determination of possible rights of third parties in relation to the financial collateral in securities in electronic form, as well as determining whether the rights of the recipient of the collateral have been acquired in good faith; procedures for the realization of a financial collateral in securities in electronic form, after the occurrence of an enforcement event.

of the legal system of Serbia with the standards of the European Union), S. Đorđević ed., Kragujevac: Univerzitet u Kragujevcu, Pravni fakultet, 2014, 586–587.

II. Goods in Transit

387. The PIL Act, as well as the former LRCL,[283] regulates that the acquisition and loss of the rights in rem in respect of goods in transit shall be governed by the law of the State of their destination. Furthermore, now it is envisaged a special rule for the rights in rem in respect of personal belongings that the passenger carries with him – the law of his habitual residence.[284]

388. According to the doctrine if the transit is interrupted as the goods have been seized, a general rule should be applied – the *lex situs*.[285]

389. In practice, there will rarely be a need for the application of this rule, except in the case where the seller sells the same goods several times or in the case of bankruptcy or forced execution, when it is necessary to determine whether his goods are included in this property.[286]

III. Cultural Property

390. The protection of cultural property in Montenegro is realized on the basis of the Constitution, international treaties and legislation. The Constitution of Montenegro in its section on economic, social and cultural rights and freedoms stipulates that everyone is obliged to protect the natural and cultural heritage of general interest, and it also establishes the obligation of the State to protect the natural and cultural heritage (Article 78).

391. Montenegro is bound by the following international conventions adopted under auspices of UNESCO: Convention on the Means of Prohibiting and Preventing the Illicit Import, Export and Transfer of Ownership of Cultural Property (1970), Convention on the Protection of the World Cultural and Natural Heritage (1972), Convention on the Protection of the Underwater Cultural Heritage (2001) and the UNIDROIT Convention on Stolen or Illegaly Exported Cultural Objects (1995).

392. Pursuant to the substantive law of Montenegro, cultural property is any immovable, movable and intangible good for which, based on the Law on the Protection of Cultural Property,[287] it has been established that it is of a permanent historical, artistic, scientific, archaeological, architectural, anthropological, technical or

283. Article 18 para. 2 of the LRCL.
284. Article 30 of the PIL Act.
285. Mihajlo Dika, Gaša Knežević, Srđan Stojanović, *Komentar Zakona o međunarodnom privatnom i procesnom pravu* (Commentary of the PIL Act), Belgrade: Nomos, 1991, 70. *See also* Varadi, Bordaš, Knežević, Pavić, *Međunarodno privatno pravo, 14. izdanje* (Private International Law, 14th edn), Belgrade: Univerzitet u Beogradu, Pravni fakultet, 2012, 360.
286. Slavko Đorđević, *Rešavanje mobilnih sukoba zakona u stvarnopravnim odnosima sa elementom inostranosti* (Solving Mobile Conflict of Laws in Real Right Relations with a Foreign Element), Kragujevac: Univerzitet u Kragujevcu, Pravni fakultet, 2015, 121–122.
287. Podgorica, Službeni list Crne Gore No. 49/10, 40/2011 – other law, 44/2017 and 18/2019.

other social significance, irrespective of whether it is State or private property (Article 2(1)). Montenegro is obliged to ensure the protection and preservation of all cultural property located on its territory, including inland water and territorial waters, as well as to protect and preserve properties abroad, if they are of significance to its history or culture. The law also contains special provisions for the return of a cultural object to a Member State of the EU (Articles 63–66). In addition to this law, the special laws regulating certain segments of this matter include: the Law on Archival Activities, the Law on Library Activity, the Law on Culture, the Law on Museum Activity and the Law on Memorials.[288]

393. The PIL Act introduced a special conflict rule on cultural property (Article 33) which is in line with international and comparative law standards. Actually, it mirrors Article 90 of the Belgian PIL Act and the first paragraph of Article 33 is identical to Article 70 of the Bulgarian PIL Act. The Montenegrin conflict rule on cultural property applies only to a request by a State for return of an illicitly removed object that belongs to its own cultural heritage. Such request shall be governed by the law of the State of the origin of the cultural property unless it opts for the application of the law of the State where the item is located at the time of the submission of the request for revindication. However, the interest of a good faith possessor is also taken into account. Thus, if the law of the State that has designated the object as its cultural heritage does not provide for protection of the rights of a good faith possessor, the protection provided by the law of the country where the object is located at the time of the submission of the request for revindication shall apply. Furthermore, the provisions for the protection of cultural property are of imperative nature and their application may be imposed regardless conflict rules, as overriding mandatory rules.

IV. Other

A. *Means of Transport*

394. The basic solution for real right relations – the *lex situs*, is not appropriate for items that are constantly on the move and constantly cross the State boundaries, and also have great value and security significance. The category of things that perform their function by crossing State borders, and are usually located in no one's area (in the open sea or in free airspace) includes ships and aircraft. Property rights or pledge rights on a ship or aircraft are acquired only after registering and their legal position becomes similar to immovables. This special legal regime is followed by a special conflict rule for means of transport. Unlike the LRCL,[289] the PIL Act besides ships and aircraft provides the rules for means of transport in railway and commercial road transportation. The PIL Act stipulates that the acquisition, transfer and termination of real rights on means of transport shall be governed by: the law

288. *See infra* Table of Statutory Instruments.
289. Article 18 para. 3 of the LRCL.

of the flag of vessel; the law of the State of registration of an aircraft; the law of the State where the person exploiting the means of railroad or road transport conducts business.[290]

395. Pursuant to the LMIN ownership and other real rights (interests) in ships are governed by the law of the State to which they belong (Article 1034). Furthermore, real rights (interests) in ships under construction which are constructed in a domestic shipyard are governed by Montenegrin law (the LMIN, Article 1035). The LMIN recognizes the following real rights on ships and ships under construction: ownership, contractual mortgage and statutory charges (Article 235, paragraph 1). Foreigners may become owners of ships registered in Montenegro (Article 223, paragraph 1, item 1). A ship partially or wholly owned by a foreigner may be registered in Montenegro if certain conditions have been met (i.e., if Montenegro conducts supervision of the ship and if the registration is approved by the Ministry of Transportation, Sea Navigation and Communications; the decision of the Ministry is discretionary in nature; if the registration is not approved the ship acquired by foreigner will be erased from the register; *see* Articles 211 and 215). Foreigners may also acquire a mortgage over a ship registered in Montenegro (Article 237). A mortgage over a ship constituted by contract must be entered in the register in order to take effect in relation to third parties (Article 226, paragraph 3). A contractual mortgage over a ship which was recorded in a foreign public register will be provisionally recorded in the Montenegrin register when the ship acquires nationality of Montenegro if duly noted on the certificate on the erasure of the ship from the foreign register (Article 251, paragraph 1). The creditor in favour of whom the provisional registration has been made has to justify it within sixty days from the date of receiving a notification of entry by submitting the necessary documents (Article 251, paragraph 2). The time when such right was acquired under foreign law will be recognized when determining the order of priority of various rights on the ship (Article 251, paragraph 1). A foreigner having a duly registered contractual mortgage for a debt expressed in foreign currency is entitled to freely dispose of assets obtained from the public auction of the ship (Article 250). Statutory charges on ships are enumerated in Articles 252 and 255 of the LMIN.

396. In 2007 Montenegro adopted the Law on Yachts[291] and that law now applies to nationality and registration of yachts.

397. The LOPRAT equals the rule from the PIL Act that ownership, pledge and other interests in aircraft are governed by the law of the State in which the aircraft was registered (Article 181). The provisions of the Convention on the International Recognition of Rights in Aircraft (1944) which has been ratified by Yugoslavia in 1991 are relevant in that respect as well. An aircraft acquires nationality of Montenegro by registration in the register of civil aircraft (the LOPRAT, Article 137). An aircraft owned by a legal person with its seat in Montenegro must be registered

290. Article 31 of the PIL Act.

291. Podgorica, Službeni list Republike Crne Gore No. 46/2007 and Službeni list Crne Gore No. 73/2010, 40/2011, 42/2015 and 16/2016.

in the Montenegrin register while for foreign natural person domiciled in Montenegro the same applies if the aircraft habitually reside in Montenegro (the Law on Aerial Traffic,[292] Article 58, paragraphs 1 and 2 respectively). There are similar provisions on recognition of contractual mortgages recorded in foreign public registers prior to recording in the domestic register, as were mentioned with respect to ships (the LOPRAT, Article 157).

§3. Immoveable Property

398. The Law on Ownership Relations grants national treatment to foreigners in regards to acquiring ownership of movables and succession of immovables situated in Montenegro. The reciprocity as the requirement for acquisition of residential property by a foreign natural person is abolished, while different requirements apply to acquisition of immovables depending on several issues (legal regime of the immovable, its location, whether prospective buyer is a foreign country or organization). Moreover, different regimes apply to foreigners from the EU and the rest of the world. According to the Stabilization and Association Agreement signed between EU and Montenegro they enjoy national treatment with no exceptions and additional requirements. On the contrary, Article 415 of the LOR provides for explicit limitations on the rights of foreign citizens to acquire ownership on: natural wealth, goods in common usage, agricultural land, forest and forest land, culture monuments of special and extraordinary significance, immovables situated at certain protected locations (one kilometre deep area of land frontier and islands, as well as restricted territory for the protection of interests and security of Montenegro proclaimed as such by a special law). However, the law provides for an exception when foreign natural person may acquire ownership on agricultural land, forest and forest land but under two conditions: that the area is not exceeding 5,000 square metres and only if the object of the contract (on sales, gift, exchange and so forth) is residential building situated on that land. The special regime applies to ownership of foreign countries and organizations. Article 418 states that upon the consent of the Ministry of Foreign Affairs they may acquire buildings and flats for official use and construction land for building such premises.

399. Traditionally, the issue of determining the applicable law to real rights on immovable property has been treated uniformly by legislation, doctrine and practice. The law of the State on the territory of which the property is situated is generally accepted and practically the only rule for the right in rem in respect of immovable property. Therefore, the PIL Act envisages the *lex situs* for the acquisition, termination, content and exercise of the right in rem in respect of immovable property as the only conflict rule.[293] However, in the case of special legal grounds for the acquisition of property, on the basis of the contract on the acquisition of

292. Podgorica, Službeni list Republike Crne Gore No. 30/2012 and 30/2017.
293. Article 26 of the PIL Act.

property, succession or division of the common property of a spouse in the case of divorce or death of one of the spouses, the conflict rules for these, respective types of legal relations shall apply.

400. By applying the *lex situs* rule on real property rights on immovables, certain national interests are protected: territorial sovereignty, security, economic interests and so forth. In the domain of law, legal certainty[294] for the holder of real right is ensured, since in most countries for the acquisition, termination and change of real rights it is necessary to perform certain official actions of the State authority where the real estate is located (registration with the land register). It also provides legal certainty for third parties who can easily access information on a certain real estate in the land registry in the country where the real estate is situated.

I. Mortgage

401. The *lex situs* as a general rule for acquiring, termination, content and exercise of the real right also governs mortgage on real estate. The same law shall govern the creation of a mortgage, the rights and obligations of the owner of the real estate and the creditor, the order of secured creditors and the termination of the mortgage.[295]

402. The *lex contractus* (the party autonomy or subsidiary the law of the place of habitual residence of the debtor of the characteristic performance or the principle of the closest connection) applies to contract on mortgage.

II. Immissions

403. Protection against immissions is carried out according to the rules on non-contractual liability. Pursuant to Article 56 of the PIL Act the law applicable to a non-contractual obligation arising out of environmental damage or damage sustained by persons or property as a result of such damage shall be the *lex loci damni* unless the person seeking compensation for damage chooses to base his claim on the law of the State in which the event giving rise to the damage occurred.

404. The Law on Ownership Relations contains detailed rule on immissions. Pursuant to Article 266 paragraph 1 of the LOR the owner of the real estate is obliged to refrain from the activities when using the real estate and to remove the causes that arise from his immovable property, which makes it difficult to use other real estate (transmission of smoke, unpleasant smells, heat, soot, trembling, noise,

294. Varadi, Bordaš, Knežević, Pavić, *Međunarodno privatno pravo, 14. izdanje* (Private International Law, 14th edn), Belgrade: Univerzitet u Beogradu, Pravni fakultet, 2012, 350; Гавроска, П., Дескоски Т., *Меѓународно приватно право (The Private International Law).* Скопје: Правен факултет 'Јустинијан Први' , 2010, 301.

295. Maja Stanivuković, Petar Đundić, *Međunarodno privatno pravo, posebni deo* (Private International Law, Special Part), Novi Sad: Univerzitet u Novom Sadu, Pravni fakultet, 2008, 53.

swelling wastewater and so forth) to a greater extent than it is customary with regard to the nature and purpose of the immovable and local circumstances, or which causes significant damage or which are inadmissible under a special regulation. This provision is of imperative character and is an overriding mandatory rule.

405. Owners of immovables that are exposed to excessive emissions shall be authorized to require from the owner of immovable property that emits them to remove the causes of these emissions and compensate the incurred damage, as well as to refrain in the future from the activities that represent the cause of excessive emissions, until he undertakes all measures to make them impossible. Exceptionally, when excessive immissions come from an activity for which there is a permit from the competent authority, the owners of immovable property which are exposed to them have no right, while that permit lasts, to require a ban on the performance of that activity, but may request compensation for damages as well as taking appropriate measures in the future to prevent or reduce excessive immissions, or the occurrence of damage.[296]

III. Easements

406. The *lex situs*, as the only connecting factor for immovable property, whether it is the acquisition, termination, content or exercise of real rights, also applies to the easements. The problem with the application of the *lex situs*, can possibly be if it is a matter of real right relations on immovables that are situated in the territory of several States (e.g., in the case of predial servitude, there is a praedium serviens and a praedium dominium, and thus the possibility of applying two *lex situs*). Even in comparative law, the legislation usually says nothing about this issue, and some authors[297] advocate for the application of the law of the country where the immovable property that faces restrictions is situated.

§4. SECURITIES

407. Securities according to the legal nature of the rights that they contain can be securities of obligatory nature, that is, negotiable instruments (bills of exchange, checks), property securities, that is, documents of title (bill of lading, warehouse bond) and securities with the right of participation (financial instruments: stocks, bonds, warrants, derivatives and so forth). The bill of lading and the warehouse bond incorporate the right of ownership or lien on movable or immovable items. The law of Montenegro does not contain a special conflict rule for acquiring and terminating ownership rights on securities. In the doctrine, the unanimous attitude is that the *lex cartae sitae* shall apply.[298] For the status, and obligations arising from securities, the applicable law is determined on the basis of the relevant conflict rule for these legal relations, respectively.

296. Article 266, paras 3 and 4 of the LOR.
297. Varadi, Bordaš, Knežević, Pavić, *Međunarodno privatno pravo, 14. izdanje* (Private International

408. The new Law on Capital Market introduces conflict rule for financial instruments. Its Article 406, paragraph 1 stipulates that if financial instruments or rights to financial instruments are given as an instrument of insurance to participants, system operators and /or the Central Bank of Montenegro, and their rights to such financial instruments or the rights of other persons who perform business for their account, are legally entered into the registry, in the account or in a centralized depository system, the rights of those entities shall be governed by the law of the State in which the registry, account or central depositary is located.

§5. Trust

409. Montenegrin law does not recognize the concept of trust. Therefore, neither doctrine nor case law addresses this legal concept.

§6. Expropriation

410. Property rights are guaranteed as fundamental human rights by the Constitution of Montenegro. It explicitly states: 'No one shall be deprived of or restricted in property rights, unless when so required by the public interest, with rightful compensation' (Article 58). The socialist legacy giving primacy to the broadly defined public interest over individual property rights was abandoned as early as in the late eighties of the twentieth century. Presently, more important concerns raise the issue of restitution[299] than expropriation.

411. The LOR stipulates in Article 7 that no person may be deprived of the ownership right, unless when it is required so by a public interest determined by law or on the basis of law, with a compensation that cannot be lower than a fair one. Pursuant to the Law on Expropriation[300] the government cannot expropriate property unless there is a 'public interest' to do so, such as the construction of roads, bridges and so forth, and the compensation must be according to the market value. These provisions are the overriding mandatory rules.

412. The issue of protection against expropriation is particularly present in the area of foreign investments. LFI provides express guarantees to foreign property owners against unlawful expropriation and rights to adequate compensation in case

Law, 14th edn), Belgrade: Univerzitet u Beogradu, Pravni fakultet, 2012, 351.

298. Maja Stanivuković, Petar Đundić, *Međunarodno privatno pravo, posebni deo* (Private International Law, Special Part), Novi Sad: Univerzitet u Novom Sadu, Pravni fakultet, 2008, 48. *See also* Maja Stanivuković & Mirko Živković, International Encyclopedia of Laws – Private International Law, Supplement 55: Serbia, B. Verschraegen ed., Alphen aan den Rijn: Kluwer Law International, 2018, 200.

299. Ivana Jelić, Siniša Bjeković & Maja Kostić-Mandić, *Grundrechte in Montenegro,* In *Handbuch der Grundrechte* Band IX, Merten/Papier, Hg., Heidelberg: C.F. Müller, 2016, 520–521.

300. Law on Expropriation, Podgorica, Službeni list Crne Gore No. 55/00, 12/02, 28/06, 21/08, 30/17 and 75/18.

of lawful expropriation (Article 29). There is also a number of bilateral agreements on the protection and improvement of foreign investments in Montenegro, which also contain provisions on the protection of foreign investors from expropriation.[301] Furthermore, Montenegro is a party to the Convention on Establishing Multilateral Investment Guarantee Agency (MIGA) since 2007 which also guarantees protection to the foreign investors.

413. The expropriation being one of the ways of the termination of the property right shall be governed by the *lex situs*.

301. *See supra* National Law.

Chapter 4. Intangible Property Rights

§1. Rights of Personality

414. Rights of personality are guaranteed as basic rights by the Constitution of Montenegro and the ECHR. They are also protected by criminal and civil law remedies in domestic law. Pursuant to LO, Article 207, rights of personality include: life, physical and mental integrity, freedom, honour, reputation, protection of private life, dignity, one's own character and voice, correspondence and personal records, personal identity, the moral component of copyright, 'as well as other rights of personality prescribed by the Constitution, ratified and published international treaties and generally accepted rules of international law and special laws'.

I. Applicable Law

415. The PIL Act contains a specific conflict rules only for infringement of the rights of personality by way of the media (especially newspapers, radio, television or other means of information) and infringement of rights related to personal data protection. These rules are contained in a single article of the PIL Act (Article 55) of Chapter VI on non-contractual obligations and addressed in more details *supra*. Paragraph 1 stipulates that the injured party may elect as applicable the law of the country in which his habitual residence is located, or in whose territory the damage occurred or where the habitual residence or place of residence *(mjesto stanovanja)* of the responsible person is located. The same rule applies to obligations arising out of the infringement of rights relating to the protection of personal data (Article 55 paragraph 4).

416. The PIL Act also provides for a special rule on the right to publish a correction for violation of rights of personality by way of the media: governing law is the law of the State where the violation occurred (Article 55 paragraph 3).

II. Remedies

417. The PIL Act does not provide for a specific conflict rule for infringement of other rights of personality (except for infringement of the rights of personality by way of the media). Therefore, those infringements should be qualified as non-contractual obligations and the provisions of Chapters VI and VII of the PIL Act shall apply.

418. The LO, Article 151 stipulates remedies for civil and legal protection of rights of personality. They include requests for: prohibition of unlawful injury if it is immediately anticipated; establishing an unlawful injury; termination of an unlawful injury if it is in progress; abstaining from future unlawful violations or removing the consequences of unlawful injury; compensation of material and non-pecuniary damage, as well as other legal remedies and measures that can protect the rights of personality. Furthermore, other remedies peculiar in this field include request to publish certain information or to provide such information to specific persons or bodies, as well as to publish a correction of published information, judicial or other decisions of the competent authority.

419. In Montenegro, traditionally non-pecuniary damages consisted of two elements: the violation of rights of personality, and suffering of physical or mental pain (evidenced by neuropsychiatric expertise). By adopting amendments to LO in 2017 non-pecuniary damage is defined as the very violation of rights of personality, while mental pain can be of importance for ascertaining the amount of compensation.

420. The Principled legal position of the Supreme Court of Montenegro[302] reads that when ascertaining the amount of fair compensation for damages due to violation of rights of personality all the circumstances of a particular case must be considered. Furthermore, the amount of the awarded compensation should be, as a rule, in line with the practice of the ECtHR, and not in an amount that would discourage the media.

421. In the Criminal Code of Montenegro,[303] Chapter 15 (Crimes against the freedom and rights of man and citizen), there are already a number of criminal offences related to infringement of rights of personality.

422. The great majority of the cases adjudicated by Montenegrin courts[304] address actions for non-pecuniary damages for violation of honour and reputation of the plaintiff via printed media and Article 10(2) (Freedom of expression) and Article 8 (Right to respect for private and family life) of the ECHR which are the far most cited provisions. Judges in the pronouncement of the judgment do not refer to the decisions of international courts, but in the reasoning cite decisions, most often of the ECtHR in connection with Article 10(2). In most of the cases the reasoning list the legal sources which are grounds for the decision (such as Article 6 of the Constitution, Article 207[305] of LO and so forth) and then reinforce their position in decision-making by referring to international law.

302. Su. I No. 64-1/11 from 29 Mar. 2011.

303. Podgorica, Službeni list Crne Gore No. 70/2003, 13/2004 – exc. and 47/2006 and Službeni list Crne Gore No. 40/2008, 25/2010, 32/2011, 64/2011 – other act, 40/2013, 56/2013 – correct., 14/2015, 42/2015, 58/2015 – other act, 44/2017, 49/2018, 3/2020, 26/2021, 26/2021, 144/2021 and 145/21.

304. Maja Kostić-Mandić, *Implementation of International and European Law in Montenegro*, In European Union Law Application by the National Courts of the EU-Membership Aspirant Countries from South-East Europe, Skopje: South East European Law School Network, GIZ, 2014, 136–137.

305. This article on pecuniary damages is substantially amended in 2017. *See* Art. 210a of the LO, available at: https://www.paragraf.me/propisi-crnegore/zakon-o-obligacionim-odnosima.html (accessed 14 Apr. 2022).

§2. PATENTS

423. The main statutory source of patent law in Montenegro is the Law of Patents.[306] Also, the Regulation on the Implementation of Intellectual Property Rights applies. In addition, the following international conventions are in force in Montenegro:

- the Paris Convention for the Protection of Industrial Property (1883);
- the Patent Cooperation Treaty (1980), Strasbourg Agreement Concerning the International Patent Classification (1971);
- the Budapest Treaty on the International Recognition of the Deposit of Microorganisms for the Purpose of Patent Procedure (1977).

Montenegro is also a party to the 1994 Agreement on Trade-Related Aspects of Intellectual Property Rights (TRIPS).

424. The LRCL did not provide any rule regarding patent and the only conflict rule on IP rights was on the applicable law to the transfer of technology contracts, licence contract included, as a common instrument for transfer of patent rights.

425. Pursuant to the PIL Act's general rule (Article 35(2)) applicable to all industrial property rights, the existence, validity, scope, ownership, transferability, duration and infringement of a patent shall be governed by the law of the State which has granted or registered this right. The law applicable to employment contract governs the right to inventions created by an employee (Article 36) while the contracts relating to patent shall be governed by the law designated for contractual relations (Article 37).

I. Creation

426. Pursuant to the PIL Act's general rule (Article 35(2)), the creation of a patent shall be governed by the law of the State which has granted or registered this right. Previously, the LRCL did not provide any rule regarding patent. The Law on Patents contains provisions on the legal position of foreign natural and legal persons with respect to registration of patents. They enjoy the same right as domestic natural and legal persons, provided that international treaties guarantee such treatment or that it follows from the principle of reciprocity. The party relying on reciprocity has to prove that reciprocity exists (Article 3).

427. The Law on Patents primarily adheres to the principle of territoriality (Article 2). However, it deviates from this principle in case of priority rights. Thus, any natural person or legal entity who files in any Member State of the Paris Union

306. Podgorica, Službeni list Crne Gore No. 42/2015, 2/2017 and 146/21.

for the Protection of Industrial Property or in any Member State of the WTO, a correct application for the same invention shall be granted priority right in Montenegro, if so requested within twelve months counting from the date of filing the first application (Article 32(1)) and the filing date is established in accordance with the national legislation of the Member State of the Paris Union or the Member State of WTO in which it was filed or in accordance with an international treaty concluded among the Member States regardless of the subsequent outcome thereof (Article 32(3)). Furthermore, the European patent application and the European patent, under the conditions determined by this law have the same legal effect and are subject to the same conditions as the national patent application and the national patent (Article 150 a).

II. Protection

428. Pursuant to the PIL Act's general rule (Article 35(2)), the protection of a patent shall be governed by the law of the State which has granted or registered this right. The Law on Patents contains provisions on the legal position of foreign natural and legal persons with respect to protection of patents. They enjoy the same right as domestic natural and legal persons provided that international treaties guarantee such treatment or that it follows from the principle of reciprocity. The party relying on reciprocity has to prove that reciprocity exists (Article 3).

429. In case of legal proceedings before the institute for intellectual property of Montenegro, a foreign legal or natural person under Article 4 of the Law on Patents needs to name an authorized representative, a natural or legal person entered in the Register of Representatives which is maintained by the institute or an attorney at law entered in the Register of the Chamber of Commerce of Attorneys of Montenegro.

III. Ownership and Transfer

430. Pursuant to the PIL Act's general rule (Article 35(2)), the ownership and transfer of a patent shall be governed by the law of the State which has granted or registered this right. The law applicable to employment contract governs the right to inventions created by an employee (Article 36) while the contracts relating to patent shall be governed by the law designated for contractual relations (Article 37).

431. Previously, the LRCL provided that the transfer of technology contracts, licence contract included, as a common instrument for transfer of patent rights, is subjected to the general rule for contracts (law chosen by the parties, and in the absence of choice, the law of domicile or seat of the party that acquires the technology (licensee) at the time of receipt of the offer) governs the contract, unless the circumstances of the case point to a different law (Article 20(18)). This special rule was aimed to protect the weaker, presumable domestic party acquiring the foreign technology and it was a precedent regarding the party performing characteristic performance.

IV. Infringement

432. Pursuant to the PIL Act's general rule (Article 35(2)) the infringement of a patent shall be governed by the law of the State which has granted or registered this right. Thus, *lex protectionis* enables legal security, as previously, under the LCLR, it was not clear which law should apply to infringement of a patent. The Law on Patents under Chapter X provides for civil law protection before the competent court so that patent holder may request: the determination of the patent infringement; cessation of the infringement and the prohibition of such or similar infringement in the future, under the threat of payment of a fine; that the products infringing the patent be withdrawn from circulation, confiscated or destroyed. The patent holder may claim for damages, usual compensation and restitution of the acquired without grounds. At the request of the patent holder who makes it probable that the patent has been infringed or that there is an imminent threat of infringement of the patent, the court may order an interim measure aimed at terminating or preventing the infringement. The Law on Patents also provides for misdemeanour responsibility of a legal person in case of infringement of a patent and stipulates fines (Article 160).

§3. Copyright

433. The main sources of copyright law in Montenegro are the Law on Copyright and Related Rights (LCRR)[307] and the Law on Protection of Integrated Circuit Topographies.[308] In this field the following international conventions are in force in Montenegro:

- the Berne Convention for the Protection of Literary and Artistic Works (1886), and the Universal Copyright Convention (1952);
- International Convention for the Protection of Performers, Producers of Phonograms and Broadcasting Organizations (1961);
- Convention for the Protection of Producers of Phonograms Against Unauthorized Duplication of Their Phonograms (1971);
- Convention Relating to the Distribution of Programme-Carrying Signals Transmitted by Satellite (1974);

307. Podgorica, Službeni list Crne Gore No. 37/2011, 53/2016 and 145/2021. The Law on Copyright and Related Rights regulates the right of authors of literary, scientific and artworks (copyright), rights of interpreters, producers of phonograms, film producers, broadcasting organizations, and publishers (related rights), special (sui generis) rights of database producers, copyright contractual rights, the collective exercise and the protection of copyright, related rights and the special rights of database producers (Article 2).

308. Podgorica, Službeni list Crne Gore No. 2/2007, 53/2011 and 44/2016.

– the World Intellectual Property Organization[309] (WIPO) Copyright Treaty (1996);
– the WIPO Performances and Phonograms Treaty (1996).

Montenegro is also a party to the 1994 Agreement on Trade-Related Aspects of Intellectual Property Rights (TRIPS).

434. The PIL Act introduces special tale: property rights and intellectual property rights. It provides three distinctive articles addressing: general rule on applicable law for existence, validity, scope, ownership, transferability, duration and infringement of copyrights, related rights and other non-registered intellectual property rights (Article 35(1)) where the law of the territory in which such protection is sought applies and special rules on intellectual property rights arising in the context of employment (Article 36) and contracts relating to intellectual property (Article 37) where the *lex contractus* applies.

I. Creation

435. Pursuant to the PIL Act applicable law for existence of copyrights, related rights and other non-registered intellectual property rights is the law of the territory in which such protection is sought (Article 35(1)). The basic reasoning for special rules for intellectual property is that due to its intangible nature, it is not appropriate to ascertain where its *lex situs* is and therefore the connecting factor should be easily ascertainable *lex loci protectionis*.

The Law on Copyright and Related Rights normally applies to nationals of Montenegro or those who have a domicile or seat in Montenegro but it also devotes a separate chapter (Chapter IX) to the rights of authors involving an international element. Those three articles[310] implement solutions adopted in international conventions in the domain of rights of foreign nationals. Foreign authors enjoy copyright protection if an international treaty ratified by Montenegro protects them, or if there is factual reciprocity between Montenegro and the country to which the author belongs (Article 196, paragraph 2). Non-material rights are recognized to foreign authors irrespective of existence of a treaty or of reciprocity (Article 196, paragraph 3).

II. Protection

436. Pursuant to the PIL Act protection of copyrights shall be governed by the law of the State in respect of which protection is sought (Article 35(1)). In principle, copyright protection lasts for the life of the author and expires seventy years after his death (Article 62(1) of the LCRR). Deadlines for protection of rights determined by the LCRR shall also apply to foreign natural and legal persons who have

---

309. http://www.wipo.int/wipolex/en/profile.jsp?code=ME (accessed 14 Apr. 2022).

310. Other two articles address the prescription dates for protection of authors' rights (Article 197) and the rights of authors in satellite transmission (Article 198).

the right to protection under this law, provided that the deadlines expire on the day of termination of protection of rights in the State whose citizenship or seat they have and cannot be longer than the deadlines set by this law (Article 197).

III. Ownership and Transfer

437. Pursuant to the PIL Act, ownership and transferability of copyrights shall be governed by the law of the State in respect of which protection is sought (Article 35(1)). Copyright law includes moral rights, property rights and other rights of the author. Copyright is independent and aligned with property law or other real rights to the subject matter of the copyrighted work, unless otherwise provided by law. The law applicable to a labour contract shall also apply to a holder of an intellectual property right if the subject of the right was created in the context of employment (Article 36). Contracts relating to copyright shall be governed by the law designated for contractual relations (Article 37).

438. Previously, the LRCL determined the law applicable to contract on assignment of copyright (Article 20(14)). If the parties have not made their choice, the governing law was the law of the author's domicile or seat at the time of receipt of the offer, unless the circumstances of the case point to another law.

IV. Infringement

439. The Law on Copyright and Related Rights in case of infringement of those rights provides for different legal remedies, among others claims for material or non-material damages (Articles 193–194), as well as misdemeanours connected with fines (Articles 200–202). Proceedings for a claim for copyright and related rights infringement are urgent (Article 195). In the course of 2018–2021, by applying the Law on Copyright and Related Rights, the Law on Obligations, and in one case by referring to the Berne Convention, the Commercial Court established copyright infringement in two cases: for publishing photos taken by the defendant on the Internet portal and in daily newspapers without the knowledge and permission of the plaintiff, without indicating the name of the author and copyright fee payment.[311] In both cases, the judgments are final.

§4. Trademarks

440. The main sources of trademark law in Montenegro are the Law of Trademarks[312] and the Regulation on the Implementation of Intellectual Property Rights.

The following international conventions are in force in Montenegro:

311. P.br. 48/19, Pž br.742/19; P.br. 318/20, Pž br.202/21.
312. Podgorica, Službeni list Crne Gore No. 72/2010, 44/2012, 18/2014, 40/2016 and 2/2017.

- Trademark Law Treaty (1994);
- Madrid Agreement Concerning the International Registration of Marks (1891);
- Protocol Relating to the Madrid Agreement Concerning the International Registration of Marks (1989);
- Nice Agreement Concerning the International Classification of Goods and Services for the Purposes of the Registration of Marks (1957).

I. Creation

441. Pursuant to the PIL Act's general rule (Article 35(2)) the creation of a trademark shall be governed by the law of the State which has granted or registered this right. Previously, the LRCL did not provide any rule regarding trade mark. The Law on Trademark contains provisions on the legal position of foreign natural and legal persons with respect to registration of trademarks. They enjoy the same right as domestic natural and legal persons provided that international treaties guarantee such treatment or that it follows from the principle of reciprocity. The party relying on reciprocity has to prove that reciprocity exists (Article 4). An applicant who files in any Member State of the Paris Union for the Protection of Industrial Property or in any Member State of the WTO, a correct application for the same trademark shall be granted priority right in Montenegro, if so requested within six months counting from the date of filing the first application (Article 23(1)).

II. Protection

442. The protection of a trademark shall be governed by the law of the State which has granted or registered this right (Article 35(2) of the PIL Act). Pursuant to the Law on Trademarks foreign natural and legal persons enjoy national treatment with respect to protection of trademarks provided that international treaties guarantee such treatment or that it follows from the principle of reciprocity. The party relying on reciprocity has to prove that reciprocity exists (Article 4). In case of legal proceedings before the institute for intellectual property of Montenegro, a foreign legal or natural person needs to name an authorized representative, a natural or legal person entered in the Register of Representatives which is maintained by the institute or an attorney at law entered in the Register of the Chamber of Commerce of Attorneys of Montenegro.

III. Ownership and Transfer

443. Pursuant to the PIL Act's general rule (Article 35(2)), ownership and transferability of trademarks shall be governed by the law of the State which has granted or registered this right. The law applicable to employment contract governs the right to trademarks created by an employee (Article 36). Contracts relating to trademarks shall be governed by the law designated for contractual relations: party autonomy, while the subsidiary rules include the application of the habitual residence of the debtor of the characteristic performance and the principle of the closest connection (Article 37).

IV. Infringement

444. Infringement of a trademark shall be governed by the law of the State which has granted or registered this right (Article 35(2) of the PIL Act). Civil protection of a trademark includes a lawsuit for annulment of trademark, a lawsuit for revocation of trademark, a request for determination and a request for termination of the trademark infringement, a request for confiscation and destruction of items, a request for compensation, usual compensation and restitution and interim measures. The procedures are urgent (Chapter IX of the Law on Trademarks). The Law on Trademarks envisages also misdemeanour responsibility where fines are prescribed (Article 62d). In addition to the trademark holder (or his representative), protection of the trademark from infringement may be requested by the acquirer of the exclusive license to the extent that he has acquired the right to use the trademark, as well as a professional organization for protection of rights entitled to represent the intellectual property right holder (Article 59b).

445. In the period from 2018 to 2020, there were five cases related to trademark infringement with a foreign element before the Commercial Court and all the judgments are final.[313]In three trademark protection cases, the reasoning of the judgments refer to the case law of the Court of Justice of the EU.

446. Thus, in the case of *Scott USA Limited v. Venera Bike Limited, Serbia*[314] where the request for annulment of the registered trademark of the defendant protected in the words of Scout Venus was rejected, in addition to the binding international agreements (Madrid Agreement Concerning the International Registration of Marks, Agreement on Trade-Related Aspects of Intellectual Property Rights, Nice Agreement Concerning the International Classification of Goods and Services for the Purposes of the Registration of Marks and the National Trademark Law), the court also stated the criteria for determining the identity of the signs explained in the judgment of the ECJ in the case of *LTJ Diffusion SA v. Sadas Vertbaudet CJEU* (C-291/00 of 20 March 2003)[315] and the arguments are reinforced on the basis of another decision of the same court in *OHIM v. Shaker* (C-334/05 of 12 July 2007).

313. P.no. 26/18, Pž.no. 644/19; P.no. 1171/18, Pž.no. 600/19; P.no. 1171/18, Pž.no. 600/19; P.no.1170/19, no appeal; P.no.167/20, no appeal; P.no. 463/20, Pž.no. 120/21.

314. P.no. 1171/18, Pž.no. 600/19.

315. 'The term "identical" should be given a strict interpretation. The protection afforded to trademark owners exists if the mark has been reproduced without any addition, omission or modification other than those which are either minute or wholly insignificant. In assessing this, the court must make a global assessment of the features of the mark and the sign and the overall impression created by them, in particular by their distinctive and dominant components, so as to determine whether they would be perceived by the average, reasonably well-informed, observant and circumspect consumer as identical.'

However, the reasoning of Commercial Court's decision is lacking the precise reference to particular paragraphs of the ECJ decisions.

447. In the case of *Jaffa Limited, Serbia v. Lidl Stiftung, Germany*[316] in which the claim for annulment of the defendant's trademark for the territory of Montenegro was upheld, the court found that there is a possibility of confusion among the average consumer about the origin of the product. Among other reasons, the plaintiff is the holder of a total of 24 trademarks for the territory of Montenegro that contain the words 'jaffa', or 'jaffa cake' and the defendant's trademark also contains these words. The court applied the criteria for determining the similarity of the signs of the previous trademarks of the plaintiff and the disputed trademark of the defendant on the basis of the criteria from the judgment of the ECJ in the case *SABEL BV v. Puma AG* (C-251/95 of 11.11.1997).

448. In the case of *Gallup International Association, Zurich v. Gallup, Inc. Omaha, Nebrasca, USA*,[317] the registered trademark was entirely revoked because the defendant did not actually use the stated trademark in Montenegro for a continuous period of 5 years without a justified reason. The Court referred to the legal understanding of the CJEU in the case of *Ansul BV v. Ajax Brandebeveiliging BV* (C-40/01 of 11 March 2003).[318]

§5. Industrial Designs

449. The main sources of law on industrial designs in Montenegro are the Law on Legal Protection of Industrial Design[319] and the Regulation on the Implementation of Intellectual Property Rights.

The following international conventions are in force in Montenegro:

- the Locarno Agreement Establishing an International Classification for Industrial Designs (1968);
- the Hague Agreement Concerning the International Deposit of Industrial Designs (1960) and the Complementary Act of Stockholm (1967);
- the Hague Agreement Concerning the International Registration of Industrial Designs (1999).

---

316. P.no.167/20, there was no appeal.
317. P.no.26/18, Pž.no.644/19.
318. In Ansul, the CJEU held that for the use to be 'genuine' it must be: in accordance with the essential function of a trademark which is to guarantee the identity of the origin of the goods and services for which it is registered; use must be by way of real commercial exploitation on the market for the relevant goods and services; exploitation that is aimed at creating and maintaining a market share / outlet for the goods and services and that the genuine use does not include 'token' use for the sole purpose of preserving the rights conferred by the mark. All the relevant market factors must be taken into account in this assessment, particularly the: nature of the goods or services; the characteristics of the market and the scale and frequency of the use of the mark.
319. Podgorica, Službeni list Crne Gore No. 80/2010, 27/2013, 42/2016 and 2/2017.

I. Creation

450. The creation of industrial designs shall be governed by the law of the State which has granted or registered this right (Article 35(2) of the PIL Act). The Law on Legal Protection of Industrial Design contains provisions on the legal position of foreign natural and legal persons with respect to registration of industrial design. They enjoy the same right as domestic natural and legal persons provided international treaties guarantee such treatment or that it follows from the principle of reciprocity. The party relying on reciprocity has to prove that reciprocity exists (Article 3). An applicant who files in any Member State of the Paris Union for the Protection of Industrial Property or in any Member State of the WTO, a correct application for the same industrial design shall be granted priority right in Montenegro, if so requested within six months counting from the date of filing the first application (Article 29).

II. Protection

451. The protection of industrial designs shall be governed by the law of the State which has granted or registered this right (Article 35(2) of the PIL Act). In case of legal proceedings before the Institute for intellectual property of Montenegro a foreign legal or natural person under Article 3(3) of the Law on Legal Protection of Industrial Design needs to name an authorized representative, a natural or legal person entered in the Register of Representatives which is maintained by the Institute or an attorney at law entered in the Register of the Chamber of Commerce of Attorneys of Montenegro.

III. Ownership and Transfer

452. Pursuant to the PIL Act's general rule (Article 35(2)) the ownership and transfer of industrial designs shall be governed by the law of the State which has granted or registered this right. The law applicable to employment contract governs the right to industrial design created by an employee (Article 36). The contracts relating to industrial design shall be governed by the law designated for contractual relations: party autonomy, while the subsidiary rules include the application of the habitual residence of the debtor of the characteristic performance and the principle of the closest connection (Article 37).

IV. Infringement

453. Infringement of industrial designs shall be governed by the law of the State which has granted or registered this right (Article 35(2) of the PIL Act). Civil protection of industrial designs includes a lawsuit for annulment design rights, a lawsuit for challenging design rights, a request for designation of a designer, a request for determination and a request for termination of the trademark infringement, a request for confiscation and destruction of items, a request for compensation, usual compensation and restitution and interim measures. The procedures are urgent (Chapter IX of the Law on Legal Protection of Industrial Design). In addition to the industrial design holder (or his representative), protection of the industrial design from infringement may be requested by the acquirer of the exclusive license to the extent that he has acquired the right to use the industrial design, as well as a professional organization for protection of rights entitled to represent the intellectual property right holder (Article 50b).

Chapter 5. Family Law

454. Changed political and economic circumstances that occurred in Montenegro after regaining independence in 2006 led to the fact that family law relations are increasingly characterized by the existence of a foreign element. Some persons from the former State (Yugoslavia, that is, the State Union of Serbia and Montenegro) became foreign nationals, a number of foreigners who purchased immovable property settled in Montenegro, especially on the Adriatic coast, while a significant number of Montenegrins emigrated looking for a better standard of living. Furthermore, from some rural areas of the country, young people traditionally emigrate to the United States or to the countries of Western Europe (Germany, Luxembourg), while nowadays, in most cases, the whole family emigrates. For all those reasons it is becoming more common to have different citizenship of family members, different domiciles or habitual residence, possession of property in different countries and so forth. Regulating family relations with a foreign element is of particular importance because, although the exact number of Montenegrin emigrants and their descendants around the world is not known, it is estimated that there are as many as the population living in Montenegro, and a significant number holds Montenegrin citizenship.[320]

455. The Constitution of Montenegro guarantees gender equality, equality of legitimate and illegitimate children and prohibits any form of discrimination in accordance with the highest international standards. The right to marriage is a universal human right, and the special articles of the Constitution are dedicated to the family, the protection of mother and child, and the rights of the child (Articles 72–74). One of the characteristics of the substantial law of Montenegro in this area is that, after the Second World War, under the influence of the ideology of socialism, the patriarchal tradition of submitting a wife to the right of a spouse is abandoned, and a special attention is paid to the interests of the child. However, Montenegrin law does not recognize the effects of certain new rights legally established abroad, such as registered (same-sex) partnership, same-sex marriage, surrogate maternity and related adoption, because these rights are not acknowledged in its national law.

456. The family law area is the most regulated area in the PIL Act, and the Hague conventions that bind Montenegro are:

- Convention on the Civil Aspects of International Child Abduction;
- Convention on the Protection of Children and Co-operation in Respect of Intercountry Adoption;
- Convention on Jurisdiction, Applicable Law, Recognition, Enforcement and Co-operation in Respect of Parental Responsibility and Measures for the Protection of Children; and

320. Cooperation strategy with the Diaspora for the period 2020–2023, Government of Montenegro, June 2020.

– Convention on the International Recovery of Child Support and Other Forms of Family Maintenance.

457. Montenegro is also a member of the European Convention on Recognition and Enforcement of Decisions concerning Custody of Children and on Restoration of Custody of Children.

§1. State Law – Religious Law

458. Montenegro is a secular State in which religious institutions[321] are separated from the State (Constitution, Article 14). Family relations are regulated by LF and it does not recognize the influence of religion on family relations. The only provision in the LF where religion is addressed is the one on foster care, and Article 160 states: 'When placing the child into another family, the custodial body has an obligation to pay special attention to the national, religious and cultural origin of the child, its age, health and social status.'

459. In the period after the Second World War, under the influence of the socialist ideology in Montenegro, the practice of religious rituals in urban areas was reduced to a minimum, and mostly in the privacy of the home. However, even then religion has retained a significant place with some believers in rural and coastal areas. Nevertheless, today, in practice, in some, traditional parts of the State, there is a certain influence of customary and religious law. The most common is the dominant position of the husband and father in the family, the custom of giving dowries, the conclusion of marriage in religious form (the conclusion of a marriage in a civil form in domestic law is mandatory), as well as the custom that male heirs inherit the entire property and that the females denounce the succession in their favour. These customs are present among the members of all religions in Montenegro, and apart from marrying in a religious form, which has become more common in the last two decades, they are more present in the older population.

460. A foreign religious law may be primarily discussed in marital law, for example, if the foreign national wants to get married before our registrar and his national law in the field of family law applies Sharia law. This religious law, with the fulfilment of certain conditions, allows the possibility that a man may have at the same time a valid marriage with up to four women. If a person already has a marriage, a new marriage could not be concluded in Montenegro, because both the Constitution of Montenegro and LF stipulate that marriage can only be concluded with the free consent of men and woman (singular), and that marriage is based on the equality of spouses (Article 71, Article 3, respectively), and the LF provides that no one can conclude a new marriage until his earlier marriage ends (Article 19). The

321. Pursuant to the 2011 Census, the Montenegrins are predominantly Christian Orthodox (72%), Muslim (19%), and Roman Catholics (3,5%), https://www.monstat.org/userfiles/file/popis2011/saopstenje/saopstenje(1).pdf (accessed 14 Apr. 2022).

existence of a previous marriage as a marital impediment is imposed as an overriding mandatory rule, irrespective of the applicable law.

461. The situation is different with the religious form of marriage. If domestic citizens concluded marriage in a religious form abroad, marriage will be recognized in Montenegro if a religious marriage is prescribed in that foreign country as a valid legal form. Foreign marriage is not subject to distinctive recognition procedure (as applicable to foreign judgments). However, recognition can be refused on the grounds of violation of public policy.

462. On the contrary, a divorce decision made abroad can produce effects in Montenegro only if it is recognized. There is no exclusive jurisdiction of the domestic judiciary for ruling on divorce, but the general framework is set out in Article 141 of the PIL Act. Montenegro adheres to the system of bilateralization and therefore upon the recognition, a foreign judgment shall produce the same legal effect in Montenegro as a domestic judgment. The concept of 'judgment' is laid down in a broad manner since it encompasses a settlement made before a court of law ('court settlement'), as well as a decision of other authority which, in the State in which it was rendered, is equalized with a court judgment, or court settlement.

463. In principle, the decision of a foreign authority, which, pursuant to the law of that country is competent for the divorce, even if it is a religious institution, will not constitute an obstacle to the divorce, unless there are other impediments to recognition.

464. In practice, the greatest challenge can be recognition of the effects of relations based abroad on Sharia Law. The mere fact that a decision was based on religious law does not lead to a violation of the public policy of Montenegro, because the application of this institute in the field of the applicable law and recognition and enforcement of court decisions may occur only if the effects of the relevant law or decision obviously contradicted to the domestic public policy.

465. The impossibility of entering into a polygamous marriage in Montenegro should not be interpreted as a complete denial to give legal effect to such marriages entered into abroad. Certain effects of such marriages should be recognized. For example, all children born in a polygamous marriage (from the first, second, third, fourth wife) should be considered to be legitimate, they should all have the right to inherit from their father, to receive maintenance from their father as long as they are acquiring regular education, and so forth. The position of the second (third, fourth) wife should also be brought into harmony with the logically sustainable substantive result by applying the method of adaptation, or transposition.

466. On the basis of Yugoslav case law,[322] in one case, the recognition of a foreign court decision which was based on Sharia law was rejected, whereby after the

322. Milan Pak *Međunarodno privatno pravo* (Private International Law), Belgrade: Nomos, 1991, 111–112.

divorce the child is entrusted with custody only to the father, because the decision did not contain reasoning and it was not possible to ascertain whether it was made having in mind the best interest of the child.

467. In addition, a violation of a public policy may arise in the form of decisions based on discrimination in relation to sex, religion or any other form of discrimination (if it is obvious, and if the facts of the decision indicate so).

§2. Marriage

I. Engagement

468. In Montenegrin substantive family law engagement is not perceived as a legal concept. The principle of free assent to marriage is one of the basic principles of family law and engagement cannot create a legal obligation to marry.[323] However, certain legal effects of breach of engagement are recognized in domestic family law, such as the compensation of pecuniary damages in connection with costs incurred for organizing the expected wedding and the obligation to return the engagement and wedding gifts.[324]

469. The PIL Act does not provide for a distinctive conflict rule for engagement. The general conflict rule for non-contractual liability for damages (Article 52) should govern compensation of damages and the conflict rule for unjustified enrichment (Article 60) should govern the returning of engagement gifts.[325]

II. Heterosexual Marriage

A. *Form*

470. In marriages with a foreign element, the form gives reasons to distinguish two situations. The first concerns the conclusion of a marriage before a domestic authority, in the domestic territory, when the foreign element appears in the citizenship of the person. The second situation relates to the recognition of marriages that are concluded abroad, when the foreign element occurs in the place of legal act. In both cases, the basic conflict rule is that the form of marriage will be valued by the law of the country of marriage (*lex loci celebrationis*).[326]

---

323. The principle of free assent to marriage is expressly provided in the Constitution of Montenegro (Art. 71), and in the Law on Family (Art. 18).

324. Kluwer Monograph on PIL of Montenegro of 2013, paras 353–355.

325. Bernadet Bordaš, *Porodičnopravni odnosi u međunarodnom privatnom pravu* (Family Relations in Private International Law), Novi Sad: Forum, 2000, 22–23.

326. *See* Art. 13(3) of the German PIL Act, Art. 16 of the Austrian PIL Act, Art. 45 of the Swiss PIL Act, Art. 28 of the Italian PIL Act, Art. 170 of the French Civil Code etc.

471. The same rule applies to marriages with a foreign element concluded in Montenegro and to the recognition of marriages concluded abroad. For both situations, the same conflict rule applies, the sole difference being the role of the domestic authority. In the case of marriages concluded before the Montenegrin competent authority, it acts in the manner prescribed by domestic law. In the case of foreign marriages, the competent Montenegrin authority should recognize the marriage as valid or refuse to recognize it. Marriage concluded abroad is not subjected to the recognition procedure, as is the case with foreign court or arbitral decisions. In fact, the validity of the marriage certificate from the civil record of marriage is acknowledged.

472. Marriage can also be concluded in a diplomatic-consular form. The diplomatic or consular office is considered an extraterritorial part of the country of appointment; therefore, the law of the appointing country applies to such a marriage. In order for a marriage to be concluded in a diplomatic-consular office, it is necessary that certain conditions are fulfilled. The PIL Act addresses only conditions for concluding marriages in Montenegrin diplomatic or consular office (Article 159). First, Montenegro as the country of appointment of a diplomatic or consular office has to give special authorization on the basis of which this activity can be performed, as it does not fall under the regular functions of the diplomatic or consular offices. Second, the host country has to give its consent or it should be provided for by an international agreement that Montenegrin diplomatic or consular office may perform marriages in a foreign form on its territory or in order for the marriage to be valid in that country. And third, a special condition relating to diplomatic and consular marriages concerns the Montenegrin citizenship of persons who want to conclude a marriage.

473. The foreign diplomatic or consular offices in Montenegro must also act upon authorization of the country of appointment, as well as Montenegro as a host country. These issues are usually regulated by bilateral treaties. Diplomatic and consular offices of foreign countries must have special authorization from the Ministry of Foreign Affairs of the Government of Montenegro regarding marriage. Moreover, certain conditions in terms of employees and equipment for the realization of such an act must be met. Unlike the previous two conditions, some countries do not require that persons who wish to marry in diplomatic and consular offices to be of the same nationality. In some diplomatic and consular offices in Montenegro (e.g., of France and Greece), the marriage can be concluded by persons, one of whom can be a foreign, as well as a citizen of Montenegro. In the diplomatic-consular office of the Federal Republic of Germany, as well as in the diplomatic-consular office of the United States of America in Podgorica, marriages cannot be concluded, while, for example, in the diplomatic-consular office of the Russian Federation in Podgorica, only Russian citizens may conclude marriage.[327]

474. One of the basic consular functions of the representative offices of Montenegro abroad is registration of the concluded marriages of Montenegrin citizens

327. Article 4, para. 2 of the Law of the Russian Federation 143-FZ of 11/15/1997 on civil status acts.

before the authorities in the host country, but for the time being a marriage cannot be concluded in our diplomatic or consular offices abroad.

B. Substance

475. LF specifies the substantive conditions that must be fulfilled in order to conclude the valid marriage: the diversity of the sexes of future spouses; the consent of the declared wills for marriage; the absence of marital impediments envisaged by law (preexisting marriage, mental incapacity and kinship) and the conclusion of marriage for the purpose of the community of living.[328]

476. The PIL Act, adheres to the nationality principle,[329] envisaging the application of distributive cumulation. Article 77 of the PIL Act reads as follows: 'As regards the conditions for entering into marriage the governing law for each person is the law of the State whose citizen that person is at the time of marriage.' In practice, registries in Podgorica[330] tend to disregard the rules of PIL and apply LF instead.[331] However, when a foreign national wants to conclude a marriage in Montenegro, he is obliged to attach a certificate of free marital status, which confirms that there are no marital impediments on the part of that person for marriage, under the law of his citizenship.[332] So, for example, an American citizen who wishes to marry in Montenegro (before the Montenegrin local registry office) needs to submit a document showing that he is free to marry. Given that such a document is not issued in the USA, their citizens who want to marry in Montenegro should schedule a meeting at the US Consular Section in Podgorica to fill out 'Free to Marry' statement which it would then be certified by a consular officer before the wedding.

477. Certain conditions envisaged by Montenegrin legislation, as the law of the country in which the marriage is concluded, shall apply even when two foreign citizens marry in Montenegro before the Montenegrin local registry office and regardless of our conflict rule (Article 77 of the PIL Act). Here we refer to the overriding mandatory rules of Montenegro's law, which relate in the first place to absolute marital impediments (the existence of an earlier marriage, kinship and mental incapacity).[333] Relative marital impediments, such as the 16 years that our substantive

328. Articles 16–24 of the Family Law.
329. *See also* Art. 13(1) of the German PIL Act, Art. 17(1) of the Austrian PIL Act, Art. 19 of the Swiss PIL Act, Art. 27 of the Italian PIL Act, Art. 3 of the French Code Civil.
330. http://podgorica.me/licna-stanja/ (accessed 14 Apr. 2022).
331. The most popular touristic resort in Montenegro, Budva is also a popular spot for marriage ceremonies with Montenegrins and foreigners alike. According to the data of the Budva Registrar Office, in 2015 there were a total of 302 weddings, and even in 193 cases one of the partners was a foreigner, while foreigners entered into 97 marriages. In 2017, foreigners entered into 68 marriages while in 66 cases one of the spouses was a foreigner. In the same period there were only 19 marriages in which both spouses were Montenegrin citizens with permanent residence in Budva.
332. Information available at: https://me.usembassy.gov/u-s-citizen-services/local-resources-of-u-s-citizens/marriage-in-montenegro/ (accessed 14 Apr. 2022).
333. On the contrary, Varadi, Bordaš, Knežević, Pavić refer to public policy, and Jakšić refers to a special clause of the public policy. *See* Varadi, Bordaš, Knežević, Pavić, *Međunarodno privatno*

law prescribes as the minimum age for marriage to be approved by the court, does not constitute an overriding mandatory rule, but the application of our law would be imposed as an obstacle for marriage to a person who is 12 years old.

478. On the basis of overriding mandatory rules, the conclusion of a marriage between two foreign nationals would be refused, and regardless of the fact that under their national law none of the above facts constitutes an absolute marital impediment (e.g., Russian citizens, uncle and a niece could not marry before of our registrar, but that would not be an obstacle for marriage in the Russian diplomatic and consular office in Montenegro, which would apply the substantive law of the Russian Federation).

479. In this area, there may be a departure from the application of regularly applicable law, if its effects would be incompatible with the basic values of our public policy.

480. Bilateral agreements containing provisions on the applicable law to substantive conditions for the conclusion of marriage provide for the same solutions as the PIL Act (treaties with the Czech Republic, Slovakia, France, Hungary, Poland and Romania).

III. Same-Sex Marriage

A. Form

481. Montenegro is among the legal systems that do not allow same-sex marriages, regardless of whether the same-sex partners are domestic citizens or there is an international element in that marriage as the 2007 Constitution of Montenegro bans same-sex marriage. Also, if the conclusion of the same-sex marriage falls under PIL, the domestic authority does not take into account the position of foreign law, but the application of domestic law is imposed. In Montenegro, same-sex marriage cannot be concluded before the local authorities because the Constitution of Montenegro stipulates that marriage is the union of a man and a woman, and this rule, as well as the equivalent provision of LF, are overriding mandatory rules.

482. However, given the fact that the laws of several countries permit the conclusion of the same-sex marriage, there is a possibility of concluding the same-sex marriage in certain diplomatic-consular offices in Montenegro. Thus, in the Embassy of the United Kingdom in Podgorica, British citizens can conclude not only a heterosexual marriage but the embassy is also authorized to conclude same-sex marriages and to convert the existing civil partnership into marriage. Based on the nota verbale of the Ministry of Foreign Affairs of Montenegro, it is specified that

pravo, 14. izdanje (Private International Law, 14th edn), Belgrade: Univerzitet u Beogradu, Pravni fakultet, 2012, 294–295; Aleksandar Jakšić, *Međunarodno privatno pravo* (Private International Law), Belgrade: Dosije, 2008, 383.

the same-sex marriage between two British citizens, as well as the conversion of civil partnership into marriage, constitutes a sovereign act within the territory of the Embassy.

B. Substance

483. In Montenegro, the heterosexuality of the spouses is considered to be a substantive requirement and the marriage may be concluded only between a woman and a man. Thus, there is no conflict rule on same-sex marriages in the PIL Act and partners of the same sex cannot validly enter into the marriage before Montenegrin local authorities. If the conclusion of the same-sex marriage or its effects fall under PIL, the domestic authority does not take into account the position of foreign law, but the application of domestic law is imposed. Furthermore, even marriages registered in the premises of the British Embassy would not produce a legal effect on the territory of Montenegro (they cannot be the basis for any other legal action in Montenegro: annulment, renunciation, divorce or termination of marriage due to death, separation and division of succession).

484. A same-sex marriage, validly concluded abroad, neither could be recognized nor produce effects in Montenegro, since the recognition of such a marriage would constitute a violation of the public policy of Montenegro. Similarly, the termination of the same-sex marriage concluded abroad by divorce or annulment could also not be pronounced by domestic courts because initiating this procedure is conditioned upon this marriage being recognized in our country (by recognition of the probative force of a foreign document, or by an entry of marriage in the register of civil status if one of the partners is a domestic national).

485. However, the question may arise whether the indirect effects of same-sex marriages concluded under foreign law (e.g., judgment on maintenance between the same-sex partners) may constitute impediment to recognition and enforcement of a foreign judicial award. Having in mind the wording of Article 147 of the PIL Act which stipulates narrow preconditions for triggering this impediment (the effect of recognition of a foreign judgment is manifestly contrary to the public order of Montenegro), in our view, it shouldn't be the case.

IV. Personal Effects of Marriage

486. Montenegrin doctrine addresses personal, personal-property (maintenance) and property relations of spouses, and the latter are divided into statutory and contractual property relations. The law of Montenegro contains specific conflict rules for each of these relations. The rights and duties of a spouse of a personal nature, among others, include: running a life together, independence in the choice of work and occupation, determining family name(s), determining the place of permanent residence and so forth.

487. In Montenegro, the same conflict rule applies to personal and property effects of marriages (legal property relations), thereby eliminating the problem of legal qualification. The law of Montenegro traditionally adheres to the common citizenship of the spouses as a primary rule for personal and property relations of spouses. However, the PIL Act introduces innovations in relation to the rules of the previous LRCL, that is the previous subsidiary rules the common domicile or the last common domicile are now replaced with the common or the last common habitual residence. Thus, the rule for the personal effects of the marriage is set in the form of subsidiary connections (Article 80 of the PIL Act): common citizenship, or common habitual residence, or the last common habitual residence, or the law of Montenegro. The competent authority starts from the first connection (the common nationality of the spouses), and if there are no conditions for the application of that connecting factor because the persons do not have a common citizenship, they apply the next connection (their common habitual residence, or the last common habitual residence), and if the spouses do not fulfil any of the above conditions, the law of Montenegro will ultimately be applied.

488. Effects of marriage on capacity of the spouses are subject to the law that governs the status of each of the spouses pursuant to Article 11 of the PIL Act.

V. Dissolution

A. *Annulment*

489. The marriage that is concluded without the fulfilment of positive substantive conditions, in the presence of negative substantive conditions (marital impediments), or when a legally prescribed form is violated, is null and void. Absolutely null and void is the marriage in which the conditions which are prescribed in the general interest are not fulfilled, and which can therefore be annulled upon the lawsuit of a broader circle of persons, with no time limits. These conditions are stated exhaustively and the marriage will be absolutely null: if it is concluded by persons of the same sex, if there was no consensus on the will of fiancées, if it was not concluded for the purpose of the community of life, if it was concluded despite the existence of some marital impediment (preexisting marriage, kinship[334] and mental incapacity) and if the marriage is not concluded before the competent authority. Relatively null and void marriages are annulled by a private lawsuit of spouses, and this right is timely limited. A relatively nullified marriage can be revived not only at the expiration of the time-limit for the lawsuit, but also with subsequent court approval. Relatively null marriages arise from disrespecting marital impediments, such as: when a juvenile older than 16 concludes marriage without a court permission, or in case of a mental incapacity that has ceased during a marriage. Regarding the legal consequences of a nullity, an invalid marriage takes place and, as a rule, produces effects until a judgment becomes final.

334. The marriage concluded between the civil relatives from incomplete adoption is also null and void, but it can be convalidated by the court granting the subsequent approval.

490. Article 79 of the PIL Act reads: 'The annulment of a marriage shall be governed by the law of the State the law of which applied to the terms of conclusion of the marriage.' When Montenegrin court is competent to decide on the annulment of a marriage, on the basis of the PIL Act, the issue of form as a reason for the annulment will be valued according to the law of the country where the marriage has been concluded, and the validity of substantive conditions for the conclusion of marriage will be valued according to the law of citizenship of persons at the time of concluding the marriage. In practice, it may happen that for concluding the marriage, two or more laws are applicable. One of the laws may, while others may not stipulate the specific reason for the annulment. The reason for the annulment is to be valued according to the law applicable to the conclusion of a marriage. In case of double-sided material impediments (such as kinship), a marriage will be annulled if conditions under any of the two applicable laws of citizenship of spouses are met. In case the question is raised before a domestic court, it is sufficient that the impediment is foreseen by domestic law because it is an overriding mandatory rule.

491. In addition to the causes of the invalidity of marriage, the following questions are also determined by this applicable law: whether the cause makes marriage non-existent, null or void; whether the cause of invalidity has *ipso iure* effect, or the marriage will be considered valid until it is declared invalid by the competent authority; whether marriage, depending on the cause, can be convalidated or not.[335]

B. Divorce

492. For divorce, the LRCL envisaged the application of the laws of citizenship of the spouses at the time of filing a lawsuit, which, in the case of persons having different citizenship, resulted in the cumulative application of the two laws, a situation that is to be avoided in modern law. The emphasis was also on the dissolution of marriage,[336] while the possibility of choice of law in this area was not foreseen.

493. The PIL Act aims to prevent the cumulative application of the law and to ensure the application of one law, which is common to spouses, and to prevent the mobile conflict of law, by precisely applying the fact (citizenship, habitual residence) that was actual at the time of filing a divorce application. The conflict rule of Article 85 of the PIL Act gives priority to the common citizenship of the spouses over common habitual residence. This differs from approach present in other fields, where contemporary comparative and EU law solutions were transposed in the PIL Act. Here, national interests prevailed having in mind the number of Montenegrin citizens in Montenegro and those living abroad. However, this attachment to the nationality principle can be corrected by the parties who now, for the first time, have possibility of choice of law for their divorce. In addition to the common citizenship of the spouses the conflict rule for divorce provides for four subsidiary connections:

335. Varadi, Bordaš, Knežević, Pavić, *Međunarodno privatno pravo, 14. izdanje* (Private International Law, 14th edn), Belgrade: Univerzitet u Beogradu, Pravni fakultet, 2012, 302.
336. Article 35, paras 3 and 4 of the LRCL.

the law of their common habitual residence, or the law of their last common habitual residence, or the law of Montenegro, if the applicable law cannot be determined, or the law of Montenegro, if the marriage could not be divorced under the foreign law and either of the spouses is a Montenegrin citizen who does not have a habitual residence in Montenegro. This very detailed rule with several subsidiary connections covering plenty of situations is motivated by the fact that dissolution of marriage is one of the general principles of the Montenegrin family law. Thus, the statutory regime stipulates that for the divorce, the law of a common citizenship of the spouses is the applicable law; or if they are nationals of different countries, the law of a common habitual residence of spouses, in both cases at the time of filing a divorce application. If neither of these rules can be applied, the law of the country in which the spouses had the last common habitual residence shall apply, and if there is no basis for the application of this rule, the law of Montenegro shall apply. In order to respect the principle of a marriage dissolution, it is also foreseen that in case one of the spouses is a Montenegrin citizen who does not have a habitual residence in Montenegro, and the marriage could not be divorced under the applicable law pursuant to the aforementioned rules, the applicable shall be the law of Montenegro.[337]

494. Furthermore, the PIL Act for the first time envisages the possibility of choice of law for divorce. This is a limited choice of law because the parties can only choose as the applicable law one of the laws listed by the legislator, the criterion being significant connection to the spouses. In addition to the laws already listed in the conflict rule for divorce in the absence of party autonomy (the law of common citizenship, common habitual residence, last common habitual residence, Montenegrin law, the choice does not depend on the sequence of connecting factors), spouses may also choose the law of citizenship of either of them at the time of filing a divorce application. In all cases, the agreement on the selection of the applicable law must be made in writing and certified by the competent authorities, at the latest at the time of filing a divorce application.[338]

495. In practice, the largest number of cases with a foreign element are disputes for divorce between Montenegrin nationals who are habitually resident abroad. Pursuant to the principle of attribution of jurisdiction, when deciding on divorce, the judges also in the same litigation often decide on parental rights (custody, contact), deprivation of parental rights and maintenance.[339] And in some cases, they may also decide on the division of property acquired in marriage (when the parties reach an agreement on the division of property and when the interest of minor children is not impaired). Thus, in one case the Higher Court in Podgorica[340] upheld the decision

337. Article 85 of the PIL Act.
338. Article 86 of the PIL Act.
339. Higher Court in Podgorica, Gž.br. 5360/18 of 29.10.2018 rendered a decision revoking the judgment of the Basic Court in Podgorica P. br.1536/17 of 26.07.2018 on divorce, entrusting the exercise of parental rights, maintaining the father's personal relations with children, the father's legal obligations on maintenance of minor children and remand the case to the trial court for retrial.
340. Higher Court in Podgorica, Gž.br.3573/19 of 25.06.2019.

of the Basic Court in Podgorica[341] and the judgment of the same Court[342] as the first instance court properly dismissed the plaintiff's claim to order the defendant to hand out the keys to the apartment in question, and the Court refers to a special procedure for determining ownership, as the ongoing procedure is urgent in order to protect the interests of the children, and thus any delay would be detrimental to their interests.

496. One of the challenges for the first instance judges is to recognize that it is a dispute with a foreign element, as these persons usually formally retain their domicile in Montenegro. Moreover, some judges do not recognize that the governing law for legal relations in Montenegro between the citizens of Montenegro and the citizens of the states created by the breakup of the former Yugoslavia should be ascertained by applying Private International Law rules, instead of Montenegrin substantive and procedural law. An illustrative example of the said practice of the basic courts can be found in a case law of the Higher Court in Podgorica, as a second instance court. In a case in which the plaintiff filed a lawsuit for entrusting him to exercise parental rights over a minor child, the Higher Court on three occasions revoked the decision of the Basic Court in Bar[343] and referred back the case to the first instance court for retrial. The facts of the case are as follows: the plaintiff and the defendant previously lived in an extramarital cohabitation with their minor child, in Bar, Montenegro; the defendant left Montenegro and took the child to Novi Sad, Republic of Serbia, where they still live; and the minor child has dual citizenship – Montenegrin and Serbian. In this case the Basic Court: did not apply the PIL Act but the LCP and its rules of local jurisdiction and lis pendens without an international element; in the repeated proceedings applied the rules of applicable law instead of rules on international jurisdiction and did not properly appreciate whether there was international lis pendens; it also did not apply the Agreement between the Republic of Serbia and Montenegro on Legal Assistance in Civil and Criminal Matters.

§3. Matrimonial Property

497. Spouses may have separate and common property. Common property is property acquired through work in the course of a marriage, as well as any income from that property. The subject of common property is widely interpreted on the basis of court practice and doctrinal attitudes.[344] On the contrary, separate property is the property acquired by a spouse before marriage, as well as property acquired during marriage through succession, gift or other forms of non-intangible acquisition (LF, Articles 285–288).

341. Basic Court in Podgorica P. br. 6293/18 of 08.04.2019.
342. Basic Court in Podgorica P. br. 6293/18 of 08.04.2019.
343. Basic Court in Bar Gž. br. 4798/15 of 08.10.2015, Gž. br. 3504/16 of 06.09.2016; Gž. br. 2257/17 of 09.05.2017.
344. *See* Radoje Korać, *Porodično pravo* (Family Law), Podgorica: Štamparija 3 M Makarije, 2011, 459–463.

498. As to the applicable law, the same rules governing the personal relations of spouses apply to the spouses' legal property relations (PIL Act Article 81, paragraph 1). The law determined in accordance with Article 80 governs the effects of marriage on property, without distinguishing between movables or immovables. This is the principle of unity of the patrimonial relations between the spouses that applies regardless of where the immovable is situated. The purpose of this principle is to avoid the undesirable application of different statutes to matrimonial property depending on its location.

499. The competent authority applies to matrimonial property the law of the common citizenship of the spouses, and if persons do not have a common citizenship, they apply their common habitual residence, or the last common habitual residence, and if there are no conditions for the application of any of these laws, the law of Montenegro will ultimately be applied.

500. In order to avoid a mobile conflict of laws, it is specified that, in the case of property relations of spouses, a change in the citizenship or habitual residence of one or both spouses trigger the change of the applicable law and the new applicable law applies to the property of the spouses independently from the moment of its acquisition.[345]

I. Choice of Law Agreement

501. LF expressly allows the spouses, or future spouses, to regulate their mutual relations on the existing or future property by contract. However, this substantive party autonomy is limited only to exclusion of the application of the domestic statutory régime, while conflictual autonomy is explicitly forbidden (Article 303). In our view this provision should not be treated as a rule of the forum that may not be derogated from and it should apply only when Montenegrin law governs the marital property relations. LF also addresses the legal form of the contract. The contract has to be in writing and certified by a notary, who has a duty to read the contract to the spouses before they sign it, and to warn them that they thereby exclude the application of the statutory régime of a common property. Based on the experience of a notary from Podgorica,[346] several pre-nuptial agreements were concluded between Montenegrin and EU citizens in the form of a notarial deed. In all cases separate property has been stipulated.

502. As to the applicable law, as well as in the domain of a statutory matrimonial property relations, in the domain of contractual property relations of spouses

345. Article 81 of the PIL Act. For mobile conflicts for this kind of relationship *see* Maja Stanivuković, Petar Đundić, *Međunarodno privatno pravo, posebni deo* (Private International Law, Special Part), Novi Sad: Univerzitet u Novom Sadu, Pravni fakultet, 2008, 241–244.

346. Courtesy of Mr. Darko Curić, Vice President of the Notary Chamber of Montenegro.

(marital contract, but also other contracts that spouses can conclude between themselves, such as a donation contract or a contract on the partition of a common property) the choice of law is restricted to the legally prescribed options. The PIL Act in its Article 82 also provides for the possibility of selecting the applicable law. The choice of law is limited to one of the following options: the law of a country whose citizenship has one of the spouses, or the law of a country whose habitual residence has one of the spouses, or the law of the country in which they intend to establish a common habitual residence, or for immovable property, the law of a place where this property is situated. The choice of law should be made before or after marriage, in writing, and the spouses can change or revoke it. If the choice of law is made after the marriage has been concluded, it begins to produce an effect from the moment of marriage, except as otherwise agreed by the parties.[347]

II. Relationship to Succession Law

503. Division of common property of the spouses may be sought during marriage and after its dissolution. Not only the spouses have the right to seek a division of common property, but also the heirs of a deceased spouse (LF, Article 295). When one of the spouses dies, apart from the right to inherit, the living spouse has the right to determine the extent of his share of matrimonial property, which then stands out and is not subject of the succession. If, in the procedure relating to succession matters, as a matter of dispute, the issue of matrimonial property arises, the procedure relating to succession matters will be stayed and the interested party will be directed to the litigation for ascertaining of the matrimonial property.

504. If the deceased was married, the authorities dealing with a given succession (court, notary) should first determine the law applicable to the matrimonial property regime. When the settlement of the estate takes place in Montenegro, the conflict rules of this country will in fact decide which law applies to the matrimonial property regime.

§4. Registered Partnership: Partnership/Civil Unions

505. Montenegro decriminalized same-sex sexual activity in 1977. Same-sex couples who live together openly in Montenegro are still rare but their legal status has started to be regulated by the Law on Same-Sex Life Partnership (LSSLP).[348] The first life partnership was concluded in July 2021, in touristic resort Budva between two young women, originally from the Balkans, who live and work abroad.[349] However, it is still necessary to harmonize more than 20 laws with the said law. Regarding amendments to the PIL Act, it is proposed that the conflict rule

347. Article 82 of the PIL Act.
348. Podgorica, Službeni list Crne Gore No. 67/2020.
349. https://www.slobodnaevropa.org/a/budva-istopolno-partnerstvo-crna-gora/31376219.html (accessed 14 Apr. 2022)

for same-sex partners be the common habitual residence of the partner, and that the subsidiary conflict rule be the right of joint citizenship. The adoption of this solution avoids examining whether the state of which the citizens are partners knows the registered partnership in its legislation.[350] The Law on Same-Sex Life Partnership regulates the community of two persons of the same sex on the basis of which they are granted part of the rights of the marital community: the right to health insurance under the partnership, the maintenance right of a partner, the right to inherit property. The law does not recognize life partners as a family, but only 'as a community of two persons of the same sex'. Life partners will neither be able to adopt, nor be caregivers or foster parents, while the rights of one partner regarding the child of the other partner encompass only decision-making on daily issues such as taking a child to a doctor, to a school and so forth.

I. Personal Effects

506. The PIL Act does not stipulate a conflict rule for personal effects of Registered Partnership (Partnership/Civil Unions), so in our view, the conflict rule on non-marital cohabitation from Article 84 should be applied. However, one must bear in mind that this provision regulates only property effects of that union in a way that it stipulates the application of the conflict rules on property effects of marriage by analogy (Articles 81–83). It should not be an impediment to its application as generally, PIL Act provides for the same conflict rules for both personal and property relations of marital spouses (except for the contractual property relations). To the maintenance which is in Law on Life Partnership regulated under the personal rights of partners should be, accordingly, applied conflict rule for marital spouses (Article 92).

507. The current best practices, in relation to new legislation encompass primarily the 2021 amendments to the Law on Pension and Disability Insurance[351] and the Law on Compulsory Health Insurance[352] so that the right to a survivor's pension may be exercised by the life partner of the deceased insured, i.e., a pension beneficiary who has entered into a life partnership with a person of the same sex, in accordance with the LSSLP.[353] In addition, the right to a survivor's pension can be exercised by the children of these persons. Furthermore, same-sex partners are equated with marital spouses in terms of rights and obligations in the health insurance system, as well as in terms of social and child protection rights.

350. Tomić, M. Zakon o životnom partnerstvu lica istog pola – korak naprijed ka evropskom javnom poretku (Law on Life Partnership of Sane Sex Persons – a step forward to European public policy), Podgorica: Pravni zbornik, No. 1/2021, 204.

351. Article 43a of the Law on Pensions and Disability Insurance, Podgorica, Službeni list Crne Gore Nos. 54/2003, 39/2004, 79/2004, 47/2007, 79/2008, 14/2010, 78/2010, 34/2011, 66/2012, 38/2013, 61/2013, 60/2014, 10/2015, 42/2016, 55/2016, 80/2020 and 145/2021.

352. Article 9(2) of the Law on Compulsory Health Insurance, Podgorica, Službeni list Crne Gore No. 145/2021.

353. The application of this law has started on 15 July 2021.

508. Registered partnership (partnership, civil union) based on the law of another country still does not produce a legal effect in Montenegro. Any contract that registered partners may enter into between themselves would probably be treated as an ordinary contract rather than a family law contract by domestic judiciary, and the applicable law would be determined accordingly, by means of relevant conflict rules for contracts.

II. Dissolution

509. The PIL Code does not contain any provisions on the dissolution of a registered partnership (partnership or civil union). Having in mind that the LSSLP explicitly stipulates that the provisions of the law governing family relations – LF shall accordingly apply to disputes concerning the annulment and termination of a partnership (Article 31), it is reasonable to suggest that accordingly the conflict rules on annulment and divorce of the PIL Act (Article 79 and 85) should be applied on PIL relations. If that is the case, in spite of cascade rules, the outcome would in most cases be the application of the Montenegrin substantive law. However, it is controversial whether partners could benefit from the choice of law for the divorce (Article 86), as it could make things more complicated especially bearing in mind that according to the LSSLP the partners cannot agree on the application of the law of another state to their property relations (Article 64) as this provision may be considered as an overriding mandatory rule.

III. Property

510. The PIL Code does not contain any provisions on the property of a registered partnership (partnership or civil union). According to the LSSLP, the partners cannot agree on the application of the law of another state to their property relations (Article 64) and this provision may be considered as an overriding mandatory rule. As a result, only Montenegrin law can govern property relations of the same-sex registered partners if the partnership is established under the LSSLP.

§5. Extramarital Cohabitation

I. Personal Effects

511. Extramarital cohabitation is regulated by substantive provisions of LF. If certain conditions are met, extramarital cohabitation produces legal effects of a pecuniary character. These effects are the mutual obligation to pay maintenance and the creation of the system of community property. Cohabitation has to last longer (three years) and there have to be no impediments to enter into a valid marriage at the time when the cohabitation started as preconditions for exercising those rights.

512. Montenegrin law does not equate this community with marriage, yet it gives priority to marriage. The law of Montenegro, both substantive and conflict rules, traditionally regulates in detail only the property effects of the extramarital cohabitation: property relations and maintenance obligation after the dissolution of this community, and not the personal effects of this community.

513. The PIL Act does not provide a special conflict rule regarding the parent-child relations stemming from extramarital cohabitation. As equality of children born out of the wedlock with the children born in the wedlock is one of the main principles of Montenegrin family law these relations shall be governed by the general rules that apply to parent-child relationship. The applicable law shall be the law of the country in which the child has habitual residence or the law of the child's citizenship, if it is more favourable to the child (PIL Act, Article 88). Similarly, neither the PIL Act nor the LCP[354] contains an explicit provision on jurisdiction for these matters. Montenegrin judicial or other authority shall have jurisdiction in respect of decisions on the care, raising and upbringing of children who have parental care in addition to the defendant's domicile, which is the basis for general jurisdiction, if the child is a Montenegrin citizen or has habitual residence in Montenegro, as well as if the child needs protection (PIL Act, Article 132).

II. Dissolution

514. LF does not regulate the creation and the dissolution of an extramarital cohabitation. The effects of dissolution of an extramarital cohabitation which produce legal obligation relate to the obligation of maintenance, which is treated as a personal-property right. LF regulates this issue in detail (Articles 266(1), 268, 270).

III. Property

515. LF defines an extramarital cohabitation as a lifelong relationship between a man and a woman of at least three years (or shorter if a child was born, or if it was converted to marriage) and is equated with the marital community in terms of the right to mutual maintenance and other property-legal relations (Article 12). The substantive law of Montenegro for the extramarital cohabitation, as well as for the marital community, envisages the community of assets. Property acquired through the work of a person in an extramarital cohabitation that lasts for a longer time is considered as their common property (LF, Article 306).

516. The conflict rules in relation to the property effects equal an extramarital cohabitation with a foreign element with the effects of marriage with a foreign element. Thus, the same conflict rules that apply to the property relations of the spouses also apply to extramarital cohabitation.

354. For this category of disputes the LCP does not provide explicit provision on territorial jurisdiction of the domestic court pursuant to Art. 29.

517. The Supreme Court of Montenegro, by applying Article 39 of the LRCL and the substantive law of the Republic of Serbia in the case of 2016,[355] decided on the property claim of the person who claimed to have lived in an extramarital cohabitation with a man who was not formally divorced. In the reasoning, the court states:

Since at the time of the establishment of the extra-marital cohabitation the defendant was married, the real estate that the defendant was able to dispose of cannot be regarded as their common property, and the claim was properly rejected as unfounded.

It is not of any importance for a different decision the statement of the claimant that the community of life between the defendant and his ex-wife ended in 1999. It is true that the property acquired by spouses after the dissolution of the community of life constitutes their separate property … Property relations of persons living in an extra-marital cohabitation enjoys legal protection only if they were able to marry, which is not the case in this dispute since the defendant was already married.

It is also of no importance that the claimant and defendant concluded a contract on the regulation of property relations dated September 1 1999 because this contract cannot change the statutory regime in regard to which extra-marital cohabitation produces legal effects of a mandatory character.

In the above case, the substantive law of both Montenegro and the Republic of Serbia envisages the same legal impediment for the establishment of the extramarital cohabitation. Otherwise, characterization of extramarital cohabitation would be made pursuant to the *lex fori*. This means that domestic authorities will apply the standards prevailing in the domestic law to resolve the question whether a certain extramarital relationship represents an extramarital cohabitation on the basis of which, for instance, one may seek partition of the common property.

518. In a more recent case[356] the plaintiff filed a lawsuit seeking to determine her right to co-ownership of the disputed real estate on the basis of the acquisition in the extramarital cohabitation. The plaintiff proposed to the court to stay the civil proceedings pending until the termination of civil proceedings between the same parties and on the same matter before the court in Serbia.[357] The first instance court[358] rejected the plaintiff's motion to stay the proceedings in this legal matter, finding that the conditions for staying of the proceedings were not fulfilled in accordance with the provisions of Article 114 of the PIL Act[359] due to the fact that the subject of the dispute, as the trial court states, is no longer the determination of the property right over the real property in question, but compensation for the damage,

355. Judgment of the Supreme Court of Montenegro, Rev 436/2016 (2), Podgorica, 26 May 2016.
356. Higher Court in Podgorica Gž.br.2980/17-09 of 21.11.2017.
357. Higher Court in Belgrade, Serbia P. br.26/15.
358. Basic Court in Podgorica P. br.3170/13 of 30.12.2013.
359. Pursuant to Article 114 of the PIL Act a court of Montenegro shall stay the proceedings at the request of a party when an action involving the same cause and the same parties is pending before a foreign court, provided that: the action in that matter was first brought before the foreign court; it is an action which is not under exclusive jurisdiction of a Montenegrin court; it is may be reasonably expected that the foreign court decision will be amenable to recognition and enforcement in Montenegro.

as requested by the plaintiff's submission dated 13 January 2016 in which he reversed the claim in this legal matter. The Higher Court in Podgorica stated as the first instance court did not decide on the modification of the claim, its reasoning that the subject matter of this dispute was no longer determining the ownership of the disputed real estate could not be accepted. Therefore, it is the duty of the trial court to decide, first and foremost, in the retrial, on the reversal of the claim and then on the plaintiffs' motion to stay this procedure.

519. A partner from a recognized extramarital cohabitation is equated with their spouse in relation to succession (LS, Article 9). He/she is also entitled to compensation for non-pecuniary damages in the case of death or serious disability if he/she has been in a recognized extra-marital cohabitation with the deceased or injured (LO, Article 210b(4)). Unmarried spouses have the right under the same conditions as spouses to treat infertility using Assisted Reproductive Technologies procedures.[360] The Montenegrin substantive law recognizes the right to a pension after death of a partner if the extramarital union lasted for at least the last three years before the death of the insured or beneficiary, or if child was born in that extramarital union.[361]

§6. Maintenance Law

520. Out of a number of international conventions dealing with the maintenance with a foreign element[362] Montenegro is a party to the Hague Convention on the International Recovery of Child Support and Other Forms of Family Maintenance (2007). This convention supersedes the New York Convention on the Recovery Abroad of Maintenance (1956) to the extent that the scope of application of these Conventions coincides. The aforementioned Hague Convention does not contain rules on applicable law, but as instrument of international legal assistance facilitates and accelerates implementation of maintenance obligation.

521. In the domain of applicable law, the most important instrument on the international level is the Hague Protocol on the Law Applicable to Maintenance Obligations of 2007. Montenegro has not ratified the protocol but has imported its main provisions into the PIL Act whose provision on the scope of the applicable law (Article 97) is identical to Article 11 of the Hague Protocol. This may be of particular importance in relation to the maintenance matters connected not only with the EU countries but also with Serbia, which ratified the Hague Protocol even before the PIL Act was adopted.

522. The PIL Act applies to maintenance obligation with international element (Articles 90–98) and those provisions literally mirror the relevant provisions of the Hague Protocol (Articles 3–8 and 10–11). The law establishes common provisions

360. The Law on Medically Assisted Fertilization Podgorica, Službeni list Crne Gore No. 145/21.
361. Article 43 of the Law on Pension and Disability Insurance.
362. *See* https://www.hcch.net/en/instruments/conventions (accessed 14 Apr. 2022).

on the law applicable to maintenance obligations arising from a family relationship, marriage, parentage or affinity, including the obligation to support the child, regardless of the marital status of his or her parents. Thus, the Montenegrin law, in the same manner as the Hague Protocol establishes a complex system of conflict rules on maintenance containing the general rule providing for the law of the country of habitual residence of the creditor as applicable law. However, the PIL Act also stipulates special rules favouring certain creditors in case of maintenance obligation of parents towards their children, of persons other than parents towards the persons who have not turned 21 ((claims based on a direct or collateral relationship (e.g., a claim made by a grandchild, sister or brother, nephew or niece) or affinity (e.g., a child towards his or her parent's spouse)),[363] and of children towards their parents (Article 91 of the PIL Act). The aim of these special rules is to provide additional opportunities for protecting these categories of creditors. The characteristic of these rules is that they are taking into account the substantive content of the applicable law and provide for the application of law that is more favourable to the party when, by rule which should be applied, a person cannot obtain maintenance.

523. The first advantage envisaged for the benefit of these categories of creditors is the application of the law of the State of the court before which the proceedings were initiated in cases where the creditor cannot obtain maintenance based on the law of the country of his habitual residence. The *lex fori* should also apply when the creditor has initiated proceedings before the competent authority of the country of the habitual residence of the debtor. However, if under this law, the creditor cannot obtain maintenance, the law of the habitual residence of the creditor will be applied. Another advantage occurs if the creditor cannot obtain maintenance from the debtor, either under the law of the country of his habitual residence, either under the law of the court, and then the law of the country of their joint nationality shall apply, provided that persons have the same nationality.

524. The PIL Act (Article 95) also mirrors Hague Protocol's Article 8 thus providing for the possibility of limited choice of law for the maintenance obligation. The maintenance creditor and debtor may at any time choose between the listed laws closely connected to the case: the law of a State of nationality or habitual residence of either party at the time of choice of law; the law that applies to their property regime or their divorce or legal separation, either on the basis of their choice of law or de facto.

525. In Montenegrin law the decision on the obligation to provide maintenance is made by the court, at the request of the person who needs maintenance. However, in marital disputes on the upbringing of children, the court ex officio decides on child support. According to LF, maintenance is awarded in money, and otherwise it can be determined if the creditor and the debtor agree on it.

---

363. Andrea Bonomi, *Explanatory Report on the Hague Protocol of 23 November 2007 on the Law Applicable to Maintenance Obligations*, The Hague Conference on Private International Law: 2013, 5, available at: https://assets.hcch.net/docs/9975314d-3097-41e3-91b8-f5913d14ffb7.pdf (accessed 14 Apr. 2022).

I. Spousal Maintenance

526. The PIL Act stipulates as the basic connecting factor for maintenance obligations the law of the country of habitual residence of the creditor. The advantage of this connection in comparison with citizenship is that it allows the decision on the existence and amount of the obligation to be determined on the basis of the social environment of the country where the creditor lives. This connecting factor also allows for equal treatment among creditors living in the same country, regardless of their citizenship. In the event of a change in the habitual residence of the creditor, the law of the country of a new habitual residence shall apply *pro futuro*. Claims of the creditor from the period before the change remain the subject of the law of the previous habitual residence.

527. In the case of the obligation to provide support between spouses, ex-spouses or parties in marriage that has been annulled, the general rule shall not apply provided that one of the parties opposes it, and the law of another country, in particular the law of the last common habitual residence, is in closer connection with marriage. In this case, the law of the country with which the closest connection exists shall apply. The PIL Act, modelled on the Hague Protocol, provides this peculiar exception clause.

528. The PIL Act introduces limited choice of law, so for the first time in the positive PIL of Montenegro there is an option of choosing the applicable law to maintenance obligations. The choice of law rules are contained in two separate articles. Article 94 of the PIL Act applies only to the needs of a particular procedure, while Article 95 refers to the choice of law in any other case. In the first case, the parties can explicitly choose as the applicable law for the maintenance obligation the law of the country in which the proceedings are conducted. The agreement designating applicable law made before a procedure is instituted must be in writing and signed by both parties or recorded on another medium. In the second case, a limited party autonomy is envisaged, and the creditor and the debtor of maintenance can, at any time, choose as relevant for the maintenance obligation, one of the following laws: the law of any State of which either party is a citizen at the time of the choice; the law of the State of habitual residence of either party at the time of the choice; the law that they select as applicable, or the law actually applied to their property relations; the law that they select as applicable, or the law actually applied to their divorce or separation. The PIL Act stipulates that the agreement must be in written form and signed by both parties or recorded on some other medium.

529. The same article also provides specific rules aimed at protecting a certain category of persons. It is not allowed to choose the law for the maintenance obligation of a person under the age of 18 or an adult who, because of personal incapacity or inability, is not able to protect their interests. A rule is also established that, regardless of the possibility of choice of law, issue of whether a maintenance creditor may waive his right to maintenance shall be governed by the law of the State in which maintenance creditor has habitual residence at the time of the choice.

II. Partnership Maintenance

530. For the time being Montenegro does not recognize partnership maintenance with or without international element.

III. Maintenance of Cohabitees

531. The substantive law of Montenegro regulates in detail the maintenance of the extramarital partner,[364] as a result of termination of an extramarital cohabitation recognized by the law. The conditions for obtaining maintenance are the same as required for the maintenance of the spouse. Also, the precondition is that the extramarital cohabitation has ceased, because domestic law does not acknowledge the alimony right as long as that community exists. The Montenegrin conflict rules on maintenance obligation mirror the conflict rules of the Hague Protocol. Neither of them defines family relations nor explicitly stipulates maintenance of cohabitees. However, right to maintenance from an extramarital cohabitant falls within the definition of a 'family relationship' from Article 1 of the Hague Protocol. Similarly, LF addresses mutual maintenance of family members in a very general way, but extramarital partners are explicitly listed as family members (Article 10). Therefore, the PIL Act's conflict rules provisions establishing general rule (Article 90), as well as special rule with respect of spouses and ex-spouses (Article 92) and/or special rule on defence (Article 93 may be applicable to the maintenance of cohabitees (the last two by way of analogy).

§7. Child Law

532. Traditionally, in the substantive regulation of the relationship between parents and children, emphasis was placed on the duties (and rights) that parents have in relation to the personality and property of the child.[365] The manner of substantive regulation of these relations also influenced conflict of law rules. In modern times, when there are frequent cases where members of the same family have different citizenship, and sometimes also domicile or habitual residence, designation of the applicable law to their relations is gaining more attraction. The original idea that the personal law of a husband and a father should apply to all family members loses importance, and the same holds true for the more modern concept of the application of the personal law of both parents (and the child). Following the adoption of the 1989 Convention on the Rights of the Child, the best interests of the child principle plays a prominent role in PIL.

364. Articles. 266(1), 268 and 270 of the Law on Family.
365. Pursuant to Art. 69, para. 2 of the Law on Family, childcare includes: guarding, raising, educating, schooling, advocating, supporting and managing and disposing of a child's property.

533. The PIL Act follows the trend present in modern PIL, starting from the principle of the best interests of the child aiming at providing for alternative connecting factor that better suits the needs of the modern family. Pursuant to Article 88 of the PIL Act the parent-child relations shall be governed by the law of the State in which the child has habitual residence or the law of the State of the child's citizenship, depending on which one is more favourable to the child.[366]

I. Determination of Parenthood

534. The principle of the best interests of the child is also present in designating applicable law for the family status of the child. The PIL Act stipulates thoroughly the recognition, establishment or contestation of parentage providing for several connections which are all fixed in time. Pursuant to its Article 87(1) applicable law for these matters is the law of the State whose citizenship the child obtained at the time of birth. However, if the substantive law of the child's citizenship or habitual residence at the time his family status is determined or the law that at the time of birth applies to personal relations of the spouses is more favourable to the child, one of these laws shall prevail. Thus, the competent body should be well prepared to cope with possible several different national substantive family laws, in order to ascertain which law is the most favourable to the child. The effect of recognition and its form are regulated separately. Thus, in order that the recognition of the child produces effect it has to be done in compliance with: the law of the citizenship of a father/mother; or the actual citizenship of a child; or the actual habitual residence of the child (Article 87(2)). The applicable law for the form of recognition is the law of the State where the recognition has been exercised or the law applicable to the effect of recognition (Article 87(3)).

535. Earlier, the LRCL predicted that 'the law governing recognition, establishment or contesting parentage shall be the law of the State whose citizen was, at the time the child was born, the person whose paternity or maternity is recognized, established or contested' (Article 41).

II. Custody and Contact

536. The question of entrusting custody (care and bringing up) of a minor that has at least one living parent is governed by the law determined pursuant to Article 88 of the PIL Act (the law of the State of habitual residence or citizenship of the child, depending on which one is more favourable to the child). This provision determines the applicable law to the broader question of relations between parents and children, including the question of custody. It applies to custody of either legitimate or illegitimate children, custody of children after divorce and after the death

366. Article 88 of the PIL Act.

of a parent and custody in case of separation of parents during marriage.[367] Ascertaining of the law that is more favourable to the child necessarily implies a value judgment which will have to be made in accordance with the prevailing value system of the forum.[368] These connecting factors are aligned with the basis for international jurisdiction (Article 132 of the PIL Act).[369] Furthermore, a Montenegrin judicial or other authority shall also have jurisdiction when the child needs the protection. In this area, the following international conventions are also applicable:

– the 1996 Hague Convention on Jurisdiction, Applicable Law, Recognition, Enforcement and Co-operation in Respect of Parental Responsibility and Measures for the Protection of Children. Rights of custody and rights of access to children are of great importance when parents are separated and living in different countries. The term 'access' encompass the contacts at a distance which a parent is authorized to maintain with the child by correspondence, telephone or telefax.[370] In the domain of the applicable law, the Convention stipulates that the attribution, exercise or extinction of parental responsibility is governed by the law of the State of the child's habitual residence. It also regulates situations where a change in the habitual residence occurs.[371]
– the 1980 European Convention on Recognition and Enforcement of Decisions concerning Custody of Children and on Restoration of Custody of Children.

537. In practice,[372] courts in Montenegro pay considerable attention to international sources of law when deciding on the best interests of the child. In their decisions, the judges refer to the Convention on the Rights of the Child, as well as to the ECtHR's decisions. Thus, in one case the Higher Court in Podgorica[373] revoked the judgment of the Basic Court in Podgorica[374] and remanded the case to the trial court for retrial in a case on divorce, entrusting the exercise of parental rights, maintaining the father's personal relations with children, and the father's legal obligations on maintenance of minor children. The Higher Court stated that the first instance judgment was not guided by the best interests of the minor children of the litigants, as required by the provision of Article 3 of the Convention on the Rights of the Child, and that Article 12 of this Convention stating 'child will be given a

367. Kluwer Monograph on PIL of Montenegro of 2013, para. 404.
368. Mirko Živković, *Poveravanje dece na čuvanje i vaspitavanje u međunarodnom privatnom pravu* (Custody and Care of Minors in Private International Law), Niš: Institut za pravna i društvena istraživanja Pravnog fakulteta u Nišu, 1991, 90.
369. In addition, a Montenegrin judicial or other authority shall also have jurisdiction when the child needs the protection from such authority.
370. Explanatory Report by Paul Lagarde, para. 20, 547, https://assets.hcch.net/upload/expl34.pdf (accessed 14 Apr. 2022).
371. Article 16 pars. 3 and 4 and Art. 17 of the Convention.
372. Courtesy of Ms. Mirjana Popović, judge of the Higher Court in Podgorica and a member of the Consultative Council of European judges in respect of Montenegro who provided for the complete files to the author, the facts of these, as well as numerous other cases are now available to the public.
373. Higher Court in Podgorica, Gž.br. 5360/18 of 29.10.2018.
374. Basic Court in Podgorica P. br.1536/17 of 26.07.2018.

special opportunity to be heard in any judicial proceedings or administrative proceedings concerning the child, either directly or through a representative or appropriate body, in a manner consistent with the procedural rules of national law' should have been applied. Furthermore, the Higher Court in Podgorica[375] upheld the decision of the Basic Court in Podgorica[376] and the judgment of the same Court,[377] that it was necessary to conduct expert evaluation of a team of expert witnesses in order to give a proposal and opinion on the purposefulness of deprivation of parental right of the father, as well as a proposal on entrusting minor children. This reasoning is line with the practice of ECtHR as expressed in the judgment of that court *Sommerfeld v. Germany*[378] which emphasizes the need and necessity of engaging expert opinion in all situations when it is necessary to decide on a model of contacting a child with a parent with whom the child does not live.

III. Guardianship

538. LF does not provide an explicit answer to the question of whether a foreign national can be a guardian to a foreign or domestic person. In our view considering the content of this legal institute, in cases where a foreigner has a domicile in Montenegro, and if the conditions prescribed by law are met, the issue of foreign citizenship should not be an obstacle to the establishment of guardianship.

539. Article 16 of the PIL Act regulates the appointment of guardian, the relationship between the guardian and the ward, and the termination of guardianship by a single conflict rule. Placement under guardianship and termination of guardianship as well as relationships between a guardian and persons under guardianship shall be governed by the law of the State of which the person under guardianship is a citizen. The same article addresses provisional protection measures with respect to a foreign citizen or a stateless person present in Montenegro, or the protection of property of an absent foreign citizen and of a stateless person present in the territory of Montenegro. In both cases the governing law is the law of Montenegro and those measures last until the State whose judicial or other authority is competent has given a decision and taken necessary measures.

IV. Adoption

540. As a general rule, pursuant to LF, a citizen of Montenegro cannot be adopted by a foreign citizen. However, such adoption may, exceptionally, be allowed if adopters could not be found among domestic citizens. In that case a prior approval of adoption by the ministry in charge of social welfare is needed (Article 125).

375. Higher Court in Podgorica, Gž.br.3573/19 of 25.06.2019.
376. Basic Court in Podgorica P. br.6293/18 of 08.04.2019.
377. Basic Court in Podgorica P. br. 6293/18 of 08.04.2019.
378. ECtHR *Sommerfeld v. Germany*, No. 31871/96 of 8 Jul. 2003.

541. The PIL Act, for the conditions of establishment, effect and termination of the adoption of a child, starts from the law of the country of which the adopter is a citizen. If spouses jointly adopt a child, in order to avoid cumulation of laws, the law applicable to the personal relations of spouses applies. For the consent of the child, in addition to the citizenship law of the adopters, the citizenship of a child shall also be applied, and the form of adoption shall be governed by the law of the place where the adoption is established.[379]

542. Substantive law regulates in details the possibility that extramarital partners adopt a child (LF Articles 127, 132(2), 134). If the law of Montenegro is applicable child can be adopted even by partners living in an extramarital community, as well as by a partner of the parent of a child who is adopted if he/she lives with the child's parent in an extramarital community (Article 132(2)).

543. Earlier, according to the LRCL, various solutions were envisaged. The conditions for the establishment and termination of adoption were based on the cumulative application of the laws of citizenship of the adopter and adoptee, which in a situation when adopters are spouses who have different citizenship in relation to the adoptee could lead to ordinary cumulation of three laws. The form was governed by the law of the place where the adoption is established, and for the effects of adoption, the cascading application of one law was envisaged.[380]

544. Montenegro is also a party to the Hague Convention on Protection of Children and Co-operation in Respect of Intercountry Adoption of 1993, which does not contain conflict rules.[381]

V. Artificial Insemination, Surrogacy

545. The Law on Medically Assisted Fertilization (LMAF)[382] regulates the maternity and paternity in case of Medically Assisted Fertilization (MAF) procedure. Article 41 provides that the mother of the child that was conceived using MAF procedure is the woman that gave birth to the child. If the child has been conceived with a donated egg cell, the maternity of the woman that donated the egg cell cannot be searched. As for paternity, the husband of the mother is considered to be the father of a child conceived with MAF procedure, provided that the procedure was effectuated in conformity with the law. His paternity (whether he is a spouse or an extramarital cohabitant) may not be contested unless it is determined that the child was not conceived by the application of the MAF procedure and then the provisions

379. Article 89 of the PIL Act.

380. Articles 44 and 45 of the LRCL.

381. *See* Valerija Šaula, *Haška konferencija i međudržavno usvojenje*, u: *Državljanstvo i međunarodno privatno pravo; Haške konvencije*, urednici: G. Knežević, V. Pavić *(Serbian Private International Law at the time of transition: the changed significance of citizenship and residence,* In *Citizenship and International Private Law; The Hague Conventions),* G. Knežević, V. Pavić, eds., Belgrade: Univerzitet u Beogradu, Pravni fakultet, Službeni glasnik, 2007, 151–171.

382. Podgorica, Službeni list Crne Gore No. 145/2021.

of the law governing family relations and the law governing civil proceedings apply (Article 42). Finally, if the child was conceived with donated sperm cells, the donor has no rights or obligations towards the child conceived by the application of the MAF procedure and the child must not find out his identity (Article 40). In addition, LF (Article 118) regulates the contesting of legitimate paternity in case of 'artificial insemination'. According to this rule, the husband may contest paternity of the child born by his wife in the course of marriage or within 300 days from the date of dissolution of marriage, if the child was conceived without his consent by artificial insemination of the mother with another man's sperm. The claim can be filed within six months from the date of finding out about the circumstances that give the plaintiff a cause of action, but not after the child reaches the age of 5.

546. In contesting of legitimate and establishing of illegitimate paternity, the cited provisions of the Montenegrin statutes could be considered as overriding mandatory rules, while family status of the child is regulated by Article 87 of the PIL Act.

547. Although the LMAF allows the donation of gametes, it very strictly prohibits surrogacy in any form. Thus, the prohibition includes performing the MPO procedure for a surrogate mother, mediation, as well as advertising the offer and need for a surrogate mother, and concluding contracts or other legal transactions on the birth and transfer of a child to another person, both with and without compensation (Article 37). As these rules should be considered as overriding mandatory rules, consequently, the child could not legally enter in the Personal Registry.

VI. Child Support

548. The PIL Act mirrors relevant solutions of the Hague Protocol and envisages as the basic connecting factor for the maintenance obligations the law of the country where the creditor of the maintenance obligation has their habitual residence. In the case of a change in the habitual residence of the creditor, from the moment of the occurrence of that change, the law of the country of a new habitual residence shall apply. The governing law changes from the moment of changing the habitual residence, but only for the future. Claims of the creditor from the period before the change remain the subject of the law of the previous habitual residence.

549. The PIL Act also provides for specific rules to the advantage of certain maintenance creditors. Pursuant to Article 91 specific maintenance rules shall apply also to maintenance obligations of parents to their children. If the law of the habitual residence of the creditor does not grant him a right to maintenance, the maintenance obligation shall be governed by the law of the State in which the court before which the proceeding is initiated is located. Notwithstanding the general rule (habitual residence of the creditor) if the maintenance creditor initiated a procedure before the competent authority of the State in which the maintenance debtor has his habitual residence, the law of that State shall apply. If that law does not grant the creditor a right to maintenance, the law of the creditor's habitual residence shall govern the maintenance obligation. If neither of the listed laws grants the creditor a right to maintenance, the maintenance obligation shall be governed by the law of the State of their common citizenship, provided that such common citizenship exists.

550. Choice of applicable law is excluded for maintenance obligations over a minor (Article 95(3)).

551. The PIL Act provisions on scope of the law applicable to maintenance obligation as well as on setting the amount of maintenance mirror the relevant provisions of the Hague Protocol.[383]

VII. Child Abduction

552. Montenegro is a party to the Hague Convention on the Civil Aspects of International Child Abduction,[384] which is one of the most successful instruments adopted under the auspices of the Hague Conference on Private International Law. The scope of application of this Convention are the cases in which a child before the violation of the right to custody or visits, had a habitual residence[385] in a Contracting State, if it was taken or retained in a Contracting State by a parent who was not granted custody. The Convention does not apply when a child reaches 16 years of age. This Hague Convention does not deal with the applicable law, but provides international legal assistance to the Member States with a goal of an urgent return of children who have been unlawfully detained or held in any Contracting State, as well as respect in other Contracting States of the right to custody and the right of visits,[386] which are established in the Contracting State concerned. It is particularly important to provide the recognition of the effects of decisions of foreign courts and administrative bodies entrusted to the child care, without conducting a recognition procedure.[387]

383. *See* Arts 97 and 98 of the PIL Act and Arts 11 and 14 of the Hague Protocol.

384. For the implementation of this Convention in Montenegro *see* Maja Kostić-Mandić, *an on Application of the Hague Child Abduction Convention, Montenegro*, In *Private International Law in the Jurisprudence of European Courts: Family at Focus*, M. Župan ed., Osijek: Faculty of Law Osijek, 2015, 251–257.

385. *See also* Petar Đundić, *Redovno boravište deteta u praksi primene Haške konvencije o gra anskopravnim aspektima međunarodne otmice dece od 25. oktobra 1980. godine* (The Habitual Residence of a Child in the Practice of Applying the Hague Child Abduction Convention of 25 October 1980), Zbornik radova Pravnog fakulteta u Novom Sadu, No. 2/2004, 551–570; Beaumont, Holliday, *Recent Developments on the Meaning of 'Habitual Residence' in Alleged Child Abduction Cases*, In *Private International Law in the Jurisprudence of European Courts – Family at Focus*, M. Župan ed., Osijek: Faculty of Law Osijek, 2015, 39–58.

386. *See* Maja Stanivuković, Petar Đundić, *Pravo na viđanje deteta i Haška konvencija o gra anskopravnim aspektima međunarodne otmice deteta (1980)* (Access Rights and the Hague Convention of 25 October 1980 on the Civil Aspects of International Child Abduction), Pravni život, No. 10/2010, 25–45.

387. Article 14 of the Child Abduction Convention.

553. However, the application of this Convention in Montenegro has its own specificities. Ministry of Justice as a Central Authority for Hague Child Abduction Convention in its work basically does not comply with Article 7 of the Convention, limiting its actions only to:

- forwarding applications for return or rights of access to a Central Authority of a country were the child is situated after the abduction or retention;
- providing for information of a general character;
- forwarding applications obtained from a foreign central authority to the competent courts in Montenegro which are seized with the respective cases, which will be addressed in more detail.

554. Once when Ministry of Justice as a Central Authority forwards application to the competent court it communicates with the police in order to access the information on the whereabouts of the child. In order to deter the removal or re-abduction of the child the court may order (e.g., child's passport(s) to be deposited with authorities; alleged abductor's passport to be deposited with authorities; obtain orders to prevent the removal of the child).

555. The child has an opportunity to be heard in return proceedings in Montenegro through the administrative organ Center for Social Welfare in every case. All basic courts in Montenegro may comply with applications under the Convention. The procedure before the court can be slow (it takes time to locate a child, timeframes from LESC have to be complied with, appeal procedure takes up to three months, and forced enforcement can sometimes take up to several years). In general, the expected time from the commencement of the proceedings for return to a final order (excluding appeals) is up to six weeks.

556. The applicant is generally not required to participate in the return proceedings, but it is the common case in practice (via telephone, through a legal representative). Judicial or administrative authorities take provisional or interim measures to enable an applicant to exercise contact or access in respect of the child while return proceedings are pending.

557. Mediation and conciliation are becoming an important tool in those procedures in Montenegro. There is general piece of legislation relating to mediation[388] which also applies to mediation in family matters. Mediated agreements in family disputes involving children are immediately enforceable without any additional formalities being required. Mediation and conciliation mechanisms have a positive impact on the length of proceedings since the forced execution procedure may take years (such as ECtHR case *Mijusković v. Montenegro*[389] – child abduction case in a national context).

388. Law on Alternative Dispute Resolution, Podgorica, Službeni list Crne Gore No. 77/2020.
389. Application No. 49337/07.

558. An overview of two cases[390] of international child abduction, which were adjudicated by the courts of Montenegro will show different approaches in obtaining the final goal. In both cases, that took place shortly one after another, a father, a citizen of Montenegro unlawfully took a minor child, Swiss citizen in Montenegro, without the consent of the mother, the Swiss national. However, the second case benefited from mediation.

559. In the first case, the father of the child before the Basic Court in Podgorica started divorce proceedings, which was stayed due to the lis pendens (Swiss court issued a ruling in the proceedings for divorce on 5 May 1999). The wife has initiated proceedings for recognition of foreign court decisions (two final court orders of the Civil Division of the Court in Solothurn – Lebern entrusting the custody of the minor daughter to her mother and ordering the father to return daughter to the mother, as well as the judgment[391] laying divorce and awarding child custody to the mother and regulating the obligation of support. The appeal proceedings against the decision on the recognition of the above decision included revision before the Supreme Court of Montenegro. The procedure for execution ended by a decision which ordered the father of a child to return it to the mother. The attempt of alternative dispute resolution (handing the child to the mother without carrying out mandatory execution, with a proposal on the conclusion of agreements on access with the child's father) failed. Meanwhile, in the criminal proceedings before the Basic Court in Podgorica husband was convicted of a criminal offence 'Revocation of the minor' under the Criminal Code of Montenegro and sentenced to a suspended sentence. Finally, after thirteen attempts of mandatory execution, after two and a half years the child was returned to her mother.

560. In the second case, the marriage between a Swiss citizen and a Montenegrin citizen with a permanent residence in Switzerland was divorced by the judgment of the District Court Pfaffikom, Switzerland[392] and a custody of a minor child was awarded to the mother. The same judgment provided for the manner of exercising rights of access. The father acted in compliance with the court's decision for the following three years. During one of the arranged visits, the father removed the child to Montenegro without the consent of the mother, with the intention to permanently retain him there. The Swiss decision granting the custody to the mother is then recognized as enforceable judgment in the former Yugoslavia (FRY) by the District Court in Pančevo.[393] The wife has applied for the child's return under the Hague Child Abduction Convention. Swiss Federal Departments of Justice and Police ordered the Swiss Embassy in Belgrade to forward the request to the Ministry of Justice of the Montenegrin Government. Basic Court in Herceg Novi delivered a judgment that the father is guilty of a criminal offence – 'Revocation of the

390. Courtesy of Attorney at Law Vanja Mugoša, from the Law Office 'Jovović, Mugoša & Vuković' who provided for the complete files to the author, the facts of two case where the Convention applied are now available to the public.
391. Judgment of the Municipal Court Solothurn – Lebern of 5 May 1999.
392. U.1/CE960121 of 3 Dec. 1996.
393. R. br.10/97 of 17 Mar. 1997.

minor' of the Criminal Code of Montenegro and sentenced him to a suspended sentence. At the Center for Social Welfare Municipality of Herceg Novi, the procedure for arranging contacts between the mother, who came to Montenegro and son for the duration of the execution procedure was started. The Basic Court in Herceg Novi in several occasions decided on requests for provisional measures (the requests were submitted both by the mother or the father). One of the rulings complied with the proposal of the seizure of child's passport (and not the father's passport) while another temporary relief was issued regarding protection and placement of the minor child, which prohibits the child's mother to leave Montenegro with her son before the termination of the litigation, initiated by the father before the same court demanding modifying of the decision on custody. However, the procedure regarding custody never came to an end because the father willingly returned the child and the parents amicably arranged their relations – for the sake of their son who during the situation suffered from severe psychological problems.

561. The recent practice[394] in the application of the Convention shows that judges are increasingly aware of the mechanism and provisions of the Convention. Thus, in a case from 2018, the Basic Court in Ulcinj stated that there was no basis for a decision on the urgent return of the child within the meaning of Article 1 of the Convention as the court could not determine that the minor child was actually present in Montenegro.[395]

562. In a case from 2019[396] the Basic Court in Podgorica issued a decision refusing the application to return minor children to Germany as unfounded. The Court argues that in a proceeding on a request for the return of children under the Convention, the court is limited to determining whether there has been a wrongful removal or detention of a child and possibly any exceptions to the return of children under Article 13 so therefore the petition should be the subject of an assessment by the court deciding on the exercise of parental rights in proceedings before the Basic Court in Kolašin.

563. And, surely the most interesting is a case from 2014. The father of the minor child has filed the application, through the US central authority, for the return of the minor child to the US on the ground that removal and retention of the child are wrongful under Article 3 of the Convention. His application was accompanied by the court decisions on custody. The court also ruled that the mother wrongfully removed and retained the child.[397] Mother did not dispute that she brought the minor

394. Courtesy of Mr. Ibrahim Smailović, ex Director General, Directorate for Civil Litigation and Supervision, Ministry of Justices of Montenegro who provided for the complete files to the author, the facts of the cases are now available to the public.
395. Basic Court in Ulcinj Rs. Br. 43/17, 23.01.2018.
396. Basic Court in Podgorica Rs 200/18 of 22.03.2019.
397. According to the decision of the Basic Court - Divisions of the Essex County Divisional and Family Court no. 12W1029WD from 31.08.2012 the parties have joint custody of the minor child and the removal and retention of the minor child by the mother was wrongful. The subsequent judgment of the same court no. 12W1029WD from 14.11.2013 granted sole legal and physical custody of a child to the father.

child to Montenegro without the consent of the child's father but argued that his consent was not required in the first place since the State of Massachusetts does not recognize extramarital cohabitation. She argued that although the applicant was loving and caring father, the 2-year-old child was not safe when the father was looking after her and she was at work as he suffered from post-traumatic stress due to his involvement in the war and his misusing of the alcohol; that he refused to be treated; that she reported him several times to the US police when he was verbally aggressive towards her, each time that he was intoxicated. The child's father refused to provide medical records.

The first instance court based its decision[398] on ECHR instead of the Hague Abduction Convention. In the court's view, the return of a minor child to the US would not be in the best interest of the child and would constitute a violation of Article 8 of the ECHR over the mother and the minor daughter. In the court's view, the deciding factor in this legal matter is the time and integration of the minor child in the new environment, since more than three years have elapsed since the moment of bringing the minor child to Montenegro until the decision is made, and the Court referred to the case law of the ECtHR *Neulinger & Shuruk v. Switzerland and Raban v. Romania*.[399] However, the Higher Court in Podgorica revoked this decision and referred the case back to the Court of First Instance for retrial.[400] The Higher Court points out that before reaching a decision on the best interest of the child the Basic Court has to establish whether the removal of a child was wrongful under Article 3. That is a preliminary issue for deciding on the urgent return of a child under Article 12 of the Convention when the Court must also take into account exceptions to Article 13 paragraph 1 point b of the Convention in order to protect the best interest of the child.

§8. PROTECTION OF ADULTS

564. Montenegro is not a party to the 2000 Hague Convention on the International Protection of Adults. PIL of Montenegro in the field of conflict of laws for the protection of adults traditionally adheres to the same rule. Pursuant to Article 16 of the PIL Act, provisional protection measures with respect to a foreign national or a stateless person present in Montenegro are governed by the law of Montenegro and last until the State whose judicial or other authority is competent has given a decision and taken necessary measures. The same rule applies to the protection of property of an absent foreigner and of a stateless person present in the territory of Montenegro.

565. However, placement under guardianship and termination of guardianship as well as relationships between a guardian and persons under guardianship shall be governed by the law of the State of which the person under guardianship is a citizen.

398. The Basic Court in Podgorica Rs.br. 247/14 of 06.07.2015.

399. ECtHR *Neulinger & Shuruk v. Switzerland*, Application No. 41615/07 and *Raban v. Romania* Application No. 25437/08.

400. The Higher Court in Podgorica Gž. Br. 3233/14 of 21. 10. 2014.

Chapter 6. Succession Law

566. In Montenegro, the *lex nationalis* used to be a traditional conflict rule for succession. The LRCL submitted succession and the testator's capacity to make a Will to the national law of the deceased (Article 30). The citizenship of a deceased was fixed to the moment of his death/of making the Will, respectively. In modern times, the habitual residence became the most important objective connecting factor for succession especially in the conventional and EU law, as well as in some national legislations. The primary goal of the Montenegrin PIL Act in following this trend was to harmonize its legislation with the EU law in the course of EU integration process. Nevertheless, the new rules have a special value since now it is possible to apply the same law to members of an international family (persons with different citizenships living in the same country). The PIL Act abandons the LRCL legal tradition and adopts completely new rules. In addition to introducing the last habitual residence of the deceased, it provides for the choice of the applicable law. A provision on an estate without a claimant is also envisaged (the law of the State where the succession property is located) and the provision on the field of application is introduced,[401] which were modelled after the rules of the Succession Regulation.

567. The main legal source for succession matters is the PIL Act. Furthermore, Montenegro has ratified two multilateral conventions concerning the form of testamentary dispositions: the Hague Convention on the Conflicts of laws relating to the Form of Testamentary Dispositions and Convention providing a Uniform Law on the Form of an International Will (the provisions of the second convention are, as required by the Convention, directly transposed into LS).[402] A commitment to an international form of testament ensures that, in the States parties to this convention, the testament will be considered valid as to the form, irrespective of the applicable law.

568. Provisions on the applicable law of the PIL Act are to a large extent inspired by the Succession Regulation, but the Code does not contain a provision, as it is a case for contractual and non-contractual obligations, that domestic authorities shall interpret and apply the provisions of the PIL Act in accordance with EU law. Nevertheless, it is expected that the new rules will contribute to the better enforcement of law and timely capacity building of judiciary.

569. The right of foreigners to inherit property situated in Montenegro is regulated by LS and the Law on Ownership Relations. Although both laws were passed in the course of two months their provisions on succession of immovables contradict. Thus, the Law on Ownership Relations provides in Article 414 that a foreign natural person may acquire ownership of immovables situated in Montenegro on the basis of succession in the same manner as Montenegrin nationals while the LS contains a provision according to which foreign heirs in Montenegro have the same

401. Article 76 of the PIL Act.
402. Articles 74–87 of the LS.

position as heirs who are domestic nationals (the provision is addressing both, immovables and movables) but under the condition of reciprocity, unless otherwise provided by an international treaty (Article 5). Moreover, pursuant to LS there is a presumption of reciprocity, so the burden of proof is on the person having legal interest. In order to prevent this kind of conflict of laws Article 5 of LS should be amended and the reciprocity condition deleted.

570. The rights of foreigners to inherit property in Montenegro are guaranteed by provisions of certain bilateral treaties. Most of them grant national treatment to nationals of the other Contracting Party with respect to succession to movable and immovable property alike.[403]

§1. *Lex Successionis*

571. Pursuant to the PIL Act, the general rule for succession is that the law of the habitual residence of the deceased at the time of his death will apply to the succession as a whole (Article 71). The PIL Act does not contain a specific definition of the habitual residence for succession, but the general definition from Article 12 of the Code applies. The habitual residence is determined on the basis of an assessment of the life circumstances of the deceased during the last years of his life and at the time of death, taking into account all relevant facts, and in particular the duration and permanence of the presence of the deceased in the country concerned, as well as the conditions of stay and reasons for that presence.[404] The established habitual residence should have a close and stable relationship with the country concerned. The decisive reason for making habitual residence a decisive connecting factor was to achieve legal certainty – since the applicable law can be determined in advance and there is a close relationship with that law. In addition, in order to avoid mobile conflict of laws, relevant is the habitual residence at the time of the death of the deceased. Also, in the interests of legal certainty, the applicable law relates to the succession as a whole, regardless of the type and location of assets. The question arises: How do you determine a habitual residence when deceased for professional or economic reasons, lived abroad for many years, but retained a close and stable relationship with country of origin?[405] In such a case, it could still be deemed, depending on the circumstances of a particular case that the deceased had had his habitual residence in his country of origin in which was the centre of his family's interest and his social life. Other complex cases can occur if the deceased lived in several countries alternately or if he travelled from one State to another without having permanently settled in any of them. If the deceased was a citizen of

403. *See,* e.g., bilateral treaties on judicial assistance with Austria (Art. 29, para. 2), Bulgaria (Art. 19, para. 2), Czech Republic (Art. 35, para. 1), Hungary (Art. 40, para. 1), Poland (Art. 35, para. 2), Romania (Art. 34, para. 1).

404. *See* Recitals 23, 24, 37 and 38 of the Succession Regulation.

405. Recital 24 of the Succession Regulation.

one of those States or if he had all his main property in one of these States, the citizenship or place of that property could be a significant factor in the overall assessment of all factual circumstances.

572. The General rule – the last habitual residence of the deceased is applied to the succession as a whole. However, this rule should be seen in the light of the PIL Act's rule of jurisdiction for succession according to the place of location of the assets and the rules on the choice of jurisdiction.[406] Furthermore, the general rule applies only if the party autonomy is not exercised or some of the general institutes of PIL have been applied (such as escape clause) which would lead to the application of some other law.

§2. Scope of Application

573. Regarding its scope of application, the PIL Act mirrors Article 23(2) of the Succession Regulation. Some minor differences, which derive from the national style of drafting legal norms, do not prejudice the preceding paragraph.[407] Furthermore, pursuant to Article 76(4) of the PIL Act the law applicable to succession also governs the particular causes of the incapacity to dispose or receive, which is not explicitly stated in the exempli causa listing of the Succession Regulation Article 23(2). According to Article 76[408] of the PIL Act the law applicable to succession governs in particular: the causes and time of the opening of succession; the circle of heirs and legatees, inheritance shares, and other rights resulting from the opening of succession; the capacity to inherit; the particular causes of the incapacity to dispose or receive (the inheritance);[409] disinheritance and debarment from succession; the transfer of assets making up the succession to the heirs and legatees, including the conditions and effects of accepting or waiving the succession or legacy; the powers of the heirs, the executors of the wills and other administrators of the succession, in particular the sale of property and the payment of creditors; responsibility for the debts under the succession; the freely disposable portion, the reserved portions and the other restrictions on the freedom to dispose of property upon death, including the allocations deducted from the succession by a court of other authority to the advantage of the relatives of the deceased; any obligation to return or calculate the value of a gift and their calculation in the succession parts; sharing the inheritance.

In regards to the responsibility for the debts under the succession, in Montenegrin substantive law the maintenance obligation, as well as maintenance right cannot be transferred to another person. The only exceptions to this rule are the due receivables which as a common obligation can be the part of inheritance.[410]

406. *See* Arts 127–129 of the PIL Act.

407. The differences are primarily reflected in the way of formulating points 1 (the place' is not listed) and 2 ('the succession rights of the surviving spouse or partner' is not listed).

408. Unofficial translation by Professor Dr Vesna Bulatovic, Encyclopedia of PIL of 2017, Vol. 4, 3530–3531. *See infra* Annex I for the updated version of the PIL Act.

409. The words in the brackets are added by the author.

410. *See* Radoje Korać, *Porodično pravo* (Family Law), Podgorica: Štamparija 3 M Makarije, 2011, 402–403.

§3. TESTAMENTARY DISPOSITION

I. Legal Capacity

574. Legal capacity to make a testamentary disposition is governed by the law of habitual residence of the testator at the time of death or by the law he has chosen to be applicable law (the law of the State whose nationality he possesses or the law of the State in which he has habitual residence at the time of choice of applicable law or at the time of his death, and for immovables *lex situs*) (Article 74(3) of the PIL Act). This capacity is not affected by the subsequent change of the applicable law.

II. Choice of Law

575. In accordance with the contemporary tendencies in the domain of the applicable law for succession in comparative law, the PIL Act provides for a prominent role for choice of law. However, this choice of law has its limits: a significant connection between the deceased and the chosen law is required. Based on the principle of a unitary succession, Article 72 of the PIL Act provides that a testator for his succession as a whole may choose the *lex nationalis* or the law of the country in which he habitually resides at the time of the choice of the applicable law or at the time of his death. The possibility of deviation from the rule that the entire property is subject to a unitary succession regime is also envisaged and it is possible for the testator for the immovable property to choose the law of the country where it is situated.[411] Such a solution should contribute to legal predictability and stability and it enables to synchronize with the applicable law for property relations of immovable. Although the basic idea of a unitary system of succession is to apply a single law to the succession as a whole even when a deceased has assets in several countries, when the testator chooses otherwise, this is considered to be acceptable.[412]

576. The explicit choice of law must be made in the form intended for disposing of property in case of death (Will, Joint Will or Succession Agreement). It should be noted that there is no Joint Will in the substantive law of Montenegro, and the Succession Agreement is null and void.[413] Tacit choice of law stems from the provisions of such disposition of property upon death (if, for example, deceased referred to certain provisions of the law of the State of his nationality or otherwise mentioned that law).[414]

411. Article 72 para. 2 of the PIL Act.
412. See *Comments on the Succession Proposal,* Max Planck Institute for Comparative and International Private Law, Hamburg: Offprint, 2010, 71.
413. Article 121 of the LS.
414. Recital 39 of the Succession Regulation.

577. The existence and material validity of the very act of choosing the applicable law is valued according to the chosen law.[415]

III. Compulsory Portion

578. In the law of Montenegro, the legislator defines the compulsory portion as a part of the estate with which the testator cannot dispose (Article 28(1) LS). In Montenegro, the compulsory heirs are: descendants, adopted and his offspring, spouse, parents, adoptive parents, brothers, sisters, grandparents (Article 27 LS). The rights of the compulsory heirs are protected by the provisions of LS and these provisions cannot be excluded by the testator, because the court, at the request of the heirs, will amend the testament, except in case of fulfilment of the legal requirements for exclusion from the right to the compulsory portion, or for depriving the right to the compulsory portion.[416]

579. As previously stated *lex successionis* is applied, among other things to: compulsory heirs, right to the compulsory portion, size of the compulsory portion, exclusion from the right to the compulsory portion, violation and protection of the compulsory portion.

IV. Interpretation

580. Pursuant to Article 74 of the PIL Act interpretation shall be governed by the law which was applicable to the succession to the deceased at the time when the disposition was made. This law may be: the law of the habitual residence of the testator at the time of his death (the law that was applied through the application of an escape clause included) or the law he has chosen as governing law (the law of the State whose nationality he possesses or the law of the State in which he has habitual residence at the time of choice of applicable law or at the time of his death or the law of the State in which the immovable property is located).

V. Last Will

A. *Formal Validity*

581. In Montenegrin positive law, the provisions on the applicable law for the formal validity of Will are contained in the Hague Convention on the Conflicts of Laws Relating to the Form of the Testamentary Dispositions and the PIL Act. Montenegro became a member of this convention by the way of succession, and Yugoslavia was the first country to ratify it in 1962. Some of the main rules of the Convention (its Articles 1(1), 2, 5) are incorporated into the provisions of Article 73

415. Article 74 of the PIL Act.
416. Article 46 of the LS.

of PIL Act. The basic idea of the Convention, and therefore of the relevant provisions of the Code, is the application of the principle of *favor testamenti*. The Convention in its Article 1(1) envisages a large number of alternative connections in order to maintain the Will in force. The total list of connecting factors includes all the facts that may be relevant. Additionally, personal connections (nationality, domicile and habitual residence) are fixed at two points: the time of disposition or the time of the death of the testator, which can be significant when there is a change of legislation. A mobile conflict of laws is prevented also by other connections (the place of disposition, the place where immovables are located).

582. The PIL Act, beside the connecting factors stipulated by the Convention, contains the additional two: the law of Montenegro and the law which was applicable or would have been applicable to succession at the time of disposition. The list contains alternative connecting factors and therefore the order of their application is not derived from the text of the provision of the PIL Act. For example, if the Will would be valid according to the law of Montenegro as the *lex nationalis* of the testator, and it was made in the United Kingdom, it is not necessary to engage in ascertaining of the content of foreign law (UK law), but it suffices to ascertain that the Will is valid by one of the alternative applicable laws.

583. In the domain of the applicable law for the formal validity of a Will, the possibility of applying the renvoi is excluded under both, the Convention and the Code.[417] The revocation of a Will shall be adhered to the same law applicable to their formal validity. Issues that are explicitly qualified as matters of form include: the existence of restrictions in terms of age, citizenship and other personal characteristics of the testator; the fulfilment of the requirements regarding witnesses, as well as the prohibition of certain types of disposal in the case of death.[418]

584. Montenegro succeeded to the 1973 UN Convention providing a Uniform Law on the Form of an International Will, ratified by the Former Yugoslavia in 1977. The Convention provides that a Will shall be valid as regards form, irrespective particularly of the place where it is made, of the location of the assets and of the nationality, domicile or residence of the testator, if it is made in the form of an international will complying with the provisions set out in its Articles 2–5. Moreover, LS incorporates its integral text.

585. In addition to the previously mentioned rules, Article 104 of the PIL Act provides the possibility of making a Will in the form of a Judicial Will before an authorized consular office or Embassy of Montenegro that conducts consular affairs as a privilege of Montenegrin citizens.

417. Article 1 of the Convention states 'a testamentary disposition shall be valid as regards form if its form complies with the internal law', and Art. 4 para. 2(2) of the PIL Act provides that renvoi is excluded for the form of legal transactions.
418. Article 5 of the Convention and Art. 76 of the PIL Act.

B. Substantive Validity

586. The admissibility and substantive validity of the Will are to be governed according to the law of habitual residence or, if the choice of the applicable law is exercised, by the law of citizenship of the person on the day when the disposal was made, starting from the presumption that that day is the day of the death of the person. The substantive validity of the Will (the existence of legally relevant and free declaration of will, the appointment of the heiress and legators, the provisions for the exclusion of legitimate heiress from the heritage, the modalities and deadlines for acquiring the succession, the possibility and condition of the will's revocation and so forth)[419] is most often governed by the same law which is applicable to statutory succession. However, the testator may make a choice of law. Unlike the substantive choice of law, which in the field of inheritance occurs in the form of incorporation of the provisions of a foreign law into the text of the Will, the choice of the applicable law implies the possibility that the testator chooses the applicable law in the form prescribed for the Will (e.g., by introducing a provision in the Will that succession shall be governed by his *lex nationalis* at the time of making the Will).

587. It has long been considered that in the domain of succession, the choice of applicable law is not desirable because it can be motivated by the intention to apply the law that does not protect the rights of the compulsory heirs or otherwise seek to avoid the exercise of rights on the basis of an objective connecting factor, which is usually domestic law. However, the general trend of liberalization of PIL gives the right to those who believe that in the field of succession, an individual can more successfully than the State, represented in the legislature, determine the applicable law.[420]Also, by allowing the limited choice of law, the change of citizenship, domicile or habitual residence does not affect the applicable law, which contributes to legal certainty.

VI. Legacy

A. Formal Validity

588. The PIL Act does not contain a special rule on the form of legacy. The formal validity of the legacy should be governed by the law applicable to the form of the Will.

419. *See* Edin Muminović, *Međunarodno privatno pravo* (Private International Law), Sarajevo: Univerzitet u Sarajevu, Pravni fakultet, 2006, 189–190; Milorad Ročkomanović, *Međunarodno privatno pravo* (Private International Law), Niš: Univerzitet u Nišu, Pravni fakultet, 2012, 330. Unlike national law which usually does not contain a definition of what is included in the questions of the material validity of the Will, the Succession Regulation specifies this term in its Art. 26.

420. Jürgen Basedow, The Recent Development of the Conflict of Laws, In *Japanese and European Private International Law in Comparative Perspective*, Basedow, Baum, Nishitani eds., Tübingen: Mohr Siebeck, 2008, 4–18.

B. *Substantive Validity*

589. The PIL Act does not contain a special rule on the substantive validity of the legacy. The applicable law should be the law applicable to the substantive validity of the Will.

VII. Testamentary Contract

A. *Formal Validity*

590. Pursuant to the substantive law of Montenegro, testamentary contract is absolutely null regarding both, formal and substantive validity.[421] However, the PIL Act explicitly recognizes testamentary contracts (Articles 72(3), 74(4)) so that, when the applicable law provides for this type of contract, the Montenegrin court/ notary will have to ascertain its formal validity. The PIL Act does not explicitly address formal validity of a testamentary contract but in our view, this type of contract should be governed by the general conflict rule on formal validity of last wills (Article 73 of the PIL Act), which was modelled after the rules of the Hague Testamentary Convention of 1961. However, the matter related to the form of testamentary contract is tackled in a conflict rule addressing the party autonomy, stipulating that the choice of law must be expressed in the form provided for disposal in case of death (will, joint will or testamentary contracts) (Article 72(3)).

B. *Substantive Validity*

591. The PIL Act explicitly addresses substantive validity of the joint will or testamentary contracts. It provides the possibility for the parties from the joint will or testamentary contracts to agree that for substantive validity (as well as the existence, effects and interpretation) of their disposal the applicable law is the law that one of them may designate, in accordance with the rules on choice of law from Article 72(1, 2, and 5).[422] Thus, the same rules apply to substantive validity of all disposals in case of death, and that is: the law to govern the succession as a whole may be the law of the state whose nationality he possesses or the law of the state in which he has habitual residence at the time of choice of applicable law or at the time of his death, while he may choose *lex situs* to govern the succession to immovable property. The same rules also apply to a modification or revocation of an earlier choice of applicable law.

421. Article 121 of the LS.
422. Article 74(4) of the PIL Act.

§4. Inheritance and Liability

592. The law applicable to the succession also governs liability for debts (Article 76(8) of the PIL Act). The same law applies to ascertaining what makes the deceased's debts. The obligation that may not be subject to the inheritance, such as, the obligation of maintenance of a divorced spouse is extinguished at the moment of his death.

593. If the law of Montenegro is governing law, pursuant to Article 140 of the LS, the heir is responsible for the deceased's debts up to the value of the inherited property at the moment of the deceased's death.

§5. Case Law

594. The amendments to the Law on Extra-Judicial Procedure[423] (Article 94) that came into effect as of 1 May 2015 introduced the obligatory jurisdiction of the notary to rule on succession. This authority is granted by a court decision, and they act as commissioners of a court, competent for running the inheritance proceedings. If there are no contentious issues, the procedure before the notary lasts on average less than sixty days.[424]

595. Even if it is still too early to draw conclusions regarding tendencies of the practice of Montenegrin notaries in the succession matters with foreign element an overview of two cases may point to some different practices. In one case[425] the deceased at the time of her death, in 2015, had a habitual residence in Montenegro, and she also had Montenegrin citizenship. Her property consisted of two real properties in Sarajevo (Bosnia and Herzegovina), a car, with Montenegrin registration plates, and a bank deposit in Montenegro. The competent notary in Podgorica, Montenegro, applied the principle of a unique succession and ruled on a succession as a whole in accordance with Article 71 of the PIL Act by applying the Montenegrin LS. Following the proceedings, the heirs registered as owners of immovable property in the Republic Administration for Geodetic and Property Affairs of Bosnia and Herzegovina. In other case[426] the deceased at the time of his death, in 2017, had a habitual residence in Montenegro, and he was a citizen of Serbia. His property consisted of real estate in Podgorica (not registered with the Cadaster of Immovable Property), real estate in Peć (Kosovo), a deposit in a bank and a pistol. The competent notary in Podgorica applied Article 71 of the PIL Act but only ruled on the succession of the movable property.

---

423. Podgorica, Službeni list Crne Gore No. 27/2006, 20/2015, 75/2018 and 67/2019.
424. *Analiza rada notara u ostavinskim predmetima i rasterećenje sudova od ove vrste predmeta (maj 2016 – decembar 2017)*, (Analysis of the work of notaries in probate cases and relieving the courts of this type of case (May 2016 - December 2017)), Podgorica: Ministarstvo pravde Vlade Crne Gore, September 2018.
425. Final decision of the court of 20 Jan. 2016.
426. Final decision of the court of 30 Mar. 2018.

596. One of the notaries from Podgorica provided for information regarding the practice of competent authorities of some European countries relating to Montenegro.[427] In one case the deceased at the time of his death, in 2018, had a habitual residence in the Republic of Croatia, of which he was a citizen. His properties were located in the Croatian municipality of Labin and in the Montenegrin municipality of Danilovgrad. The Croatian notary refused to rule on the immovable property in Montenegro, and instructed the successors to address the local court/notary in Montenegro. In another case the deceased at the time of his death, in 2015, had a habitual residence in France, and the citizenship of Montenegro. In the probate procedure, which was conducted in France, the ruling encompassed only the property that was located in France.

597. According to the data obtained from the Notary Chamber of Montenegro from July 2020 to July 2021 the provisions of the PIL Act were applied in 127 succession proceedings conducted by notaries as commissioners of the court. However, further information on those cases is not publicly available. It is striking information that in most of these cases only four notaries acted, all of them from the coastal region (Bar, Budva, Kotor and Ulcinj). Moreover, out of a total of 56 notaries, 36 notaries reported no cases of succession proceedings with a foreign element.

427. Information provided by Mr Đorđije Lakić, practitioner with the notary.

Part III. Annex: International Civil Procedure

Chapter 1. Sources of ICP

598. The most important sources of International Civil Procedure in Montenegro have already been enumerated in the section on Sources of PIL. The PIL Act is the most important source in the field of jurisdiction and recognition and enforcement of foreign judgments in Montenegro. This law introduces significant innovation in relation to the LRCL. The new provisions are to a large extent inspired by the 2001 Brussels I Regulation and the Lugano Convention. Some solutions from other EU regulations in this area[428] as well as from comparative, primarily German law, also influenced the final text of the codification. Furthermore, statutory provisions on international jurisdiction are found in LCP (Articles 19 and 29), the LOPRAT (Article 174), the LMIN (Article 1051), the Law on Insolvency (Articles 14, 180, 183 and 185), LBE (Article 91), LC (Article 28), LFI Investment (Article 30). The rules on international jurisdiction also exist in the following multilateral treaties: Convention on Jurisdiction, Applicable Law, Recognition, Enforcement and Co-operation in Respect of Parental Responsibility and Measures for the Protection of Children (1996) and Convention on Choice of Court Agreements (2005). They are also present in some conventions relating to international transport and liability for damages.[429] Finally, the rules on international jurisdiction in status, family and succession matters can be found in bilateral treaties on judicial assistance with Austria, Czech Republic, France, Greece, Hungary, Poland, Romania and Slovakia. Some of these treaties also contain rules on international jurisdiction in disputes for compensation of damages (e.g., the bilateral treaty with Hungary, Article 39(a), paragraph 3), and in disputes relating to real rights on immovables (e.g., the bilateral treaties with Czech Republic, Hungary, Poland and Slovakia).[430]

599. International judicial assistance is regulated by different international conventions and the most important are conventions developed by the Hague Conference on PIL. Most of them binding Montenegro address civil procedure. The basic rules for acting upon the Letter of Request of foreign courts are set out in the

428. The Brussels II bis Regulation, The Succession Regulation and The Maintenance Regulation.
429. Kluwer Monograph on PIL of Montenegro of 2013, para. 460.
430. *Ibid.*

Convention on civil procedure (1954) and elaborated by the Convention on the Service Abroad of Judicial and Extrajudicial Documents in Civil or Commercial Matters (1965) and the Convention on the Taking of Evidence Abroad in Civil or Commercial Matters (1970). Montenegro is also bound by the following Hague conventions: the Convention on Abolishing the Requirement of Legalisation for Foreign Public Documents (1961), the Convention on International Access to Justice (1980), the Convention on the Civil Aspects of International Child Abduction (1980), the Convention on the International Recovery of Child Support and Other Forms of Family Maintenance (2007). The other important conventions are the European Convention on Information on Foreign Law (1968) and Additional Protocol (1978), the European Agreement on the Transmission of Applications for Legal Aid (1977), etc. Bilateral treaties related to the area of international judicial assistance regulate service of process and the taking of evidence, contain provisions dispensing with the requirement of legalization of documents and security for costs (cautio iudicatum solvi), and provide for access to courts, legal aid and exchange of information on the content of laws of the contracting parties or all of it. Bilateral treaties on judicial assistance in civil matters binding on Montenegro are with Austria, Belgium, Bosnia and Herzegovina, Czech Republic, Greece, Italy, Cyprus, France, Macedonia, Poland, Romania, Slovakia and Serbia. As already mentioned, the Ministry of Justice of Montenegro factually applies the treaties of the former Yugoslavia with the Russian Federation and Croatia. If a bilateral agreement has not been concluded with a particular country and that country is not a member of a multilateral agreement, the provisions of the Law of Civil Procedure (e.g., service of judicial documents, Chapter 11 of the Law) shall apply.

600. The PIL Act regulates recognition and enforcement of foreign judgments in Montenegro in detail. Also, some provisions from the Law on Extrajudicial Procedure and LESC are applied to certain issues. A number of bilateral treaties that refers to judicial assistance and binds on Montenegro include provisions on the recognition and enforcement of foreign (and/or arbitral) decisions (agreements signed with: Austria, Bosnia and Herzegovina, Bulgaria, Czech Republic, Cyprus, Hungary, Macedonia, Slovakia, Poland, Romania, Serbia) and there are four separate treaties dealing with the recognition and enforcement of foreign judgments in civil and commercial matters (with France and Greece), that is, the recognition and enforcement of maintenance judgments (with Austria and Belgium).[431] In a few multilateral international treaties, there are certain provisions that are significant in this area. Thus, recognition and enforcement of foreign judgments are subject of the Hague Convention on Jurisdiction, Applicable Law, Recognition, Enforcement and Co-operation in Respect of Parental Responsibility and Measures for the Protection of Children, the Hague Convention on the International Recovery of Child Support and Other Forms of Family Maintenance and the Hague Convention on Choice of

431. *See supra* National Law.

Court Agreements, while, e.g., the Hague Conventions Relating to Civil Procedure and the Hague Convention on International Access to Justice contain rules on the recognition and enforcement of judgments relating to the costs of the judicial proceedings, and the Hague Convention on Civil Aspects of International Child Abduction provides the recognition of judgments by foreign courts and administrative bodies entrusting the child with custody and care, without conducting a recognition procedure.

Chapter 2. The Principle of *Lex Fori*

601. Generally, the principle of *lex fori* is the ruling principle in conducting civil proceedings with an international element. The Montenegrin courts conduct civil proceeding pursuant to the *lex fori* irrespective of the existence of international element in a subject matter as the specificities of these proceedings refer to only a few issues where a foreign procedural rule may apply, by the way of exception.

602. As a rule, civil proceedings before the court in Montenegro, in a matter with a foreign element, will be conducted pursuant to the domestic rules of procedure: LCP, the Law on Extra-Judicial Procedure, and LESC, except when an issue is regulated by an international treaty (bilateral or multilateral) or by the PIL Act (or other special statutes).

603. Courts provide judicial assistance to foreign courts in the manner provided for in domestic law. However, by the way of exception domestic courts may act pursuant to procedural rules of a foreign court when they are rendering judicial assistance, provided that the requested procedure is not contrary to domestic public policy (the LCP, Article 174) such as if the evidence is admissible through a witness who can testify under oath.[432]

604. In civil proceedings with a foreign element, the issue of a party's capacity to a lawsuit implies the question of whether that entity is entitled to be a party to the proceedings under the law which is applicable to it. This is an exception to the rule that all court proceedings must always be subjected to the *lex fori*. Pursuant to the PIL Act, the capacity of a natural person to be a party in a lawsuit before the court of Montenegro is governed by their national law. The capacity of a foreign legal person to be a party in a lawsuit before the court of Montenegro is governed by the law of the country to which this person belongs. However, if a legal person has its actual seat in a country other than the country where it was established and where according to the law of that other country, the law of that country is applicable, the applicable law shall be the law of the country of the actual seat.[433]

605. If, according to the law of their nationality, natural person has the capacity to be a party in a lawsuit, the content and scope of such capacity is determined by the law of the country in which the proceedings are conducted – *lex fori*.[434]

606. The litigation capacity of foreign nationals is governed by the law of the country of their citizenship. However, unlike the capacity to be a party, Montenegrin law provides the possibility of applying domestic law. According to the PIL Act, if a foreign national does not have the litigation capacity in civil proceedings,

432. *See*: Milisav Čizmović & Biljana Đuričin, *Građansko procesno pravo* (Civil Procedural Law), Podgorica: Faculty of Law in Podgorica, 1994, 105.
433. Article 19, para. 3 of the PIL Act.
434. Varadi, Bordaš, Knežević, Pavić, *Međunarodno privatno pravo, 14. izdanje* (Private International Law, 14th edn), Belgrade: Univerzitet u Beogradu, Pravni fakultet, 2012, 521.

but has such capacity under the law of Montenegro, the person shall be considered to have litigation capacity.[435] This means that if the *lex nationalis* sets more stringent requirements than the law of Montenegro, a foreign national shall be considered to have litigation capacity if that is so according to the *lex fori*.

435. Article 136, para. 2 of the PIL Act.

Chapter 3. National Jurisdiction

607. During the proceedings, the court shall, ex officio, have due regard to whether the dispute falls within the jurisdiction of the court because the lack of international jurisdiction can lead to the non-recognition of court judgments,[436] while in the case of an error regarding local jurisdiction the court would not react at a later stage of the procedure.[437]

608. The PIL Act contains a number of rules on international jurisdiction, and the application of domestic rules on local jurisdiction in the function of the rules of international jurisdiction is possible in case of a legal gap.

609. Presently, Article 29 of the LCP provides that the court of Montenegro will have international jurisdiction if its jurisdiction for a dispute with an international element is expressly provided by a statute or an international treaty or if its jurisdiction arises from the provisions on local jurisdiction of the domestic court. The second option is available if there is no express provision on jurisdiction of the domestic court neither in a statute nor in an international treaty for the specific type of dispute with an international element.

610. The courts tend to stick to the express provisions on international jurisdiction contained in the PIL Act and other statutes, and show general reluctance to base their international jurisdiction on analogous application of the rules on local jurisdiction.[438]

611. The PIL Act explicitly provides analogous application of the rules on local jurisdiction for family law disputes with a foreign element which do not fall under the cases regulated by the special rules contained in that code.[439]

436. Article 19, para. 2 of the Law on Civil Procedure states: 'When, in the course of proceedings, the court finds that another body has jurisdiction for resolving the dispute, it shall declare that it is not competent, annul the actions conducted and reject the claim.'
437. *See* Art. 18, para. 3 of the LCP.
438. Kluwer Monograph on PIL of Montenegro of 2013, para. 210.
439. Article 135 of the PIL Act. This law contains specific rules on international jurisdiction for: marital and related disputes, child family status, parental care, adoption and maintenance (Arts 130–134).

Chapter 4. International Jurisdiction

612. The international jurisdiction of judiciary of Montenegro is of an abstract nature, but it is a preliminary issue and a precondition for determining subject matter and territorial jurisdiction. In most cases the provisions of the PIL Act on international jurisdiction will apply. Jurisdiction shall be established on the basis of the facts and circumstances present at the time the procedure is initiated and any subsequent changes of the facts upon which the jurisdiction was established that may occur in a later stage of a procedure do not impact jurisdiction (Article 112). If international jurisdiction is provided by a ratified international treaty it will have the supremacy over the PIL Act or any other, special law containing the provisions on international jurisdiction and shall apply directly when it regulates relations differently than the national legislation.[440] In case that a foreign court has jurisdiction under the provisions of an international treaty, the domestic court should only declare itself incompetent and it should not deliver to the foreign court the case files.

§1. Statutory Forums

I. General Jurisdiction

613. General jurisdiction of the judiciary of Montenegro for all types of litigious and non-litigious matters with a foreign element is based on the domicile of the defendant. The most significant exceptions to the said rule are cases where the law prescribes the exclusive jurisdiction of the domestic judiciary or when the parties have selected the court to adjudicate their dispute. If the defendant is a legal person, according to the rule of general jurisdiction, he may be sued in the country in which he has his seat. The qualification of the notion of the seat (as well as the place of domicile) of the defendant is done under domestic law. In trials relating to legal persons, in case of doubt, the place where their management is located shall be considered their seat. In the disputes against Montenegro or local government units, the seat of its parliament is relevant.[441]

614. In certain cases, the residence of the defendant can also be the basis for this type of jurisdiction, but only when defendant is natural person. If a defendant neither has a domicile in Montenegro nor in the other State, a court in Montenegro shall have jurisdiction if the defendant has his residence in Montenegro.[442]

615. The PIL Act, like its predecessor LRCL[443] extends the general jurisdiction of domestic courts in the case of the existence of material co-defendants, as well as for non-litigious matters, if certain requirements are met. In the event of a lawsuit

440. Pursuant to Art. 9 of the Constitution of Montenegro.
441. Article 40 of the PIL Act.
442. Article 99, para. 2 of the PIL Act.
443. Article 46, paras 4 and 5 of the LRCL.

with multiple defendants and with the status of material co-defendants, a Montenegrin court shall also have jurisdiction when one of the defendants has his domicile or seat in Montenegro.[444] Where a legal relationship is decided upon in non-litigious procedure involving several parties, a Montenegrin court shall have jurisdiction if the party against whom the claim is filed has his domicile or seat in Montenegro, and where the procedure involves only one person, if that person has his domicile or seat in Montenegro.[445] In the non-litigious procedure, there is no defendant so court starts from the domicile of a person whose role in the procedure is similar to the defendant's role. Also, there is no alternative application of the defendant's residence to natural persons who do not have a domicile.

II. Specific Jurisdiction

616. In addition to the defendant's domicile, which is the basis for general jurisdiction, other facts on which specific jurisdiction can be based include: citizenship, habitual residence, place where the property is situated, place of performance of a contract, place of harmful event and so forth. The rules of specific jurisdiction are formulated for certain types of relationships based on the connection and strength of the relationship between a person, res or an event, and one country. The establishment of specific jurisdiction in order to protect a certain category of persons, usually the weaker party, which is in the role of the plaintiff, is based on the place of domicile of the consumer, the place of habitual work of the employee, the habitual residence of the creditor of the obligation of maintenance and so forth. A close relationship between relations and territory occurs, for example, when establishing specific jurisdiction according to the place of performance of the contract or the place where the property is situated.

617. The PIL of Montenegro in principle provides a generally accepted basis for international jurisdiction,[446] providing for the compliance of these rules with the facts that occur as connections in determining the applicable law for certain types of relationships.

618. The PIL Act introduces habitual residence as a basis of jurisdiction for certain matters. Pursuant to the general definition (for the applicable law), 'habitual residence of a natural person is a place where a natural person habitually resides, independently of the registration with the competent body and independently of residence or domicile permit, and irrespective of whether the residence is restricted

444. Article 100 of the PIL Act.
445. Article 109 of the PIL Act.
446. Maja Kostić-Mandić, *The New Private International Law Act of Montenegro*, Yearbook of Private International Law, Vol. XVI, 2014/2015, 437–438.

in advance'. The Code specifies that 'in determining habitual residence, due consideration should be taken of the circumstances of personal or professional nature that show durable connections with that place or indicate the intention to create such connections'.[447]

619. Jurisdiction of the court of Montenegro in status of persons[448] and family law disputes[449] is regulated in a way that in addition to the citizenship of Montenegro, the special jurisdiction of the Court of Montenegro can be based on the habitual residence in Montenegro. This also applies to disputes on establishment or contestation of parentage, in the matter of parental care and adoption.[450]

620. The role of habitual residence is prominent especially in the field of maintenance and succession, influenced by the EU regulations. Thus, a Montenegrin court shall have jurisdiction to hear maintenance disputes if the defendant has habitual residence in Montenegro or the maintenance creditor has habitual residence in Montenegro or maintenance is decided in an action brought before a Montenegrin court on status matters or parental care (Article 134 of PIL Act).

621. In matters of succession a Montenegrin court shall have jurisdiction if the deceased person had his habitual residence in Montenegro at the time of his death. If that is not a case, a Montenegrin court shall have jurisdiction on the basis of the assets that make part of his inheritance being located in Montenegro and if one of the conditions is additionally met: the law of Montenegro was designated as applicable; or the deceased person was a Montenegrin national at the time of his death; or that this article applies only to such assets (Article 128 of PIL Act).

622. In some fields the PIL Act adheres to the traditional rules:
the jurisdiction to hear disputes on rights in rem in movable property shall be conferred on a Montenegrin court if:

- the movable property is located in the territory of Montenegro (Article 120);
- for disputes arising from contractual relations,[451] the domestic court is competent if the place of performance of the obligation is in Montenegro (Article 123);
- for disputes on non-contractual liability for damages, the domestic court is competent as a place where the harmful event occurred or may occur (Article 126).

623. The rules on specific jurisdiction are for the first time regulated by the PIL Act for disputes from intellectual property rights,[452] consumer contracts[453] and individual employment contracts.[454] Special protection for certain categories of weaker parties (consumers, employees) is basically based on the premises that:

447. Article 27 of the PIL Act.
448. Articles 115–117 of the PIL Act.
449. Article 130 of the PIL Act.
450. Articles 131–133 of the PIL Act.
451. *See* Davor Babić, *Međunarodna nadležnost prema mjestu ispunjenja ugovorne obveze u europskom i hrvatskom pravu (International jurisdiction according to the place of fulfillment of the contractual obligation in European and Croatian law),* In: 'Republika Hrvatska na putu prema europskom pravosudnom području – Rješavanje trgovačkih i potrošačkih sporova', Tomjenović/Čulinović

(1) the weaker party as the plaintiff institutes the procedure in Montenegro: in the case of consumer contracts, if the consumer has domicile in Montenegro, and in the employment contract, if the employee habitually performs his job in Montenegro;[455]
(2) the other party to the contract (company, employer) may initiate the procedure only in Montenegro as the place of domicile of the weaker party;
(3) in order to avoid disturbing this system, the possibility of parties designating jurisdiction is limited.

624. The review of the case law of the Higher Court in Podgorica, from 2013 to 2015, in the application of the LRCL indicates that the largest number of cases is related to two areas: contracts for the purchase of immovable property and exercising parental rights. Other cases are related to: contractual liability for damages, unjust enrichment, divorce, division of the joint property, succession, *cautio judicatum solvi* and tenancy of immovable property.[456]

III. Exclusive Jurisdiction

625. In comparison with the LRCL, the PIL Act regulates exclusive jurisdiction in a completely new manner. The most significant innovation concerning exclusive jurisdiction is abandonment of exclusive jurisdiction for the status relationships of natural persons, family and succession matters (stipulated by the LRCL)[457] and introduction of new rules mirroring Article 22(1) of the Lugano Convention.

626. The PIL Act specifies that a Montenegrin court shall have exclusive jurisdiction when so explicitly provided for by that or another piece of legislation. Based on the PIL Act, judiciary of Montenegro is exclusively competent for two groups of relations: those related to immovable property located in Montenegro and procedures where exercising of certain private rights depends on the authorities of Montenegro.

627. The first area includes the exclusive jurisdiction of our judiciary for proceedings relating to the acquisition, transfer, alteration and termination of real rights in immovable property in Montenegro, as well as for the tenancy of immovable property located in our country. Here, the difference between the proprietary and obligatory legal effects of the contract should be made. If the rights in rem in

Herc/Butorac Malnar eds., Rijeka: Pravni fakultet u Rijeci, 2009, 89–130.

452. Article 122 of the PIL Act.

453. Article 124 of the PIL Act.

454. Article 125 of the PIL Act.

455. Also, even if the employee does not regularly does not or did not do the job only in one country, if the business unit that engaged the employee is or was located in Montenegro.

456. Gž. br. 1478/13; Gž. br. 3490/13; Gž. br. 3110/14; Gž. br. 4418/14; Gž. br. 5353/14; Gž. br. 4228/14; Gž. br. 970/14; Gž. br. 2575/14; Gž. br. 4478/15; Gž. br. 3129/15–14; Gž. br. 2014/15; Gž. br. 4430/15, Gž. br. 4798/15.

457. Articles 61, 64, 66, 70–73, 78 of the LRCL.

immovable property are transferred by contract, exclusive jurisdiction applies only to the proprietary effects of the contract.[458] Regarding the tenancy of immovable property located in Montenegro, the exclusive jurisdiction of our judiciary exists only in the proceedings regarding the long-term tenancy. If a tenancy of immovable property is concluded for temporary private use for a period of not more than six consecutive months, if the tenant is a natural person and that both the landlord and tenant have their domicile in another country, there will be no exclusive jurisdiction of our judiciary.[459]

628. As for the other group of relations, for which the exclusive jurisdiction of our judiciary exists, they include disputes with respect to validity of registration with public registers kept in Montenegro[460] (Cadaster of Immovable Property, Central Registry of Business Entities, National registers of patents, trademarks and industrial designs); validity, nullity or dissolution of a company or other legal person and the validity of decisions of their organs, if they have their seat in Montenegro,[461] as well as procedures related to the registration or validity of industrial property rights in Montenegro.[462] Deleting and inserting into public registers can be done only in procedures regulated by national legislation. For the judicial protection of industrial property rights, which are registered in our country, there is exclusive jurisdiction of our judiciary. Exclusive jurisdiction is also provided for the validity of decisions of legal person's bodies, since these decisions are published in the country where the legal person is based and available to the public in that country.[463]

629. The PIL Act does not provide exclusive jurisdiction for the disputes in respect of the rights in rem in aircraft, vessels, as well as disputes in respect of a lease of aircraft and vessels even the register where the aircraft or vessel is registered is kept in Montenegro.[464]

630. The PIL Act also provides for cases of relative exclusive jurisdiction on the basis of the party's prorogation agreement. The law explicitly states that an exclusive jurisdiction is based on an agreement on the jurisdiction of a domestic or foreign judiciary, unless the parties have otherwise agreed.[465] Here, in the first place, is the situation when, despite the existence of a prorogation agreement, one party initiates proceedings in another country, and not in the one whose jurisdiction was

458. Aleš Galič, *Uredba Brisel I: temelj evropskog građanskog procesnog prava (The Brussels I Regulation – the base of European civil procedural law)*, In Recent trends in European PIL – challenges for the national legislations of the South East European countries, T. Deskoski ed., Skopje: Faculty of Law Skopje, 2011, 50.
459. Article 119, para. 2 of the PIL Act.
460. Article 111 of PIL the Code.
461. Article 118 of the PIL Act.
462. Article 122 of the PIL Act.
463. Vesna Rakić-Vodinelić & Gaša Knežević, *Građansko procesno pravo Evropske unije* (Civil Procedural Law of the European Union*)*, Belgrade: Univerzitet u Beogradu, Pravni Fakultet, 1998, 105.
464. Article 121 of the PIL Act.
465. Articles 103–104 of the PIL Act.

determined by agreement, and the other party files a written answer to the claim or a complaint against a payment order, or pleas to the merits without having contested jurisdiction. In this case, the parties took the opportunity to change the choice of competent jurisdiction based on their party autonomy (which can be expressed by conclusive actions) for their case that no longer has the character of the rules on exclusive jurisdiction.

631. The relative exclusive jurisdiction also includes rules for certain types of contracts where the legislator protects the weaker party. Thus, in the case of a consumer contract, the legislator protects the consumer, that is, in the case of an individual employment contract, an employee, by stipulating that an economically stronger party (trader or employer) can sue a weaker party that have domicile in Montenegro only in Montenegro, unless the parties designate the jurisdiction of another judiciary by a prorogation agreement.[466]

IV. Exceptional Jurisdiction (*Forum necessitatis*)

632. The PIL Act introduces the concept of exceptional jurisdiction and provides for the possibility of establishing jurisdiction of the courts and bodies of Montenegro when such jurisdiction is not prescribed by law. The ability to establish the jurisdiction of judiciary in Montenegro although the PIL Act does not provide for the competence of our bodies for this type of relationship is motivated by securing the access to justice as one of the fundamental human rights. Nevertheless, this possibility is of exceptional character and requires fulfilment of certain conditions: the proceedings cannot be initiated abroad or it would be unreasonable to demand that the action be brought abroad and that the case has a sufficient connection with Montenegro.[467]

§2. Choice of Forum Agreement

633. Provisions on prorogation on jurisdiction in the PIL Act are inspired by the rules of the Lugano Convention, the Brussels I Regulation (before the 2012 recast) and the Hague Convention on Choice of Court Agreements (in force in Montenegro since 8 January 2018). The basic ideas of those international documents were costumed to a national piece of legislation.

634. The PIL Act addresses the possibility of choice of forum agreements of both, Montenegrin and foreign judiciary. Pursuant to the PIL Act parties may agree on the jurisdiction of a foreign judicial authority (one or more foreign courts) or domestic courts (one or more national courts), in matters in which they may freely

466. Articles 124–125 of the PIL Act.
467. Article 113 of the PIL Act.

decide, irrespective of their citizenship, domicile or residence,[468] as long as there is an international character in their relationship. This wording goes well beyond the former rule of the LRCL. (Pursuant to Article 49 of the LRCL, in order to be able to agree on the jurisdiction of the domestic judiciary, at least one of the parties had to be a citizen of Montenegro or in case of a legal person, has its seat in Montenegro. For the contracting of the jurisdiction of a foreign judiciary, foreign citizenship, or seat in a foreign country and the lack of exclusive jurisdiction of Montenegrin judiciary were required.) The PIL Act is thus in line with Article 1(2) of the Hague Convention on Choice of Court Agreements on scope, which provides a definition of an international case[469] (the jurisdictional rules of the Convention will apply either if the parties are not resident in the same State, or if some other element relevant to the dispute (the location of the chosen court excluded) has a connection with some other State).

635. An agreement on jurisdiction of a court may be stipulated before the dispute arises, for example, as a clause in the sales contract, which provides that all disputes arising out of that contract may be settled by the courts of a particular country, or after the dispute has arisen, in the form of a prorogation contract. In both cases, the emphasis is on contracting jurisdictions for disputes from a particular relationship. A general prorogation clause, on the basis of which it would have been assumed a particular jurisdiction for all future disputes arising out of all legal relations of the parties, irrespective of the subject matter of the dispute, is not allowed.[470] The jurisdiction of either domestic or a foreign court shall be exclusive, except when otherwise agreed by the parties.

636. Under the PIL Act, the prorogation agreement will not produce effects if there is exclusive jurisdiction of the judiciary of Montenegro for a certain type of dispute and if it is a type of relationship for which parties cannot agree on the jurisdiction because they cannot freely dispose of their rights.[471] Thus, for example, for the dispute over the transfer of property rights to immovable property located in Montenegro, there is exclusive jurisdiction of the Montenegrin judiciary and the agreement of jurisdiction of a foreign court for this dispute will not produce legal effects in our country. But, if it is a matter of choice of forum agreement for dispute on payment of damages due to non-execution of a contract for the sale of this immovable, since this type of dispute does not fall under the exclusive jurisdiction

468. Under the Hague Convention on Choice of Court Agreements (Art. 1(2)), it is provided that in the domain of jurisdiction a case is considered to be international unless the parties are resident in the same Contracting State and the relationship of the parties and all other elements relevant to the dispute, irrespective of where the chosen court is located, are connected only with that State.

469. *Ibid.*

470. Siniša Triva & Mihajlo Dika, *Građansko parnično procesno pravo, 6. izdanje* (Civil Litigation Law, 6th edn.), Zagreb: Narodne novine, 2004, 286; Aleksandar Jakšić, *Građansko procesno pravo* (Civil Procedural Law), Belgrade: Univerzitet u Beogradu, Pravni fakultet 2010; Đuro Vuković, *Me unarodno građansko procesno pravo* (International Civil Procedural Law), Zagreb: Informator, 1987, 29.

471. Article 104 of the PIL Act.

of our judiciary, a judgment based on such agreement could be recognized in our country if it meets other, legally prescribed conditions.[472]

637. An agreement on jurisdiction is concluded or confirmed: (1) in writing; (2) in a form compliant with the practice that the parties have already established; or (3) in international trade and exchange, in a form compliant with the custom that the parties knew or ought to have known and which is generally known in that area of trade and is regularly adhered by the parties in agreements of the same type. An agreement on jurisdiction is deemed to be concluded in writing if it is concluded by electronic means of communication that may create a permanent record of the agreement.[473]

638. The prorogation contract is at the same time a contract on excluding the legally defined competences (derogation contract). Unless otherwise agreed, the prorogation contract excludes the jurisdiction of any jurisdiction other than the one contracted.

639. In addition to the explicit agreement of the parties, in matters in which an agreement on jurisdiction of a Montenegrin court is allowed, jurisdiction of a Montenegrin court may be established with the consent of the defendant. A defendant is deemed to have given his consent for a Montenegrin court to have jurisdiction if he has filled a written answer to the claim or a complaint against a payment order, or by pleading to the merits without having contested jurisdiction.[474]

§3. Procedural Requirements

I. Security for Defendant's Costs

640. A foreign national who initiates civil proceedings before a Montenegrin court, if certain conditions are met, has to pay security for defendant's costs. In addition to the PIL Act, which regulates the security for costs in the same way as the previous LRCL[475] numerous multilateral[476] and bilateral agreements[477] binding on Montenegro contain rules on excluding the application of security for costs.

472. Milan Pak, *Međunarodno privatno pravo, 4. izdanje* (Private International Law, 4th edn.), Belgrade: Službeni list SRJ, 2000, 56.
473. Article 105 of the PIL Act.
474. Article 106 of the PIL Act.
475. Articles 82–84 of the LRCL, *See* Mihajlo Dika, Gaša Knežević, Srđan Stojanović, *Komentar Zakona o međunarodnom privatnom i procesnom pravu* (Commentary of the PIL Act), Belgrade: Nomos, 1991, 263–273; Arts 137–139 of the PIL Act.
476. The Hague Convention of 1954 on Civil Procedure, the Hague Convention of 1980 on International Access to Justice, the Convention of 1956 on the Recovery Abroad of Maintenance, the Hague Convention of 2007 on the International Recovery of Child Support and Other Forms of Family Maintenance.
477. *See infra* Table of International Treaties.

641. According to the PIL Act, Article 137, in order to oblige a foreign national to pay the security for costs, certain requirements must be met:

- the plaintiff must be a foreign national or a stateless person domiciled abroad. The PIL Act does not specify whether this also applies to foreign legal entities, but the prevailing opinion of the doctrine is affirmative,[478] which is explicitly defined in some international treaties;[479]
- the defendant must state the request for security costs. The court cannot, ex officio, bind the foreign plaintiff to pay security for costs.

642. The defendant has to state their request for payment of security for costs by the plaintiff at the preparatory hearing or at the latest before they plead to the merits. However, a later request will be granted, as well, if it was filed as soon as the defendant learned of the circumstances authorizing them to request the security for costs (e.g., if he was not aware that the plaintiff was a foreign national).

643. The defendant has no right to request security for costs in the following cases (Article 138):

1. if the nationals of Montenegro are not obligated to give security for costs in the plaintiff's home country. The exemption from this duty is provided in all multilateral and bilateral treaties indicated in the preceding paragraphs. However, the existence of a treaty is not indispensable since factual reciprocity suffices:
2. if the plaintiff enjoys the right of asylum in Montenegro;
3. if the claim is based on the employment relationship of a foreign worker in Montenegro;
4. in divorce, annulment of marriage, paternity or maternity disputes;
   in actions brought on a bill of exchange or cheque, counterclaim actions and actions for issuance of a summary order for payment of a debt.

644. Upon request of the defendant, the court will issue a ruling which will determine the amount of security and the period within which it should be deposited. The proceedings shall be stayed until the security was deposited by the plaintiff. If the plaintiff fails to deposit security within the period ordered by the court, the action or the appeal (if the request for security for costs was filed only in the appeal proceedings) is considered to be withdrawn.

---

478. Siniša Triva, Velimir Belajac, Mihajlo Dika, *Građansko parnično procesno pravo* (Civil Litigation Law), Zagreb: Narodne novine, 1986, 390; Milan Pak, *Međunarodno privatno pravo, 4. izdanje* (Private International Law, 4th edn.), Belgrade: Službeni list SRJ, 2000, 109; Mihajlo Dika, Gaša Knežević, Srđan Stojanović, *Komentar Zakona o međunarodnom privatnom i procesnom pravu* (Commentary of the PIL Act), Belgrade: Nomos, 1991, 264.
479. The Hague Convention on International Access to Justice provides that natural and legal persons who have a habitual residence in a Contracting State and appear in the role of a plaintiff in another may not request the payment of security for costs (Art. 14).

645. In the practice of the Commercial Court there were several cases of deciding on security for costs. There is a steady practice in deciding on security for costs as provided for by an international treaty,[480] but there are also frequent cases that the representative of the defendant ask for the security for costs even in cases they know it cannot be granted on the basis of valid international agreements (when a plaintiff is the national of Albania, France, Germany),[481] while in other situations courts normally determine the obligation of securing litigation costs (when a plaintiff is the national of the Republic of Ireland, Australia and USA).[482] Otherwise, judges tend to interpret wording of Article 138, paragraph 1, point 1: 'if, in the State of which the claimant is a national, Montenegrin nationals are not under duty to provide security' as an exemption not encompassing factual reciprocity. This line of reasoning is best illustrated in the following example. In this case,[483] it was concluded that there is no legal basis for exemption from giving security for costs of a party domiciled in the United Kingdom, since there is no bilateral agreement, the UK is neither a member of the Hague Convention on Civil Procedure nor Hague Convention on International Access to Justice, and according to the opinion of the Ministry of Justice, it cannot be considered that the Convention between the Kingdom of Yugoslavia and the United Kingdom on judicial assistance in civil and commercial matters of 1936 is in force since the conditions laid down in the provision of Article 24 of the Vienna Convention on the Succession of States in respect of treaties of 1978 were not met. In this case the court did not address factual reciprocity: whether the security for costs is requested from domestic nationals in the practice of the UK courts. Similar reasoning has been expressed in two other cases where the plaintiff was domiciled in the Republic of Ireland.[484]

646. Even the Higher Court in Podgorica addressed security for defendant costs. The Higher Court in Podgorica[485] confirmed the decision of the Basic Court in Kotor[486] founded on Article 17 of the Hague Convention on Civil Procedure (1954). In the complaint, the respondent stated that there was no reciprocity between Ukraine and Montenegro because they were new states and were not subject to the provisions of international treaties that bound the USSR and Yugoslavia.

II. Legal Aid

647. The conditions for granting legal aid (exemption from payment of costs of civil proceedings) are laid out in Article 140 of the PIL Act. In the positive law of Montenegro, this right may be used by foreign natural persons irrespective of whether they are in the role of the plaintiff or defendant. The general framework for

480. Commercial Court P. br.1014/15, P.br. 574/18-15.
481. Commercial Court P.br. 572/19, P.br. 345/19 and P.br. 574/18-15, respectively.
482. Commercial Court P. br. 234/18, P. br. 463/20 and P. br. 478/20, respectively.
483. Commercial Court P. br. 1016/15
484. Commercial Court P. br. 234/18, P. br. 336/17.
485. Higher Court in Podgorica Gž.br.2154/17 of 05.05.2017.
486. Basic Court in Kotor P.br.703/16/16 of 25.01.2017.

granting legal aid is provided by LCP, while LFLA[487] deals with the right to free legal aid even in matters with international element.

648. The PIL Act prescribes that the foreign citizens are entitled to exemption from the payment of costs of civil proceedings on the condition of reciprocity.[488] Bearing in mind the fact that even factual reciprocity suffices,[489] and that there are several multilateral and bilateral treaties establishing diplomatic reciprocity (formal by its content), this condition can rarely lead to an unequal position of foreigners before the domestic court. Older international treaties adhere to the national treatment principle. Thus, the Hague Convention on Civil Procedure of 1954, as well as the Hague Convention on International Access to Justice of 1980,[490] guarantee national treatment to citizens of Contracting States in civil and commercial cases in accordance with the law of the State in which free legal aid is sought.[491]

649. The LFLA, in relation to the PIL Act explicitly expands the number of persons who potentially can enjoy this right. The LFLA also states for which types of procedures legal aid is not provided for, such as: (1) proceedings before commercial courts and procedure involving registration of the type of economic activity performed; (2) procedure for the award of damages in relation to defamation and insult; (3) proceedings initiated on the basis of the lawsuit for reducing the amount of child support.[492] The LFLA also contains a separate chapter on disputes with a foreign element, and in particular regulates situations in which a foreign element originates from a Member State of the EU.[493]

§4. International Service

650. Provisions of international treaties that bind Montenegro apply to international service, and if there is no such treaty, the provisions of LCP shall apply. Montenegro is a member of the Convention on the Service Abroad of Judicial and Extrajudicial Documents in Civil or Commercial Matters of 1965 from 2012 (the Convention on Civil Procedure of 1954 is still in force). The central body for the Hague Service convention is the Ministry of Justice. Montenegro has used the opportunity provided by the Convention to exclude the application of certain provisions of the Convention, primarily those relating to direct service. Montenegro

487. Podgorica, Službeni list Crne Gore No. 20/2011.
488. Article 140 of the PIL Act. According to the LRCL, the condition of reciprocity was not required if a foreign national or stateless person had a domicile in Montenegro (Art. 85, paras 3–4).
489. Mihajlo Dika, Gaša Knežević, Srđan Stojanović, *Komentar Zakona o međunarodnom privatnom i procesnom pravu* (Commentary of the PIL Act), Belgrade: Nomos, 1991, 238.
490. Under Art. 22 of the Hague Convention on International Access to Justice, its provisions replace Arts 17–26 of the Hague Convention on Civil Procedure of 1954 for countries Parties to the both conventions.
491. Article 20 para. 1 of the Hague Convention on Civil Procedure.
492. *See* Arts 12, 25 and 7 of Hague Convention on International Access to Justice.
493. Chapter 10 and Arts 59–61 of LFLA.

made declaration that it opposes service of judicial documents through foreign diplomatic or consular agents, unless the document is to be served upon a national of the State in which the documents originate (Article 8, paragraph 2). Also, Montenegro does not accept the methods of direct service specified in Article 10 of the Convention (servicing by postal channels, judicial officers or other competent persons).

651. The judge in Montenegro may give judgment even if no certificate of service or delivery has been received, under the condition that the document was transmitted by one of the methods provided for by the Hague Service Convention, and that after at least six months of the date of the transmission of the document no certificate of any kind has been received through the competent authorities of the State addressed (Article 15, paragraph 2). Montenegro has also stated that *restitutio in integrum* will not be entertained after one year following the date of the judgment (Article 16, paragraph 2).

652. Montenegro is a party to the numerous bilateral treaties on legal aid.[494]

653. If neither multilateral nor bilateral treaty is applicable, service to persons or institutions abroad, as well as to foreign nationals enjoying immunity, has to be conducted through diplomatic channels (the LCP, Article 130, paragraph 1). If the service to a citizen of Montenegro abroad is needed, it may be accomplished through the consul or diplomatic representative of Montenegro that performs consular functions in the relevant country, but this type of service is valid only if the recipient voluntarily assents to receive the process (the LCP, Article 130, paragraph 2). If a party or his legal representative are abroad and have no attorney in Montenegro, the court will invite them to appoint an attorney for purposes of service of process in Montenegro within an appropriate time period. If they fail to do so, the court will appoint a temporary representative authorized to receive process on the party's behalf, and will give the party or its legal representative a notice thereof (the LCP, Article 143).

§5. Rules of Evidence

654. If evidence has to be taken abroad, the court will request legal assistance from a foreign court in the country where the evidence is located.[495] If a treaty, neither multilateral nor bilateral is applicable, service of the Letter of Request has to be conducted through diplomatic channels, in accordance with the provisions of the LCP.

---

494. *See supra* National Law.

495. On practice of Montenegrin courts *see* Maja Kostić-Mandić, *Izvođenje dokaza po zamolnicama stranih sudova* u: *Državljanstvo i međunarodno privatno pravo; Haške konvencije*, urednici: G. Knežević, V. Pavić (Letters of Request and Taking of Evidence, In *Citizenship and International Private Law; The Hague Conventions*), G. Knežević, V. Pavić, eds., Belgrade: Univerzitet u Beogradu, Pravni fakultet, Službeni glasnik, 2007, 254, n. 67.

655. Montenegro is a Member State of the Convention on the Taking of Evidence Abroad in Civil or Commercial Matters of 1970, from 2012. The central body is the Ministry of Justice. Montenegro has used the opportunities provided by Article 33 of the Convention and has made reservations regarding the application of certain articles. Thus, members of the judicial personnel of the requesting authority may be present at the execution of a Letter of Request only with the prior authorization by the competent authority; Letter of Request in either English or French, or a translation into one of these languages will not be accepted: it is necessary that the letter is made in the Montenegrin language or that it is accompanied by a translation into that language (Article 4, paragraph 2); in Montenegro, Articles 16 and 18 of the Convention will not apply, so that a diplomatic officer or consular agent accredited in Montenegro may not take the evidence in relation to citizens of Montenegro or a third country; Letters of Request issued for the purpose of obtaining pretrial discovery of documents as known in common law countries will not be executed (Article 23).

656. Pursuant to the LCP[496] the request for legal assistance has to be delivered through diplomatic channels, unless provided otherwise by an international treaty. The request and enclosed documents have to be made in the language of the requested State or accompanied with an official translation into that language (the LCP, Article 176). In its request the court will describe the circumstances of the case as determined at the main hearing and indicate the circumstances that should be observed with special attention when evidence is taken (the LCP, Article 221, paragraph 3). In its ruling on taking evidence abroad, the court will determine the time until which it will wait for the evidence to be taken. When this time expires, the hearing may be conducted although the specific evidence has not been taken (the LCP, Article 222). Foreign official documents, if they are duly legalized, have the same evidentiary value as domestic official documents, on the condition of reciprocity (the LCP, Article 227). The requirement of legalization may be dispensed with, if there is an international treaty to this effect with the country of origin. The basic courts in Montenegro will take evidence upon request of a foreign court if there is an international treaty on legal assistance, or reciprocal practice of rendering legal assistance with the courts of the relevant country (the LCP, Article 173, paragraph 1). The request for legal assistance has to be submitted through diplomatic channels and written in Montenegrin or accompanied by an official translation into that language, if not provided otherwise by an international treaty (the LCP, Article 175). If the requested procedural action would be contrary to public policy of Montenegro, the court will deny legal assistance to the foreign court. However, in such a case the court must send the request to the Supreme Court that will make a final decision on this issue (the LCP, Article 173, paragraph 2). The courts render legal assistance to foreign courts in the manner defined by domestic law. The procedural action may be conducted in the manner requested by the foreign court, if that would not countervail the public policy of the forum (the LCP, Article 174).

496. The following paragraphs elaborating provisions of the LCP mirror paras 481–482 of Kluwer Monograph on PIL of Montenegro of 2013.

657. Montenegro has signed numerous bilateral agreements on legal aid. In all of the above cases, with the exception of Serbia, Bosnia and Herzegovina and Macedonia,[497] Montenegro, by the way of succession, took over the treaties of the former Yugoslavia, that is, the State Union of Serbia and Montenegro. Now we will briefly look at the content of the two bilateral agreements that apply between Montenegro and the States of the former Yugoslavia, which go a step further than the solutions of previously elaborated Hague conventions. This is especially important for a treaty concluded with Serbia.

658. The agreement between Montenegro and the Republic of Serbia on Legal Assistance in Civil and Criminal Matters of 2011[498] stipulates that for general types of provision of legal assistance related to the service and service of certain acts, documents and information, as well as for performing of certain procedural actions (hearing parties, witnesses, taking inheritance statements and so forth), the cooperation takes place directly between the courts and other competent authorities of the Contracting States. For all other forms of legal aid, communication takes place through the central authority. The contract stipulates the scope and method of providing legal assistance, the refusal of legal aid, the costs of the legal aid procedure and special provisions regulate the procedure for providing legal assistance in civil and criminal matters. Thus, the provisions on legal aid in civil matters of this treaty provide for the exemption from payment of costs of civil proceedings and exemption from security for costs, exemption from legalization of public documents, service of documents on personal status and the procedure for recognition and enforcement of judgments and arbitral awards.

659. The agreement between Montenegro and Bosnia and Herzegovina on Legal Assistance in Civil and Criminal Matters of 2011[499] contains very similar provisions as the one with Serbia. The most significant difference in this area is the narrow field of possible direct communication between the courts and other competent authorities of the two countries which is limited to providing legal assistance in the administrative matters provided for in the treaty, as well as to the service of invitation for succession proceedings or taking inheritance statement.

660. In practice, based on the information from the Ministry of Justice of Montenegro[500] for the period 2019–2021 most of the cases of acting upon the Letter of Request were related to service and legal aid was the most frequent in relations with the EU member countries, as bilateral agreements with some of the countries of the region which previously used to account to the highest number of requests, namely Serbia and Bosnia and Herzegovina, envisage direct cooperation between judicial authorities. The highest intensity of cooperation was recorded in cases related to the

497. This includes the Protocol with Slovakia from 2015. *See infra* Table of International Treaties.
498. Podgorica, Službeni list Crne Gore – Međunarodni ugovori No. 4/2009. The treaty entered into force on 11 Jun. 2010.
499. Podgorica, Službeni list Crne Gore – Međunarodni ugovori No. 15/2010.
500. Luris, as a system of electronic records of cases of international legal assistance in civil and criminal matters, was introduced at the Ministry of Justice in 2015.

service of documents (e.g. in 2021 there were in total 153 outgoing and 252 incoming requests from the EU, Western Balkans and other countries). There is a steady decrease in the total number of outgoing requests in 2021 and 2020 compared to 2019 (237, 283 and 394, respectively), as well as in the total number of incoming requests for the same period (303, 293 and 408, respectively).

§6. Temporary Relief

661. LESC, in its Part XXIX (Articles 278–291) regulates the security procedure which is aimed at ensuring the future coercive satisfaction of the creditor's claim. This law introduced public enforcement officers who are in charge of execution while the role of the court is significantly reduced.

662. Among various security measures enumerated in Article 254 of the LESC, the provisional measures are the closest equivalent to the notion of temporary relief (the LESC, Articles 278–291).[501] Provisional measures can be ordered before the litigation commences, in the course of the litigation, or after the end of the litigation, and can last until the time the coercive execution if effected (the LESC, Article 279). There are two types of provisional measures: those intended for securing monetary claims (the LESC, Articles 287–288), and those for securing non-monetary claims (the LESC, Articles 289–291). In order to obtain a provisional measure, the creditor must at least show that he has a credible claim and that there is a risk that the debtor will prevent the future satisfaction of the claim, or make it considerably more difficult, for example, because he will dispose of his assets or conceal them (the LESC, Article 287). It is presumed that such a risk exists if the claim has to be realized abroad. When the litigation or other equivalent proceeding has not yet been initiated the jurisdiction in that case lies with the court that would have jurisdiction for deciding on the motion for coercive execution. Provisional measures for securing monetary and non-monetary claims are exemplified in the LESC, Articles 288 and 290, respectively. The list of provisional measures given in those articles is not exhaustive and any appropriate measure which would provide security for future realization of the claim may be ordered.

663. Security procedures on ships and aircraft are regulated by the LMIN (Articles 1005–1032) and the LOPRAT (Articles 169–176).

501. This paragraph is literally taken from paragraph 483 of the 2013 edition of this monograph, with only a legislative update.

Chapter 5. Recognition and Enforcement of Foreign Decisions

664. In Montenegro the subject of recognition may be foreign court decision, court settlement or decision of other authority which in the country of their origin are equalized with a court judgment, and regulate private legal relations with an international element.[502] Only meritorious decisions may be recognized, irrespective of their name in the country where they were rendered, and irrespective of which type of authority, possibly even a non-judicial, may make that decision, as long as that decision is made in the form, procedure and by the authority competent for the adoption of this kind of decision pursuant to the law of the country of the decision-making (e.g., the decision of a foreign administrative or religious body on the divorce can be recognized if it meets the conditions for recognition).[503] The foreign character of the decision relates to the moment when the decision has become final, which means that, for example, the decisions of courts in Slovenia or Croatia that became valid during the existence of SFR Yugoslavia could not now be considered foreign decisions.[504]

665. The basic courts of Montenegro decide on recognition and enforcement of foreign court decisions, except for commercial matters where the Commercial Court of Montenegro is competent.[505] The procedure for the recognition of foreign judgments has now been regulated in detail,[506] and a new remedy has been introduced: an objection against the decision declaring the recognition.[507] The other legal remedies include appeal against a decision on recognition or a decision on objection (before Higher Court or Court of Appeal) and the extraordinary legal recourse: an application for reopening the proceedings. By way of exception, the court shall not serve a decision on the recognition of a foreign judgment on divorce to the other party if the party seeking recognition is a Montenegrin citizen, and the other party has no domicile or habitual residence in Montenegro.[508]

666. In order for foreign judgment to produce the effect in Montenegro, it has to pass through a formal recognition process called 'exequatur'. The PIL Act in Article 141, as well as the LRCL, stipulates that a recognized foreign court decision in

502. Article 141of the PIL Act.
503. Milan Pak, *Međunarodno privatno pravo* (Private International Law), Belgrade: Nomos, 1991, 104.
504. For the case law in Serbia, *see*: Varadi, Bordaš, Knežević, Pavić, *Međunarodno privatno pravo, 14. izdanje* (Private International Law, 14th edn), Belgrade: Univerzitet u Beogradu, Pravni fakultet, 2012, 583.
505. The Commercial Court decides on the recognition and enforcement of foreign judicial decisions rendered by commercial courts, as well as of foreign arbitration awards (Art. 14(4) and Art. 18 para. 2(4) of the Law on Courts.
506. Articles 152–157 of the PIL Act.
507. Article 153, paras 3, 4 and 5.
508. Article 153, para. 6.

Montenegro is equalized with decisions of domestic courts. This means that a foreign judgment in Montenegro can produce only those effects stipulated by our legal system and could not produce any effect that would have under the law of the State of origin.

667. In its procedure for recognition of a foreign judgment, the court shall limit itself to examining whether the conditions from Articles 142–147 of the PIL Act are met. The conditions for the recognition of a foreign court decision are largely formulated in the same way as in the LRCL, except for reciprocity which is no longer required, and a special basis for refusing recognition of a court decision made in a foreign country by applying the rule of excessive jurisdiction. In the field of recognition and enforcement of foreign court decisions, Montenegrin law did not take solutions from the EU law. The provisions of the PIL Act should apply independently of the country of origin of the decision for which recognition is sought, of course, if the primacy in application does not have any ratified international agreement. Therefore, the EU rules in this field aimed at ensuring the free movement of court decisions on the territory of the Union with minimum control possibilities, have not influenced the PIL Act rules in this field.

668. In Montenegro, the preconditions for the recognition of a foreign judgment are formulated as impediments to recognition, that is, in a negative way. The only one positively formulated, is that applicant for the recognition submits the certificate of the competent foreign court or other authority that the judgment has become final. Therefore, except in the above case, the burden of proof is on the opponent of the applicant and if they prove the existence of an obstacle, the recognition of the foreign judgment shall be denied. A different rule applies for impediments proven ex officio by the court. If the court fails to determine the existence or absence of those preconditions that are accounted for ex officio, it will be considered that there are no obstacles and therefore a decision on the recognition of a foreign decision will be issued.

669. Pursuant to the PIL Act, the preconditions for the recognition of a foreign judgment relate to: finality under the law of the State of origin, international jurisdiction, the right of the defence, the existence of a final judgment in the same matter and between the same parties and the effects of lis pendens and public policy.

670. A foreign judgment shall be recognized if the person seeking recognition submits, together with the judgment (or its certified transcript, certified translation of the foreign judgment) a certificate by a foreign court or other competent authority that the judgment has become final pursuant to the law of the country of origin.[509] If the applicant for the recognition fails to submit the certificate even after a postponed deadline, the application for the recognition of a foreign court decision will be rejected.

509. Article 142 and Art. 149 para. 2 of the PIL Act.

671. International jurisdiction involves two cases: the lack of exclusive jurisdiction of the Montenegrin judiciary and the lack of excessive jurisdiction of the foreign judiciary. The law specifies that a foreign judgment shall not be recognized if the subject matter is within exclusive jurisdiction of a judicial or other authority of Montenegro,[510] as well as if the foreign court based its jurisdiction on the facts not recognized by the law of Montenegro as the facts that may serve as grounds for the establishment of international jurisdiction of a Montenegrin court in handling the same dispute.[511]

672. Respecting the rights of the defence in the law of Montenegro implies that a Montenegrin court shall refuse to recognize a foreign judgment if upon party's request, the court finds that the defendant could not take part in the foreign proceedings due to irregularities in the procedure. The inability to participate in the proceedings should be interpreted narrowly, that the party was not able to participate in a certain stage of the procedure and that later it could not achieve different result in the appellate procedure or using extraordinary legal remedies. If a party had at its disposal an effective remedy at the later stages of the proceedings but did not use it, it is not entitled to invoke a violation of the right of the defence in the procedure for the recognition of a foreign judgment.[512] The PIL Act specifies that irregularities relate 'especially' to adequate service and sufficient time to prepare for defence,[513] which opens the possibility for a wider interpretation of the content of this institute. In the first case, the person against whom the decision was made should prove that he could not take part in the procedure because he was not served in person with the summons, lawsuit, or decision which instituted the proceedings, or if no attempt of service has been made. If personal delivery was tried, but it was not successful, the opponent of the applicant cannot rely on for this reason. This objection is characteristic of the decisions made in the absence of the defendant.[514] In the second case, the opponent of the applicant for the recognition in the foreign procedure was not given sufficient time to prepare the defence as, for example, the deadlines for addressing the allegations of the other party were too short.[515] The opponent of the applicant for the recognition cannot invoke on this basis if he has in any way took part in the hearing on the merits in the first instance proceeding.

673. Article 146, paragraph 1 of the PIL Act stipulates: 'A foreign judgment shall not be recognized if a judicial or other authority of Montenegro gave a final judgment involving the same cause of action, or if another foreign judgment on the same cause of action was recognized in Montenegro.' Therefore, Montenegrin law gives priority to domestic final judgment irrespective of the time of rendering, and if there is a valid domestic decision, or a previously recognized foreign judgment in

510. Article 144 of the PIL Act.
511. Article 145 of the PIL Act.
512. Mihajlo Dika, Gaša Knežević, Srđan Stojanović, *Komentar Zakona o međunarodnom privatnom i procesnom pravu* (Commentary of the PIL Act), Belgrade: Nomos, 1991, 290.
513. Article 143 of the PIL Act.
514. Maja Stanivuković & Mirko Živković, *Međunarodno privatno pravo: opšti deo* (Private International Law: General Part), Belgrade: Službeni list SCG, 2004, 453.
515. *Ibid.*

the same legal matter, between the same parties, this will constitute an unavoidable impediment to the recognition of a foreign judgment.

The PIL Act, as well as the former LRCL, prescribes that the court shall stay the proceedings for a recognition of a foreign judgment if before a Montenegrin court the proceedings instituted earlier and involving the same cause of action and between the same parties are still pending. The proceedings will be stayed until the earlier proceedings have been completed.[516] What will happen next with the recognition procedure depends on the outcome of the domestic lawsuit. If the domestic litigation results in issuing of a meritorious decision, we would have a situation of existence of the adjudicated matter (res iudicata) and a foreign judgment could not have been recognized. If the procedure in Montenegro did not end with the issuing of a meritorious decision, the recognition procedure would continue.

674. A foreign court judgment will not be recognized if the effect of its recognition, and not the judgment itself, would be manifestly contrary to the public policy of Montenegro.[517] The court shall act ex officio. In this segment, it can be examined both, the merits of the decision, and the existence of important procedural legal irregularities in the making of a foreign judgment. In both cases, one should always bear in mind the effect of the foreign decision and its relationship with the basic principles of the domestic legal system.

675. The basic courts and the Commercial Court have exclusive jurisdiction to decide in enforcement procedure and enforce the court decisions: to hand over or take away a child; to reinstate an employee to work; pursuant to which judgment debtor is obliged to perform an act that no other person can perform instead of him/her in accordance with law or legal transaction; on a petition to create security; on petition for counter-enforcement and on request of a judgment creditor for payment of unliquidated damages (LESC Article 4).

676. On the other hand, a public enforcement officer shall be competent to decide on enforcement procedure, to levy enforcement[518] as well as to enforce securing of claims, except in the cases that competency of the court is prescribed for by law. However, the competence for recognition of foreign judgments remains exclusively with the competent court (PIL Act, Article 152 (1), (2), (3)) and therefore public enforcement officer may not decide on the recognition of the foreign judgments as a preliminary question in enforcement procedure as it may even trigger their criminal responsibility.

677. The local jurisdiction of public enforcement officer is decisively governed by the provisions of the LESC. Thus, the public enforcement officer determines and enforces the execution on the basis of the executive document of the court or authority whose seat is in the official area of the public enforcement officer, while for the

516. Article 146 para. 2 of the PIL Act.
517. Article 147 of the PIL Act.
518. See in more detail Ranka Račić, *Sprovođenje stranih izvršnih naslova u Crnoj Gori* (Enforcement of Foreign Executory Titles in Montenegro), Podgorica: Pravni zbornik, No. 3/2019, 63–88.

determination and implementation of the execution resulting from the authentic document, the competence of the public enforcement officer is related to the residence(s) or seat of the executive debtor. Here, one must also have in mind the provision of the PIL Act stating 'the enforcement of court and arbitration decisions shall fall within the territorial jurisdiction of the court in territory of which the enforcement is to be carried out (Article 152 (4))'. This inconsistency of the two pieces of legislation is a clear mistake which should not have occurred in the first place. It is the fact that both the PIL Act and the LESC have been drafted for several years and then had a long vacatio legis but both of them started to be applied in 2014. According to the public enforcement officers it does not make a problem in their practice as they simply disregard this provision but can be misleading to the general public, so this provision of the PIL Act should be amended for the sake of legal security.

§1. Case Law

678. In Montenegro, it is still difficult to obtain information on case law regarding the application of laws or conventions in the field of PIL, and international treaties in general, since specialized software used by the courts only recognizes the application of the ECHR and is generally not user-friendly (the search presupposes one already has information on a specific judgment, and search by keywords is not effective). Court decisions are generally published on the official website of courts,[519] but in practice this does not apply to all decisions. Also, sometimes it takes years before the decision is available on the website. Before filing for request on access to information the author of this monograph was able to access only one relevant judgment published on the official website of courts. However, some judges were helpful in providing for information for academic purposes on their own motion. Therefore, the author received information on the application of the PIL Act and bilateral treaties before the Higher Court in Podgorica, the Commercial Court of Montenegro, the Basic Court in Podgorica and the Basic Court in Cetinje. The cited decisions of the Higher Court in Podgorica and the decisions of the Basic Court in Cetinje collected on the basis of requests for access to information are now available on the above site, after they were anonymized.

679. The survey on the practice of the basic courts in Podgorica and Cetinje for the period from January 2015 to November 2018 shows that cases where recognition and enforcement of foreign judgments were sought make most of the cases involving international element in private law issues. The judges are, generally, proficient in these matters, the most challenging cases being those originating from common law countries (the USA or the UK), where they face difficulties regarding ascertaining finality of a foreign judgment. The Basic Court in Podgorica mainly ruled in divorce cases[520] and in the field of succession, a decision of the District

519. https://www.sudovi.me/sdvi/odluke (accessed 14 Apr. 2022).
520. Basic Court in Podgorica Pso. br. 11/18; Pso. br. 41/17.

Court in Ljubljana,[521] as well as a decision of the notary in Skopje, Macedonia[522] both relating, *inter alia*, to immovable property in Montenegro obtained exequatur. The Basic Court in Cetinje ruled on recognition of a judgment on divorce in Germany,[523] and on the recognition of a foreign judgment on the basis of a bilateral agreement.[524] In one case on the division of marital property, this court did not have local jurisdiction.[525]

680. For the same period the Higher Court in Podgorica applied the PIL Act on three occasions. In the case relating to the exercise of parental rights over a minor child[526] the court confirmed the judgment of the Basic Court in Bar[527] on termination of proceedings in Montenegro for international lis pendens. Previously, in another case,[528] it reversed the judgment of the Basic Court in Bar[529] and remanded the case to the first instance court for retrial because the first instance court applied the rules of the PIL Act on the applicable law to the issue of international jurisdiction. In another case,[530] the court dealt with the condition for recognition under Article 146, paragraph 2 of the PIL Act. In the cited case, the Higher Court found that there is still pending litigation procedure relating to the contract on the division of the joint property from 1975 before the Basic Court in Bar. Therefore, the fact that the judgment on the same matters has been already rendered in the procedure conducted before the court in Ljubljana, Slovenia, whose recognition is sought does not affect the domestic procedure and exequatur procedure was stayed. Referring to the case law of the ECtHR,[531] the Higher Court in Podgorica reversed the judgment[532] and remanded the case to the first instance court. The Basic Court in Bar rejected the application for the recognition of a foreign decision on the maintenance obligation which did not contain data on the name and surname, domicile or place of residence of the parties, as an incomplete submission in accordance with the provisions of Article 106 paragraph 4 of LCP. The Higher Court pointed out that along with the application for recognition, a court decision, whose recognition was sought and which contained all the necessary information about the parties, was attached. According to the court, 'by refusing recognition of the judgment due to the lack of information in the application itself the right of the party to access to justice, which includes the right to a final decision in the court proceedings, would be impaired, and these restrictions would not be proportionate to the legitimate aim pursued'.

521. Basic Court in Podgorica Rs. br. 168/15.
522. Basic Court in Podgorica Rs. br. 183/15.
523. Basic Court in Cetinje Rs. br. 44/2016; Rs. br. 13/2017.
524. Basic Court in Cetinje Pso. br. 1/16, Rs. br. 37/2016.
525. Basic Court in Cetinje P. br. 378/2014.
526. Higher Court in Podgorica Gž. br. 2257/17.
527. Basic Court in Bar P. br. 749 /16.
528. Higher Court in Podgorica Gž. br. 3504/16.
529. Basic Court in Bar P. br. 840/15.
530. Higher Court in Podgorica Gž. br. 6291 /16.
531. ECtHR *Golder v. United Kingdom,* 4451/70, § 25, 21.02.1975, *Hornsby v. Greece,* 18357/91, § 40, 19.03.1997, *Kreuz v. Poland, 28249/95,* § 52, 19.06.2001, *Sotiris and Nikos Koutras ATTEE v. Greece,* 39442/98, § 15, 16.11.2000, *Běleš and Others v. Czech Republic, 47273/99,* § 61, 12.11.2002, *Ateş Mimarlik Mühendislik A.Ş v. Turkey*, 33275/05, § 48, 25.09.2012.
532. Higher Court in Podgorica Pso. br. 18/17, Gž. br. 3987/17.

681. In its practice in the period from January 2015 to November 2018, the Commercial Court in Podgorica decided mostly on the recognition of decisions from Serbia, referring to the bilateral agreement with this country,[533] and in one case on the recognition of a decision from Croatia, according to the PIL Act.[534]

682. The case law of the Basic Court in Podgorica, the Higher Court in Podgorica and the Supreme Court of Montenegro for the period from the end of 2018 to 2021 reinforces the above statement that the judges are well trained to apply relevant legal sources to recognition and enforcement of the foreign court decisions as they regularly apply the PIL Act, and also often bilateral[535] agreements. The largest number of applications for recognition still refers to family relations and specially to divorce, and those decisions are of a typical character. However, there is an impression that the legal counsellors of the parties often do not have enough knowledge on the subject and that sometimes the relevant sources of law are not treated as complementary. The case where the recognition of a notarial deed as a court decision was requested also speaks in favour of the above.[536] In this case, no account was taken of Article 141 of the PIL Act (addressing the court and similar decisions of other bodies which, according to the law of the country of origin, are equated with court decisions) and Article 8 of the Law on Notaries, which stipulates that a foreign notarial deed has, subject to reciprocity, the same legal effect as a notarial deed drawn up under this law, and that it can be an enforceable document, if it refers to the rights that are not contrary to the legal order of Montenegro and if it contains all the elements that are legally necessary for enforcement. And above all, on the Convention Abolishing the Requirement of Legalisation for Foreign Public Documents (HCCH 1961 Apostille Convention).

683. In the mentioned period, there were several decisions that also refer to the conditions for the recognition of the foreign court decisions where the court practice adhered to the above addressed prevalent doctrinal views.

684. In several cases, the courts ruled whether the decision has become final pursuant to the law of the country of origin. In a case relating to the recognition of a divorce decision from Denmark,[537] the applicant for the recognition failed to submit the certificate by a foreign court that the judgment has become final even after a postponed deadline, so the court concluded that the application for recognition

533. Commercial Court Rs. br. 16/15, Rs. br. 19/16, Rs. br. 2/17, Rs. br. 19/17, br. 20/17, Rs. br. 23/17, Rs. br. 13/18.

534. Commercial Court Rs. br. 20/16.

535. Higher Court in Podgorica Gž.br.5001/18, Higher Court in Podgorica Gž. br. 4462/19.

536. Basic Court in Podgorica Pso br. 4/17. Before refusing to recognize the foreign notarial record on the publication of the will, the Basic Court in Podgorica sent a request to the Ministry of Justice to diplomatically determine and inform that court whether the said notarial record was equated with the court decision according to the Italian law. The reply states that the relevant rules are set out in the HCCH 1961 Apostille Convention, to which Montenegro is a signatory, and since the notarial deed in question contains an apostille, it should be recognized as a notarial deed, in accordance with Article 1, item c) of the said Conventions.

537. Higher Court in Podgorica Gž br. 2527/18.

should be considered withdrawn. In another case,[538] the court granted exequatur to the decision from England and Wales as the court ruled that it was clear from the case file that the application for recognition of the foreign court decision was accompanied by a certificate from the competent court, that the time for appeal against the decision had expired, and the certificate was translated by a judiciary sworn translator for the English language. In the third case,[539] the court ruled that the fact that the party filed a request for extraordinary review of the decision of the district court in Trebinje before the Supreme Court of Republic Srpska did not affect the procedure of recognizing a foreign court's decision that became final and enforceable, because the applicant submitted a certificate of finality of that decision.

685. However, based on the practice of domestic courts, in most cases the opponent of the applicant for the recognition alleges a violation of the defence rights in the foreign procedure.[540] In one case,[541] The Higher Court in Podgorica ruled that it has not been proven that the right to defence of defendant was violated during the adoption of the relevant foreign court decision, in terms of Article 143 of the PIL Act, having in mind the fact that the defendant stated only in the objection procedure against the decision declaring the recognition of a decision that he could not participate in the procedure that preceded the adoption of the disputed decision.[542] In another case,[543] the Higher Court in Podgorica annulled the decision of the basic court and returned the case to the first instance court for retrial because the first instance court while deciding on the application for recognition of the foreign court judgment inspected a photocopy of the court delivery note in question, which was not certified. Furthermore, here we list in more detail a typical case[544] in the objection procedure, where the decision of the first instance court on refusing the recognition of the decision from Germany due to procedural irregularities was confirmed,

538. Higher Court in Podgorica Gž br. 4379/19.
539. Higher Court in Podgorica Gž br. 6013/18.
540. Higher Court in Podgorica Gž br. 4379/19, Higher Court in Podgorica Gž br. 5184/17, Higher Court in Podgorica Gž br. 6185/19, Higher Court in Podgorica Gž br. 6357/19, Higher Court in Podgorica Gž br. 6737/17.
541. Higher Court in Podgorica Gž br. 4379/19.
542. 'The fact that the court decision in question indeed states that the hearing is held in the absence of the opponent of the applicant does not mean that he was not informed about the hearing and did not have the opportunity to participate in that procedure, either personally or through his attorney. Therefore, the first-instance court correctly assessed that the opponent of the applicant did not submit any evidence even in the procedure regarding the recognition of a foreign court decision that he disputed the content of the court decision before the court that rendered it, so in accordance with the provisions of Article 365 of the LCP, new facts and new evidence cannot be pointed out in the appeal. It follows from all the above that the opponent of the applicant did not prove that he could not participate in the proceedings due to irregularities in the proceedings.' Higher Court in Podgorica Gž br. 4379/19.
543. Higher Court in Podgorica Gž br. 5184/17.
544. Basic Court in Podgorica Rp.br. 3/20. In this case, *Deutche Rentenversicherung Bayern Süd* from Germany sought recognition of a decision obliging the opponent of the applicant to return the certain amount of the money to the applicant in the name of the approved and paid pension to her father within four months, because she failed to report the death of the beneficiary.

but without the application of the PIL Act.[545] The court pointed out that the decision had to be delivered to the opponent of the applicant residing in Montenegro in accordance with the Convention on the Service Abroad of Judicial and Extrajudicial Documents in Civil and Commercial Matters (HCCH 1965 Service Convention) through the Ministry of Justice as the central body, because Montenegro had declared a reservation to Article 10 that is, it excluded the possibility of judicial and extrajudicial acts being delivered directly to persons on its territory, by mail, and in this way the applicant sent certain letters to the opponent of the applicant. The court also points out that the decision in question was rendered without participation in the proceedings of the opponent of the applicant, who was therefore not given the right to raise objections that could possibly release her from the claim or give her a more favourable position in the proceedings resulting in the decision whose recognition is sought, and the recognition of the decision as such was contrary to the imperative regulations of the state in which recognition is sought, i.e., contrary to Article 20 of the Constitution of Montenegro, which guarantees everyone the right to a legal remedy against a decision deciding on his right or on a legally based interest, and contrary to Article 6 of the European Convention for the Protection of Human Rights and Fundamental Freedoms. Namely, the basis of the decision whose recognition is sought is the unjust enrichment, that is, a non-contractual obligation, so there is no place to apply Article 30 of the Agreement concluded between the SFRY and the Federal Republic of Germany on Social Security, since it is not an enforceable court decision or an enforceable title of the holder or body of a Contracting State on contributions or other social security claims, and even if it were, paragraph 2 of the same article provides that recognition may be refused if the decision is contrary to the public policy of the Contracting State in which the decision or document is to be recognized.

686. In one case,[546] the objection of the opponent of the applicant stating that the effect of recognition of that decision would obviously be contrary to the public order of Montenegro was rejected as unfounded and the court explained the restrictive application of this institute in accordance with the wording of Article 147 of the PIL Act. The court confirms the allegations in the objections relating to the fact that the decision to sell the disputed real estate was made on the basis of the institute of personal bankruptcy which does not exist in domestic law. However, this circumstance does not automatically presuppose that the decision is in itself contrary to the imperative rules of law of the state in which the foreign court decision is recognized. In the court's view:

545. 'The decision cannot be recognized in this legal system, because its enforceability is also questionable, so the first instance court correctly decided when it rejected the applicant's request as unfounded, without examining whether under German law this decision can be equated with a foreign court decision in terms of Article 142 paragraph 3 of the PIL Act.'

546. Basic Court in Podgorica Rp.br. 4/19. The decision of the Basic Court in Podgorica (Pso.br. 7/2018) confirming the final decision of the District Court in Plymouth no. 172/2011, brought in a case between the personal bankruptcy trustee A.A. and responsible parties H.M.M. and S.M.M.

the prohibitions which should be taken into account in assessing whether a particular final decision of a foreign court should be recognized, must be essential, and in conflict with a specific rule of domestic law or, in absence of that, with basic civil law principles. The fact is that the personal bankruptcy procedure was conducted against the opponents of the applicant in the home country, in a legal manner, and the sale of real estate in Montenegro is only a consequence of that specific procedure. If this consequence is in accordance with domestic law in the part relating to the enforcement, and does not deny or restrict the opponents of the applicants of their essential human and then procedural rights, this Panel sees no reason why the decision should not be recognized in this legal system.

687. In another case,[547] the granting of exequatur was refused due to the existence of exclusive jurisdiction because the real estate to which the disputed relations are related in the stated legal matters is located in Montenegro. The court referred to the provisions of the Agreement between Montenegro and Bosnia and Herzegovina on Legal Assistance in Civil and Criminal Matters, the Law on Civil Procedure and the PIL Act.

688. There is also a case when the Higher Court issued a decision revoking the decision of the panel of the basic court in Bar and returned the case to the first instance court for retrial due to international lis pendens under Article 146 paragraph 2 of the PIL Act, because of the previously initiated procedure in Montenegro.[548]

547. Higher Court in Podgorica Gž br. 4462/19.

548. Higher Court in Podgorica Gž. br. 6291/16. The Higher Court states that the opponent of the applicant pointed out in all legal remedies that since 1975 the civil proceedings between same parties and in the same matter are being conducted before the same court in Montenegro, so that final judgment of the Ljubljana court cannot be recognized.

Chapter 6. International Insolvency Law

689. In 2011 the new LB, influenced by the EU Regulation No. 1346/2000 on Insolvency Proceedings, came into force. The 2011 LB provides for a special chapter on international bankruptcy (Chapter IX, Articles 178–207).[549]

690. LB regulates bankruptcy proceedings with a foreign element in a detailed manner. Chapter IX of LB applies when assistance is sought in Montenegro by a foreign court or a foreign representative in connection with a foreign proceeding, or when the foreign and domestic proceeding are taking place concurrently, or when creditors in a foreign State have an interest in requesting the commencement of bankruptcy proceeding or participating in such proceeding (Article 178). According to the law, the provisions of the chapter dealing with bankruptcy proceedings with a foreign element should be interpreted in accordance with international standards (Article 185). Commercial courts are competent for deciding on recognition of foreign proceedings and for cooperation with foreign courts (*see* Articles 180 and 181).[550] Public policy exception is also introduced so that the court may refuse to take an action required by this law if the action would be contrary to the public policy of Montenegro (Article 183).

549. Kluwer Monograph on PIL of Montenegro of 2013, para. 369.
550. For recognition of foreign insolvency proceedings *see* Vladimir Savković, *Universalism and the recognition of group proceedings under the UNCITRAL Model Law in Montenegro*, International Insolvency Review, 2019, 103–125.

Chapter 7. International Arbitration

691. Sources of law on international arbitration in Montenegro include multilateral and bilateral treaties and statutory instruments. Montenegro became a party to the New York Convention on the Recognition and Enforcement of Foreign Arbitral Awards of 1958 and the European Convention on International Commercial Arbitration of 1961 by the way of succession. Montenegro is also a party to the Washington Convention on the Settlement of Investment Disputes Between States and Nationals of Other States of 1965 (ICSID Convention). A number of bilateral treaties on international legal assistance contain provisions on the recognition and enforcement of foreign arbitral awards,[551] and relevant provisions can also be found in some bilateral trade and navigation agreements. Also, many Bilateral Investment Treaties (BIT) contain arbitration clauses that give investors the opportunity to initiate arbitration procedure against the host country of investment. In this short overview the focus will be on provisions of the statute law.

692. International Commercial Arbitration is regulated by the Law on Arbitration[552] (LA) of 2015, which is modelled after the UNCITRAL Model Law on International Arbitration. In addition to international arbitration, this law also regulates internal arbitration, recognition and enforcement of arbitral awards, as well as the jurisdiction and conduct of courts in relation to arbitration. Until the adoption of the Law on Arbitration in this area, the relevant provisions of LCP (Part IV) and the PIL Act (for Recognition and Enforcement) were applied.[553] The Law on Arbitration applies to domestic and international arbitration alike. Montenegrin law stipulates that the parties to arbitration may be natural persons with domicile or habitual residence in Montenegro, and/or legal persons established under Montenegrin law. Under the LA, international arbitration implies conduct of arbitral proceedings before an arbitral tribunal for the resolution of a dispute with an international element in which one of the parties is a natural person with domicile or habitual residence in another country or a legal person established under a foreign law whose seat is in another country.[554]

693. International Commercial Court of Arbitration attached to Montenegro Chamber of Commerce with its seat in Podgorica is the sole arbitration centre in Montenegro, established in 2003.[555] Its latest, 2015 arbitration rules are drafted in accordance with the UNCITRAL enactments.[556] This institutional arbitration is becoming more popular in recent years.

551. Treaties with: Austria, Bosnia and Herzegovina, Bulgaria, Czech Republic, Italy, Hungary, Macedonia, Poland, Serbia and Slovakia. *See* the section dedicated to the sources of PIL of Montenegro.

552. Podgorica, Službeni list Crne Gore No. 47/2015, https://www.paragraf.me/propisi-crnegore/zakon_o_arbitrazi.html (accessed 14 Apr. 2022).

553. Title XIII of the PIL Act, Arts 150–151 ceased to be in force.

554. Article 2 of the Law on Arbitration.

555. Vesko Božović, *Montenegro*, Global Arbitration Review, 13 Oct. 2017.

556. http://www.privrednakomora.me/sites/pkcg.org/files/multimedia/main_pages/files/2012/09/arbitrazna_pravila1.pdf (accessed 14 Apr. 2022).

§1. Arbitration Agreement

694. The validity of the arbitration agreement as to form is regulated by the New York Convention Article II, and the European Convention, Article 1(2)(a). When none of these conventions is applicable, the form of the arbitration agreement is governed by the provisions of the Law on Arbitration.

695. The LA stipulates arbitration agreement shall be concluded in writing, but this rule is softened by the provisions of Article 9. Those provisions were modelled after the UNCITRAL Model Law Article 7, option I (2006) which provide that arbitration agreement may be even oral as long as the content of the agreement is recorded and that signatures of the parties or an exchange of messages between the parties is no longer required.[557] However, they are not fully in compliance with it since according to the Explanatory report of the LA, they were considered to be too advanced for Montenegro at the time of the adoption of the LA. Thus, according to the LA, Article 9(4), an arbitration agreement has been concluded in writing if it is contained in documents signed by the parties or has been concluded in an exchange of messages by means of communication which provide a written record of the agreement of the parties, whether or not those messages have been signed by the parties; after an orally concluded arbitration agreement one party sends to the other party a notice in writing referring to a previously concluded oral agreement and the other party fails to object to the contents of the received notice in a timely manner, which is considered to constitute acceptance of the offer according to the usages of the trade; the parties in a written contract make a reference to another document containing an arbitration agreement (general terms of business, general terms for conclusion of legal transaction, text of another agreement, etc.) provided that the purpose of such reference is to make the arbitration agreement an integral part of the main contract; a bill of lading contains an express reference to an arbitration clause in a charter party; the claimant initiates arbitral proceedings in writing, and the respondent expressly accepts arbitration and agrees to it in writing or in the statement made on the record at the hearing or takes part in arbitral proceedings and does not deny the existence of the arbitration agreement or fails to object to the jurisdiction of the arbitral tribunal before raising issues related to the substance of the dispute.

696. Other provisions of the LA providing for the principles of Kompetenz-Kompetenz and separability of the arbitration clause from the underlying contract are fully in compliance with the international standards in the field.

§2. Rules of Procedure and Rules Applicable to Substance of Dispute

697. The rules of procedure of the Law on Arbitration generally mirror Chapter V on Conduct of Arbitral Proceedings of the UNCITRAL Model Law, with some

557. Explanatory Note by the UNCITRAL Secretariat on the 1985 Model Law on International Commercial Arbitration as amended in 2006, 5.

supplement provisions (e.g., regarding the place of arbitration in Article 32(3) and Article 32(4); commencement of arbitral proceedings before institutional or ad hoc arbitration in Articles 33 and so forth). Thus, Article 31 stipulates the parties are free to agree on the procedure to be followed by the arbitral tribunal in conducting the proceedings or in referring to specific rules of arbitration. If the parties fail to agree on the rules of arbitration proceedings, the arbitral tribunal may conduct the arbitration proceedings in such manner as it considers appropriate (the power to determine the admissibility, relevance and weight of any proposed and adduced evidence included).

698. The rules applicable to substance of dispute are also modelled after the UNCITRAL Model Law. Pursuant to Article 40 of the LA, the arbitral tribunal shall decide the dispute in accordance with such rules of law as are chosen by the parties as applicable to the substance of the dispute (unless the parties have agreed on the application of conflict of laws rules), and in case of failing any designation of the applicable law by the parties, the arbitral tribunal shall apply the law determined by the conflict of laws rules which it considers applicable. The arbitrators shall decide ex aequo et bono only when parties explicitly stipulate so.

§3. Judicial Review of Arbitral Awards

699. Judicial review of arbitral awards may arise in proceedings for setting aside domestic arbitration award, initiated by an application before a domestic court, and in the procedure for the recognition and enforcement of a foreign arbitral award. The court of the country of arbitration (the place of arbitration and the place of rendering of an award) is competent to decide on the setting aside of the award. Thus, in Montenegro, the Commercial Court of Montenegro is competent to decide on setting aside of domestic arbitration award issued through the institutional or ad hoc arbitration in Montenegro, irrespective of whether it is a domestic or international arbitration, even in the case of an arbitration award rendered in arbitration administered by The International Court of Arbitration which is part of the International Chamber of Commerce in Paris, if the place of arbitration is Montenegro.

700. The reasons for setting aside arbitration award are provided for in Article 48 of the Law on Arbitration. The conditions for setting aside defined by this law are modelled after the European Convention on International Commercial Arbitration. These taxable conditions are formal, procedural, and the merits of the decision can only be examined on the basis of the institute of public policy. An arbitral award may be set aside if the party making the application furnishes proof in one of the following six cases: the arbitral tribunal was not competent, disadvantages of the parties in the proceedings, violation of the right of defence, the award deals with a dispute not contemplated by the arbitration agreement or contains decisions on matters beyond the scope of the arbitration agreement, deficiencies in the composition of the arbitral tribunal or the arbitral procedure and the award does not contain the statement of reasons or has not been signed.

701. The existence or validity of an arbitration agreement is a prerequisite for the validity of arbitral awards, since without the existence of a valid arbitration agreement, there is no basis for the jurisdiction of arbitration. Pursuant to the Law on Arbitration, this condition will be valued according to the law that the parties have agreed upon or under the law of Montenegro, unless the parties have otherwise agreed.

702. The procedural deficiencies on the side of the party include cases when the party to the proceedings did not have the capacity to conclude the arbitration agreement and to be a party to the dispute or a party was not duly represented.

703. The right of defence traditionally covers situation where the party making the application was not given proper notice of the initiation of the arbitral proceedings or was otherwise unlawfully unable to present his case before the arbitral tribunal.

704. Another condition is that the award deals with a dispute not contemplated by the arbitration agreement or contains decisions on matters beyond the scope of the arbitration agreement, provided that only the part of the award on matters not submitted to arbitration may be set aside if that part of the award can be separated from the decision on matters submitted to arbitration. This is the most common reason for the annulment of arbitration decisions. Arbitrators are obliged to act in accordance with the expressed will of the parties in the arbitration agreement. The decision could be annulled if the arbitrators make a decision over the requests submitted by the parties. For example, if the parties agreed that the arbitration will be competent to resolve disputes solely from the main contract, and the decision is made on the obligations regarding the secondary contracts and relations with the subcontractors.

705. Another condition relates to the composition of the arbitral tribunal or that arbitral procedure was not in accordance with the Law on Arbitration or a permissible agreement of the parties, and that fact could have affected the content of the arbitral award. A violation of the procedure that would lead to the setting aside of arbitral award should be relevant, and could affect the content of the award.

706. In the law of Montenegro, it is presumed that all arbitral awards contain the statement of reasons. The European Convention allows the parties to release the arbitrators from this obligation.[558] Parties may explicitly or implicitly consent that reasons need not be stated. An agreement is implicit when litigants have accepted an arbitral procedure under which it is customary not to state reasons, unless one of them requests the arbitral tribunal to do so.

707. The court shall also set aside an arbitral award if it finds ex officio that:

558. Article 8, indent a) of the European Convention on International Commercial Arbitration.

- the subject matter of the dispute is not capable of settlement by arbitration under the legislation of Montenegro;
- The LA, as arbitral, lists the contractual and non-contractual relations. The doctrine[559] lists as potentially controversial arbitrability of disputes in the field of competition law, intellectual property law and bankruptcy law.
- the award is contrary to the public policy of Montenegro.

708. An application for setting aside arbitral award may be instituted within three months from the date on which the award had been served on the party. The parties may not waive their right to make an application for setting aside arbitral award. New arbitral proceedings between the same parties in relation to the same matter may be conducted only on the basis of a new arbitration agreement. Exception from this rule exists in case the court set aside an arbitral award on the grounds other than those related to the existence and validity of the arbitration agreement not specifying the names of the arbitrators, since such agreement is still binding upon the parties until they agree otherwise.[560]

I. Recognition and Enforcement of Foreign Arbitral Award

709. In order for a foreign arbitral award to produce legal effect in Montenegro, it is necessary to obtain an exequatur by a domestic court. In the procedure for recognition and enforcement, the domestic court exercises control of a foreign arbitral award, but the powers of the court are limited to establishing the existence of conditions provided for by national law.[561] The most important sources of law in Montenegro in this area are the Law on Arbitration and the New York Convention. Previously, the provisions of the LRCL, and then the PIL Act, were applied to the recognition and enforcement of foreign arbitral awards.

710. The Law on Arbitration in Article 52 provides for the conditions for the recognition and enforcement of a foreign arbitral award, modelled after the New York Convention so that the same conditions apply to all arbitral awards irrespective of their origin. The conditions for the recognition and enforcement of a foreign arbitral award are negatively formulated (as reasons for the refusal of enforcement). Montenegro, on the basis of succession, became a member to this Convention and is still bound by reservations made by the former State (restrictions requiring the existence of reciprocity with the State of origin of the award and that a dispute is of commercial character).[562] However, the applicant for the recognition has the right to cite more favourable provisions of the Law on Arbitration which does not stipulate these two conditions.

559. *See* Maja Stanivuković, *Međunarodna arbitraža* (International Arbitration), Belgrade: Službeni glasnik, 2013, 106–113.
560. Article 49 of the Law on Arbitration.
561. Gaša Knežević, *Izvršenje arbitražnih odluka sa posebnim osvrtom na Ex-YU element* (Enforcement of Arbitral Awards with Special Regard on Ex-YU Element), Belgrade, Pravni život, No. 9-10/1994, 1448.
562. Article I(3) para. 1 of the New York Convention.

711. Upon the request of a party, exequatur may be refused for the following reason: if the arbitration agreement is not valid; in case of violation of the right of defence; when the arbitrators in the decision-making exceeded the limits of the arbitration agreement; if the composition of the arbitral tribunal and the arbitration procedure are not in accordance with the arbitration agreement; and if the decision whose exequatur is sought is not final.

712. Two conditions for which the court is charged ex officio relate to: arbitrability and public policy. The court shall refuse recognition and enforcement of an arbitral award if it finds that the subject matter of the dispute is not capable of settlement by arbitration under the law of Montenegro. Under the Law on Arbitration, arbitrable are disputes with an international element arising from a contractual or non-contractual relationship in which one of the parties is a natural person with domicile or habitual residence in another country or a legal person established under a foreign law whose seat is in another country.[563] The court shall refuse recognition and enforcement of an arbitral award if it finds that the effects of the arbitral award would be contrary to the public policy of Montenegro. In the procedure for the recognition and enforcement of foreign arbitral award, the domestic court only protects the national public policy.[564] Unlike the earlier LRCL,[565] the possibility of re-examining the possible violation of the public policy is now limited only to the effects of the decision.

713. The recognition and enforcement of foreign arbitral award in Montenegro are decided by the Commercial Court in the contradictory proceedings. A decision on recognition and enforcement of an arbitral award shall contain statement of reasons. An appeal against a decision rendered in the proceedings for recognition may be submitted to the Court of Appeal of Montenegro within fifteen days from the date of service of the decision on recognition.[566]

§4. CASE LAW

714. In this brief overview of the arbitration practice relevant for Montenegro we will look at fairly recent decisions of the Court of Appeal of Montenegro and the cases brought against Montenegro under the ICSID Convention.

715. In 2017 the Court of Appeal of Montenegro[567] reversed the decision of the Commercial Court of Montenegro and by granting exequatur upheld the award of the International Arbitration Court of the International Chamber of Commerce

563. Article 2 para. 1 of the Law on Arbitration.
564. Aleksandar Goldštajn & Siniša Triva, *Međunarodna trgovinska arbitraža* (International Commercial Arbitration), Zagreb: Informator, 1987, 18.
565. *See* Art. 99 para. 3 of the LRCL.
566. Article 54(5) of the LA.
567. Court of Appeal of Montenegro P.ž. br. 637/17; Rs. br. 18/16, available at: http://www.cin-cg.me/wp-content/uploads/2018/09/LINK-5-Apelacioni-sud-pravosna%C5%BEna-presuda.pdf (accessed 14 Apr. 2022).

(ICC) in Paris number 17146, rendered on 12 March 2013.[568] The second instance court agreed on findings of the Arbitral Tribunal that arbitration clause is not ambiguous, but incomplete because it neither expressly mentions the name of the arbitral institution referred to in Sub-Clause 20.6(a) of the General Conditions of the Contract (GC), nor the location of the place of arbitration (Sub-Clause 20.6(b) of the GC). The Court of Appeal finds that the interpretation of the arbitration clause also requires the interpretation of contract, contractual documents, as well as the examination of the overall circumstances. However, the Court did not address the fact that the clause stipulates application of the UNCITRAL Arbitration Rules. In the court's view the interpretation of Sub-Clause 20.6 of the GC was confirmed, among others, by the FIDIC Multilateral Development Bank Harmonized Conditions of Contract for Construction 2006, which provided for the ICC as the default institution (CII, paragraph 18). Finally, in its reasoning the court states: 'unlike the first-instance court that performed a strict linguistic interpretation of the arbitration clause, this court having in mind that the aim of our legal system is to harmonize with European legal standards and adapt to contemporary trends in the field of law ... accepted an interpretation that when it comes to incomplete arbitration clause they should be salvaged' (through interpretation).[569] The European Convention which contains a specific mechanism[570] to ensure the constitution of an arbitral tribunal even if no seat was designated in the arbitration clause was not even addressed in the Arbitral Tribunal's reasoning. To the best of our knowledge this is the first time that such or a similar clause was upheld by the ICC and the Court of Appeal of Montenegro alike.

716. Finally, after four identical decisions of the Commercial Court refusing the exequatur of the arbitral award,[571] a decision of the Constitutional Court[572] that revision as an extraordinary legal remedy in this case is permissible and the decision of the Supreme Court[573] that the revision is not permissible, the decision of the Court of Appeal[574] was executed in the amount of EUR 12 million.

717. It is worth mentioning that in his paper[575] published in a Montenegrin law journal, one of the arbitrators in this case, with dissenting opinion, addressed in details all arguments of the Court of Appeal proving them wrong. Among others, the author pointed out that the parties have not agreed to the ICC arbitration but agreed only that their disputes prospective will be resolved by an arbitration applying the UNCITRAL Arbitration Rules, the court's ignorance of the proceedings

568. Available at: www.cin-cg.me/wp-content/uploads/2018/.../LINK-1-Odluka-arbitraže-MTK-Pariz.pdf (accessed 14 Apr. 2022).
569. The words in brackets were added by the author.
570. Article IV(3) to IV(7) of the European Convention.
571. Commercial Court Rs.br.30/14 of 20.03.2015, Rs.br.19/15 of 28.09.2015, Rs.br. 29/15 of 31.03.2016, Rs.br.18/16 of 23.03.2017.
572. Constitutional Court U-III br.1624/18 of 29.01.2019.
573. Supreme Court Rev. br. 101/18 of 13.06.2018.
574. Court of Appeal Pž.br. 637/17 of 28.04.2018.
575. See in more detail Časlav Pejović, *O jednoj odluci Apelacionog suda: Rušenje mita o 'domaćinskoj pravdi'* (About one decision of Appellate Court: breaking the myth of 'domestic justice'), Podgorica: Pravni zbornik, No. 3/2019, 137–169.

before the ICC arbitration with respect to the effects of the challenge of jurisdiction, as well as their invoking the wrong FIDIC enactment and miscitation of the European Convention's Article IV.

718. Recently, Montenegro has been a party to the several proceedings conducted under the ICSID Convention. In 2016 Montenegro prevailed in a dispute with MNSS BV and Recupero Credito Acciao,[576] Netherlands-registered investors in a bankrupt steel plant. The Arbitral Tribunal dismissed the claim against Montenegro partly on jurisdiction and partly on the merits. The arbitral tribunal declined its jurisdiction over the contract and the investment law claims and rejected all BIT claims except for the breach of the full protection and security standard, while ruling that the investors had suffered no loss as a result of a violation of this treaty standard.[577]

719. Montenegro was also successful in a claim brought by the Central European Aluminum Company ('CEAC').[578] The main contentious issue was whether CAEC had its seat in Cyprus and accordingly whether CEAC was a protected investor within the meaning of the applicable Cyprus–Serbia and Montenegro Bilateral Investment Treaty of 2005. Montenegro argued that the claimant had no office in Cyprus, that the address provided was in fact an abandoned residence and the tribunal accepted the view that a certificate of tax residency was insufficient to establish a seat for the purposes of a BIT claim. The Arbitral Tribunal declined its jurisdiction on the ground that Claimant had failed to establish a seat, registered office or any premises of its own open to the public at the claimed address in Cyprus.

---

576. *MNSS BV and Recupero Credito Acciaio NV v. Montenegro* (ICSID Case No. ARB(AF)/12/8).

577. https://www.acerislaw.com/montenegro-icsid-arbitration-track-record/ (accessed 14 Apr. 2022).

578. *CEAC Holdings Limited v. Montenegro* (ICSID Case No. ARB/14/8). *See* Inna Uchkunova et al., *The Requirement of 'Effective Seat' in CEAC Holdings Limited v. Montenegro: Are We Moving Towards a Double-Barreled Test for Protected 'Investor'?* 8 Dec. 2016, http://arbitrationblog.kluwerarbitration.com/2016/12/08/requirement-effective-seat-ceac-holdings-limited-v-montenegro-moving-towards-double-barreled-test-protected-investor/ (accessed 14 Apr. 2022).

Annex I. Private International Law – Act[579]

('Official Gazette of Montenegro', Nos. 1/2014, 6/2014 – revised version, 11-2014 – revised version, 14/2014 and 47/2015 – revisions relevant to this act made in another act)

PART ONE

APPLICABLE LAW

Chapter I

GENERAL PROVISIONS

Scope

Article 1

The present Act shall govern the rules designating applicable law in private law matters having international implications ('conflict provisions'), the rules on the jurisdiction of judicial and other authorities to hear such actions, and the rules of procedure, as well as the rules for the recognition and enforcement of foreign judgments and arbitration awards, and of decisions of other authorities.

Supremacy of international treaties and other legislation

Article 2

The provisions of the present Act shall not apply to the matters from Art. 1 of the present Act where such matters are governed by an international treaty or other legislation.

579. Unofficial translation by Professor Dr. Vesna Bulatović, University of Montenegro, Podgorica. Updated version as of 8 Dec. 2018.

Annex I

Legal gaps

Article 3

In the absence from the present Act of a rule to designate law applicable to a matter from Art. 1 of the present Act, such matter shall be subject to provisions and principles of the present Act, the principles of legal order of Montenegro and the principles of international private law.

Reference to foreign law

Article 4

Where under the present Act reference is made to foreign law, the legislation, including conflict provisions, of that state shall apply, unless otherwise provided for by the present or other act.

Reference to the law of Montenegro or to the law of a third state is not allowed where the case is relating to any of the following:

1. legal status of legal persons and forms of organisation without legal personality;
2. form of legal transactions;
3. choice of applicable law;
4. maintenance;
5. contractual relations;
6. non-contractual relations.

Where the conflict provisions of a foreign state make reference to the law of Montenegro or make reference to the law of a third state, the substantive law of Montenegro and substantive law of the third state shall apply.

States with multiple legal systems

Article 5

Where the applicable law is from a state with multiple legal systems, and where the provisions of the present Act do not refer to a particular jurisdiction within that state, applicable law shall be designated according to the rules of that legal system.

Where applicable law of a state with multiple legal systems may not be designated as provided for in paragraph 1 of this Article, the law of the jurisdiction within that state which has closest connections with the legal relationship shall apply.

Determination of content of foreign applicable law

Article 6

A judicial or other authority duly empowered by law ('judicial or other authority') shall act ex officio to determine the content of applicable law.

The judicial or other authority from paragraph 1 of this Article shall determine the content of applicable law in accordance with international treaties, and may seek information on foreign law from the ministry responsible for justice affairs as well as opinions from experts and specialised institutions.

Parties to a proceeding may also file documents on the content of foreign law or otherwise assist the judicial or other authority.

The judicial or other authority may commit the parties to cooperate in determining the content of a foreign law when the parties have decided which foreign law shall apply.

Interpretation and application of foreign law

Article 7

Foreign law shall be interpreted and applied in the way it is interpreted and applied in its state of origin.

Where foreign law is not applied, or where foreign law is interpreted and applied wrongly, legal remedies shall be allowed.

Exception clause

Article 8

By way of exception, the law designated according to the present Act shall not apply where, taking into account all the circumstances of the case, the connection to that law is manifestly weak, and where there is significantly stronger connection to other law.

This provision shall not apply when the parties themselves have designated the law applicable to their relationship.

Public order

Article 9

Where a provision of foreign law is manifestly contrary to the public order of Montenegro, that provision shall not apply.

Direct application of certain provisions

Article 10

The provisions of Montenegrin law whose application is deemed particularly significant to the protection of public interest, such as political, social, or economic system of the state, shall apply to all the cases that the provisions refer to, irrespective of the applicable law designated.

By way of exception, a court may take into account the direct application provisions of another state that the legal relationship is closely connected to.

In deciding to take into consideration the provisions from paragraph 1 of this Article, the court shall take into account their nature and purpose, as well as the consequences of their application or non-application.

Annex I

Chapter II

LEGAL STATUS OF PERSONS

I. LEGAL STATUS OF A NATURAL PERSON

Nationality

Article 11

The issue whether a natural person has the nationality of a state shall be governed by the law of that state.

Where a person who is a Montenegrin national also holds nationality of another state, the person shall be deemed to have Montenegrin nationality only.

Where a person who is not a Montenegrin national has two or more nationalities, the person shall be deemed to have the nationality of the state with which that person, taking all circumstances and notably his habitual residence into account, has the closest connections.

Where a person is stateless or his nationality cannot be established, applicable law shall be designated according to his habitual residence.

Where a person has the status of a refugee or asylee, applicable law shall be the law of the state where that person has habitual residence.

Where the habitual residence of a person cannot be established, applicable law shall be the law of a state that the person has closest connections to.

Habitual residence

Article 12

For the purpose of the present Act, habitual residence of a natural person is a place where a natural person habitually resides, independently of the registration with the competent body and independently of residence or domicile permit, and irrespective of whether the residence is restricted in advance. In determining habitual residence, due consideration should be taken of the circumstances of personal or professional nature that show durable connections with that place or indicate the intention to create such connections.

For the purpose of the legal relationships from Chapters V and VI of the present Act, habitual residence of a natural person pursuing a business activity shall be subject to Articles 40 and 51 of the present Act.

Legal capacity

Article 13

Legal capacity of a natural person shall be governed by the law of the state of which the natural person is a national.

Civil capacity

Article 14

Civil capacity of a natural person shall be governed by the law of the state of which the natural person is a national. Where applicable law for a particular matter envisages specific provisions on civil capacity, that law shall apply.

Where a contract was signed by persons present in the same state, the person who according to the law of that state has civil capacity may not claim his civil incapacity according to the law of a third country, except where the other contractual party was aware of civil incapacity at the time the contract was concluded, and where the person was not aware of it for reason of gross negligence.

Paragraph 2 of this Article shall not apply to legal transactions related to family and succession relations, or to legal transactions relating to the rights in rem in immovable property located in a third state, rather than a state where the contract was concluded.

Civil capacity of entrepreneurs

Article 15

Civil capacity of a natural person pursuing a business activity without establishing a legal person shall be governed by the law of the state where the person is registered as an entrepreneur. Where no registration is required, civil capacity shall be governed by the law of the state where the natural person has the principal place of business.

Guardianship

Article 16

Placement under guardianship and cessation of guardianship as well as relationships between a guardian and persons under guardianship shall be governed by the law of the state of which the person under guardianship is a national.

Provisional protection measures with respect to a foreign national or a stateless person present in Montenegro are governed by the law of Montenegro and last until the state whose judicial or another authority with decision-making powers has given a decision or taken necessary measures.

Paragraph 2 of this Article also applies to the protection of property of an absent foreign national and of a stateless person present in the territory of Montenegro.

Name

Article 17

Determination or change of name shall be governed by the law of the state of which that person is a national.

The effect that a change in nationality has on one's name shall be governed by the law of the state of which that person has obtained nationality. In case of a stateless person, the effect of a change in habitual residence on the name shall be governed by the law of the state where the person has his new habitual residence.

The protection of name shall be governed by the law designated pursuant to Chapter VI of the present Act.

Notwithstanding paragraph 1 of this Article, spouses may subject the determination or a change in name on the occasion of or after the conclusion of their marriage in Montenegro, to the law of the state of which one spouse has nationality, or to the law of Montenegro if one of the spouses has habitual residence in Montenegro. Where the affidavit on the change of name is given after the conclusion of marriage, that statement must be in the form of a public document.

Notwithstanding paragraph 1 of this Article, holders of parental rights may make a statement before the registry officer that the child's surname shall be governed by the law of the state in which one of the spouses has habitual residence in Montenegro. Where the statement on the change of name is made after the birth certificate is issued, the statement must be in the form of a public document.

The effects on a child of the determination of name, or of surname made pursuant to paragraphs 4 and 5 of this Article, where the change is made in a surname of a minor who has turned ten, require the consent of the child on condition that the child is capable of expressing his opinion.

Declaring a missing person dead

Article 18

Declaring a missing person dead shall be governed by the law of the state of which the person was a national at the time he disappeared. Where the person is stateless, the terms and effects of declaring the missing person dead shall be governed by the law of the state in which the person had his last habitual residence.

Provisional measures for the preservation and protection of property owned by the person present in the territory of Montenegro shall be governed by Montenegrin law.

A person who has habitual residence in Montenegro may be declared dead according to Montenegrin law where so required by the person who has a legal interest in it.

II. LEGAL STATUS OF A LEGAL PERSON, ORGANISATIONAL FORMS WITHOUT LEGAL PERSONALITY AND OF THE STATE

Legal person

Article 19

A legal person shall be governed by the law of the state where it was established.

Where a legal person has its actual seat in a state other than the state where it was established and where according to the law of that other state the law of that state is applicable, applicable law shall be the law of the state of the actual seat.

Organisational forms without legal personality

Article 20

Organisational forms without legal personality shall be governed by the law of the state where they were registered or established.

Scope of application of applicable law

Article 21

The law applicable under Articles 19 and 20 of the present Act refer in particular to the following:

1. establishment, legal nature and legal form;
2. name or title;
3. legal subjectivity and system of management;
4. establishment, competence and functioning of the bodies of the legal person or of other organisational form;
5. agency;
6. acquisition and loss of membership, and related rights and obligations;
7. liability for obligations;
8. consequences of any violations of law or of founding documents;
9. reorganisation and cessation of a legal person or of other organisational form.

State as an entity in private law relationships with an international element

Article 22

Provisions of the present Act also apply to private law relations with an international element in which one party is a state unless otherwise provided for by law.

Chapter III

LEGAL AFFAIRS, REPRESENTATION AND STATUTE OF LIMITATIONS

Form of legal transactions and legal actions

Article 23

Unless otherwise provided for by the present Act, a legal transaction and a legal action are deemed valid with respect to their form if they are valid either according to the law of the place where the legal transaction is concluded or the legal action initiated or according to the law applicable to the content of the legal transaction or of legal action.

Contractual representation

Article 24

Relationships between the grantor of attorney and a third party, the existence and scope of authority given to a representative, as well as effects arising out of the usage or alleged usage of such authority, shall be governed by the law chosen by the grantor and the third party, on condition that the choice made is known or could have been known to the representative.

In the absence of a choice of law, the matters from paragraph 1 of this Article shall be governed by the law of the state where the representative acted. If the representative acted in the conduct of his professional activity, applicable law shall be the law of the place where the representative had his statutory seat, on condition that the place is known or could have been known to the third party.

Notwithstanding paragraphs 1 and 2 of this Article, where the subject of representation is the right to immovable property, the matters from paragraph 1 of this Article shall be governed by the state where the immovable property is located.

The right established pursuant to paragraphs 1 and 2 of this Article shall also apply to the relationship between the representative and the third party that arise out of the fact that the representative acted within the scope of his authority, that he has exceeded such authority, or that he has acted without any authority.

Statute of limitations

Article 25

The statute of limitations shall be governed by the law applicable to the content of the legal matter or of the legal transaction.

Chapter IV

RIGHTS IN REM AND INTELLECTUAL PROPERTY RIGHTS

I. RIGHTS IN REM

Rights in rem in in respect of immovable property

Article 26

The acquisition, loss, content and exercise of the right in rem in respect of immovable property shall be governed by the law of the state on the territory of which the property is located.

Rights in rem in respect of movable property

Article 27

The acquisition and loss of the right in rem in respect of movable property shall be governed by the law of the state on the territory of which the movable property is located when the action or facts that are invoked as basis of the acquisition or the loss occur.

Where particular actions or circumstances, that are prerequisite to acquisition or loss of the right in rem in respect of movable property, were initiated in one state, they shall be deemed also consummated in another state where the last action or circumstance occurred thereby initiating acquisition or loss of the right in rem.

The content and exercise of the right in rem in respect of movable property shall be governed by the law of the state on the territory of which the movable property is located.

Type of property

Article 28

The determination of whether a property is considered to be movable or immovable shall be governed by the law of the state where the property is located.

Transfer of movable property to Montenegro

(conflict of laws in respect of movable property)

Article 29

Where a movable property, in respect of which the right in rem has been acquired in another state, is transferred to Montenegro, the acquired right in rem shall be recognized in Montenegro on condition that Montenegrin law knows the right in rem which in terms of its content and effects is equivalent to the right in rem which has been acquired in another state.

The content, exercise and registration of the right in rem in respect of movable property from paragraph 1 of this Article shall be governed by Montenegrin law.

Where Montenegrin law requires the registration of the right in rem from paragraph 1 of this Article and where the right is registered within 30 days of the date the property arrived in Montenegro, the date of registration shall be deemed to be the date when the property arrived in the territory of Montenegro.

Goods in transit

Article 30

The acquisition and loss of the rights in rem in respect of goods in transit shall be governed by the law of the state of destination.

The rights in rem in respect of personal belongings that the passenger carries with him shall be governed by the law of the state of his habitual residence.

Annex I

Means of transport

Article 31

The acquisition, transfer and loss of the rights in rem in respect of means of transport shall be governed by:

1. the law of the flag of vessel;
2. the law of the state of registration of an aircraft;
3. the law of the state where the person exploiting the means of railroad or road transport does business.

Validity of registration

Article 32

The validity of registration by which the rights in rem are acquired, transferred or lost shall be governed by the law of the state in the territory of which the property was located at the time the legal transaction was concluded.

Cultural property

Article 33

If an item, which is proclaimed as being cultural heritage of a state, has unlawfully left the territory of that state, the revindication by the state shall be governed by the law of that state except where the state chooses the law of the state on the territory of which the property is located at the time of the revindication claim.

If the law of the state that has proclaimed an item as being its cultural heritage does not grant any protection to the possessor in good faith, the latter may invoke the protection that is attributed to him by the law of the state on the territory of which the item is located at the time of the revindication claim.

Scope of application of the law applicable to the rights in rem

Article 34

The law applicable to the rights in rem refers to the following in particular:

1. existence, type, content and scope of rights;
2. holders of the rights;
3. transferability of the rights;
4. manner of acquisition, transfer and loss of the rights;
5. registration requirements and possibility to oppose third parties.

IV. INTELLECTUAL PROPERTY RIGHTS

General provisions

Article 35

The existence, validity, scope, property, transferability, duration and violations of copyrights, related rights and other non-registered intellectual property rights shall be governed by the law of the state in respect of which protection is sought.

The existence, validity, scope, property, transferability, duration and violations of a registered industrial property right shall be governed by the law of the state which has granted or registered this right.

Intellectual property rights arising in the context of employment

Article 36

The law applicable to a labour contract shall also apply to a holder of an intellectual or industrial property right if the subject of the right was created in the context of employment.

Contract relating to intellectual property rights

Article 37

Contracts relating to intellectual or industrial property rights shall be governed by the law designated under Chapters V and VII hereof.

Chapter V

CONTRACTUAL RELATIONS

Choice of applicable law

Article 38

A contract shall be governed by the law chosen by the parties to the contract. The choice of law must be exclusive and be clearly arising from the provisions of the contract or the circumstances of the case. The contractual parties may choose applicable law for the contract in its entirety or only for a part thereof.

Contractual parties may agree at any time on another law as the law applicable to their contract. The change of applicable law following the conclusion of a contract shall be without effect on the validity of the form within the meaning of Article 45 of the present Act and on the rights of third parties.

Where all other elements of the facts at the time of choice of applicable law are related to another state rather than the state whose law has been chosen, the choice of law cannot exclude the application of regulations that cannot be derogated from by agreement of the law of that other state.

Annex I

The existence and validity of the agreement of the parties on applicable law shall be governed by Articles 14(2), 44 and 45 of the present Act.

Absence of choice of applicable law

Article 39

To the extent that the law applicable to the contract has not been chosen by the parties in accordance with Article 38 of the present Act, and without prejudice to the contracts from Articles 41, 42 and 43 of the present Act, the governing law shall be designated as follows:

1. a contract for the sale of goods shall be governed by the law of the state where the supplier has his habitual residence;
2. a contract for the provision of services shall be governed by the law of the state where the service provider has his habitual residence;
3. a contract relating to a right in rem in respect of immovable property or to a tenancy of immovable property shall be governed by the law of the state where the property is located;
4. a contract relating to a tenancy of immovable property concluded for temporary private use for a period of not more than six consecutive months shall be governed by the law of the state where the landlord has his habitual residence, provided that the tenant is a natural person and has his habitual residence in the same state;
5. a franchise contract shall be governed by the law of the state where the franchisee has his habitual residence;
6. a distribution contract shall be governed by the law of the state where the distributor has his habitual residence;
7. a contract for the sale of goods by auction shall be governed by the law of the state where the auction takes place, if such a place can be determined.

Where the contract is not covered by any of the categories from paragraph 1 of this Article or where the elements of the contract would be covered by more than one of the points from paragraph 1 of this Article, the contract shall be governed by the law of the state where the party required to effect the characteristic performance of the contract has his habitual residence.

Where it is clear from all the circumstances of the case that the contract is manifestly more closely connected with a state other than the state indicated in paragraphs 1 or 2 of this Article, the law of that other state shall apply.

Where the law applicable cannot be designated pursuant to paragraphs 1 or 2, the contract shall be governed by the law of the state with which it is most closely connected.

Habitual residence

Article 40

Within the meaning of the present chapter, habitual residence of companies and other business establishments, whether they are legal persons or organisational forms without the capacity of a legal person, shall be the place of their administration.

Habitual residence of a natural person pursuing a business activity shall be the place which is the principal place of its business and activities.

Where a contract is concluded within the framework of business activities of a branch, representative unit or secondary establishment, or where the contract stipulates that a branch, representative office, or secondary establishment is responsible for execution of the contract, habitual residence shall be the place where the branch office, representative office or secondary establishment is located.

The designation of habitual residence shall be governed according to the time the contract was concluded.

Contracts of carriage

Article 41

To the extent that the law applicable to a contract for the carriage of goods has not been chosen by the parties in accordance with Article 38 of the present Act, the law applicable shall be the law of the state of habitual residence of the carrier, provided that the place of receipt or the place of delivery or the habitual residence of the consignor is also located in that state. Where those requirements are not met, the law of the state where the place of delivery as agreed by the parties is located shall apply.

The parties may choose as the law applicable to a contract of carriage only the law of the state where:

1. the passenger has his habitual residence;
2. the carrier has his habitual residence;
3. the carrier has his place of central administration;
4. the place of departure is located, or where
5. the place of destination is located.

To the extent that the law applicable to a contract for the carriage of passengers has not been chosen by the parties in accordance with paragraph 2 of this Article, the law applicable shall be the law of the state where the passenger has his habitual residence, provided that either the place of departure or the place of destination is located in that state. Where these requirements are not met, the law of the state where the carrier has his habitual residence shall apply.

Annex I

Consumer contracts

Article 42

Consumer contracts shall be governed by the law of the state where the consumer has his habitual residence, provided that the supplier:

1. pursues his commercial or professional activities in the state where the consumer has his habitual residence; or
2. by any means, directs such activities to that state or to several states including that state, and the contract falls within the scope of such activities.

The parties may choose other law as applicable but such a choice may not have the result of depriving the consumer of the protection afforded to him by provisions that cannot be derogated from by agreement by virtue of the law which, in the absence of choice, would have been applicable pursuant to paragraph 1 of this Article.

Where the requirements under paragraph 1 of this Article are not met, the law applicable to a consumer contract shall be designated pursuant to Articles 38 and 39 of the present Act.

Paragraphs 1 and 2 of this Article shall not apply to:

1. service contracts where the services are to be supplied to the consumer exclusively in a state other than that in which he has his habitual residence;
2. contracts of carriage other than a contract relating to package travel (contracts providing a combined service of travel and accommodation for a single price);
3. contracts relating to a right in rem in immovable property or a tenancy of immovable property other than timeshare contracts.

Individual employment contracts

Article 43

An individual employment contract shall be governed by the law chosen by the parties in accordance with Article 38 of the present Act. Such a choice of law may not have the result of depriving the employee of the protection afforded to him by provisions that cannot be derogated from by agreement under the law that, in the absence of a choice of law, would have been applicable pursuant to paragraphs 2 and 3 of this Article.

To the extent that the law applicable to the individual employment contract has not been chosen by the parties, the contract shall be governed by the law of the state in which or, failing that, from which the employee habitually carries out his work in performance of the contract. In case of an employee's temporary employment in another state, he shall be deemed to be working in a state in which he habitually carries out his duties.

Where the law applicable cannot be designated pursuant to paragraph 2 of this Article, the contract shall be governed by the law of the state where the place of business through which the employee was engaged is located.

Existence and material validity

Article 44

The existence and validity of a contract, or of any term of a contract, shall be determined by the law which would govern it if the contract or term were valid.

A party, in order to establish that he did not consent, may rely upon the law of the state in which he has his habitual residence if it appears from the circumstances that it would not be reasonable to determine the effect of his conduct in accordance with the law specified in paragraph 1 of this Article.

Form of contract

Article 45

A contract concluded between the persons who, or whose agents, are in the same state at the time of its conclusion, is formally valid if it meets the formal requirements of the law which governs it in substance under the present Act or the law of the state where it was concluded.

A contract concluded between persons who, or whose agents, are in different countries at the time of its conclusion is formally valid if it satisfies the formal requirements of the law which governs it in substance under the present Act, or of the law of either of the countries where either of the parties or their agent is present at the time of conclusion, or of the law of the country where either of the parties had his habitual residence at that time.

A unilateral act intended to have legal effect relating to an existing or contemplated contract is formally valid if it satisfies the formal requirements of the law which governs or would govern the contract in substance under the present Act, or of the law of the state where the act was done, or of the law of the state where the person by whom it was done had his habitual residence at that time.

The form of consumer contracts shall be governed by the law of the state where the consumer has his habitual residence.

A contract the subject matter of which is a right in rem in immovable property or a tenancy of immovable property shall be subject to the formal requirements of the law of the state where the property is located if by that law:

1. those requirements are imposed irrespective of the state where the contract is concluded and irrespective of the law governing the contract; and
2. those requirements cannot be derogated from by agreement.

Annex I

Assignment of claims

Article 46

The relationship between a creditor (assignor) who has assigned his claim against another person (debtor) and a new creditor (assignee) shall be governed by the law that applies to the contract of assignment of claims.

The law governing the assigned claim shall determine its assignability, the relationship between the new creditor and debtor, the conditions under which the assignment can be invoked against the debtor and the conditions under and the manner in which the debtor can discharge his obligations.

The assignment of claims within the meaning of this Article includes outright transfer of claims, transfers of claims by way of security and pledges or other security rights over claims.

The duty of third person to satisfy the creditor

Article 47

Where the duty of a third person to satisfy the creditor is not provided for by the contract, it shall be governed by the law applicable to claims in respect of which the duty is stated.

Scope of applicable law

Article 48

The law applicable to contractual relations shall govern in particular:

1. interpretation of the contract;
2. performance of the obligations arising from the contract;
3. within the limits of the powers conferred on the court by its procedural law, the consequences of a total or partial breach of obligations, including the assessment of damages in so far as it is governed by rules of law;
4. the various ways of extinguishing obligations;
5. statute of limitations;
6. extinguishing of rights due to expiry of the time limits;
7. the consequences of nullity of the contract.

In relation to the type and manner of performance and the steps to be taken by the creditor in the event of defective performance, account shall be taken of the law of the state in which performance takes place.

Interpretation and application of this chapter

Article 49

The provision under this chapter shall be interpreted and applied in accordance with Regulation of (EC) No. 593/2008 of the European Parliament and of the Council of 17 June 2008 on the law applicable to contractual obligations - Rome I.

Chapter VI

NON-CONTRACTUAL RELATIONS

V. GENERAL PROVISIONS

Definitions

Article 50

For the purposes of this chapter, damage shall be interpreted to mean any consequence arising from tort/delict, unjust gain, management without an order or pre-contractual obligation.

The provisions of this chapter shall also apply to non-contractual obligations that are likely to occur.

Any reference in this chapter to a tort/delict, shall also include torts/delicts that are likely to occur.

Any reference in this chapter to damage, shall also include damage that is likely to occur.

Habitual residence

Article 51

For the purposes of this chapter, habitual residence of companies and other bodies pursuing a business activity, whether they are legal persons or organisational forms without legal personality, shall be the place of their central administration.

Where the tort/delict, or the damage arises, in the course of operation of a branch, representative unit or secondary establishment, the place where the branch, representative unit or secondary establishment is located shall be treated as the place of habitual residence.

The habitual residence of a natural person pursuing a business activity shall be his principal place of business.

II. NON-CONTRACTUAL OBLIGATIONS ARISING OUT OF TORT/DELICT

General rule

Article 52

The law applicable to a non-contractual obligation arising out of a tort/delict shall be the law of the state in which the damage occurs irrespective of the state in which event giving rise to the damage occurred and irrespective of the state or states in which the indirect consequences of that event occurred, unless otherwise provided for in the provisions of this chapter.

Where the person claimed to be liable and the person sustaining damage both have their habitual residence in the same country at the time the damage occurs, the law of that country shall apply.

Where it is clear from all the circumstances of the case that the tort/delict is manifestly more closely connected with a state other than that indicated in paragraphs 1 or 2 of this Article, the law of that other state shall apply. A manifestly closer connection with another state might be based in particular on a pre-existing relationship between the parties, such as a contract that is closely connected with the tort/delict in question.

Unfair competition and acts restricting competition

Article 53

The law applicable to a non-contractual obligation arising out of an act of unfair competition shall be the law of the state where competitive relations or the collective interests of consumers are, or are likely to be, affected.

Where an act of unfair competition affects exclusively the interests of a specific competitor, Article 52 of the present Act shall apply.

The law applicable to a non-contractual obligation arising out of a restriction of competition shall be the law of the state where the market is, or is likely to be, affected.

When the market is, or is likely to be, affected in more than one state, and the defendant has his domicile in Montenegro, the person seeking compensation for damage may choose to base his claim on the Montenegrin law, provided that the market of Montenegro is amongst those directly and substantially affected by the restriction of competition out of which the non-contractual obligation on which the claim is based arises. Where the claimant sues more than one defendant, he can choose to base his claim on the Montenegrin law if the restriction of competition on which the claim against each of these defendants relies directly and substantially affects also the market in Montenegro.

The law applicable under paragraphs 1, 2, 3 and 4 of this Article may not be derogated from by an agreement on the choice of applicable law under Article 63 of the present Act.

Environmental damage

Article 54

The law applicable to a non-contractual obligation arising out of environmental damage or damage sustained by persons or property as a result of such damage shall be the law designated pursuant to Article 52, paragraph 1 of the present Act, unless the person seeking compensation for damage chooses to base his claim on the law of the state in which the event giving rise to the damage occurred.

Breach of right of person

Article 55

The law applicable to obligations arising out of the breach of the right of person by way of the media, the press in particular, radio, television and other media, shall, at the choice of the injured party, be the law of the state:

1. in which he has his habitual residence;
2. in the territory of which the damage occurred; or
3. in which the person responsible has his habitual residence or domicile.

In the cases from subparagraphs 1 and 2 of paragraph 1 of this Article, the person claimed to be responsible needs to have been able to reasonably expect that the damage will occur in the state of habitual residence or in the territory of which the damage occurred.

The law applicable to the right to publish a correction in case of a breach of right of person through the media shall be the law of the state in which the right of person was breached through the media.

Paragraph 1 of this Article shall also apply to obligations arising out of the breach of rights relating to the protection of data on person.

Industrial action

Article 56

Without prejudice to Article 52 of the present Act, the law applicable to a non-contractual obligation in respect of the liability of a person in the capacity of a worker or an employer or the organisations representing their professional interests for damages caused by a strike or other form of industrial action, pending or carried out, shall be the law of the state where the strike or other form of industrial action is to be, or has been, taken.

Product liability

Article 57

The law applicable to non-contractual obligations arising out of damage caused by a product shall be designated in accordance with the 1973 Convention on the Law Applicable in Cases of Product Liability ('Official Gazette of SFRY - International Treaties', No. 8/77).

Road accidents liability

Article 58

The law applicable to non-contractual obligations arising from road accidents shall be designated in accordance with the Convention on the Law Applicable to Road Accidents ('Official Gazette of SFRY - International Treaties', No. 26/76).

Damage on vessel in open sea or on aircraft

Article 59

If the event giving rise to an obligation to compensate for the damage caused on a vessel in an open sea or on an aircraft, the law of the place where the facts giving rise to the obligation of compensation of damage occurred shall be considered the law of the state of the flag or the law of the state in which the aircraft is registered.

III. UNJUST ENRICHMENT, NEGOTIORUM GESTIO AND CULPA IN CONTRAHENDO

Unjust enrichment

Article 60

If a non-contractual obligation arising out of unjust enrichment, including payment of amounts wrongly received, concerns a relationship existing between the parties, such as one arising out of a contract or a tort/delict, that is closely connected with that unjust enrichment, it shall be governed by the law that governs that relationship.

Where the law applicable cannot be designated on the basis of paragraph 1 of this Article and the parties have their habitual residence in the same state when the event giving rise to unjust enrichment occurs, the law of that country shall apply.

Where the law applicable cannot be designated on the basis of paragraphs 1 or 2 of this Article, it shall be the law of the state in which the unjust enrichment took place.

Negotiorum gestio

Article 61

If a non-contractual obligation arising out of an act performed without due authority in connection with the affairs of another person concerns a relationship existing between the parties, such as one arising out of a contract or a tort/delict, that is closely connected with that non-contractual obligation, it shall be governed by the law that governs that relationship.

Where the law applicable cannot be designated on the basis of paragraph 1 of this Article, and the parties have their habitual residence in the same state when the event giving rise to the damage occurred, the law of that country shall apply.

Where the law applicable cannot be designated on the basis of paragraphs 1 or 2 of this Article, it shall be the law of the country in which the act was performed.

Culpa in contrahendo

Article 62

The law applicable to a non-contractual obligation arising out of dealings prior to the conclusion of a contract, regardless of whether the contract was actually concluded or not, shall be the law that applies to the contract or that would have been applicable to it had it been entered into.

Where the law applicable cannot be designated on the basis of paragraph 1 of this Article, it shall be:

1. the law of the country in which the damage occurs, irrespective of the state in which the event giving rise to the damage occurred and irrespective of the state or states in which the indirect consequences of that event occurred; or

2. where the parties have their habitual residence in the same country at the time when the event giving rise to the damage occurs, the law of that country.

IV. GENERAL PROVISIONS ON NON-CONTRACTUAL OBLIGATIONS

Choice of applicable law

Article 63

The parties may agree to submit non-contractual obligations to the law of their choice:

1. by an agreement entered into after the event giving rise to the damage occurred; or
2. where all the parties are pursuing a commercial activity, also by an agreement freely negotiated before the event giving rise to the damage occurred.

The choice shall be expressed or demonstrated with reasonable certainty by the circumstances of the case and shall not prejudice the rights of third parties.

Where all the elements relevant to the situation at the time when the event giving rise to the damage occurs are located in a state other than the state whose law has been chosen, the choice of the parties shall not prejudice the application of provisions of the law of that other country which cannot be derogated from by agreement.

Non-contractual obligations arising from an infringement of an intellectual property right are not subject to the rule on the freedom of choice of applicable law.

Scope of applicable law

Article 64

The law applicable to non-contractual obligations shall govern in particular:

1. the basis and extent of liability, including the determination of persons who may be held liable for acts performed by them;
2. the grounds for exemption from liability, any limitation of liability and any division of liability;
3. the existence, the nature and the assessment of damage or the remedy claimed;
4. within the limits of powers conferred on the court by its procedural law, the measures which a court may take to prevent or terminate injury or damage or to ensure the provision of compensation;
5. the question whether a right to claim damages or a remedy may be transferred, including by inheritance;
6. persons entitled to compensation for damage sustained personally;
7. liability for the acts of another person;

8. the manner in which an obligation may be extinguished and rules of prescription and limitation, including rules relating to the commencement, interruption and suspension of a period of prescription or limitation.

Application of rules of safety and conduct

Article 65

In assessing the conduct of the person claimed to be liable, account shall be taken, as a matter of fact and in so far as is appropriate, of the rules of safety and conduct which were in force at the place and time of the event giving rise to the liability.

Direct action against the insurer of the person liable

Article 66

The person having suffered damage may bring his claim directly against the insurer of the person liable to provide compensation if the law applicable to the non-contractual obligation or the law applicable to the insurance contract so provides.

Interpretation and application of this chapter

Article 67

The provisions of this chapter shall be interpreted and applied in accordance with Regulation (EC)/864/2007 of the European Parliament and of the Council of 11 July 2007 on the law applicable to non-contractual obligations - Rome II.

Paragraph 1 of this Article shall not apply to Articles 57, 58 and 59 of the present Act.

Chapter VII

COMMON RULES ON CONTRACTUAL AND NON-CONTRACTUAL RELATIONS

Subrogation

Article 68

Where a creditor has a non-contractual claim upon a debtor, and a third person has a duty to satisfy the creditor, or has in fact satisfied the creditor in discharge of that duty, the law which governs the third person's duty to satisfy the creditor shall determine whether, and the extent to which, the third person is entitled to exercise against the debtor the rights which the creditor had against the debtor under the law governing their relationship.

Multiple liability

Article 69

If a creditor has a claim against several debtors who are liable for the same claim, and one of the debtors has already satisfied the claim in whole or in part, the question of that debtor's right to demand compensation from the other debtors shall be governed by the law applicable to that debtor's obligation towards the creditor.

Burden of proof

Article 70

The law governing contractual and non-contractual obligations shall apply to the extent that it contains rules which raise presumptions of law or determine the burden of proof.

The legal effect of a contract or act may be proven by any mode of proof recognised by the law of the forum or by any of the laws referred to in Article 45 of the present Act under which that act is formally valid, provided that such mode of proof can be administered by the forum.

Chapter VIII

SUCCESSION

General Rule

Article 71

The law applicable to the succession as a whole shall be that of the state in which the deceased had his habitual residence at the time of his death.

Choice of applicable law

Article 72

A person may choose as the law to govern the succession as a whole the law of the state whose nationality he possesses or the law of the state in which he has habitual residence at the time of choice of applicable law or at the time of his death.

A person may choose as the law to govern the succession to immovable property the law of the state in which the property is located.

The choice of law must be expressly determined or clearly inferred from the circumstances of the case and in the form of a disposition of property upon death (will, joint will or inheritance agreement).

The existence and material validity of the choice of applicable law shall be governed by the determined law.

Paragraphs 1 through 3 of this Article shall also apply to a modification or revocation of an earlier choice of applicable law.

Annex I

Validity of the form of will

Article 73

A will shall be valid as to form if its form complies with the law:

1. of the place where it was made;
2. of the state of which the testator had nationality at the time of disposition or at the time of his death;
3. of the place in which the testator had his domicile at the time of disposition or at the time of his death;
4. of the place of habitual residence of the testator at the time of disposition or at the time of his death;
5. of Montenegro;
6. so far as immovable property is concerned, also of the place where the property is located;
7. which was applicable or would have been applicable to succession at the time of disposition.

The revocation of a will shall be valid as to form if its form complies with any of the laws according to the terms of which, under paragraph 1 of this Article, the will could have been validly drawn up.

The validity of form of a will is also affected by:

- existence of limitations as to age, nationality or other personal characteristics of the testator;
- fulfilment of conditions in respect of witnesses;
- prohibition of certain types of dispositions in the event of death.

Existence, material validity, effects and interpretation of disposition of estate in the event of death

Article 74

The existence, material validity, effects and interpretation of disposition of estate in the event of death shall be governed by the law which was applicable to the succession to the deceased person at the time when the disposition was made.

The disposition shall also be valid when it is valid according to the law applicable to the succession at the time of death of the deceased person. In that event, the same law shall be applicable to the effects and interpretation of disposition with the estate in the event of death.

Paragraphs 1 and 2 of this Article shall also apply to the capacity to make a testamentary disposition. Subsequent change of applicable law shall have no effect on this capacity.

The parties to a joint testamentary disposition or an inheritance agreement may agree to subject the existence, material validity, effects and interpretation of their disposition to an applicable law that one of them can designate under Article 72, paragraphs 1, 2 and 5 of the present Act.

Estate without a claimant

Article 75

An estate without a claimant shall be governed by the law of the state where it is located.

Scope of applicable law

Article 76

The law applicable to succession shall govern the following in particular:

1. the causes and time of the opening of succession;
2. the circle of heirs and legatees, inheritance shares, and other rights resulting from the opening of succession;
3. the capacity to inherit;
4. the particular causes of the incapacity to dispose or receive;
5. disinheritance and debarment from succession;
6. the transfer of assets making up the succession to the heirs and legatees, including the conditions and effects of accepting or waiving the succession or legacy;
7. the powers of the heirs, the executors of the wills and other administrators of the succession, in particular the sale of property and the payment of creditors;
8. responsibility for the debts under the succession;
9. the freely disposable portion, the reserved portions and the other restrictions on the freedom to dispose of property upon death, including the allocations deducted from the succession by a court of other authority to the advantage of the relatives of the deceased;
10. any obligation to return or calculate the value of a gift and their calculation in the succession parts;
11. sharing the inheritance.

Annex I

Chapter IX

FAMILY RELATIONS

I. MARRIAGE

Terms of conclusion of marriage

Article 77

The terms of conclusion of a marriage shall be governed, for respective persons, by the law of the state of which the respective person has nationality at the time marriage is concluded.

Form of marriage

Article 78

The form of marriage shall be governed by the law of the place in which marriage is concluded.

Annulment of marriage

Article 79

The annulment of a marriage shall be governed by the law of the state the law of which applied to the terms of conclusion of the marriage.

Relations between spouses

Article 80

The personal relations between the spouses shall be governed by the law of state of their nationality.

Where the spouses are nationals of different states, the law of the state where they both habitually reside shall apply.

Where the spouses do not have the same nationality, or the same habitual residence in the same state, the law of the state where the spouses were last habitually resident shall apply.

Where applicable law cannot be designated pursuant to paragraphs 1, 2 and 3 of this Article, the law of Montenegro shall apply.

Law applied to property relations between spouses

Article 81

The property relations between the spouses shall be governed by the law of the state which also applies to their personal relationships.

Where the change of nationality or habitual residence of one or both spouses results in a change of applicable law, the new applicable law shall apply to the property of the spouses independently of the time it is acquired.

Contractual relations between spouses

Article 82

The spouses may agree in writing to subject their contractual property relations to the law:

1. of the state of nationality of either of the spouses;
2. the state of habitual residence of either of the spouses;
3. the state in which they intend to establish their common habitual residence;
4. in relation to immovable property, the law of the place in which the immovable property is located.

The spouses may modify or revoke their choice of law. The choice made after the marriage is concluded shall start producing effect from the moment of conclusion of marriage, except as otherwise agreed by the parties.

Protection of third parties

Article 83

With their choice of law as applicable to their matrimonial property regime, the spouses may not oppose the rights of third parties, except where such parties knew or could have known of the application of that law.

Where in respect of rights in rem in immovable property the registration requirements are met under the law of the state in which the immovable property is located, the third parties are deemed to know of the application of the designated law.

Property regime of common law marriage

Article 84

Property relations between the persons living in common law marriage shall be governed by the law under Articles 81 through 83 of the present Act.

Divorce

Article 85

Divorce shall be governed by the law of the state of which the spouses are nationals at the time the divorce application is introduced.

Where the spouses do not have the same nationality, the law of the state where they have their common habitual residence at the time the divorce application is introduced.

Where the spouses do not have the same nationality, or common habitual residence at the time the divorce application is introduced, the law of the state where the spouses had their last common habitual residence shall apply.
Where applicable law cannot be designated under paragraphs 1, 2 and 3 of this Article, the law of Montenegro shall apply.
Where either of the spouses is a Montenegrin national who does not habitually reside in Montenegro, and the marriage could not be divorced under the law designated under paragraphs 1, 2 and 3 of this Article, the divorce shall be governed by the law of Montenegro.

Choice of law

Article 86

The spouses may at any event choose the law applicable to a divorce, and in addition to one of the laws from Article 85 of the present Act may also choose the law of nationality of either spouse at the time the divorce application is made.
The agreement designating the applicable law must be made in writing and certified in accordance with law, not later than at the time the divorce application is made.

II. PARENTAL RIGHT

Family status of child

Article 87

The recognition, establishment or contestation of parentage shall be governed by the law of the state the nationality of which the child obtained at the time of birth.
Where that is more favourable to the child, the following may apply:

1. the law of the state of which the child is a national or in which he has habitual residence, at the time his family status is determined;
2. the law that at the time of birth applies to personal relations of the spouses.

The recognition of parentage shall produce effect provided it is made in accordance with the law of the state of which the person whose parentage is invoked is a national, or the law of the state of nationality of the child at the time of recognition, or the law of the state in which the child habitually resides at the time of recognition.
The form of recognition shall be governed by the law of the state where the recognition was made or the law determined in accordance with the law from paragraph 2 of this article.

Relations between parents and child

Article 88

The parent child relations shall be governed by the law of the state in which the child has habitual residence or the law of the state of the child's nationality, where so more favourable to the child.

Adoption

Article 89

The terms of establishment, effect, and termination of adoption of a child shall be governed by the law of the state of nationality of the adoptive parent.

Where the spouses jointly adopt a child, the law under Article 80 of the present Act shall apply.

The child's consent, in addition to the applicable law as designated under paragraph 1 of this Article, shall be governed by the law of the state of the child's nationality.

The form of adoption shall be governed by the place where the adoption is established.

III. MAINTENANCE

General rule

Article 90

The maintenance obligation shall be governed by the law of the state on the territory of which the maintenance creditor has his habitual residence, unless otherwise provided for by the present Act.

In the event of change of habitual residence of the maintenance creditor, the law of the state of the new habitual residence shall apply as of the moment the change takes effect.

Specific rules to the advantage of certain maintenance creditors

Article 91

Specific maintenance rules shall apply to maintenance obligations:

1. of parents to their children;
2. of persons other than parents to the persons who have not turned 21, except for the obligations from Article 92 of the present Act; and
3. of children to their parents.

If the law designated by Article 90 of the present Act does not grant the creditor a right to maintenance, the maintenance obligation shall be governed by the law of the state in which the court before which the proceeding is initiated is located.

Notwithstanding the general rule from Article 90 of the present Act, if the maintenance creditor initiated a procedure before the competent authority of the state in which the maintenance debtor has his habitual residence, the law of that state shall apply. If that law does not grant the creditor a right to maintenance from the debtor, the maintenance obligation shall be governed by the law of the creditor's habitual residence.

If the law designated by Article 90 of the present Act and paragraphs 2 and 3 of this Article does not grant the creditor a right to maintenance, the maintenance obligation shall be governed by the law of the state of their common nationality, provided that such common nationality exists.

Specific rule applying to spouses and former spouses

Article 92

The maintenance obligation between spouses, former spouses or parties to a marriage which is cancelled shall not be governed by Article 90 of the present Act in case of opposition by either of the parties and if the law of another state, the law of the state of their last common habitual residence in particular, is more closely connected to the marriage, in which case that law with which there is a closer connection shall apply.

Contestation of right to maintenance of certain persons

Article 93

In case of maintenance obligation other than maintenance obligation of the parents toward their children, and the obligations from Article 92 of the present Act, the maintenance debtor may contest the creditor's claim on the basis of the fact that no such maintenance obligation is envisaged according to either the law of debtor's habitual residence or the law of common nationality of the parties.

Choice of law applicable to a procedure

Article 94

Notwithstanding the general rules from Articles 90 through 93 of the present Act, and exclusively for the purpose of a specific procedure, maintenance creditor and maintenance debtor may choose as the exclusive law applicable to maintenance obligation the law of the state in which the procedure is instituted.

The agreement designating applicable law made before a procedure is instituted must be made in writing and signed by both parties or recorded in any other way which makes its content accessible for use and later reference.

Choice of applicable law

Article 95

Notwithstanding the general rules from Articles 90 through 93 of the present Act, the maintenance creditor and maintenance debtor may at any time subject the maintenance obligation to any of the following laws:

1. law of any state of which either party is a national at the time of the choice;
2. law of the state of habitual residence of either party at the time of the choice;
3. law that they select as applicable, or the law actually applied to their property relations;
4. law that they select as applicable, or the law actually applied to their divorce or separation.

The agreement designating applicable law must be made in writing and signed by both parties or recorded in any other way which makes its content accessible for use and later reference.

Paragraph 1 of this Article shall not apply to maintenance obligations over a minor or an adult who for reason of his incapacity or inability cannot protect his interests.

Irrespective of the choice of law within the meaning of paragraph 1 of this Article, the issue of whether a maintenance creditor may waive his right to maintenance shall be governed by the law of the state in which maintenance creditor has habitual residence at the time of the choice.

The right designated by the parties shall not apply if the application of that law would result in manifestly unfair or unreasonable consequences to either party, except where at the time of designation the parties are fully informed and aware of the consequences of their choice.

Public bodies

Article 96

The right of state authorities and other entities exercising public authority ('public bodies') to a repayment claim in respect of the allowance given to the creditor instead of maintenance shall be governed by the law that such public bodies are subject to.

Scope of the law applicable to maintenance obligation

Article 96

The law applicable to the maintenance obligation governs, notably:

1. whether, to what extent, and from whom the maintenance creditor can claim maintenance;
2. within which delay the maintenance creditor can lodge a claim for maintenance;

3. the basis for fixing the amount of maintenance and indexation;
4. who can lodge a claim for maintenance, except for the issues of civil capacity and representation in the procedure;
5. statute of limitations or terms for initiating the procedure;
6. the limits of the duty of the maintenance debtor when a public body claims repayment for the allowance paid to the creditor instead of maintenance.

Setting the amount of maintenance

Article 98

Both the creditor's needs and the debtor's financial standing as well as any allowance that the creditor received instead of a regular payment of maintenance shall be taken into account, even where otherwise provided for by applicable law.

PART TWO

JURISDICTION AND PROCEDURE

Chapter X

JURISDICTION OF JUDICIAL AND OTHER AUTHORITIES OF MONTENEGRO IN CIVIL MATTERS WITH AN INTERNATIONAL ELEMENT

I. GENERAL PROVISIONS

General jurisdiction

Article 99

A court of Montenegro shall have jurisdiction if the defendant has his domicile or statutory seat in Montenegro.

If the defendant does not have his domicile in Montenegro or in the other state, a court in Montenegro shall have jurisdiction if the defendant has his residence in Montenegro.

Material co-defendants

Article 100

In the event of a civil case with multiple defendants with the status of material co-defendants, a Montenegrin court shall also have jurisdiction when one of the defendants has his domicile or statutory seat in Montenegro.

Jurisdiction for mutually related actions

Article 101

A Montenegrin court, with jurisdiction to hear one of several actions, shall also have jurisdiction to hear other actions if they are related to the action that the Montenegrin court has jurisdiction for.

The actions shall be deemed related if the connections among them are so close that it is justified to hear and determine them together to avoid the risk of irreconcilable judgments if the actions were heard separately.

Jurisdiction according to the place of business

Article 102

A Montenegrin court shall have jurisdiction over a dispute arising out of business operation of a branch, representative unit or secondary establishment located in Montenegro even when the defendant does not have his statutory seat in Montenegro.

Agreement on the jurisdiction of a Montenegrin court

Article 103

In a matter in which, according to Montenegrin law, parties can freely dispose of their rights, they may agree to confer jurisdiction on a Montenegrin court or Montenegrin courts to hear the disputes which have arisen or may arise in connection with a legal relationship.

The Montenegrin court from paragraph 1 of this Article shall have exclusive jurisdiction, except when otherwise agreed by the parties.

Agreement designating jurisdiction to a foreign court

Article 104

In matters in which parties can freely dispose of their rights, the parties may agree to confer jurisdiction on a foreign court or foreign courts to hear disputes which have arisen or may arise in connection with a legal relationship, provided that a Montenegrin court does not have exclusive jurisdiction.

The jurisdiction of a foreign court from paragraph 1 of this Article shall be exclusive, except when otherwise agreed by the parties.

Form of agreement on jurisdiction

Article 105

An agreement on jurisdiction is concluded:

1. or confirmed in writing;

2. in a form compliant with the practice that the parties have already established; or
3. in international trade and exchange, in a form compliant with the custom that the parties knew or ought to have known and which is generally known in that area of trade or exchange and is regularly followed by the parties in agreements of the same type.

An agreement on jurisdiction is deemed to be concluded in writing if it is concluded by electronic means of communication that may create a permanent record of the agreement.

Defendant's silent consent to jurisdiction

Article 106

In matters in which an agreement on jurisdiction of a Montenegrin court is allowed pursuant to Article 103 of the present Act, jurisdiction of a Montenegrin court may be established with the consent of the defendant.

A defendant is deemed to have given his consent for a Montenegrin court to have jurisdiction provided that he has filed his counterclaim or a complaint against a payment order, that at the preliminary hearing, or where there was no such hearing, at the first hearing on the merit he entered into discussion without having contested jurisdiction, or that he has filed a counterclaim.

Exclusive jurisdiction

Article 107

A Montenegrin court shall have exclusive jurisdiction when so explicitly provided for by the present or another Act.

Jurisdiction to hear counterclaims

Article 108

A Montenegrin court shall also have jurisdiction to hear the counterclaim arising from the same agreement or facts on which the original action is based.

Jurisdiction over non-litigious procedures

Article 109

Where a legal relationship is determined in a non-litigious procedure involving several parties, a Montenegrin court shall have jurisdiction if the party against which the claim is filed has his domicile or statutory seat in Montenegro, and where the procedure involves only one person, if that person has his domicile or statutory seat in Montenegro, unless when otherwise provided for by the present Act.

Jurisdiction to grant provisional, protective and executory measures

Article 110

A Montenegrin court shall have jurisdiction to grant provisional, protective and executory measures with respect to persons present in Montenegro at the time the action was introduced, even if, under the present Act the Montenegrin court would not have jurisdiction to adjudicate the merits.

Jurisdiction to hear registration disputes

Article 111

A Montenegrin court shall have exclusive jurisdiction to hear disputes with respect to validity of registration with public registers kept in Montenegro.

Establishment of jurisdiction

Article 112

Jurisdiction of a judicial or other authority of Montenegro in matters with an international element shall be established ex officio on the basis of the facts and circumstances present at the time the procedure is initiated.

Jurisdiction of a judicial or other authority of Montenegro shall also exist when the facts that it is based on change during the procedure.

Exceptional jurisdiction

Article 113

If the present Act does not attribute jurisdiction to a judicial or other authority in Montenegro, and the proceedings cannot be initiated abroad or when it would be unreasonable to demand that the action be brought abroad, jurisdiction shall be conferred on a judicial or other authority in Montenegro in a place with which the case has a sufficient connection.

International lis pendens

Article 114

A court of Montenegro shall stay the proceedings at the request of a party when an action involving the same cause and the same parties is pending before a foreign court, provided that:

1. the action in that matter was first brought before the foreign court;
2. it is an action which is not under exclusive jurisdiction of a Montenegrin court;
3. it is may be reasonably expected that the foreign court decision will be amenable to recognition and enforcement in Montenegro.

Annex I

II. SPECIFIC PROVISIONS

1. Status of persons

Jurisdiction to hear guardianship issues

Article 115

A Montenegrin authority shall have jurisdiction to hear guardianship cases involving persons who are Montenegrin nationals or have habitual residence in Montenegro.

A Montenegrin authority shall take necessary provisional measures in order to protect person, rights and interests of a foreign national who is present or has property in Montenegro.

Name

Article 116

A court and/or authority of Montenegro shall be responsible for change and protection of the name for Montenegrin nationals or for persons who have habitual residence in Montenegro.

Declaring a missing person dead

Article 117

A court of Montenegro shall have jurisdiction to declare a missing person dead, provided that the person was a Montenegrin national or had habitual residence in Montenegro at the time of his death.

Legal persons

Article 118

A court of Montenegro shall have exclusive jurisdiction to hear proceedings on validity of incorporation, nullity or dissolution of a company or legal person, or validity of decisions of their bodies, provided that they have a statutory seat in Montenegro.

2. Jurisdiction for rights in rem and intellectual property rights

Immovable property

Article 119

A Montenegrin court shall have exclusive jurisdiction to hear proceedings involving rights in rem in immovable property or tenancy of immovable property provided that the immovable property is located in Montenegro.

The jurisdiction to hear proceedings in respect of a tenancy of immovable property concluded for temporary private use for period of not more than six consecutive months shall also be conferred on the court of the state where the defendant has his domicile, provided that the tenant is a natural person and that both the landlord and tenant have their domicile in the same state.

Movable property

Article 120

The jurisdiction to hear disputes on rights in rem in movable property shall be conferred on a Montenegrin court if the movable property is located in the territory of Montenegro.

Aircrafts and vessels

Article 121

The jurisdiction to hear disputes in respect of the rights in rem in aircrafts, vessels, as well as disputes in respect of a lease of aircrafts and vessels shall be conferred on a Montenegrin court even when the register where the aircraft or vessel is registered is kept in Montenegro.

The jurisdiction to hear disputes in respect of disturbance of possession of the aircraft and vessel from paragraph 1 of this Article shall be conferred on a Montenegrin court even when the register in which the aircraft or vessel is registered is kept on the territory of Montenegro, and when the disturbance occurred on the territory of Montenegro.

Industrial property rights

Article 122

A Montenegrin court shall have exclusive jurisdiction to hear proceedings in respect of registration or validity of a patent, trade or service mark, industrial samples and models, or other related rights that may be deposited or registered, irrespective of whether the issue was raised by action or in a counterclaim, provided that the deposition or registration claim was filed in Montenegro, or that deposition or registration has taken effect, or that on the basis of international agreement the deposition or registration is deemed to have taken effect.

3. Jurisdiction to hear contractual disputes

General rule

Article 123

The jurisdiction to hear contractual disputes shall be conferred on a Montenegrin court even when the subject matter of the dispute is an obligation that has been fulfilled or that should be fulfilled in Montenegro.

Annex I

Unless the parties have otherwise agreed, the place of fulfilment of the obligation from paragraph 1 of this Article shall be deemed to be:

- in the supply of goods, the place in which, under the contract, the goods have been delivered or should be delivered;
- in the supply of services, the place in which, under the contract, the services have been delivered or should be delivered.

Consumer contracts

Article 124

In addition to the general jurisdiction rules, a Montenegrin court shall have jurisdiction to hear action brought by a consumer against a supplier, provided that the consumer has his domicile in Montenegro.

The supplier may bring action against the consumer who has his domicile in Montenegro only before a Montenegrin court.

The derogations from paragraphs 1 and 2 of this Article shall be allowed only on the basis of a jurisdiction agreement which:

1. was made after the dispute occurred;
2. allows the consumer to bring action before another court which would have jurisdiction under the criteria which were not listed in this Article; or
3. was concluded between the consumer and supplier provided that at the time of conclusion both parties had their domicile or habitual residence in the same state, and which confers jurisdiction on the courts of that state, provided that such an agreement is not in contravention of the law of that state.

Paragraphs 1, 2 and 3 of this Article refer only to the disputes arising out of:

1. sales contract for goods to be paid in instalments;
2. loan agreements to be repaid in instalments, or any other form of loan granted to finance sales of goods; or
3. any other case in which a contract is concluded with a person who pursues his commercial or professional activity in Montenegro or who, by any means, directs such activities to Montenegro or to several states including Montenegro, and that the contract falls within the scope of such activities.

Paragraphs 1 through 4 of this Article shall not apply to contracts of carriage, save for package travel.

Individual employment contracts

Article 125

In addition to general jurisdiction rules, a Montenegrin court shall have jurisdiction to hear action brought by an employee against his employer provided that:

1. the employee habitually carries out his duties in Montenegro or that the last place in which he habitually carried out his duties was in Montenegro; or
2. the employee does not or did not habitually carry out his duties in just one state, provided that the business unit which engaged the employee is or was located in Montenegro.

An employer may bring action against an employee who has his domicile in Montenegro only before a Montenegrin court.

The provisions of this Article may be derogated from only in the event of conclusion of a jurisdiction agreement which:

1. was concluded after the dispute occurred; or
2. which allows the employee to bring action before another court which would have jurisdiction on the basis of the criteria from paragraphs 1 and 2 of this Article.

4. Jurisdiction in respect of non-contractual relations

General rule

Article 126

A Montenegrin court shall have jurisdiction to hear disputes in respect of non-contractual relations even when the tort/delict occurred or is likely to occurring the territory of Montenegro.

Paragraph 1 of this Article shall also apply to disputes against insurance company for damages to third parties on the basis of a regulation on direct liability of an insurance company, as well as to disputes in respect of repayment claims on the basis of the claim for damages from recourse debtors.

5. Jurisdiction in respect of succession

General rule

Article 127

A Montenegrin court shall have jurisdiction in respect of succession if the deceased person had his habitual residence in Montenegro at the time of his death.

Jurisdiction according to the location of assets

Article 128

When the deceased person did not have his habitual residence in Montenegro at the time of his death, a Montenegrin court shall have jurisdiction on the basis of the fact that the assets that make up his inheritance are located in Montenegro and that:

1. the law of Montenegro was designated as applicable pursuant to Article 72 of the present Act; or
2. the deceased person was a Montenegrin national at the time of his death; or
3. that this Article applies only to such assets.

Choice of jurisdiction

Article 129

In respect of disposition of property in the event of his death, a person may designate a court or courts of the state the law of which can be chosen as applicable to succession under Article 72 of the present Act to also have jurisdiction in respect of disposition of his property, in its entirety or in part. Once chosen in this way, the jurisdiction shall be exclusive.

6. Jurisdiction in respect of family law disputes

Marriage and related disputes

Article 130

A Montenegrin court shall have jurisdiction to hear actions relating to the existence of marriage, divorce or annulment of marriage, if:

1. one spouse is a Montenegrin national or was a Montenegrin national at the time the marriage was concluded;
2. both spouses have their habitual residence in Montenegro;
3. one spouse is a stateless person who has habitual residence in Montenegro; or
4. one spouse has habitual residence in Montenegro, except where it is clear that the decision of the Montenegrin court would not be recognized under the law of the state of which either of the spouses is a national.

The jurisdiction of a Montenegrin court pursuant to paragraph 1 of this Article also refers to a case when the marriage dispute seeks a decision on maintenance between the spouses or former spouses, parental care or child subsistence or marital property regime.

Paragraphs 1 and 2 of this Article shall also apply to common law marriage.

Child family status

Article 131

A Montenegrin court shall have jurisdiction to hear disputes relating to establishment or contestation of parentage provided that the child, mother, father or a person claiming to be the father or mother of the child:

1. is a Montenegrin national; or
2. has habitual residence in Montenegro.

Annex I

Parental care

Article 132

A Montenegrin judicial or other authority shall have jurisdiction in respect of decisions on the care, raising and upbringing of children who have parental care if the child is a Montenegrin national or has habitual residence in Montenegro.

A Montenegrin judicial or other authority shall also have jurisdiction when the child needs the protection from such authority.

Adoption

Article 133

A Montenegrin judicial or other authority shall have jurisdiction in respect of decisions relating to adoption if the adoptive parent, one of the adoptive parents, or adoptee:

1. is a Montenegrin national; or
2. has habitual residence in Montenegro.

Maintenance

Article 134

A Montenegrin court shall have jurisdiction to hear maintenance disputes if:

1. the defendant has habitual residence in Montenegro;
2. the maintenance creditor has habitual residence in Montenegro; or
3. maintenance is decided in an action brought before a Montenegrin court on status relationships or parental care.

Other family law relations

Article 135

A Montenegrin court shall have jurisdiction in respect of other family law relations when the court has jurisdiction under the rights of territorial jurisdiction.

Annex I

Chapter XI

OTHER PROVISIONS

Capacity of natural person to act as party to civil proceedings

Article 136

The capacity of a natural person to be a party to and act independently in civil proceedings shall be governed by the law of the state of which the person has nationality.

Where a foreign national does not have the capacity to act independently in civil proceedings pursuant to paragraph 1 of this Article, but has such capacity under the law of Montenegro, the person may act in the proceeding to defend his cause on his own.

A legal representative acting on behalf of the foreign national from paragraph 2 of this Article may act in the proceeding only until the foreign national states that he will take over the conduct of the proceeding.

The capacity of a foreign legal person to be a party to proceedings shall be governed by the law designated under Article 19 of the present Act.

Obligation to cover the cost of proceeding

Article 137

Where a foreign national or a stateless person without a domicile in Montenegro institute civil proceedings before a Montenegrin court, he shall cover the cost for the defendant, at his request.

The defendant shall file the request from paragraph 1 of this Article at the preliminary hearing at the latest, and where preparatory hearing is not held, at the first hearing on the merits before discussions on the merits begins, i.e. as soon as he learns that the requirements are met for him to seek security.

The security for the cost of proceedings shall be provided in money and the court may allow for the security to be provided in another appropriate form.

Exemption from duty to cover cost of proceeding

Article 138

A defendant shall not be entitled to security of the cost of proceedings:

1. if, in the state of which the claimant is a national, Montenegrin nationals are not under duty to provided security;
2. if the claimant enjoys the right of asylum in Montenegro;
3. if the claim is relating to the claimant's receivable arising out of his employment in Montenegro;
4. if the proceeding is relating to a marital dispute, a dispute to establish or contest parentage, or a case of statutory maintenance;

5. if the proceeding is an action upon a bill of exchange or cheque, a counterclaim or issuance of payment order.

The issue of whether Montenegrin nationals are under the duty, within the meaning of paragraph 1, subparagraph 1 of this Article, to provide security in the state of which the claimant is a national, shall be resolved by the state administration authority responsible for justice affairs.

Court decision on security of cost of proceedings

Article 139

In its decision granting the request for a security for the cost of proceedings, the court shall set the amount of security and the deadline by which it must be deposited, and warn the claimant of the consequences as provided for by law should he fail to deposit the security by the deadline.

Where the claimant does not prove by the agreed deadline that he has deposited the security, the claim will be deemed withdrawn, that is that the claimant has given up the legal remedy if the request for security was filed only during the proceeding on the legal remedy.

The defendant who filed a timely request for a security for the cost of proceedings shall not be under duty to continue the proceedings on the merits until a final decision has been reached on his request, and if the request is granted, until the claimant has deposited the security.

If the court dismisses the request for a security for the cost of proceedings, it may decide that the proceedings should continue even before the decision dismissing the request becomes final.

Exemption from cost of the proceedings

Article 140

Foreign nationals are entitled to exemption from cost of proceedings on reciprocity terms.

PART THREE

RECOGNITION AND ENFORCEMENT OF FOREIGN DECISIONS

Chapter XII

RECOGNITION AND ENFORCEMENT OF JUDGMENTS

A foreign judgment

Article 141

A foreign judgment shall be given the same effects as a domestic judgment of a Montenegrin court and shall produce legal effect in Montenegro only insofar as it is recognised by a Montenegrin court.

Annex I

A foreign judgment within the meaning of paragraph 1 of this Article shall also be deemed to be a settlement made before a court of law ('court settlement').

A foreign judgment shall also be deemed to be a decision of other authority which, in the state in which it was given, is equalised with a court judgment, or court settlement, if such a decision governs the relations from Article 1 of the present Act.

Certificate of validity

Article 142

A foreign judgment shall be recognised if the person seeking recognition produces, together with the judgment, a certified transcript and a certificate issued by the competent foreign judicial or other authority certifying the validity of the judgment under the law of the state in which it was given.

If a foreign court judgment or its certified transcript are not made in an official language or a language in the official use in the court, the person seeking recognition must also file a certified translation of the foreign judgment.

Violation of the right to defence

Article 143

A Montenegrin court shall refuse to recognise a foreign judgment if upon examining the complaint filed by the defendant from the foreign judgment the court finds that the defendant could not take part in the proceedings due to irregularities in the procedure.

The defendant from the foreign judgment shall be considered to have been unable to take part in the procedure if the defendant was not served in person with the summons, charge, or decision which instituted the proceedings, or if no attempt of service has been made, or if he was not served the documents in sufficient time in which to prepare for his defence, except where the defendant took part in the hearing on the merits in the first instance proceeding.

Exclusive jurisdiction of Montenegrin court

Article 144

A foreign judgment shall not be recognized if the subject matter is within exclusive jurisdiction of a judicial or other authority of Montenegro.

Excessive jurisdiction of a foreign court

Article 145

A foreign judgment shall not be recognised if a foreign court based its jurisdiction on the facts not recognised by the law of Montenegro as the facts that may serve as grounds for the establishment of international jurisdiction of a Montenegrin court in handling the same dispute.

Existence of a final judgment on the same cause of action and between the same parties

Article 146

A foreign judgment shall not be recognised of a judicial or other authority of Montenegro gave a final judgment involving the same cause of action, or if another foreign judgment on the same cause of action was recognized in Montenegro.

The court shall stay the proceedings for a recognition of a foreign judgment if before a Montenegrin court the proceedings instituted earlier and involving the same cause of action and between the same parties are still pending. The proceedings will be stayed until the earlier proceedings have been completed.

Violation of public order

Article 147

A foreign judgment shall not be recognised if the effect of its recognition would be manifestly contrary to the public order of Montenegro.

Foreign judgment on personal or family status of a Montenegrin national

Article 148

Where a Montenegrin court finds that a foreign judgment refers to a personal status of a Montenegrin national, for such a judgment to be recognised, the judgment must be subject to review pursuant to Articles 142 through 147 of the present Act.

Enforcement of a foreign judgment

Article 149

Enforcement of foreign judgments shall be governed by Articles 142 through 147 of the present Article.

A person seeking recognition of a foreign judgment must produce, in addition to the certificate from Article 142 of the present Act, also the certificate of enforceability of the judgment under the law of the state in which it was given.

*Chapter XIII**

RECOGNITION AND ENFORCEMENT OF ARBITRATION AWARDS

Foreign arbitration award

Articles 150–151

(repealed)

Annex I

*Chapter XIV**

PROCEDURE FOR RECOGNITION AND ENFORCEMENT OF COURT AND ARBITRATION DECISIONS

Procedure for making the application

Article 152

The procedure for the recognition of a foreign court or arbitration decision shall be initiated by an application.

The recognition of a foreign judgment relating to a personal status may be sought by any person with a legal interest.

The recognition of foreign court and arbitration decisions shall fall within the territorial jurisdiction of the court having actual jurisdiction.

The enforcement of court and arbitration decisions shall fall within the territorial jurisdiction of the court in the territory of which the enforcement is to be carried out.

Course of procedure and legal aid

Article 153

In its procedure for a recognition of a foreign court or arbitration decision, the court shall limit itself to examining whether the conditions from Articles 142 through 147 of the present Act are in place.

If the court finds no obstacles to the recognition of the foreign court or arbitration decision, it shall issue a decision declaring the recognition of the foreign decision.

The decision declaring the recognition shall be served on the other party or other participants involved in the procedure for a foreign judgment, together with a notification that the decision may be appealed against within 30 days of the date of service.

The appeal is decided by the court which gave the decision declaring the recognition, in a panel of three judges. Where the decision on the appeal depends on any disputed facts, the court shall issue its decision after a hearing.

The court decision dismissing the application for a recognition of a foreign court or arbitration decision and the court decision on appeal may be appealed against with the appellate court within 30 days of the date of service.

Notwithstanding paragraph 3 of this Article, the court shall not serve a decision recognising a foreign judgment on divorce to the other party if the party seeking recognition is a Montenegrin national, and the other party has no domicile or habitual residence in Montenegro.

Extraordinary legal remedies

Article 154

An application for a review may be filed against a decision declaring recognition or enforceability of a foreign judgment which was vacated by an extraordinary legal remedy in the state in which it was given.

Recognition or declaration of enforceability of a foreign judgment as a preliminary question

Article 155

Where a Montenegrin court handles the matter of recognition or declaration of enforceability of a foreign judgment as a preliminary question, the Montenegrin court shall have jurisdiction in respect of its recognition or declaration as enforceable in the procedure in which it decides the matter in relation to which the application is made.

Documentation

Article 156

The following must be submitted together with the application for recognition or declaration of enforceability of a foreign judgment:

1. the original judgment or its certified transcript, together with a translation by a certified court interpreter;
2. certificate that the judgment is final under the law of the state in which it was given;
3. certificate that the judgment is enforceable under the law of the state in which it was given if the declaration of enforceability of the judgment is sought.

Cost of procedure

Article 157

The cost of procedure shall be decided by the court in accordance with the rules that would apply if the matter were decided by a judicial or other authority of Montenegro.

Due application of other legislation

Article 158

In the absence of specific provisions in the present chapter on the procedure for recognition of foreign court and arbitration decisions, the provisions of the law governing non-litigious procedure shall apply accordingly.

Annex I

*The provisions of chapter XIII as well as the provisions of chapter XIV governing the procedure for recognition and enforcement of foreign arbitration awards of the International Private Law Act ('Official Gazette of Montenegro', Nos. 1/2014, 6/2014 – revised version 11/2014 – revised version and 14/2014) were repealed as of the date of enactment of the Arbitration Act ('Official Gazette of Montenegro', No. 47/2015), i.e. as of 26 August 2015.

PART FOUR

SPECIFIC PROVISIONS

Marriages concluded at diplomatic or consular missions

Article 159

Montenegrin nationals may conclude their marriage at a diplomatic or consular missions of Montenegro provided that the state in which the diplomatic or consular mission is located has no objections or where so provided for by an international agreement.

The ministry responsible for consular affairs shall designate diplomatic and consular missions of Montenegro where marriages between Montenegrin national may be concluded.

Guardianship affairs

Article 160

Guardianship affairs relating to Montenegrin nationals present abroad are handled by a diplomatic or consular mission of Montenegro, provided the state in which the diplomatic or consular mission is located has no objections, or where so provided for by an international agreement.

Drafting a will

Article 161

A Montenegrin national present abroad can have his will drafted by a diplomatic or consular mission of Montenegro pursuant to the provisions governing the drafting of a court will.

Certification of signatures, manuscripts and transcripts

Article 162

A diplomatic or consular mission of Montenegro may certify signatures, manuscripts and transcripts pursuant to international treaties and regulations of the state in which the diplomatic or consular mission is located.

More specific rules governing the conduct of activities from paragraph 1 of this Article shall be enacted by the ministry responsible for consular affairs.

Issuance of certificates on regulations of Montenegro

Article 163

A certificate on regulations that are or were applicable in Montenegro, for their use before the authorities abroad, shall be issues by a state administration body responsible for justice affairs.

The certificate from paragraph 1 of this Article shall include the name of certificate, the date of issuance, effective date, date of expiry, and the text of the relevant provisions from that regulation.

PART FIVE

TRANSITIONAL AND FINAL PROVISIONS

Jurisdiction

Article 164

A judicial or other authority of Montenegro before which the proceedings were initiated to hear private law matters with an international element before the beginning of implementation of the present Act shall retain jurisdiction even when the present Act does not confer jurisdiction on that court to hear such matters.

The procedures from paragraph 1 of this Article whereby the judicial or other authority of Montenegro declared itself as incompetent before the beginning of implementation of the present Act may be instituted again after the beginning of implementation of the present Act if the present Act provides for the jurisdiction of a court or of other authority of Montenegro, and if the application concerned can still be filed.

Pending proceedings

Article 165

Where before the beginning of implementation of the present Act a first instance decision was given whereby the proceedings before a first-instance court or other authority is finalised, the proceedings shall continue under the regulations in effect until the day the implementation of the present Act started.

Where after the beginning of implementation of the present Act the first instance decision from paragraph 1 of this Article is vacated, the proceedings will continue according to the provisions of the present Act.

Applicable law

Article 166

The first-instance proceedings on a cause of action involving an international element which is still pending on the date the implementation of the present Act begins shall be governed by the law provided for by the present Act.

Annex I

Recognition and enforcement

Article 167

The present Act shall apply to the terms of recognition and declaration of a foreign judgment enforceable provided that on the date when its implementation begins, the proceedings seeking recognition or declaration of a foreign judgment enforceable is still pending.

Legislation repealed and made ineffective

Article 168

As of the date the present Act enters into force, the Law on Resolving Conflict of Laws with Regulations of Other Countries ('Official Gazette of SFRY', Nos. 43/82 and 72/82 and 'Official Gazette of FRY' No. 46/96) shall be repealed, and the following provisions shall become ineffective: Article 15, paragraph 1, subparagraph 1 of the Law on Pledge as Security for Claims ('Official Gazette of RME', No. 38/02), Article 10 of the Law on Foreign Trade ('Official Gazette of RME' No. 28/04), and Article 3 of the Law on Consumer Protection ('Official Gazette of ME', No. 26/07).

Entry into force

Article 169

The present Act shall enter into force on the eight day of its publication in the 'Official Gazette of Montenegro', and its implementation will begin six months after its publication.

The single article of the Act Amending the International Private Law Act('Official Gazette of Montenegro', No. 14/2014)

Article 2

The present Act shall enter into force on the day of its publication in the 'Official Gazette of Montenegro'.

Annex II: Law on Maritime and Inland Navigation[580]

('Sl. list SRJ', No. 12/98, 44/99, 74/99 and 73/2000, 'Sl. list RCG', No. 46/2007 – other law and 'Sl. list CG', No. 17/2007 – other law, 51/2008 – other law, 20/2011 – other law i 62/2013 – other law)

Chapter IX. The Applicable Law and Exclusive Jurisdiction of Courts of the Federal Republic of Yugoslavia Over Relations Containing an International Feature (Element)

Article 1033

The provisions of Arts. 1034 - 1051 of the law shall apply to every craft which is a vessel under Yugoslav law and to every craft which is a vessel under the law of the vessel's flag.

Article 1034

The following are assessed according to the law of the vessel's flag:

(1) the duties and rights of the master in management of the vessel and in establishing rights and obligations on behalf of the holder of the right of possession of the vessel or ship owner or carrier;
(2) rights against a state owned vessel and real rights in the vessel;
(3) legal consequences of an event on the vessel to which the law of the place where the event occurred must be applied.

The provision of Point 3 of Paragraph 1 of this article shall apply to events which occurred on foreign vessels within the Federal Republic of Yugoslavia provided that the State of the vessel's nationality gives the same treatment to vessels which have Yugoslav nationality.

Article 1035

The Yugoslav law shall apply to real rights in a vessel under construction which is being built in the Federal Republic of Yugoslavia.

580. The author of this Monograph adapted and updated the version of the English translation of the Law on Maritime, Inland Navigation, Belgrade, Službeni list SFRJ,22 April 1977, available at: https://apps.dtic.mil/dtic/tr/fulltext/u2/a375605.pdf.

Annex II

Article 1036

The Yugoslav law shall govern employment relations of members of the crew of maritime vessels.

Article 1037

The law of the vessel's flag shall apply to limitation of liability of the carrier or other natural or legal person equivalent to the carrier under this law.

As an exception to the provision of Paragraph 1 of this article, this law shall apply if its provisions on limitation of liability are stricter than the regulations of the law of the vessel's flag.

Article 1038

The law chosen by the principals shall apply to contracts concerning shipping relations.

Article 1039

As an exception to the provision of Article 1038 of this law, this law shall apply to affreightments as follows:

(1) to the carrier's liability for damage, shortage or loss of cargo envisaged by the provisions of this law, whose application may not be excluded by agreement among the principals, if the port (or dock) of loading or destination is within the Federal Republic of Yugoslavia;
(2) if by application of another law a passenger would be placed in a less favorable position than under the provisions of this law.

An agreement concluded contrary to the provisions of Paragraph 1 of this article shall be null and void.

Article 1040

If the law whose application the principals have chosen for affreightments cannot apply to the entire contract or to some of the relations which arise out of the contract, or if the principals have not expressly stated the law which must be applied, and their intention as to application of a particular law cannot be established even from the circumstances of the case, the contract or contractual relation shall be governed by:

(1) the law at the place where the contract was concluded—as to evaluation of the principal rights and obligations of the parties to the contract;
(2) the law of the state of the carrier's nationality—if the contract of carriage of passengers or goods has been concluded on the basis of the carrier's general conditions established in advance;
(3) the provisions of this law—to a towage contract.

The law of the place where particular actions have been performed or where they should have been performed shall apply in the case referred to in Paragraph 2 of this article to the manner of performance of secondary rights and obligations of the contracting parties (manner of loading and delivery of cargo, computation of time for lay days and days on demurrage, the manner of paying freight, etc.).

Article 1041

If the law whose application the parties to a salvage contract have chosen cannot apply to the entire contract or to any of the relations which arise out of that contract, or if the principals have not explicitly chosen the law which is to be applied, and their intention as to application of a particular law cannot be established even from the circumstances of the case, the contract or contractual relation shall be governed by the law of the state of the port or dock where the salvage operation ended or the law of the first port or dock the salvaged vessel reached after the completed salvage operation.

Article 1042

As an exception to the provisions of Article 1041 of this law, the following shall apply:

(1) the provisions of this law—if lives have been saved when the ship or property on the ship was not salvaged at the same time, if all those persons were nationals of the Republic of Yugoslavia or if the salving vessel or the vessel salvaged and, if there were more vessels, one of them was a Yugoslav military vessel or Yugoslav public vessel;
(2) the provisions of Article 684, Paragraphs 1 and 2; Articles 808 through 814; and Articles 818 and 820 of this law;
(3) the provisions of the federal law regulating limitation on action concerning claims, if not otherwise stipulated by this law;
    (h) the law of the state of the salving vessel's nationality — to division of the salvage award between the holder of the right of possession of the vessel or ship owner or operator of the salving vessel and the crew of that vessel.

An agreement concluded contrary to the provisions of Paragraph 1 of this article shall be null and void.

Article 1043

The following shall apply to recovery for loss resulting from collision of ships:

(1) the law of the State in whose coastal sea or inland waters the collision occurred;
(2) the provisions of this law — if the collision occurred on the high seas.

As an exception to the provisions of Paragraph 1 of this article, the following shall apply to recovery for loss resulting from collision:

(1) if all the vessels involved in the collision are of the same nationality — the law of that State;

(2) if the vessels involved in the collision have differing nationality, but the law of all those states is the same — the law of those States.

Article 1044

As an exception to the provisions of Article 1043 of this law which indicate application of a foreign law for recovery of loss from collision, the following shall apply:

(1) the provisions of this law — if all interested persons are nationals of the Federal Republic of Yugoslavia or Yugoslav legal persons or if one of the vessels involved in the collision was a Yugoslav military vessel or Yugoslav public vessel;
(2) the provisions of Article 793, Paragraph 2; Article 794, Paragraph 1; and Articles 795 through 801 of this law;
(3) the provisions of the federal law regulating limitation on action concerning claims, if not otherwise stipulated by this law.

An agreement concluded contrary to the provisions of Paragraph 1 of this article shall be null and void.

Article 1045

In a general average case if the law which the principals have chosen cannot apply to the entire contract or to any of the relations which arise out of the contract or if the parties have not expressly chosen a law which must be applied, and their intention as to application of a particular law cannot be established even from the circumstances of the case, the law of the port (or dock) of discharge of the last portion of cargo which was on the vessel at the moment when the general average act was committed shall apply.

If all the principals in a general average case are nationals of the Federal Republic of Yugoslavia or Yugoslav legal persons, Yugoslav law shall apply in the cases referred to in Paragraph 1 of this article.

Article 1046

The law of the place of the shipyard shall apply to relations arising out of a contract concerning construction, modification or repair of vessels if the parties have not chosen the law which shall apply to those contracts or to sections of those contracts or if the law chosen is altogether or partially inapplicable.

Article 1047

The law of the insurer's seat shall apply to the marine insurance contract and relations arising from it provided as follows:

(1) that the principals have not expressly stated the law which must he applied to the contract, and their intention as to application of a particular law cannot be established even from the circumstances of the case;

(2) that the law whose application the parties have stipulated cannot apply to a portion of the contract or to some legal relation in that same contract — but only to that portion of the contract or that legal relation arising out of that contract.

As an exception to the provisions of Paragraph 1 of this article Yugoslav law shall apply to relations arising out of the marine insurance contract if all persons interested in that contract are nationals of the Federal Republic of Yugoslavia with a residence in the Federal Republic of Yugoslavia or Yugoslav legal persons with the seat in the Federal Republic of Yugoslavia, and the subject matters covered by insurance are exposed to the perils covered exclusively within the Federal Republic of Yugoslavia.

Article 1048

The form of a legal act in a shipping relation shall be evaluated according to the law of the place where the act was committed or where it should have been committed or according to the law which is applicable to the shipping relation as a whole.

Article 1049

The provisions of this law concerning recovery of sunken objects shall also be appropriately applied to recovery of objects sunk outside the coastal sea and inland waters of the Federal Republic of Yugoslavia if the object is state property or if the objects are covered by a right of property of a Yugoslav legal person or national of the Federal Republic of Yugoslavia, and the objects are recovered by a Yugoslav company, other Yugoslav legal person or national of the Federal Republic of Yugoslavia.

Article 1050

The foreign law which would be applicable under the provisions of this law shall not be applied if its application has been obtained exclusively in order to evade application of the law of the Federal Republic of Yugoslavia.

Article 1051

A Yugoslav court shall have exclusive jurisdiction to try the following:

(1) disputes concerning the award for salvage of Yugoslav military vessels and Yugoslav public vessels, recovery for loss resulting from a collision of ships in which one vessel is a Yugoslav military vessel or Yugoslav public vessel;
(2) cases as referred to in Articles 445, 446 and 447 of this law which arise in the course of and in connection with conduct of a proceeding for limitation of a carrier's liability being conducted by a Yugoslav court (Article 449);
(3) cases as referred to in Article 867 of this law which arise in the course of and in connection with conduct of a proceeding for adjustment of general average when a Yugoslav court has jurisdiction to examine objections to the final general average statement (Article 868);

(k) disputes arising in the course of and in connection with judicial execution proceeding which a Yugoslav court is conducting against maritime and inland vessels (Articles 909 and 913).

Annex III: Law on Obligations and Basics of Property Obligations in the Carriage by Air[581]

Law on Obligations and Basic Ownership Relations in Aerial Transport ('Sl. list CG', No. 18/2011, 46/2014 and 43/2018)

PART FIVE

APPLICABLE LAW AND APPROPRIATE APPLICABILITY OF REGULATIONS

Relations Created in International Civil Aviation

Article 177

Provisions hereof on contracts of carriage of passengers, baggage and cargo and providing services in the air are applied to international air traffic, if parties did not agree the application of some other law, or if it is not determined otherwise by international agreement.

Determining Applicable Law with the Contract of International Civil Aviation

Article 178

(1) If the Law the application of which was agreed between parties cannot be applied to the entire contract, or to some of the relations arising from the contract, or if the parties do not specifically determined the right to be applied, and their intention regarding the application of certain law cannot be clearly determined from the case circumstances, the law which is closely related to the contract or contractual relation shall be applied to that contract.

581. https://www.google.com/url?sa=t&rct=j&q=&esrc=s&source=web&cd=1&ved=2ahUKEwjK3fuqg_XoAhUK86YKHRWEBiEQFjAAegQIAhAB&url=http%3A%2F%2Fwww.poreskauprava.gov.me%2FResourceManager%2FFileDownload.aspx%3Frid%3D312104%26rType%3D2%26file%3DLaw%2520on%2520Obligations%2520final%2520full%25202015.pdf&usg=AOvVaw2ASk1uKd_4wy1eMhY0YoJQ.

(2) If nothing else arises from crucial circumstances, the closest law in the State in which the carrier at the time of the conclusion of contract had the seat shall apply to main rights and obligations.
(3) To secondary rights and obligations, applied shall be the Law of the place where such actions were performed, i.e. where they should have been performed.

Determining Applicable Law with the Insurance Agreement

Article 179

(1) The Law regarding the insurance company in the place of the company shall apply to the contract of air traffic insurance and relations arising thereof, under condition:
   - that parties did not clearly indicated the Law that shall be applied to the contract, and their intention regarding application of certain Law cannot be determined from the circumstances surrounding the case; and
   - that the law the application of which was agreed between the parties cannot be applied to the part of that contract or to some other relation from that contract.
(2) With exception from Paragraph 1 of this Article, domestic law shall be applied to the relations in air traffic insurance agreement, if all interested parties in such an agreement are Montenegrin nationals with the residence in Montenegro or legal persons registered and with their seat in Montenegro, and it is about insured objects exposed to covered risks exclusively on Montenegrin territory.

Determining Applicable Law According To Which the Type of Contract Is Evaluated

Article 180

Contract and any other legal action performed in the aim of realization of that contract are valid regarding the form, if the contract was concluded, i.e. the action performed in the form prescribed by the law of the State in which the contract was concluded, i.e. the action performed, or the Law according to which the main rights and obligations in the contract are assessed.

Applicable Law When Determining the Actual Rights over Aircraft

Article 181

Regarding property law and other actual laws applied to aircraft, the law of the state in which the aircraft is registered shall be applied.

Annex III

Determining Applicable Law according To Which Damage on the Ground Caused by Aircraft in Flight is Assessed

Article 182

The law of the state in which the damage was caused shall apply to the damage liability from Article 114 hereof.

Annex III

Annex IV: Law on Bill of Exchange[582]

('Sl. list RCG', No. 45/2005)

XVI

CONFLICTS OF LAWS

Article 95

The ability of a person to undertake obligations under a bill is determined by the law of that person' s country of domicile. If that law refers to a law of another country, then the laws of that country apply.

A person who, under the law specified in the paragraph 1 of this Article is regarded unable to undertake obligations under a bill, is still legally bound if that person places a signature in a country under the laws of which is regarded able to enter into relations under a bill.

Article 96

The form in which obligations under a bill are undertaken is determined in the laws on whose territory such obligations are undertaken.

As an exception to the paragraph 1 of this Article:

(1) in case obligations under a bill are not valid according to the provision of paragraph 1 of this Article, but under the laws of a certain country do represent evidence of an obligation undertaken at a later point in time, the fact that earlier obligations are in an incorrect form do not influence the validity of any such later obligations;
(2) obligations under a bill between our citizens undertaken abroad, if in accordance with the provisions in this Law, are valid even if they are not in accordance with the laws of the country in which they are undertaken.

582. Text in English available at: https://www.tobaccocontrollaws.org/files/live/Montenegro/Montenegro%20-%20Law%20on%20Bills%20of%20Exchange.pdf.

Annex IV

Article 97

The form and deadline for protesting, as well as for all other acts required for the exercise or maintenance of rights under a bill are determined in the laws of a country in which the protest is to be raised or the other acts are to be performed.

Article 98

The effects of obligations of an acceptor of a drawn bill and an issuer of a promissory note are determined in the law applicable in the place where these documents are payable.

Effects caused by obligations of the other parties liable under a bill are determined in the laws of the country on the territory of which signatures are placed to witness the acceptance of such obligations.

Article 99

Deadlines for exercise of rights to recourse with regard to all signatories of a bill are determined by the laws applicable in the place of issuance.

Laws applicable in the place of issuance are also the bases for determining whether a bill holder has a right to the claim, which is the reason for issuance of the bill.

Article 100

The issue whether acceptance may be limited to one portion of the amount of the bill or whether the bill holder is obliged to accept a partial payment, is determined in accordance with the laws of the country in which the drawn bill is payable.

The same laws apply in dealing with the issue of partial payment of promissory notes.

Article 101

The law of the country in which a bill is payable determines measures to be undertaken in case of theft or loss of a bill.
THE LAW ON CAPITAL MARKET[583]
('Sl. list CG', No. 12/2018)
http://scmn.me/images/ENG/Regulation/CapitalMarket/Law_on_Capital_Market.pdf
Applicable law
Article 406

Where financial instruments or rights in financial instruments are provided as collateral security to participants, operators of the systems and/or the Central Bank of Montenegro, and their rights or the rights of any other person acting on their behalf with respect to the financial instruments are legally recorded in a register, an account or a centralized deposit system, the rights of such entities shall be governed by the law of the state in which the register, account or centralized deposit system is located. Where financial instruments or rights in financial instruments are provided as collateral security to the central bank of a Member State or the European

583. http://scmn.me/images/ENG/Regulation/CapitalMarket/Law_on_Capital_Market.pdf.

Central Bank and their rights or the rights of any other person acting on their behalf with respect to the financial instruments are legally recorded in a register, an account or a centralised deposit system of the Member State, their rights shall be governed by the law of the Member State in which the register, account or centralised deposit system is located

Annex IV

Annex V: The Law on Arbitration

('Sl. list CG', No. 47/2015)

https://www.privrednakomora.me/sites/pkcg.org/files/multimedia/main_pages/files/2012/09/final_eng_zakon_o_arbitrazi_final_0.pdf.

Annex V

Selected Bibliography

Antić, O. *Obligaciono pravo, 8. izdanje* (*Obligations*), 8th edn. Belgrade: Pravni fakultet Univerziteta u Beogradu, Dosije studio, 2014.

Babić, D. *Međunarodna nadležnost prema mjestu ispunjenja ugovorne obveze u europskom i hrvatskom pravu (International jurisdiction according to the place of fulfillment of the contractual obligation in European and Croatian law),* In: 'Republika Hrvatska na putu prema europskom pravosudnom području – Rješavanje trgovačkih i potrošačkih sporova', Tomjenović/Čulinović Herc/Butorac Malnar eds., Rijeka: Pravni fakultet u Rijeci, 2009.

Bogišić, V. *Izabrana djela, tom: Studije i članci* (Selected works, volume: Studies and articles). Podgorica: CID, 2004.

Bordaš, B. *Porodičnopravni odnosi u međunarodnom privatnom pravu* (*Family Law Relations in Private International Law*). Novi Sad: Forum, 2000.

Čizmović, M. & Đuričin, B. *Građansko procesno pravo* (*Civil Procedural Law*). Podgorica: Faculty of Law in Podgorica, 1994.

Dika, M., Knežević, G. & Stojanović, S. *Komentar Zakona o međunarodnom privatnom i procesnom pravu* (*Commentary of the PIL ActPIL Act*). Belgrade: Nomos, 1991.

Đorđević, S. *Rešavanje mobilnih sukoba zakona u stvarnopravnim odnosima sa elementom inostranosti* (*Solving Mobile Conflict of Laws in Real Right Relations with a Foreign Element*). Kragujevac: Univerzitet u Kragujevcu, Pravni fakultet, 2015.

Đorđević, S. *Pogled na opšta koliziona pravila za stvarna prava na pokretnim stvarima u novom Zakonu o međunarodnom privatnom pravu Crne Gore, u: 'Usklađivanje pravnog sistema Srbije sa standardima Evropske unije', urednik S. Đorđević* (View of general conflict rules for real rights on movables in the new Private International Law Code of Montenegro, In *Harmonization of the legal system of Serbia with the standards of the European Union*), S. Đorđević ed., Kragujevac: Univerzitet u Kragujevcu, Pravni fakultet, 2014.

Đundić, P. *Redovno boravište deteta u praksi primene Haške konvencije o građanskopravnim aspektima međunarodne otmice dece od 25. oktobra 1980. godine* (The Habitual Residence of a Child in the Practice of Applying the Hague Child Abduction Convention of 25 October 1980), Zbornik radova Pravnog fakulteta u Novom Sadu, No. 2/2004.

Galič, A. *Uredba Brisel I: temelj evropskog građanskog procesnog prava (The Brussels I Regulation – the base of European civil procedural law)*, In Recent trends in European PIL – challenges for the national legislations of the South East

European countries, T. Deskoski ed., Skopje: Faculty of Law Skopje, 2011.

Гавроска, П., Дескоски Т., *Меѓународно приватно право* (*The Private International Law*). Скопје: Правен факултет 'Јустинијан Први' , 2010.

Goldštajn, A. & Triva, S. *Međunarodna trgovinska arbitraža* (*International Commercial Arbitration*). Zagreb: Informator, 1987.

Jakšić, A. *Međunarodno privatno pravo* (*Private International Law*). Belgrade: Dosije, 2008.

Jakšić, A. *Građansko procesno pravo* (*Civil Procedural Law*). Belgrade: Univerzitet u Beogradu, Pravni fakultet 2010.

Jelić, I., Bjeković, S. & Kostić-Mandić, M. *Grundrechte in Montenegro,* Handbuch der Grundrechte – in Deutschland und Europa, Band IX, Heidelberg: Hg. Merten/ Papier, 2016.

Katičić, N. *Ogledi o međunarodnom privatnom pravu* (*Essays on Private International Law*). Zagreb: Narodne novine, 1971.

Knežević, G. *Izvršenje arbitražnih odluka sa posebnim osvrtom na Ex-YU element* (*Enforcement of Arbitral Awards with Special Regard on Ex-YU Element*). Belgrade, Pravni život, No. 9–10/1994.

Korać, R. *Porodično pravo* (*Family Law*). Podgorica: Štamparija 3 M Makarije, 2011.

Korać, V. Notarial Form *Ad Solemnitatem* in Montenegrin Law, Annals FLB – Belgrade Law Review, Year LXIV, 2016.

Kostić-Mandić, M. *The Closest Connection Principle in 1983 PIL ActPIL Act in Theory and Practice,* In *Twenty Years of the Private International Code.* edited by M. Živković, Niš: Univerzitet u Nišu, Pravni fakultet, 2004.

Kostić-Mandić, M. *Izvođenje dokaza po zamolnicama stranih sudova* u: *Državljanstvo i međunarodno privatno pravo; Haške konvencije*, urednici: G. Knežević, V. Pavić (Letters of Request and Taking of Evidence, In *Citizenship and International Private Law; The Hague Conventions*), G. Knežević & V. Pavić, eds., Belgrade: Univerzitet u Beogradu, Pravni fakultet, Službeni glasnik, 2007.

Kostić-Mandić, M. *Mjerodavno pravo u Opštem imovinskom zakoniku za Knjaževinu Crnu Goru* u *120 godina OIZ-a u Crnoj Gori* (*The Applicable Law in the General Pecuniary Code for the Principality of Montenegro*) In *120 years of GPC in Montenegro*, Podgorica: Univerzitet Crne Gore, Pravni fakultet, Udruženje pravnika CG, 2009.

Kostić-Mandić, M. *Opšta klauzula odstupanja od redovno mjerodavnog prava: u savremenom međunarodnom privatnom pravu* (*General Escape Clause: in Contemporary Private International Law*). Podgorica: University of Montenegro, Faculty of Law, 2012.

Kostić-Mandić, M., Stanivuković, M. & Živković, M. *International Encyclopedia of Laws: Private International Law*, Supplement 38: Montenegro, edited by B. Verschraegen. Alphen aan den Rijn: Kluwer Law International, 2013.

Kostić-Mandić, M. 'Implementation of International and European Law in Montenegro', In *European Union Law Application by the National Courts of the*

EU-Membership Aspirant Countries from South-East Europe. edited by S. Georgievski & Veronika Efremova, Skopje: South East European Law School Network, GIZ, 2014.

Kostić-Mandić, M. *The New Private International Law Act of Montenegro,* Yearbook of Private International Law, Sellier European Law Publishers, Vol. XVI, 2014/2015.

Kostić-Mandić, M. 'Country Report on Application of the Hague Child Abduction Convention, Montenegro', In *Private International Law in the Jurisprudence of European Courts: Family at Focus*, edited by M. Župan. Osijek: Faculty of Law Osijek, 2015.

Kostić-Mandić, M. *Međunarodno privatno pravo* (*Private International Law*). Podgorica: Univerzitet Crne Gore, Pravni fakultet, 2017.

Kostić-Mandić, M. 'National Report: Montenegro', In *Encyclopedia of Private International Law*, vol. 4, edited by J. Basedow, G. Rühl, F. Ferrari and P. de Miguel Asensio. Chetenham, UK, Northampton, MA, USA: Edward Elgar Publishing, 2017.

Kostić-Mandić, M. *Primjena međunarodnog privatnog prava u notarskoj praksi* (Application of Private International Law in Notaries' Practice), Podgorica: GIZ, 2021.

Kostić-Mandić, M, Cross-border Recognition and Enforcement of Foreign Judicial Decisions in South East Europe and Perspectives of HCCH 2019 Judgments Convention, Skopje: GIZ, 2021.

Muminović, E. *Međunarodno privatno pravo* (*Private International Law*). Sarajevo: Univerzitet u Sarajevu, Pravni fakultet, 2006.

Pak, M. *Međunarodno privatno pravo* (*Private International Law*). Belgrade: Nomos, 1991.

Pak, M. *Međunarodno privatno pravo, 4. izdanje* (*Private International Law*, 4th edn.). Belgrade: Službeni list SRJ, 2000.

Pejović, Č. *O jednoj odluci Apelacionog suda: Rušenje mita o 'domaćinskoj pravdi' (About one decision of Appellate Court: breaking the myth of 'domestic justice'),* Pravni zbornik, No. 3/2019

Radišić, J. *Obligaciono pravo, opšti deo, 6. izdanje* (*Obligations*, general part), 6th edn. Belgrade: Nomos, 2000.

Račić, R. *Sprovođenje stranih izvršnih naslova u Crnoj Gori (Enforcement of Foreign Executory Titles in Montenegro)*, Podgorica: Pravni zbornik, No. 3/2019.

Rakić-Vodinelić, V. & Knežević, G. *Građansko procesno pravo Evropske unije* (*Civil Procedural Law of the European Union*). Belgrade: Univerzitet u Beogradu, Pravni Fakultet, 1998.

Rašović, Z. *Komentar Zakona o svojinsko-pravnim odnosima* (*Commentary on the Law on Ownership Relations*). Podgorica: Univerzitet Crne Gore, Pravni fakultet, 2009

Ročkomanović, M. *Međunarodno privatno pravo* (*Private International Law*). Niš: Univerzitet u Nišu, Pravni fakultet, 2012

Sajko, K. *Međunarodno privatno pravo* (*Private International Law*). Zagreb: Narodne novine, 2009

Savković, V. *International Encyclopedia of Laws: Contracts: Montenegro*. Alphen aan den Rijn: Kluwer Law International, 2017.

Selected Bibliography

Stanivuković, M. 'Yugoslavian PIL at the End of the 20th Century: Progress or Regress?' In *Private International at the End of the 20th Century: Progress or Regress?* edited by S. Symeonides. The Hague, London, Boston: Kluwer Law International, 2000.

Stanivuković, M. *Srpsko međunarodno privatno pravo u vremenu tranzicije: promenjen značaj državljanstva i prebivališta*, u: *Državljanstvo i međunarodno privatno pravo; Haške konvencije*, urednici: G. Knežević, V. Pavić (Serbian Private International Law at the time of transition: the changed significance of citizenship and residence, In *Citizenship and International Private Law; The Hague Conventions*), G. Knežević, V. Pavić, eds., Belgrade: Univerzitet u Beogradu, Pravni fakultet, Službeni glasnik, 2007.

Stanivuković, M. *Pojedinac pred sudom Evropskih zajednica* (*Individual Before the European Court of Justice*). Belgrade: Službeni glasnik, 2009.

Stanivuković, M. & Đundić, P. *Pravo na viđanje deteta i Haška konvencija o gra đanskopravnim aspektima međunarodne otmice deteta (1980)* (Access Rights and the Hague Convention of 25 October 1980 on the Civil Aspects of International Child Abduction), Pravni život, No. 10/2010.

Stanivuković, M. *Međunarodna arbitraža* (*International Arbitration*). Belgrade: Službeni glasnik, 2013.

Stanivuković, M. & Živković, M. *Međunarodno privatno pravo: opšti deo, 6. izdanje* (*Private International Law: General Part*, 6th edn.). Belgrade: Službeni glasnik, 2015.

Stanivuković, M. & Đundić, P. *Međunarodno privatno pravo, posebni deo, 2. izdanje* (*Private International Law, Special Part*, 2nd edn.). Novi Sad: Univerzitet u Novom Sadu, Pravni fakultet, 2015.

Stanivuković, M. & Živković, M. *International Encyclopedia of Laws: Private International Law*, Supplement 55: Serbia, edited by B. Verschraegen. Alphen aan den Rijn: Kluwer Law International, 2018.

Tomić, M. *Zakon o životnom partnerstvu lica istog pola – korak naprijed ka evropskom javnom poretku* (Law on Life Partnership of Sane Sex Persons – a step forward to European public policy), Podgorica: Pravni zbornik, No. 1/2021.

Table of Cases

Table of Cases

Court of Appeal of Montenegro

P.ž. br. 637/17 and Pž.br. 637/17, 715

Commercial Court of Montenegro

P.br. 513/10, P.br.1041/12, Pž.br. 420/20, P.br.1014/15, P.br. 574/18-15, P.br. 1016/15, P. br. 336/17, P. br. 234/18, Rs.br.19/15, Rs.br. 29/15, Rs.br.18/16, P.br. 26/18, Pž.br.864 /18, P.br.288/18, P.br. 48/19, Pž.br. 644/19, P.br. 1113/18, P.br. 1171/18, Pž.br. 600/19, P.br. 1171/18, Pž.br. 600/19, Pž.br.644/19, Pž.br.675/19, Pž br.742/19, P.br.1170/19, P.br.167/20, P.br. 318/20, P.br. 463/20, Pž.br. 120/21, Pž br.202/21, 256, 274, 344, 439, 445, 448, 645, 716

Ombudsman of Montenegro, Opinion No. 01-293/17-2, Podgorica, 30.06.2017, 206

Arbitration Court of the International Chamber of Commerce in Paris Award No. 17146 of 12 March 2013, 715

ICSID cases

CEAC Holdings Limited v. Montenegro (ICSID Case No. ARB/14/8), 719

MNSS BV and Recupero Credito Acciaio NV v. Montenegro (ICSID Case No. ARB (AF)/12/8)718

Yugoslav/Serbian Foreign Trade Arbitration

T-55/76, T-190/82, T-4/02, T-2/04, T-14/04 T-15/04, 272

ECJ

ECJ 23 November 1999, C-369/96, *Jean-Claude Arblade and Arblade & Fils SARL* and C-376/96 *Bernard Leloup, Serge Leloup and Sofrage SARL*, [1999] ECR I-08453, 163

ECJ 19 September 1995, C-364/93, *Marinari v. Lloyd's Bank*, [1995] ECR I-2719, 336

ECJ 27 October 1998, C-51/97, *Réunion Européenne v. Spliethoff's Bevrachtingskantoor*, [1998] ECR I-6511, 336

ECJ 7 March 1995, C-68/93, *Fiona Shevill and others v. Press Alliance SA* [1995] ECR I-415,359

ECtHR

Mijušković v. Montenegro Application No. 49337/07, 21. 09. 2010, 557

Golder v. United Kingdom, Application No. 4451/70, 21.02.1975, 680

Hornsby v. Greece, 18357/91, 19.03.1997, 680

Kreuz v. Poland, 28249/95, 19.06.2001, 680

Sotiris and Nikos Koutras ATTEE v. Greece, 39442/98, 16.11.2000, 680

Běleš and Others v. Czech Republic, 47273/99, 12.11.2002, 680

Ateş Mimarlik Mühendislik A.Ş v. Turkey, 33275/05, 25.09.2012, 680

Sommerfeld v. Germany, No. 31871/96, 8.07.2003, 537

Neulinger & Shuruk v. Switzerland, Application No. 41615/07, 6 .07.2010, 563

Raban v. Romania, Application No. 25437/08, 30.11.2010, 563

Ivanović v. Croatia, 13006/13, 18.09.2014, 186

Foreign decisions

Municipal Court Solothurn – Lebern, Switzerland of 5 May 1999, 559
District Court Pfaffikom, Switzerland, U.1/CE960121 of 3 December 1996, 560
District Court in Pančevo, Serbia, R. br.10/97 of 17 March 1997, 560
Basic Court - Divisions of the Essex County Divisional and Family Court, USA, no. 12W1029WD of 31 August 2012, 563
Basic Court - Divisions of the Essex County Divisional and Family Court, USA, no. 12W1029WD of 14 November 2013, 563
Higher Court in Belgrade, Serbia, P.br.26/15, 517

Table of Statutory Instruments

The list of statutes' references is valid as of 14 April 2022

Zakon o čeku ('Sl. list FNRJ', br. 105/46, 'Sl. list SFRJ', br. 12/65, 50/71 i 52/73, 'Sl. list SRJ', br. 46/96 i 'Sl. list SCG', br. 1/2003 – Ustavna povelja), 320

Law on Cheques ('Sl. list FNRJ', No. 105/46, 'Sl. list SFRJ', No. 12/65, 50/71 and 52/73, 'Sl. list SRJ', No. 46/96 and 'Sl. list SCG', No. 1/2003 – Constitutional Charter), 320

Zakon o pomorskoj i unutrašnjoj plovidbi ('Sl. list SRJ', br. 12/98, 44/99, 74/99 i 73/2000, 'Sl. list RCG', br. 46/2007 – dr. zakon i 'Sl. list CG', br. 17/2007 – dr. zakon, 51/2008 – dr. zakon, 20/2011 – dr. zakon i 62/2013 – dr. zakon). 58

Law on Maritime and Inland Navigation ('Sl. list SRJ', No. 12/98, 44/99, 74/99 and 73/2000, 'Sl. list RCG', No. 46/2007 – other law and 'Sl. list CG', No. 17/2007 – other law, 51/2008 – other law, 20/2011 – other law i 62/2013 – other law), 58

Zakon o eksproprijaciji ('Sl. list RCG', br. 55/2000, 12/2002 – odluka US i 28/2006 i 'Sl. list CG', br. 21/2008 i 30/2017), 411

Law on Expropriation ('Sl. list RCG', No. 55/2000, 12/2002 – decision of the Constitutional Court and 28/2006 and 'Sl. list CG', No. 21/2008 and 30/2017), 411

Zakon o penzijskom i invalidskom osiguranju ('Sl. list RCG', br. 54/2003, 39/2004, 61/2004 – odluka US, 79/2004, 81/2004 – ispr., 29/2005 – dr. zakon, 14/2007 – odluka US i 47/2007 i 'Sl. list CG', br. 12/2007 – dr. zakon, 13/2007 – dr. zakon, 79/2008, 14/2010, 78/2010, 34/2011, 40/2011 – dr. zakon, 66/2012, 39/2011 – dr. zakon, 36/2013 – dr. zakon, 38/2013, 61/2013, 6/2014 – ispr., 60/2014, 10/2015, 44/2015 – odluka US, 42/2016, 55/2016, 80/2020 i 145/2021), 507

Law on Pension and Disability Insurance ('Sl. list RCG', No. 54/2003, 39/2004, 61/2004 – decision of the Constitutional Court, 79/2004, 81/2004 – corr., 29/2005 – other law, 14/2007 – decision of the Constitutional Court and 47/2007 and 'Sl. list CG', No. 12/2007 – other law, 13/2007 – other law, 79/2008, 14/2010, 78/2010, 34/2011, 40/2011 – other law, 66/2012, 39/2011 – other law, 36/2013 – other law, 38/2013, 61/2013, 6/2014 – corr., 60/2014, 10/2015, 44/2015 – decision of the Constitutional Court, 42/2016, 55/2016, 80/2020 and 145/2021), 507

Krivični zakonik Crne Gore ('Sl. list RCG', br. 70/2003, 13/2004 – ispr. i 47/2006 i 'Sl. list CG', br. 40/2008, 25/2010, 32/2011, 64/2011 – dr. zakon, 40/2013, 56/2013 – ispr., 14/2015, 42/2015, 58/2015 – dr. zakon, 44/2017,49/2018, 3/2020, 26/2021, 26/2021, 144/2021 i 145/21), 421

Criminal Code of Montenegro ('Sl. list RCG', No. 70/2003, 13/2004 – exc. and 47/2006 and 'Sl. list CG', No. 40/2008, 25/2010, 32/2011, 64/2011 – other act,

Table of Statutory Instruments

Table of Statutory Instruments

Table of International Conventions

This is a non-exhaustive list of multilateral treaties in force in Montenegro, as of 14 Apr. 2022.

Table of International Conventions

Table of Bilateral Treaties

This is a non-exhaustive list of bilateral treaties on legal assistance in force in Montenegro, as of 14 April 2022,

Table of Bilateral Treaties

Index

The numbers here refer to paragraph numbers.

Index

Index

Index

www.ingramcontent.com/pod-product-compliance
Lightning Source LLC
Chambersburg PA
CBHW072242240926
51846CB00012B/138
* 9 7 8 9 4 0 3 5 1 5 8 6 1 *